YEARS

SIMON &
SCHUSTER
PAPERBACKS

T0049054

ALSO BY JOSEPH EPSTEIN

Divorced in America: Marriage in an Age of Possibility (1974)

Familiar Territory: Observations on American Life (1979)

Ambition: The Secret Passion (1980)

Middle of My Tether: Familiar Essays (1983)

Plausible Prejudices: Essays on American Writing (1985)

Once More Around the Block: Familiar Essays (1987)

Partial Payments: Essays on Writers and Their Lives (1989)

The Goldin Boys: Stories (1991)

A Line Out for a Walk: Familiar Essays (1991)

Pertinent Players: Essays on the Literary Life (1993)

With My Trousers Rolled: Familiar Essays (1995)

Life Sentences: Literary Essays (1997)

Narcissus Leaves the Pool (1999)

Snobbery: The American Version (2002)

Envy (2003)

Fabulous Small Jews (2003)

Alexis De Tocqueville: Democracy's Guide (2006)

Friendship: An Exposé (2006)

In a Cardboard Belt!: Essays Personal, Literary, and Savage (2007)

Fred Astaire (2008)

The Love Song of A. Jerome Minkoff and Other Stories (2010)

Gossip: The Untrivial Pursuit (2011)

Essays in Biography (2012)

Distant Intimacy: A Friendship in the Age of the Internet (2013)
(with Frederic Raphael)

A Literary Education and Other Essays (2014)

Masters of the Games: Essays and Stories on Sport (2015)

Frozen in Time: Twenty Stories (2016)

Wind Sprints: Shorter Essays (2016)

Where Were We?: The Conversation Continues (2017)
(with Frederic Raphael)

Charm: The Elusive Enchantment (2018)

The Ideal of Culture: Essays (2018)

Gallimaufry: A Collection of Essays, Reviews, Bits (2020)

The Novel, Who Needs It? (2023)

Never Say You've Had a Lucky Life
Especially If You've Had a Lucky Life (2024)

Familiarity Breeds Content

New and Selected Essays

Joseph Epstein

SIMON & SCHUSTER PAPERBACKS
New York   Toronto   London   Sydney   New Delhi

An Imprint of Simon & Schuster, LLC
1230 Avenue of the Americas
New York, NY 10020

First Simon & Schuster trade paperback edition April 2024

SIMON & SCHUSTER and colophon are registered trademarks of Simon & Schuster, LLC

Simon & Schuster: Celebrating 100 Years of Publishing in 2024

For information about special discounts for bulk purchases,
please contact Simon & Schuster Special Sales
at 1-866-506-1949 or business@simonandschuster.com.

The Simon & Schuster Speakers Bureau can bring authors to your live event.
For more information or to book an event, contact the
Simon & Schuster Speakers Bureau at 1-866-248-3049 or
visit our website at www.simonspeakers.com.

Interior design by Wendy Blum

Manufactured in the United States of America

1   3   5   7   9   10   8   6   4   2

Library of Congress Cataloging-in-Publication Data has been applied for.

ISBN 978-1-6680-0972-7
ISBN 978-1-6680-0973-4 (ebook)

Contents

Contents

Foreword

Being a dull but determined literary plodder, it only occurred to me as I sat down to write that the title of Joseph Epstein's thirty-fifth book is a sly double entendre. *Con*-tent, as in material; con-*tent*, as in happy. My late employer, Malcolm Forbes, had his own spin, embroidered in needlepoint on a pillow aboard his yacht: "Familiarity breeds children." He spoke with authority, having produced five bairns.

Over the course of a long and distinguished career, the hyper-productive Epstein has bred endless *con*tent, with a felicity of intellect that leaves his many admirers dazzled, grateful, and very con*tent*, indeed. The late Martin Amis wrote of his hero Saul Bellow, Epstein's fellow Chicagoan and sometime friend, "One doesn't read Saul Bellow. One can only re-read him." I venture wittily, "Ditto Epstein." Having been an Epstein votary for over four decades, I had previously read most of the essays collected here; some, many times. I confess that on setting out, I anticipated doing a bit of skipping. I did not. *Mutatis mutandis*, as my old man used to say, I re-read each essay with pleasure equal to that I derive from listening, for the hundredth time, to *Sgt. Pepper's Lonely Hearts Club Band*.

The small bookshelf by my side of the bed holds the three dozen-odd books that I'd want with me in the lifeboat. They are so dear to me that I might actually toss someone out of the lifeboat in order to accommodate them. They are my biblio-comfort zone; my literary mac and cheese: Auden, Larkin, Boswell, Waugh, Wodehouse, Stephen Potter, Clive James, Anthony Lane, Christopher Hitchens, and Joseph Epstein. When I was asked to contribute this prefatory ululation, I tallied the Epsteins and wasn't surprised to find that his volumes are the most numerous. It makes me con*tent* to think that he's made enough off me to buy . . . well, at least a half-dozen deep-dish Chicago pizzas. Familiarity also breeds royalties.

Counting my Epsteins took me back to an evening decades past but still green in memory, a first meeting with someone who would become a bosom friend and boon companion. After the Howdya-dos and What are you drinking? I spotted a number of Epsteins on his bookshelf. The connection was instantaneous. Suddenly, there we both were, on a foggy Casablanca tarmac, at "the beginning of a beautiful friendship." Forty years later, when I was asked to sing hymns at Epstein's gate, I wrote my old pal with hyperventilating jubilation. "I have *arrived*," I purred. He was duly impressed. I mention this not to preen (he lies) but to aver that Joseph Epstein's readers aren't mere readers, but devotees. They're . . . I'll stop there. In our fevered era, one must exercise caution before proclaiming oneself a member of a "cult." But what the hell. It *is*.

I read the manuscript electronically, highlighting especially delightful bits and passages, but soon gave up as I realized I was more or less highlighting the whole damn thing. To cite but a few beauts:

"The most dangerous moment for a bad government is when it begins to reform itself." Now that generalization—it is by Tocqueville—seems to me splendid. It comes at things at a near perfect level of generality, neither too high nor too low. It calls up all those governments, from Roman to French to Russian, whose

last-minute attempts at reform only made easier the way for the revolutions that toppled them.

[Franklin] remarks in his autobiography that, if you wish to insinuate yourself in the good graces of another person, the trick is not to do that person a favor but to have him do one for you. So the trick of making many friends, at least on the superficial level on which the Good Guy operates, is not to charm them but to let them charm you.

. . . the novelist of friendlessness is Joseph Conrad, whose heroes are among the loneliest figures in literature and among the most moving in part because of their solitariness, which gives them their tragic dimension.

The great gluttons of the movies of my boyhood were an Austro-Hapsburgian character actor named S. Z. ("Cuddles") Sakall and Sydney Greenstreet; Sakall played his fat man sweet, as if he were a walking piece of very creamy pastry, while Greenstreet played his menacing, as if he were a hard dumpling that, should it roll over you, could cause serious damage.

William Howard Taft, our twenty-seventh president, was built like two walruses with a single head.

Imagine my chagrin at learning, as I not long ago did, that a writer whom I rather blithely despised for what I take to be his fraudulent self-righteousness and utterly self-assured hypocrisy, had cancer. Until then I had so enjoyed loathing him, my distaste for everything about him had seemed so complete, so pure, so uncomplicatedly pleasant, and now it was incomplete, alloyed by his misfortune, complicated by my own sympathy for his illness. This was a real setback. I had counted on being able to continue disliking him for another decade or two. It was as if someone had removed a wall against which I had happily grown accustomed to banging my head. I suppose this makes me a pretty good but not a great hater.

Although it is probably the sheerest economic jealousy on my part, it lifts my spirits to discover that someone driving a Rolls Royce looks sad.

It was Evelyn Waugh who, having submitted himself to a painful and less than altogether necessary operation for hemorrhoids, claimed that his motive for doing so was perfectionism.

The best tables in the best restaurants, mail filled with offers and invitations, the feeling that the world really is at one's feet, such can be among the high, heady delights that accompany fame. "Where to?" a cab driver in Paris is said once to have asked Herbert von Karajan. "It doesn't matter," the famous conductor is said to have replied. "They want me everywhere."

I had better stop before I begin to sound like Lillian Hellman in trousers.

And I had better stop there, before I quote the entire book. If you're new to this feast, you have a splendid meal ahead. Joe Epstein is incapable of writing a boring sentence; appears to have read everything, but wears his erudition lightly; is a veritable combine harvester of of anecdotes, witticisms, apothegms, aphorisms, *bon mots*, aperçus, jokes (often Jewish), and sparkly repartee; comes equipped with a foolproof bullshit detector; and is deep down a "good guy," despite the essay in which he strives, with dark hilarity, to persuade us otherwise. He is the most entertaining living essayist in the English language. I almost wrote " entertaining and accessible," which would surely make him groan, but what the hell. He *is*. All those years as a college professor around the seminar table made him a companionable pedagogue (though no doubt he was one tough grader). As I read this book, I often found myself wishing I'd been one of his fortunate students.

Too late, alas, but his oeuvre, to use the word his idol and progenitor Montaigne would, is there, to read and re-read. You and I may have missed his class, but we can audit. The thirty-five Epsteins comprise a one-man version of *The Great Books*, another feat of Chicago intellectuality. It's too depressing to think this might be the final volume in the series, so I won't go there. His energy, even in his mid-80s shows little sign of flagging. I can hope he has another half-dozen in him yet. Joe Epstein's content will endure, making his re-readers content. To give him the last *bon mot:* "All of us would like to have said about us what I heard a eulogist say of the songwriter Yip Harburg: 'He is survived by his words.'"

—Christopher Buckley

Familiarity
Breeds
Content

Selected Essays

Jokes and Their Relation to the Conscious

My title, of course, derives from Freud's famous work *Jokes and Their Relation to the Unconscious*. In that work Freud put forth the notion that there are ultimately no jokes—and, as usual, he wasn't kidding. At bottom, he found, most jokes had as their purpose either hostility or exposure. But as Freud found it necessary, as historian Peter Gay has put it, "to be rational about irrationality," so in his book on jokes he turns out to be good-humored in his finally humorless task. *Jokes and Their Relation to the Unconscious*, in addition to being another piece of brilliant Freudian analysis, is also a compendium of quite good jokes, and from his selection of examples, it is apparent that Freud loved a joke. This should come as no great surprise. "The attitude of psychology," W. H. Auden once remarked, "should always be 'Have you heard this one?'"

As a medical student Freud wrote a histological paper of some significance in which, to make sure of the firmness of his conclusions, he went to the trouble of dissecting four hundred eels. For his book on jokes, one suspects that he must have listened to more than four times that many jokes, though in the book itself he dissects, at a rough guess, only a hundred or so of them. Being Sigmund Freud, he is never obtuse—and if not everywhere persuasive, he is never less than fascinating. Only with one joke in the book does he, to my mind at least, go askew. This is the joke about Itzig in the army, which, as Freud recounts it, goes as follows:

> Itzig had been declared fit for service in the artillery. He was clearly an intelligent lad, but intractable and without any interest in the service. One of his superior officers, who was friendlily disposed to him, took him to one side and said to him: "Itzig, you're no use to us. I'll give you a piece of advice: buy yourself a cannon and make yourself independent!"

Freud believed that what this joke is about is that "the officer who gives Artilleryman Itzig this nonsensical advice is only making himself out stupid to show Itzig how stupidly he himself is behaving." I myself think the joke is really vaguely an anti-Semitic one about Jews performing best when in business for themselves. Another joke of the same type has to do with the Israeli private who is doing poorly in the army until his sergeant tells him he can win a weekend pass if he captures an Egyptian tank. Lo, three weeks in a row he brings in an Egyptian tank, and on each occasion wins his weekend pass. One of his fellow enlisted men, hotly curious, asks him how he does it. "Very simple," he says. "I go over to our motor pool and take out a tank. Then I drive out into the desert till I spot an Egyptian tank. At this point I hoist up a white flag. When the Egyptian tank driver comes within hearing range, I call out to him, 'Hey, friend, want to win a weekend pass?'"

Freud was chiefly interested in the underlying meaning of jokes—in, as his title announces, their relation to the unconscious—but I think that the relation of jokes to the *conscious* has an interest of its own. The above paragraph, for example, touches on a number of questions about jokes at the level of consciousness. Ethnic sensitivities abraded by jokes is but the most obvious. Would the Anti-Defamation League rather not have these two jokes told? ("Incidentally," Freud noted, "I do not know whether there are many other instances of a people making fun to such a degree of its own character [as do the Jews].") Then there is the question of jokes and taste. Ought one to be making Israeli-Arab jokes at a time when life in the Middle East is dire? Can it be that the better jokes are no laughing matter?

The world is divided on the question of the value of jokes: between those who adore them and those who, if not outright offended, are left cold by them. (The world, Robert Benchley said, is divided into two kinds of people—those who divide the world into two kinds of people and those who don't.) I happen to be among those who adore jokes. In saying this, I do not mean to say that I am a fine fellow, of that caste of special and superior beings: the good-humored. I used to think that a sense of humor was an absolute requisite for friendship; and while it is true that most of the people I count as friends enjoy laughter, so, alas, do many people who are frivolous, or cynical, or even vicious. Idi Amin, I understand, enjoyed a joke, too.

Having said that a taste for jokes is no sign of superiority, I am nonetheless not going to demonstrate my mental inferiority by setting about the thankless and absurd task of seriously defining a joke and then strenuously analyzing the nature of jokes. Jokes, like beauty, are too various to capture in any but a jerry-built definition. It is enough to say that there are short jokes and long jokes, sweet jokes and sour jokes, healthy and sick jokes, and jokes that spring from whimsy, anger, or sharp observation and sometimes from all of these in combination. But finally a joke is a joke, and the way to tell if it is any good or not is to notice, after you have heard it, whether you are smiling. If you are doing so out of more than politeness, it is a pleasant joke; if you are laughing, it is a good joke; if you are rocked with laughter, your eyes watering with laughter, it is, quite possibly, a blessed joke.

Max Beerbohm, whose work as an essayist and as a draughtsman has brought so much laughter, remarked that "only the emotion of love takes higher rank than that of laughter." He makes the interesting point that love has its origin in the physical and ends in the realm of the mental, while laughter has its origin in the mental and ends in the realm of the physical. Beerbohm claimed that he could make nothing of the lucubrations of William James or Henri Bergson on the subject of laughter. ("It distresses me," he wrote, "this failure to keep pace with the leaders of thought as they pass into oblivion.") He was content to accept laughter as a great gift. He felt—rather like Freud, though for different reasons—that "nine-tenths of the world's best laughter is laughter *at*, not *with*." He held that "laughter is a thing to be rated according to its own intensity."

Max Beerbohm also said that the man who has not laughed much in life is a failure, and that he himself would rather be a man to whom laughter has often been granted but who has died in a workhouse than another who has never laughed but may be buried in Westminster Abbey. I like that exceedingly, because, measured by this standard, my own life has already been a grand success. Laughter comes easily to me. Sometimes it comes too easily. I have been seized by attacks of giddy laughter in lecture halls, worn out by costly laughter in the act of courtship. Once, as a younger man, I was actually asked to leave a restaurant because my too uproarious laughter nearly resulted in upsetting a table. I seem, moreover, to be able to laugh at almost anything, exceptions being practical jokes and the comically intended descriptions of female actresses by the theater and movie critic John Simon. Well-done slapstick—for example, a man walking into a wall or one taking a pie in the face—can send me writhing to the floor. George Meredith said, "We know the degree of refinement in men by the matter they will laugh at, and the ring of the laugh." I laugh at Henny Youngman. So much, then, for my refinement.

I should prefer to die laughing and, on more than one occasion, thought I might. The best laughs, what Mel Brooks calls the dangerous laughs (implying the possibility of a stroke or heart attack at the end of them), have invariably been private. The comic situation, the splendid off-the-cuff witticism, the unexpected fling of whimsy, the surgical puncturing of pretension, the predicament so bleak that it allows for no other response than laughter—these, which cannot be jerked from their context, make for the keenest laughter. Seldom do I laugh at the written word, although a few writers can bring me to this happy state: certain physical descriptions by Saul Bellow, patches of straight-faced dialogue by Evelyn Waugh, bizarre touches by S. J. Perelman, a mere phrase by H. L. Mencken (such as his reference, in one of his autobiographical volumes, to homosex as among "the non-Euclidian varieties of fornication"). Yet a book of jokes, of the kind that the late Bennett Cerf used to turn out, leaves me tighter lipped than a Calvinist at a porno film.

Jokes—formal, traditional jokes—are, or in my view ought to be, social acts. The best joke-tellers are those who have the patience to wait for conversation to come around to the point where the jokes in their repertoire have application. Take, for instance, the joke about

Yankel Dombrovich, the forty-five-year-old bachelor from the village of Frampol, who is terrified of women:

A match has been arranged for Yankel with a widow from a nearby village whose name is Miriam Schneider. Yankel is, dependably, terrified. His mother tells him not to worry. Women, she instructs her son, love to talk about three things: they love to talk about food, they love to talk about family, and if neither of these works they love to talk about philosophy.

Finally the day arrives upon which Yankel and Miriam are to be introduced. Miriam turns out to be four foot six and weigh well above two hundred pounds, and to be without apparent gifts for, or even inclination toward, conversation. Yankel thinks, *Oh, this is horrible, what will I say to her? What was it Momma told me women like to talk about? Oh, yes, food.*

"Miriam," he announces in a quavering voice, "let me ask you, Miriam, do you like noodles?"

"No," she replies in a bass voice drained of expressiveness, "I don't like noodles."

"Miriam," Yankel returns, remembering his mother's instructions that women also like to talk about family, "Miriam, do you have a brother?"

"No," she answers, "I don't got no brother."

Worse and worse, Yankel thinks. *What is left to talk about? Oh, yes, philosophy. Momma says women like to talk about philosophy.* "Miriam," Yankel lamely tries again, "let me ask you a final question: If you had a brother, would he like noodles?"

A more patient man than I would wait to tell such a joke until a discussion of modern philosophy arose. "Speaking of Wittgenstein," he might say, "do you know the story of Yankel Dombrovich?" But I am not that more patient man. So much did I like that joke when I first heard it that I told it, without aid of suave transition, to everyone I knew. But as I cannot await a suave transition to tell jokes, neither do I require any to have jokes told to me. In fact, I consider it a fine morning on which my telephone rings and a voice on the other end says, "Did you hear that the McCormick Company went to court to protest against the common metaphor for death being 'the Grim Reaper'?" No, I hadn't heard. "Yes, the McCormick Company has asked that henceforth death be known as 'the International Harvester.' "

My mornings are not interrupted in this way often enough. Even though I have a small band of four or five friends who share my love for a joke, and we report to each other regularly, not all that many new jokes seem to come into existence. Jokes may now, in fact, be in bad odor. I sense that nowadays people think there is something old-fashioned, square, out-of-it about them. My own generation, the one now in its forties, may possibly be the last to be interested in jokes, although perhaps here I am taking up the line of every generation as it grows into middle age. *Après nous, le déluge*, one thinks, when the generations behind one think, *Après le déluge, nous*. Yet there can be no gainsaying that certain kinds of jokes have disappeared because their subject has disappeared. The old standby jokes about the traveling salesman and the farmer's daughter are a notable example. Here the conditions that once made the jokes tenable no longer exist. Less of the population is now on the farm, more salesmen probably now fly than drive, those who do drive usually are roaring along on freeways, and the old trust that once might have allowed a farmer to be at home to a salesman in distress is now gone.

Other kinds of jokes have disappeared because a social situation has arisen that makes them no longer funny. Mother-in-law jokes, for instance, have all but vanished. Why is the subject of mothers-in-law no longer funny? Because, I should guess, the assumptions under which such jokes once seemed funny can no longer be maintained. Although marriage has long been a subject for cynical jokes—"Married men make the worst husbands" is among the mildest—still, the old assumption behind most mother-in-law jokes was that marriage was really quite all right except during those periods when men had their mothers-in-law inflicted upon them. Now that the divorce rate is up, and the troubles of marriage go beyond having mothers-in-law on the premises, the joke is over.

In "The Place of Laughter in Tudor and Stuart England," the Neale Lecture in English History for 1976, Professor Keith Thomas, arguing for the importance of jokes to the historian, notes: "Jokes are a pointer to joking situations, areas of structural ambiguity in society itself; and their subject matter can be a revealing guide to past tensions and anxieties." By the same token, they can be a guide to current tensions and anxieties. Why, for example, are there currently no jokes about Negroes in America? The history of jokes about Negroes is a mini-history of the state of whites' thinking about Negroes over the past four or five decades. In my own lifetime the radio program *Amos 'n' Andy* wrung laughs out of every stereotyped attribute of the Negro, chief among which were dumbness, malapropisms, and irresponsibility. Then, when the civil rights movement of the early 1960s got under way, something called the "Mississippi joke" began to go the rounds.

The USS *Mississippi*, a ship manned by white Mississippians, has but a single Negro aboard. One day the captain calls the first mate over to ask the whereabouts of the Negro.

"About two days ago he died, sir, and we threw his body overboard."

"Overboard?" asks the captain. "Are you sure he was dead?"

"Well, we asked him if he was dead before we did it, sir. He said he wasn't—but you know how they lie."

A fast and interesting switch: the target of this joke is no longer Negro stereotypes but the brutality and stupidity of people who hold to these stereotypes. Yet nothing significant in the way of Negro jokes has come along since. A single Negro comedian of real power, Mr. Richard Pryor, has proved too dangerous to appear regularly on television, and his work has instead been more frequently shown in the movies, where it is much blunted. The subject of Negroes has become, in Francis Bacon's phrase, "privileged from jest." Why? As an amateur sociologist, I should say because there is today a great unease and anxiety about the subject of the black population in the United States, of which a large portion has risen in the accustomed way up into the middle class, but of which a sizable segment still seems hopelessly mired in lumpen status, and this is no joking matter.

Quite apart from explicitly political jokes of the kind Mort Sahl used to tell, most jokes have something of a political implication—political insofar as they appeal to conservative or radical temperaments. A joke can be judged conservative or radical if, in its implications, it tends to reinforce the arrangements of society as it stands, or if it protests against current arrangements. By this measure the late Lenny Bruce, so beloved of intellectuals in the 1960s, was assuredly a radical comedian, even though little of his material was explicitly political. A single conservative comedian is more difficult to point out, for the work of conservative comedy is done by discrete jokes. "When we laugh," Professor Thomas notes, "we betray our innermost assumptions." Virginia Woolf made the same point from a somewhat different angle when she said that one of the nice things about having settled morals—and, one might add, settled politics—is that at least one knows what to laugh at. Tell me whether you think a good joke can be made about the subject of free enterprise or of public welfare and I will tell you a good deal about what your politics are.

Are ethnic jokes essentially political? For the most part I suspect they are, and the majority of them tend to be of a conservative cast. Their origin is evidently in xenophobia. As early as the time of Tudor England, according to Professor Thomas, "there were jokes against foreigners, whose characters had already assumed familiar stereotypes: the French were lascivious, the Spaniards proud, the Italians revengeful, the Dutch mean and the Germans drunk." Not the least item of interest about ethnic jokes is that they often serve as an index to the social standing of a particular group, and in any country. Over British television, one can still hear Irish jokes such as this one:

Paddy goes to his physician to complain that in his marriage his sexual powers appear to be diminishing. The physician puts Paddy on a seafood diet, instructs him to run ten miles a day, and asks him to call in at the end of two weeks. After two weeks on this regimen, Paddy telephones to his physician.

"Well, Paddy," the physician asks, "has your sex life improved?"

"How would I know?" answers Paddy. "I'm a hundred and forty miles from home."

Sometimes ethnic jokes can be self-reflexive, and often these are among the most bitter. "A kike," said the Jewish banker and philanthropist Otto Kahn, "is what you call the Jewish gentleman who has just left the room." This is a superior joke coming from Jewish lips, but not good at all if told by a non-Jew. Its target, certainly, is not the Jews, but their insecure place in the polite society of Otto Kahn's day. An ethnic joke told by a non-insider almost always has the curl of a sneer to it, at least in the view of the insider. "The slap in the face," said the French philosopher Alain, "is registered by the man who receives it, not the one who gives it."

One of the many ethnic jokes Freud tells in *Jokes and Their Relation to the Unconscious* is about two Galician Jews, one of whom asks the other, "Did you take a bath last week?" To which the other responds, "No, is one missing?" Today in the United States this joke would most likely be transformed into a Polish joke. In recent years the Poles have indisputably taken the brunt of ethnic humor in America.

A Pole finds a pig in the middle of the road. He brings it to his gas station attendant, whom he asks what he ought to do with the pig. The attendant tells him to take it to the local zoo, where they have a farm exhibit. Two weeks later, the Pole pulls back into the gas station. The attendant, noting the pig sitting on the front seat, says to the Pole, "I thought I told you to take that pig to the zoo." "I did," answers the Pole, "and he enjoyed it immensely. Today I'm taking him to the ball game."

Thirty years ago that would not have been a Polish but a "little moron" joke of the kind I learned in grade school. (Examples: Why did the little moron tiptoe past the medicine chest? He didn't want to wake the sleeping pills. Why does it take three little morons to replace a light bulb? One to hold the bulb, the other two to turn the ladder. Et cetera.) Now these are Polish jokes—these and, as anyone who has heard his share knows, others that are much worse. Why the Poles? Why so much contumely suddenly aimed at an ethnic group whose history in this country has largely been one of upstandingness and earnest aspiration? What seems to be the case is that the Poles, unlike other once-besieged minority groups in America, have no bank of social sympathy to draw upon. People will tell Polish jokes that they would not dare tell about the Negroes, or the Jews, or the Irish, or the Italians, or Catholics. (Jokes about Catholics, too, have largely disappeared. Anti-Catholicism, as Richard Hofstadter once remarked, used to function as the pornography of Protestantism; hence all those foul jokes about priests and nuns.) True, it is traditional to make jokes about the lower classes, as it is traditional for the lower classes to have their own jokes about the upper classes. But the Poles of the United States and of the Polish jokes are of the lower-middle and middle classes. Is it, then, middle-class aspirations that are being attacked in Polish jokes? Or is it instead, more simply, that no society can carry on without having a target for attack and that the Poles, by elimination, are at present it?

The best ethnic jokes, it seems to me, are those that use an ethnic element not as a target but as a background: the scenery for the joke, yet at the same time somehow more than mere scenery.

In the village of Tsrampel, the merchant Reb Goldman comes home early one afternoon to discover his wife being made love to on the couch in his parlor by his clerk Nathanson. Dazed, reeling with shock, he goes to his rabbi to report what he has just witnessed.

"Well," the rabbi responds, "your course is clear. You must divorce your wife."

"Divorce my wife, Rabbi?" says Reb Goldman. "Out of the question. I adore my wife."

"Then," says the rabbi, "you must fire your clerk."

"Fire Nathanson, Rabbi? Be serious. My business is up forty percent over last year. And I owe it all to Nathanson, whom I consider indispensable."

"Very well," says the rabbi. "Go. In the meantime I shall consult the commentaries to find a solution. Return to my study a week hence."

A week later Reb Goldman is back in the rabbi's study, a beaming smile upon his face.

"Well," says the rabbi, "I see that you have decided to divorce your wife after all."

"On the contrary, Rabbi. My wife is a wonderful mother and has for twenty years been a good wife to me."

"Then you have decided to fire your clerk?"

"Never, Rabbi. Nathanson remains irreplaceable."

"So," says the rabbi, "then why are you smiling so contentedly?"

"Because, Rabbi, I sold the couch."

This joke is irreducibly Jewish. It would not work if it were set in a small Italian village with a shopkeeper going to his priest; it would not work set in Harlem. It is a sweet joke, lovely in many ways, although I think there are people who would take exception to it. Yet in it is to be found much of the pleasure that can be taken from ethnic jokes which are neither squalid nor vicious. The pleasure is in reacquainting ourselves with a piece of knowledge that, in the best schools, we are trained to disregard: the knowledge that there is something intractably distinct about every group, however we might wish to believe otherwise. *Et vive la distinction!*

I do not think the world, giving way to ethnic sensitivities, would be better for the absence of ethnic jokes. Certainly such jokes are not now in the ascendant. If there is a reigning kind of humor, I should say it is psychoanalytic. Psychoanalysis—"the talking cure," as it used to be called—was once itself the subject of many jokes. (One woman to another: "My son has been to see a psychoanalyst, who tells him that he has an Oedipus complex." The other woman: "Oedipus, schmoedipus, just so long as he loves his mother!") Much of the humor of Woody Allen, surely the most admired comedian of our day, especially among the young, is psychoanalytic and not only in subject matter ("I'm never again going to a psychoanalytic conference," one Allen joke has it; "all those guys do in the evenings is sit around drinking and singing, 'I want a girl just like the girl that married dear old Dad' ") but in style. The same can be said about the humor of Philip Roth, which is at its source, as are the conflicts in his novels, psychoanalytic. Both Allen and Roth are very funny men, yet much of their humor, like psychoanalysis itself, does not bear retelling. Although the comedy team of Id & Superego—if I might so bill psychoanalytic humor—has made possible many a hardy laugh, ultimately sex is the fringe beyond which it cannot get. The pleasures that psychoanalytic humor gives seem of a different order than those of conventional jokes.

What are the pleasures of conventional jokes? Granted, a habitual joke-teller can make himself a terrible bore, and certain vigorously filthy jokes can be, as Freud rightly said, "acts of sexual aggression." The tension brought about by the prospect of bad taste emerging in a joke-telling situation is always present: "Did you hear the one about the two lesbians, the Turk, and the cocker spaniel?" The pleasures, however, do outweigh the risks. "A new joke," Freud wrote, "acts almost like an event of universal interest; it is passed from one person to another like the news of the latest victory." Freud also wrote: "Joking activity should not, after all, be described as pointless or aimless, since it has the unmistakable aim of evoking pleasure in its hearers. . . . [It is] an activity which aims at deriving pleasure from mental processes, whether intellectual or otherwise." Telling a joke is an authentic instance of how giving can be an even greater delight than receiving. How else explain that retelling the same joke to a fresh audience never becomes tiresome, although it generally is tiresome to hear the same joke retold?

When someone tells a good joke, something extraordinary can happen. Most people, I have discovered, rarely have a repertoire of more than two or three jokes. But one joke can ignite the memory of others perhaps long forgotten, and soon the cornucopia pours forth. Topical jokes—about politics, celebrities, events—fade away, meeting their just fate alongside the songs of Nineveh in oblivion. But the permanent jokes, those of universal point and interest, hang on, over the years and over the generations. Occasionally a joke will be improved by the listener's response to it. I recall once telling an economist of the Chicago School the old joke about the airplane in difficulty, whose captain, in order to land the plane safely, had to ask that passenger who was of least value to society to bail out without a parachute—at which point a disc jockey and a used-car salesman got up in the middle of the aisle and started fighting. "I would like that joke much better," said the economist, "if two sociologists got up in the middle of the aisle and started fighting."

But the great point about jokes is that they all have a point. Perhaps they are out of favor just now because the kind of pointed clarity they provide is not much valued; or, at any rate, so one assumes from its absence from so much contemporary literature, film, painting, and criticism. If an analogy is wanted, jokes may be likened to short stories of the traditional kind—not merely in their brevity but in the range of their possible effects. Jokes can be ironical, philosophical, bittersweet, satirical—anything, really, so long as they are also funny. To the connoisseur a well-told joke is a poem of sorts, having its own special rhythm. In my head, punch lines from jokes rattle around quite comfortably alongside lines of poetry, taking on a poetic status of their own. I close with a poem made up of punch lines—a joke addict's wasteland:

> Oy, was I thoisty!
> The Kuala tea of Mercey is never strained.
> You don't like my brother—eat the noodles.
> An hour later you're hungry for power.
> After lunch the captain wants to go waterskiing.
> How much do you tip the whipper?
> Comfortable, I don't know; I make a nice living.
> Hit the ball and drag Irving.
> I'm crying because we lost India.
> Patience, jackass, patience.
> Is not hell for Khrushchev—is hell for Marilyn Monroe.

And you'll keep singing it till you get it right.
What do they know about fornication in Findlay, Ohio?
So what's this vulgar crap?
Funny, you don't look Jewish.
You're velcome.

(1978)

A Man of Letters

My definition of a pessimist is a person who doesn't check his mail. Although with age my illusions about human nature become fewer, my belief that people learn from history slighter, my confidence in youth lesser, nonetheless my feelings about the mail—about *my* mail—remain what they have always been: feelings of complete, utter, and abject hopefulness. When it comes to the mail, I am a Fabian, a lifetime member of the Americans for Democratic Action, a Pollyanna perpetually aglow and atremble with optimism. I love mail, I adore mail, I cannot get enough mail. Saul Bellow, in his novel *Humboldt's Gift*, remarks on his hero's receiving "heavy mail," and that is a phrase which, as the boys and girls in literary criticism nowadays say, resonates with me.

The mail generally arrives in my neighborhood between 11:15 and 11:45 a.m. As will scarcely be surprising, this is one of the high points of my day. The postman, quite heedless of James M. Cain's novel, always rings once. At his ring I stop my work, either reading or writing, usually in mid-sentence. If I am speaking over the telephone

18

when the postman rings, my attention flags. My mind is now on that apartment building mailbox marked "Epstein" and on the small table beneath the mailboxes on which are placed magazines and packages. I walk down the stairs simulating a mien of casualness, though my heart bounds. What is it, exactly, that I expect to find in the day's mail? Notice of a large inheritance? Extravagant praise for my character? Unexpected checks for ample sums? Offers of ambassadorships in countries of gentle climate and stable government? Interesting proposals? Fascinating opportunities? Yes, all these things—and, who knows, perhaps something better.

In reality—now there is one of the coldest phrases in the English language—what generally awaits is a bill from the electric company, another from a dentist, two magazine subscription offers, and a box containing a sample of a new hair spray. Yet where there is mail there is desire, and sometimes there are surprises. Most of these derive from my occupation as a writer. Writing for publication makes for strange pen pals. People feel that writers are, somehow, in the public domain, which in a sense they are, and they write to them freely. Any sort of serious letter in response to something he has written is likely to be gratifying to a writer; I know it is to me. I suspect that I get my share of such letters: letters of touching appreciation, of correction, of untrammeled anger. "With all wishes for all kinds of bad luck," one recent correspondent ended a letter of the latter kind, which was positively charming next to the letter of an anonymous admirer that began "May God castrate you!"

Which brings me to George Santayana's wing chair. More than a decade ago I wrote an essay for the *New Republic* about George Santayana, a writer who seemed to me to represent the height of intellectual elegance. The essay appeared in print, and then, some four weeks later, a letter turned up from Austria, forwarded to me from the *New Republic*. I no longer have the letter, but, as I recall, it was written on linen of a quality out of which I should have liked to have a summer suit made. The letter itself opened with a paragraph of carefully measured praise for my essay—praise which spoke of my mental penetration and exquisite sensibility. (Certainly there was nothing here of substance that I would care to argue about.) My correspondent went on to inform me that he had been a student of Santayana's at Harvard, and had been left a number of his personal effects. Among these was the philosopher's favorite wing chair. Would I, so clearly an admirer of Santayana, be interested in having it?

I thought a good bit about that wing chair. I set it in different rooms in my home, considered the ethics of having it reupholstered, wondered if it carried any talismanic qualities. Had Santayana written *Dominations and Powers* sitting in that chair? Was it the same chair in which he sat, in the single room provided him by the Hospital of Blue Nuns outside Rome, while making his own abridgment of *The Life of Reason*? Merely to sit in such a chair could not but increase my powers of ratiocination, subtlety, serenity. Did I want that wing chair? Do graduate students wear jeans? Do South American politicians go in for sunglasses?

I wrote to my correspondent in Austria to thank him, first, for his kind words and, second, for his generous offer. I should, I wrote, want to pay the expense of shipping the chair to the United States. He returned my letter by saying that he would foot the shipping costs, which would come out of the eight hundred dollars that he wanted for the chair. Thus ended our correspondence. I could be quite wrong about this, but I imagine him waiting out a month of silence on my end, picking up the current week's *New Republic*, skimming an essay therein on, say, Mark Twain. Then he takes out a sheet of that splendid stationery and writes to its author, saying that, through his mother, who as a young girl had lived two doors down from Samuel and Olivia Clemens in Hartford, he had come into ownership of the favorite wing chair of Mark Twain. . . .

But, it occurs to me now, I may have imagined that Santayana's wing chair was offered to me only because of an authorly twist of pride. Perhaps my correspondent's first paragraph of praise for my writing lulled me into thinking that the remainder of his letter had to do with my reward—as if by writing well about Santayana I really deserved to have his chair. "I find I have enough of the author in me," the young Horace Walpole wrote, "to be extremely susceptible to flattery." As any writer knows, or anyone who has spent much time around writers, when it comes to flattery, compliments, praise generally, Walpole's "extremely susceptible" is putting the case very gently indeed. I have known many writers so extremely susceptible that, by comparison, they make George Jessel seem as modest as St. Therese of Lisieux.

The need for praise on the part of writers is probably greater than that of other workers in the arts, if only because writers never get the direct response to their work that composers, visual artists, and performing artists do. Perhaps this is why so many novelists and poets have attempted to write for the stage, where they can hear the laughter, see the tears, palpably feel the tension that their work creates. Writers receive reviews, of course, but these are of books only and hence few and far between; moreover, the reviews, for one reason or another, are likely to be unsatisfactory. Thus, most writers, especially if they do not live in New York, must take their injections of praise, if they are to get any at all, epistolarily.

This need for praise—great, heaping banana-split dishes of it—is not on the whole a thing calculated to remind one of the dignity of mankind. Lest I seem to exempt myself from the need, I had better quickly say that I am not exempt. I do have standards in praise, though they are rickety. I like my praise to be intelligent and, preferably, convincing, delivered by a person who has a respect for precision in language and a strong sense of history. If these qualities are lacking, I'll take it any other way I can. Rarely have I found the praise tendered me to be fulsome, though I do recall one instance where I thought things were getting out of hand. An editor for whom I once did a good deal of writing was hitting a crescendo of praise rather too early in our relationship, I thought; soon he would be comparing my pitiful scribblings with Dante and Homer. (Robert Southey is supposed to have said to a contemporary whose name I cannot recall, "You will be remembered long after Homer is forgot—but not until.") I requested him to cease and desist, and, in lieu of further praise, I asked him to send me a letter, on company stationery, proclaiming me and my writing a force for change in Latin America. This he promptly did, and thenceforth we were able to conduct a seemly editorial relationship, free on his side from the need to lavish further praise.

Sometimes the sunshine of epistolary praise turns into drizzles of oddly angled criticism, or, if not quite criticism, then a reaction quite other than what one had hoped for. In this category of letter I shall not soon forget the response to a segment of a book I wrote which was reprinted in the *Reader's Digest*. The segment had to do with the then new phenomenon of how-to-do-it sex manuals, a phenomenon that I, as an ethical platitudinarian, attacked on grounds aesthetic, psychological, and moral. Some months later, a letter, sent on to me from the *Reader's Digest*, arrived from a faithful subscriber in the Philippines. It read:

> I perused with extreme interest your fine article in current *Readers Digest*, in which you make strong censure on such tomes as *Everything You Ever Wanted to Know About Sex*, *The Joy of Sex*, *New Approaches to Sex in Marriage* by Dr. Eichenlaub, *Sensuous Woman* by J., and studies by Johnson and Masters. What you say is most intriguing. But, may I inquire, do you still possess these above-mentioned tomes? If so, would you send them on to me? I should be more than willing to provide the postage moneys for them. Please answer soonest.

Ah, me, another rainy day in the Republic of Letters.

But what should a perfect delivery of mail contain? This of course will differ from person to person, but for me it would include a letter from an old friend with whom I have been too long out of touch, a letter from someone I love, two letters in airmail envelopes from overseas, a letter containing some found money (an unexpected tax rebate, say, or a reprint fee), a good book that has been long awaited, a letter from someone previously unknown but obviously good-hearted and intelligent, and (finally) a letter informing me that an engagement I had foolishly committed myself to, and that has worried me ever since, has been indefinitely postponed.

What a perfectly dreary mail delivery would contain is easier to imagine. In it would be a letter from the IRS headed "Final Notice Before Seizure," a letter requesting a large loan from an acquaintance to whom all of one's own previous letters have come back stamped "Addressee Unknown," a letter thick with praise from someone certifiably despicable, and a telegram reading "Ignore last wire" when no previous wire has been received. It would also contain invitations that one does not want and that one would, if possible, be willing to expose oneself to certain short-lived yet quite painful tropical diseases to get out of. In "The Adventure of the Noble Bachelor," Conan Doyle has Sherlock Holmes remark to Watson, "Yes, my correspondence has certainly the charm of variety, and the humbler are usually the more interesting. This looks like one of those unwelcome social summonses which call upon a man either to be bored or to lie."

I can also do nicely without letters of the tutelary kind Edmund Wilson often used to send to friends. I have recently read two collections of Wilson's letters, *The Nabokov-Wilson Letters* and *Letters on Literature and Politics, 1912–1972.* They are splendid to read, full of literary history and sharp observation, but many of them cannot have been too pleasant to receive. I think here particularly of those letters in which Wilson lectured, upbraided, and generally hectored his contemporaries on their literary shortcomings, a thing he was never loath to do. Not a man long on tact, Edmund Wilson—as, for example, when he wrote to the young Scott Fitzgerald that some lines in a poem Fitzgerald had written "possess a depth and dignity of which I didn't think you capable." A bit near the knuckle, as the English say, but worse, and lengthier, examples are ready to hand. Receiving one of these stinging letters from Wilson must have made a person feel, whatever his age, like Lord Chesterfield's son, forced to take all that instruction and abuse—but without the prospect of one day coming into a title.

No, the better letters carry lighter loads. Madame de Sévigné and Horace Walpole, two of the great letter writers, almost insist upon their lightness. Walpole wrote to one Henry Seymour Conway at the close of a letter: "Well! I have here set you the example of writing nonsense when one has nothing to say, and shall take it ill if you don't keep up the correspondence on the same foot. Adieu!" And Madame de Sévigné, in a letter to the Comte de Bussy, writes: "I know not how you can like my letters; they are written in a style of carelessness, which I feel, without being able to remedy it." Of course, neither Madame de Sévigné nor Walpole is finally light. Both are truly charming and, being considerate, cannot help charming others. They are born letter writers. (Madame de Sévigné wrote nothing but letters.) They take short views, living day by day. They are cheerful without being deluded about life. Their wit, their common sense, their perspective, their generosity—all these qualities give their letters a cumulative weight.

Small splendors are the stock-in-trade of the great letter writers: anecdotes, observations, aperçus. A man named John Chute writes to Walpole about being put on a "temperate diet," which causes Walpole to rejoin with this little disquisition on the roast-beef eating habits of Englishmen:

Only imagine that I here every day see men, who are mountains of roast beef, and only seem just roughly hewn out into the outlines of human form, like the giant-rock at Pratolino. I shudder when I see them brandish their knives in act to carve, and look on them as savages that devour one another. I should not stare at all more than I do, if yonder Alderman at the lower end of the table was to stick his fork into his neighbor's jolly cheek, and cut a brave slice of brown and fat. Why I'll swear I see no difference between a country gentleman and a sirloin; whenever the first laughs, or the latter is cut, there run out just the same streams of gravy! Indeed, the sirloin does not ask quite so many questions.

The greatest letter writer among Americans, in my view, is easily Justice Holmes. He is one of the few writers who can lift me out of such brief depressions as my withering attention span will allow. Holmes is the one American model of the good life; activist and intellectual both, he was a man of wide interests and absolutely no superficiality. Of late I have been reading his correspondence with Sir Frederick Pollock, the English jurist. While stretches of these letters are taken up with matters legal, from which I am intellectually excluded, this does not in the least put me off. Instead I fall into the rhythm of Holmes's life: his vacations at Beverly Farms, the longer months when the Supreme Court is in session, his reports on his reading, his comments upon the life around him. His style is virile, and he himself is—though one scarcely ever hears the word anymore—manly in the most attractive way.

Good letters do not usually submit to the discipline of topic sentences. Thus Walpole, in a letter to George Montagu, writes, "If all the adventures don't conclude as you expect in the beginning of a paragraph, you must not wonder. . . ." Justice Holmes's letters, too, often have this pleasing jumble, this *méli-mélo*. Within the compass of a single paragraph of a letter written in 1928, when he was eighty-seven, Holmes remarks on thesis interpretations of American history of the kind produced by Charles Beard and Vernon Parrington that "belittling arguments often have a force of their own, but you and I believe that high-mindedness is not impossible to man"; that he finds Anita Loos's *But Gentlemen Marry Brunettes* dreary because "sexual talk or innuendo is displeasing from a woman, I think. Perhaps because we know, though the older literary tradition is the other way, that they take less interest in the business than we do"; and ends on yet another of his fresh, comical, yet serious metaphors for death: "Most of the places here now to me are sockets from which the occupants that I knew have been extracted by the final dentist."

In one of their exchanges Holmes and Pollock name those they deem to be literature's great letter writers. Both agree on Horace Walpole. Pollock places Samuel Johnson ahead of Charles Lamb. Holmes mentions Byron; Pollock adds Edward FitzGerald and Walter Raleigh. Neither, though, brings up the name of Justice Holmes's contemporary, Henry James, whose letters were not then as accessible as they have since become. No one surpassed Henry James for writing beautiful letters of condolence. The death of a friend was always the occasion for a moving tribute, in which James provided a celebratory portrait—making, as Leon Edel remarks in his biography of James, "his condolences into a muted epistolary elegy." So fine are these letters, so properly measured and elegantly turned, they seem almost worth dying for.

Initially, of course, the English novel was epistolary in form. Letters play an important part in much of Henry James's fiction, and one of his finest stories, "In the Cage," is about a woman who works in a post-and-telegraph office. James M. Cain's *The Postman Always Rings Twice* is only peripherally about the post; but Albert Halper, in *The Chute*, wrote a novel about workers in a Chicago mail-order house. In *Herzog* Saul Bellow deploys letters brilliantly, having his hero write to historical personages to great comic effect: *"Dear Herr Nietzsche—My dear sir, May I ask a question from the floor?" "Dear Governor Stevenson, Just a word with you, friend."* Many a novel and short story has turned on a letter sent, or discovered, or torn up at the last moment.

Nowadays such epistolary intervention in fiction will not quite do. A question of suspension of disbelief is involved; too few readers would be willing to believe that the decisive letter was actually delivered. I make this judgment on the basis of complaints I hear about postal delivery, which, to put it softly, are manifold. Postal delivery is another of those areas of civilization that give the lie to theories of progress. Currently people of cosmopolitan correspondence claim that the chance of winning in a state lottery is far better than the chance that a letter sent to Italy will reach the person it is addressed to. England once had the finest of all postal systems; fifty years ago a correspondent could send out a letter in the morning and receive an answer by evening. Edward Shils tells a story of a letter from Hungary tersely addressed to him as "Professor Edward Shils, Sociologist, England" reaching him safely at the London School of Economics. This was under the old dispensation; under the new dispensation, English mails seem scarcely better than American. Ours are erratic at best: sometimes a letter will take but a single day to make its way from the Middle West to either coast, whereas another letter will take four days to get across town.

I suppose one must partly blame the drop in the quality of postal service on the rise of what is rightly called "junk mail." The postmen's sacks are weighed down annually with some 34 billion pieces of junk mail, or roughly a third of all letters mailed in the United States. Selling through the mails is a brisk business, and there are professional brokers who deal exclusively with compiling and renting mailing lists to various firms and causes. Thus a person who subscribes to one magazine is considered fair game for all. Send in ten dollars to help save the whale, and before the year is out one is certain to be pitched for funds to put an end to the gelding of goldfish. For decades now the *New Yorker* has run, at the bottom of its slender columns, examples of silly opening gambits used in junk mail—under the rubric "Letters We Never Finished Reading." But there have been true advances in this sort of bumf. A recent letter soliciting a magazine subscription showed up in my mailbox bearing the line "Should you be punished for being born with a high I.Q.?" on the outside of the envelope. A new rubric, clearly, is called for: "Letters We Never Started Reading."

Letters I usually do finish reading are those printed in the letters columns of intellectual magazines. Controversies over some point in scholarship or in politics have an interest that transcends the points that originally gave rise to them; the interest is in seeing intellectuals in extremis, always a gaudy spectacle. Literary widows rush in to protect their husbands against what they deem defamation; disgruntled authors lash back at reviewers; intellectual kibitzers stick in their two cents' worth. Much about the character of an intellectual magazine can be discovered from the letters it prints. If most of them are congratulatory, something is amiss. Disagreement is the true oxygen of these magazines, argument and mental fencing their real exercise, intellectual bloodletting their only physic. Of present-day polemicists, I think Professor H. R. Trevor-Roper easily the best, the man most adept at laying a polemical opponent wide open; Noam Chomsky, on the subjects of Southeast Asia and the Middle East, has proved himself far and away the most boring; and the *TLS* the site of the most entertaining of these polemical picnics.

The tradition of the polemical letter goes well back, of course. Here, for example, is Oscar Wilde in 1890 in *Truth* magazine, answering Whistler's accusation of plagiarism by simply blowing Whistler off the court:

> I can hardly imagine that the public are in the very smallest degree interested in the shrill shrieks of "Plagiarism" that proceed from time to time out of the lips of silly vanity or incompetent mediocrity.
>
> However, as Mr. James Whistler has had the impertinence to attack me with both venom and vulgarity in your columns, I hope you will allow me to state that the assertions contained in his letters are as deliberately untrue as they are deliberately offensive.
>
> The definition of a disciple as one who has the courage of the opinions of his master is really too old even for Mr. Whistler to be allowed to claim it, and as for borrowing Mr. Whistler's ideas about art, the only thoroughly original ideas I have ever heard him express have had reference to his own superiority as a painter over painters greater than himself.
>
> It is a trouble for any gentleman to have to notice the lucubrations of so ill-bred and ignorant a person as Mr. Whistler, but your publication of his insolent letter leaves me no option in the matter.

I have extracted this little lyric of artful nastiness from a book entitled *Dear Sir, Drop Dead! Hate Mail Through the Ages*, edited by Donald Carroll (Collier Books). If there are 34 billion pieces of junk mail sent annually, another billion pieces of hate mail may well be aloft during the same period. A great deal of such mail is sent to people who appear on television regularly; politicians get a goodly share; athletes, authors, and others on public view come in for their epistolary abuse. Mr. Carroll remarks that the hate letter is "probably the most popular and enduring genre of folk literature in the world," adding that "it is the only literary form that has always had more practitioners than readers"—this last referring to the fact that most people who receive it throw their hate mail away unread. Although my scribblings have brought me only driblets of hate mail, such specimens of it as I have received I have read sedulously and saved. One day I plan to return each piece of hate mail in my possession to its owner, along with a note that reads:

> Sir: Out of the distant and rather dim possibility that my correspondence will one day be made public, I now return your vicious little letter to you. Odious though you may be, I see no reason why your grandchildren should have to be presented with such clear and irrefutable evidence of their forebear's ill-temper and imbecility.

This, though, is rather heavy-handed next to the crisp volley that an impudent letter provoked from Voltaire: "I am seated in the smallest room in the house. I have your letter before me. Soon it will be behind me." H. L. Mencken, a professional controversialist, apparently received enough angry mail to warrant his printing up a postcard that read "Dear Sir or Madam, You may or may not be right," which can only have left his antagonists purple with frustration.

Angry letters and sweet, Mencken used to answer all mail sent to him on the same day he received it. This is a noble ideal, to which the closest I can come is a weak sigh of aspiration. Alas, one serious drawback about letters is that, in order to get them, one must send some out. When it comes to the mail, I feel it is better to receive than to give. I suspect I am not alone in this view. Paul Horgan, in *Approaches to Writing*, suggests, "A test of characters in fiction: can you imagine how they would write letters?" This may be a good test for characters in fiction, but I know too many people who could not pass it in life.

I have never counted but I think I must write roughly eight hundred letters a year. The great majority of them have to do with business; many are little more than notes requesting this or responding to that. Almost all these letters are written in fits and starts, eight or ten at a sitting. Energy for writing letters seems, in my case, to arrive in spurts. I have on a few occasions had secretarial help, but I seem unable to dictate a letter to my own satisfaction, being one of those people who can only think with a pen in hand or a typewriter before them. I often wish it were otherwise. Along with Mencken's promptitude, I wish I could command the oil magnate Calouste Gulbenkian's method of writing letters, as described by Kenneth Clark in the first volume of his memoirs, *Another Part of the Wood*:

> "Not an office man, Mr. Clark"; and sure enough he [Gulbenkian] had no office. In summer he did his work in the park of St. Cloud. His secretaries were seated at folding card tables situated in the boscage at intervals of about half a mile. He would trot up and down between them, with two detectives,

heavily invisible, padding along in the adjoining path. I sometimes accompanied him in these walks, and his mind moved
with such precision that by the time we reached the next card
table he was ready to dictate a detailed technical letter.

Not, to be sure, that the Gulbenkian method could ever hope
to produce beautiful letters in the style of Walpole or Madame de
Sévigné, et alia. It may well be that true literary letters will soon
be—if they are not already—a thing of the past. To write chatty
letters filled with news, descriptions, observations, and anecdotes is
an activity for which people no longer seem to have the leisure or
the energy—or, perhaps more accurately, the habit. The telephone
habit has partly replaced it. Writers, editors, publishers must conduct
fully as much, or more, of their business over local and long-distance
telephone as by letter. As a result, the literary record of the future
figures to be more fragmentary than that of the past. Splendid volumes of collected letters by writers born twenty-five years from now
are not easily imagined.

Yet I should not want to write off letters as an antiquated or dead
form. Letters remain invaluable for carefully formulated thought,
for good humor, for expressions of earnest sympathy. Sentiments
that human shyness will not always allow one to convey in conversation—sentiments of gratitude, of apology, of love—can often be more
easily conveyed in a letter. Having important or amusing or detailed
information in writing, to reflect upon, to reconsider, to re-read in
tranquility, remains a fine thing. Who has not carried a gratifying
letter around with him for days after he has received it—to read it
again at free moments and feel once more something of the pleasure

it gave on first reading? Amidst the junk mail and the hate mail and the crank mail, splendid letters continue to be written. The prospect of receiving such letters still causes me to respond eagerly to the postman's ring. So write, as they used to say during the Depression, if you find work.

(1979)

Balls-Up

Three fantasies:

    Primo: A Manhattan town house at a quite good address. The women in the room are very smartly dressed; the men are in dinner clothes. My hostess comes up to ask if I will agree to play. I demur, thanking her all the same. "Oh, please do," she says, with an earnestness I cannot find it in my heart to refuse. As I move toward the piano, a well-polished Baldwin grand, I hear a woman say, "He's going to play." Across the room, another woman murmurs, "He's going to play—I was so hoping he would!" I rub my hands together briefly, bend and unbend my fingers, and proceed to toss off a flawless rendering of *Rhapsody in Blue*. As I finish, I notice that everyone seems to have gathered round the piano. Ice cubes tinkle; cigarette smoke wafts to the ceiling. I play and sing two Cole Porter songs, then follow up with Noël Coward's "Imagine the Duchess's Feelings," which has everyone in stitches. I move on to play and sing—first in English, then in French—"I Won't Dance." I close, gently and with just a touch of profundity, with "September Song." Applause envelops me. "Now that," says my hostess, handing me a fresh drink, "was simply unforgettable!"

Secondo: A hill overlooking the Loire Valley. I appear over the crest of the hill in white linen trousers, a chambray shirt, a wide-brimmed straw hat of the kind Pope John XXIII used to wear when he would go into the streets of Rome. It is a perfect day: the sun shines, flowers are everywhere in bloom, the river is a serene azure. I set up my easel, my canvas chair, and, before beginning to mix my palette, eat a lunch of what Henry James once called "light cold clever French things." After lunch, working in watercolors, I begin to paint the vista before me in a strong line and with a use of color that falls between that of Degas and Dufy. I achieve a work that is obviously representational, yet, such is the force of my character, my sensibility, my vision, is just as obviously a small masterpiece. When I am done, I put away my materials with the confidence of a man who, though he knows he is out of step with the times, knows that his own time will come.

Terzo: A large empty room, good wood floors, clean light flowing in from the windows along its north wall. On the south wall is a mirror reaching from floor to ceiling. I enter, remove my suit coat, loosen my tie. I stretch my arms out to the side, turn my head first clockwise, then counterclockwise. I bend over to pick up three rubber balls, one red, one yellow, one blue. I toss the red ball from my right hand to my left, then back again to my right hand. I feel the heft and balance of each of the balls in my hands. I begin to juggle them, flipping a new ball into the air each time the previous one reaches its peak and begins its descent, all the while softly humming to myself the strains of "Lady of Spain." After three or four minutes of this, I add a fourth ball, a green one, which joins the cascade I create by juggling the balls gingerly from hand to hand. Then I add a fifth ball, orange; later a sixth, purple. Six balls in the air! The cascade has now become a rainbow revolving before me. My control is complete, my pleasure in this control no less. My only regret is that there is not room in my hands for a seventh ball. Perspiring lightly, effortlessly keeping all these balls in the air, I smile as I hum "Over the Rainbow."

Now of these three fantasies, two are not merely improbable but, for me, utterly impossible. Although I spend a goodly amount of time listening to records and going to concerts, I can neither read music nor play a musical instrument. Worse, I was one of those children who, in grade school, was asked not to sing but just to mouth the words, lest my naturally off-key voice carry the rest of the class along with me into the thickets of dissonance. My drawing was of roughly the same discouraging caliber. In school periods devoted to art, teachers who walked up and down the aisles checking their students' sketches and paintings never stopped, or even hesitated, to gaze at mine, which were so clearly beyond help or comment. If there were an artistic equivalent to mouthing words—a colorless crayon, say, or disappearing paint—I would, I am certain, have been asked to avail myself of it.

Denied these two gifts, of song and of drawing, I have, in life's rather arbitrary lottery, been allotted a third. I am reasonably well coordinated. Delete that "reasonably": I am extremely well coordinated. ("Don't be so humble," Golda Meir once said, "you're not that great.") I was never big or fast or physically aggressive enough to be a first-class athlete, but, as a boy, I could catch anything, or so I felt. Grounders, liners, fly balls—I gobbled them up. Throw a football anywhere within fifteen yards of me, and I would be there to meet it. In tennis I was most notable for flipping and catching my racquet in various snappy routines. In my teens I mastered most of the ballhandling tricks of the Harlem Globetrotters: spinning a basketball on my index finger, rolling it down my arm and catching it behind my back, dribbling while prone. Quite simply, I had quick and confident hands. Perhaps I should be more humble about these playground skills, for I make myself sound pretty great.

Great and humble though I apparently am, juggling is something I have never been able, yet have long yearned, to do. It is one of those fantasies possible of fulfillment, like going to Greece. Besides, juggling seemed a harmless enough fantasy, involving neither the disruption of the ecosystem nor the corruption of children. And then one day not long ago, in the produce section of the grocery store where I shop, I saw the owner's wife, an Irishwoman of great high spirits, juggling three navel oranges. So filled with envy was I that I determined then and there to learn to juggle.

When an intellectual wants to learn something he goes to the library. He reads up. But it turned out that at my library there was not much to read on the subject of juggling. The library's two books on juggling had been taken out. The library also had a novel entitled *The Juggler* by Michael Blankfort, but it, too, was gone from the shelves. Doubtless this novel is not about juggling at all but instead uses the word metaphorically, as does the final entry in the library's catalogue on the subject, *Juggling: The Art of Balancing Marriage, Motherhood, and a Career.* No help there. It was beginning to look, as the English say, like a bit of a balls-up.

I remembered that William Hazlitt wrote an essay entitled "The Indian Jugglers," which I reread. It starts magnificently: "Coming forward and seating himself on the ground in his white dress and tightened turban, the chief of the Indian Jugglers begins with tossing up two brass balls, which is what any of us could do, and concludes with keeping up four at the same time, which is what none of us could do to save our lives, nor if we were to take our whole lives to do it in." Hazlitt proceeds to describe the Indian juggler's act, noting that the juggler astonishes while giving pleasure in astonishment. "There is something in all this," he writes, "which he who does not admire may be quite sure he never admired really anything in the whole course of his life." Reading this I felt one of the keenest delights that reading offers: the discovery that someone more intelligent than yourself feels about a given subject exactly as you do.

Hazlitt then moves on to compare the juggler's skill with brass balls to his own skill with words—and finds the latter paltry in comparison. Nothing in his own work is so near perfection as that which the Indian juggler can do. "I can write a book: so can many others who have not even learned to spell," Hazlitt writes. His own essays—some of the greatest written in English—he calls "abortions." "What errors, what ill-pieced transitions, what crooked reasons, what lame conclusions! How little is made out, and that little how ill!" The juggler can keep four balls in the air, but for Hazlitt "it is as much as I can manage to keep the thread of one discourse clear and unentangled." The juggler, through patient practice, has brought his skill to perfection, something which Hazlitt feels unable to come anywhere near doing with his. "I have also time on my hands to correct my opinions, polish my periods: but the one I cannot, and the other I will not do."

Anyone who does intellectual work will instantly recognize the cogency of Hazlitt's comments. So little does such work allow for a true sense of completion, or a satisfying feeling of perfection. Every artist has felt this, and the better the artist the more achingly has he felt it. "A poem is never finished," said Valéry, "but only abandoned." If Hazlitt and Valéry, two workers in diamonds, felt this way about their works, imagine how those of us who labor with zircons feel about ours! As an old costume jeweler, I must say, I appreciate the possibility that juggling holds out for perfection—for doing the small thing extremely well.

For me, though, more is involved. Within very serious limits I am a self-improvement buff, if only a failed one. Of myself in this connection I can say, every day in every way I stay pretty much the same. A few years ago, for example, I set out to learn classical Greek. Aglow with the luster of self-betterment, I enrolled myself in a course in Greek at the university where I teach—and lasted a cool and inglorious two weeks. Walking into the room on the first day of class, I was taken for the teacher, a natural enough confusion since I was more than twenty years older than anyone else in the course (except for the actual teacher, who turned out to be roughly twenty years older than I). Being the old boy, I felt a certain obligation not to appear stupid. The option taken by a likable fellow named Fred McNally, who more than two decades ago sat next to me in an undergraduate French class, and who whenever called upon answered through an entire semester, "Beats me, sir," did not seem an option open to me. Given my natural ineptitude with foreign languages and my fear of having to avail myself of the McNally ploy, I found myself studying Greek two hours a night. Add to this another hour for class and yet another hour for getting there and back, and nearly one-fourth of my waking life was given over to this little self-improvement project. The result was the general disimprovement of everything else in my life. In the end I decided that learning Greek would have to be on that long list of items I must put off until the afterlife.

Juggling balls is surely less time-consuming than juggling Greek paradigms, but is it really self-improving? Having thought a bit about this, I have concluded that it is not a whit self-improving. Juggling is in fact the recreational equivalent of art for art's sake. It is not good exercise; you do not do it in the sunshine; it is not an excuse for gambling; it does not simulate the conditions of life; it teaches no morality (you can't even cheat at it, a prospect which lends so many games, from golf to solitaire, a piquant touch). Unlike, say, playing in the outfield, you cannot even think of anything else while doing it. Juggling is all-absorbing and an end in itself: *le jeu pour le jeu.*

Juggling is play, almost with a vengeance. "We may call everything play," writes Santayana, "which is useless activity, exercise that springs from the physiological impulse to discharge energy which the exigencies of life have not called out." Juggling also satisfies some of the criteria Huizinga lays down for play in *Homo Ludens.* It does, as Huizinga puts it, "create order, *is* order. Into an imperfect world and into the confusions of life it brings a temporary, a limited perfection." And juggling is certainly, to quote Huizinga again, "invested with the noblest qualities we are capable of perceiving in things: rhythm and harmony." Excluding people who use it to make a living by entertaining others, however, juggling is neither a fine nor a useful art, but rather a delicate, slightly perverse activity. No self-improvement, no end other than itself, sheer play, exquisitely useless—these are among the qualities that endear juggling to me.

Some people can do entirely without play, but I am not one of them. Neither is Georges Simenon, who, I was surprised to learn while recently reading his journal, *When I Was Old,* is of all things a golfer. Nor was Hazlitt, who was a dedicated player of fives, an English version of handball. Matthew Arnold was an ice-skater. Ezra Pound enthusiastically—as, unfortunately, he did everything—played tennis. Edmund Wilson was a passionate amateur magician. Other artists and intellectuals, if not themselves players, were devoted followers of games: G. H. Hardy, the Cambridge mathematician, of cricket, and Marianne Moore of baseball. While I am unable to report that T. S. Eliot had a bowling average of 192 or that Einstein was a pool shark, my guess is that among the most serious mental workers there is many a hidden player.

My own small problem is that sources of play have been drying up on me. For many years now I have been unable to take any interest in mental games: crossword puzzles, chess, bridge, Scrabble. Even poker, a game I once loved, no longer retains much interest for me, unless the stakes are high enough to frighten me. Basketball, another former love, is now too vigorous a game for me, and I can today walk under a glass backboard without even wistfully looking up. As a boy, I was a quite decent tennis player, but I find I have no appetite for being a mediocre player in a game I used to play well. I do play the game called racquetball, yet if a week goes by in which I do not get on the court, I do not weep.

The reason I no longer take any interest in mental games, I have concluded, is that I do mental work, and consequently seem to have little in the way of mental energy left for mental play. I have noticed, by the way, that many people who have a great deal of zest for such games, and who are very good at them, are often people of real intelligence whose work does not require them to make strenuous demands on their mental powers. For myself, I would rather be thinking of phrases or formulations to be used in essays than of how best to get off a blitz or of a four-letter word that means payment in arrears.

As for my loss of interest in physical games, here the problem, I think, is that I have lost the power to fantasize while playing. When playing tennis or basketball, for example, I find I can no longer imagine myself at center court at Wimbledon or in the final game of the NCAA at Pauley Pavilion, the sort of thing I invariably did as a boy. Nor am I sufficiently competitive to enjoy winning for its own sake, even though on the whole it is rather better than losing. The friend with whom I play racquetball and who is a much better athlete than I—as a boy he was an all-state football player and later a Big Ten wrestling champion—is even less competitive than I. Sometimes I wonder how either one of us ever manages to win the games we play against each other, and it usually turns out that not the better man but the least tired man wins.

Nor have I ever had the discipline or concentration to play solitary games. Running, still much in vogue, is out of the question for me. I have never been able to take calisthenics of any sort seriously. I own a bicycle, which I ride occasionally and which gives me pleasure, but this is scarcely a game. In fact, it has become most useful to me as part of a riposte. Lately, when people suggest I must be making a lot of money as a fairly productive writer, I reply, "If I am doing so well, how come I'm still riding a reconditioned three-speed Huffy?"

All this makes it the more interesting to me that I am so keen about juggling—a form of play that is both solitary and requires real discipline. Despite such drawbacks, juggling thrills me. In the phrase of the bobby-soxers of the late 1940s, it really sends me. Another drawback is that juggling, unlike other games and sports—if juggling is indeed a game or a sport—does not have an established lore, a pantheon of heroes. It is, of course, a very old form of play: court jesters, I believe, had juggling in their repertoires. But if there was a Babe Ruth, a Jim Thorpe, or a Joe Louis of juggling, I have not heard of him.

True, many of the silent-movie stars, who came out of vaudeville, juggled. Charlie Chaplin did and so did Buster Keaton. I recall a hilarious Buster Keaton movie—which of his movies isn't hilarious?—in which Buster is a contestant on a radio amateur hour whose talent turns out to be juggling. Juggling, mind you, over the radio. In the movie Keaton, deadpan as always, is blithely tossing balls in the air, while in their homes the members of the listening audience are banging away on the sides of their Philco consoles, certain that the silence is attributable to a loose tube. A splendid bit.

W. C. Fields broke into show business as a juggler, a skill at which he is said to have been consummate. In Robert Lewis Taylor's biography, *W. C. Fields: His Follies and Fortunes*, Fields is said to have begun juggling at the age of nine, inspired by the vaudeville performance of a group calling itself the Byrne Brothers. Fields's father hawked fruit and vegetables in Philadelphia, and Fields practiced on his father's wares. "By the time I could keep two objects going," he said, "I'd ruined forty dollars worth of fruit." He later worked with cigar boxes, croquet balls, Indian clubs, and odd utensils. In his early adolescence he was obsessed with juggling. He worked hours and hours at it, teaching himself to keep five tennis balls in the air, catching canes with his feet, and performing any other kind of trick he could dream up.

Fields's specialty as a juggler was to appear to fumble, then recover from what had all the marks of a disastrous error. He never lost his relish for this artful bumbling. Later in life, while serving his guests at large dinner parties, Fields would fill a plate, preferably for a comparative stranger, and, as he would begin to hand it down the line, drop it, "provoking," as his biographer tells it, "a loud concerted gasp. With consummate nonchalance he would catch it just off the floor, without interrupting whatever outrageous anecdote he was relating at the moment." But the best juggling story Robert Lewis Taylor tells is about the night Fields was working on some new trick in a hotel room in Pittsburgh, when his continual dropping of a heavy object disturbed the tenant in the room below, a bruiser who came up to complain. The complainant recognized Fields as the juggler he had seen earlier that evening at a local theater. To calm the man down Fields taught him a simple trick calling for juggling two paring knives. "I hope he worked at it," Fields said in recounting the story, "because if he did, he was almost certain to cut himself very painfully." Fieldsian, absolutely Fieldsian.

Juggling today appears to be undergoing a small renaissance. Street jugglers appear in profusion along Fisherman's Wharf in San Francisco. In Manhattan they mingle among the multitudes of street vendors. Although I myself have not seen the act, there is at work nowadays a group known as the Brothers Karamazov that is said to give great satisfaction. Along with other odd-shaped objects, the Brothers K juggle running buzz saws and, most astonishing of all, live cats. A few new juggling books have recently been published: *Juggling for the Complete Klutz* is the title of one and *The Juggling Book* that of another. Have we the makings here of a wildly popular fad?

My guess is that we do not. For one thing, juggling is just too damned difficult to catch on—if you will pardon the expression—with great numbers of people. For another, it lacks manufacturing possibilities. Balls can still be bought at dime stores (if not quite, lamentably, for dimes). So far as I know, Adidas, Nike, Puma, and other sports-equipment manufacturers have yet to produce juggling shoes, juggling shorts, or juggling watches. Certainly there is no need for them. I myself, when juggling, wear the simplest costume: buskins turned up at the toes, gold pantaloons, a leathern jerkin, and a cap with bells.

But the time, surely, has come to get some balls in the air. How good a juggler am I? In two words, not very. In trying to explain my quality as a novice juggler I feel rather as Buster Keaton must have felt while juggling over the radio. I can keep three balls in the air for roughly two minutes. I do the conventional beginner's pattern known as "the cascade," in which the balls appear to be flowing over a perpetual waterfall. While juggling I can go from a standing to a kneeling position; I can juggle sitting down. I can vary the cascade pattern with the pattern known as "the half-shower," in which. . . . But I hear you banging on your Philco. Let me conclude then by saying that, as a juggler, I am far from ready for Vegas, television, or even small family parties.*

Yet such limited prowess as I have I owe to my mentor, a man who calls himself, on the title page of *The Juggling Book*, Carlo. His real name is Charles Lewis. Mr. Lewis has done a bit of this and a bit of that, from teaching math and science in public schools to leading encounter groups to founding a spiritualist newspaper to organizing a small circus troupe. From the photograph of him on the back of the book—long dark hair, a gray beard, corduroy jeans, loose-sleeved East Indian shirt—he looks rather guruish, and guruish he turns out to be. The Carlo Method, as Mr. Lewis styles his teaching, is not without a large measure of current psychobabble. Given half a chance—and as the author of his own book, he has more than half a chance—Carlo will babble on about "levels of awareness," "great

---

* Here I cannot resist bragging. Since writing this essay, I have learned all the fundamental tricks of juggling with three balls. I can also do a number of four-ball tricks, and have only recently begun to learn to juggle with plastic clubs. I am, therefore, ready for small family parties, but only useful, I fear, to end especially dull ones, as someone once suggested that two long-play records of the late Ludwig Erhard explaining the German economic miracle was, similarly, good for ending dull parties.

possibilities for creativity," "control and direction of body forces," "inner states," "healing effects on your psyche," and, natch, that old rotting botanical metaphor, "growing." Juggling, Carlo advises, will help me "continue to grow." Thank you, Carlo, but I was growing before I read your book: growing older, growing feebler, growing closer to death—growth enough, I should think.

When Carlo knocks off the psycho-spiritual palaver, which I find so *antipatico*, he is an excellent teacher. He writes clearly, and he takes the novice through each step slowly. He had me worried at first, though, when he said that juggling, like riding a bicycle or whistling, is something everyone can learn to do, since I, after repeated attempts to learn, can whistle only pitiably. Juggling turns out to be one of those activities (tennis is another) in which one benefits greatly from professional instruction at the outset. Fundamentals—how to position your body, how to hold the balls, how to toss them—are decisive. Unlike almost any other ball game, for example, you do not use your fingertips in juggling but instead toss the balls from your palms. In all these matters Carlo is very helpful. Sometimes, too, he will strike off a delicately humorous sentence, as when he advises not to reach up to catch the balls but rather to let them fall into your hands. "The balls will come down," he writes, "which I can guarantee from long experience." Sometimes he will hit exactly the right lyrical note, as when he writes: "Somehow there is a ball up there that's never going to come down. You realize suddenly that you never have to stop; you can juggle forever." He is right about that, and when it occurs, it is a golden moment. On the day it finally happened to me, after more than a week of practice, I felt sheer exhilaration and wanted to shout, "Look, Ma, both hands!"

Earlier I said that juggling does not provide much in the way of exercise. Let me amend that by saying that at the beginning you do get quite a bit of exercise—chasing the balls you drop. To cut down the chasing I began practicing in my wife's and my bedroom, juggling over the bed and thereby, as a friend remarked, turning a conjugal into a conjuggle bed. Not long afterward, by turning on our clock radio, I added music to my practice sessions and discovered that the piano rags of Scott Joplin are particularly nice to juggle to. As my juggling began to improve, so did the music. Stan Getz's saxophone makes for fine juggling accompaniment and so do Haydn's piano trios and Telemann's wind concertos. Juggling to Strauss waltzes and Glenn Miller swing is lovely. Opera is no good at all.

Part of the delight of juggling is the rhythmical pleasure created by the clear and steady beat of the balls slapping against the palms. This gives a satisfaction roughly analogous to that which a beginning pianist must feel when running through rudimentary practice exercises. Tossing the balls first high, then low, then in wide, then in narrow arcs, I can also create pleasing if altogether ephemeral designs of a kind I could never achieve with a crayon or paintbrush. In these small ways, then, juggling has compensated me for two common pleasures—those of rhythm and design—that my natural inaptitudes have hitherto prevented me from enjoying.

To drift slightly into metaphor, juggling has supplied the possibility, however small, of chaos in my life. Since beginning to juggle I now realize how exceedingly well-ordered my life has become. I read, I write, I teach, I live among family and friends whom I love. Nor would I have it otherwise. At the same time I have always marveled at, without necessarily admiring, those people who seem to have so high a threshold for chaos in their lives: people who can simultaneously carry on love affairs while behind in their alimony payments, have government liens on their businesses, and undergo chemotherapy—people who, to use a juggling metaphor, somehow manage to keep a lot of balls in the air. One such chaos merchant of my acquaintance, a man in his early fifties, recently married a woman of twenty-three while concurrently acquiring a mistress in her late forties, a brilliant reversal of the norm that had his friends surmising that he married for sex and kept a mistress for conversation. Whatever the case, the man is obviously a juggler.

At the same time, juggling is an exercise in subduing chaos. Keeping the balls in the air, making of them a fluid pattern, one achieves a pleasing kind of order. As with much art, the trick in juggling is to make the difficult look effortless. As Samuel Butler once put it,

> As lookers-on feel most delight,
> That least perceive a juggler's sleight,
> And still the less they understand,
> The more th' admire his sleight of hand.

Yet in juggling many are the moments—when a ball slips loose, when two balls collide in midair—when chaos wins and panic, for an instant, clutches the heart. At such moments one hears the knock of the house detective, feels the unopened IRS letter in the hand, sees the X-ray being slid dramatically from its envelope.

While the balls are in the air, describing their arcs, slapping gently against my hands, with everything under control, I am happy. Perhaps this happiness comes from my complete preoccupation with what I am doing. Perhaps it comes from the thrill of beginning to master a skill, however small and insignificant. It is a thoughtless happiness, an almost animal happiness, but no less real for all that.

With the balls flying about me, I am happy, but not, I must confess, altogether content. Even in my happiness I wonder if it is not time to move on and learn new tricks. Ought I to begin to master juggling four balls? What about rings and then Indian clubs? My man Carlo says that juggling on your back while on a trapeze is just about as far as one can go with this sort of thing. "Man thou art a wonderful animal," says Hazlitt, "and thy ways past finding out." William, I say, you don't know the half of it.

(1981)

But I Generalize

As a university teacher, I don't normally call students "honey," yet not long ago I not only called a student "honey," but, in a state of complete exasperation, I invited her to dance. It happened, as scandalous things frequently do, out of town. I was lecturing at a school in Ohio, and during a session with a group of freshman students, one of them, an earnest young woman, asked if I didn't think I sometimes engaged in dangerous generalizations. I allowed as how I generalized, but that I was not aware of doing so dangerously. Could she give me an example? Reading from one of my sacred and profound works, she adduced the following instance on the behavior of immigrants to America: ". . . Greeks ran restaurants, the Jews went into retailing, the Italians sold produce and became florists, the Irish (along with being policemen) worked as waiters and owned neighborhood bars, the Germans did a bit of everything." Well, those were certainly generalizations, but what, I asked, was dangerous about them?

"Wouldn't they be offensive to the people about whom you say these things?" she answered.

"Why?" I rejoined. "I myself, a member of the Hebrew extraction, as a black sergeant of mine once referred to Jews, am not in the least offended that my co-religionists went into retailing in this country. Nor do I think that the Greeks, Irish, Germans, and Italians would be in the least offended by my generalizations about them."

"Still," she said, "what you wrote isn't true of *all* Greeks, Jews, Italians, and Irish."

"True enough," I said, "Einstein didn't go into retailing but relativity, Fermi didn't go into flowers but fission. But there is enough general truth to my statements to hold up. At least I believe there is."

"Even if there is," she said, "I don't think you're entitled to say things like that."

And then it happened: "Honey," said I, "if I can't say things like that, then we may as well turn on the stereo and start dancing, because all conversation becomes impossible."

Along with demonstrating my ability to overpower an eighteen-year-old girl in argument, this incident reminds me not only of my own love of generalization but of its importance to civilized discourse. Generalization, especially risky generalization, is one of the chief methods by which knowledge proceeds. In science such generalizations are called hypotheses, and eventually these scientific generalizations have to be backed up. Apparently, though, this is not even true of all scientific generalizations; I recently learned, for example, that Gödel thought that "not everything that is true is provable." And Valéry spoke of that body of items that "are neither true nor false—in fact they could not be either." Outside of science, not all generalizations have to—or indeed can—be backed up. I sometimes think risky generalizations are the only kind that are of interest. Safe generalizations are usually rather boring. Delete that "usually rather." Safe generalizations are quite boring. But I generalize.

Generalizations have had a very bad press. Part of the reason they have been so roundly contemned is that they can so readily be pressed into service for inimical causes. What else is racism, what else anti-Semitism, but faulty generalizations organized and systematized? The most thoughtful writers have implored those who generalize to knock it off. "All general judgments are loose, slovenly, imperfect," noted Montaigne. "General notions," wrote Lady Mary Wortley Montagu, "are generally wrong." And Blake, never noted for the light touch, added, "To generalize is to be an idiot." Yet all these attacks on generalization—it will not have been missed by close readers—are themselves generalizations.

There are generalizations and there are generalizations—which is not only a generalization but very close to a tautology. Allow me to elaborate. I myself have a sharp distaste for large social generalizations, those, that is, whose pretense is to take in all of society. Lonely crowds, affluent societies, organization men are not for me. I am not too wild about Me Decades or Future Shocks, either. To pass muster with me, a generalization must not be too roomy, or cover too vast an area, or even be on too significant a subject. I despise, for instance, the notion that we are living in something called "a culture of narcissism," but I like very much John O'Hara's observation that "almost no woman who has gone beyond the eighth grade ever calls a fifty-cent piece a half-a-dollar." For me a generalization, like a friend, has to have a little modesty.

This doesn't mean that I am interested in modest generalizations exclusively. Not at all. I am afraid that I am one of those people who continues to read in the hope of sometime discovering in a book a single—and singular—piece of wisdom so penetrating, so soul stirring, so utterly applicable to my own life as to make all the bad books I have read seem well worth the countless hours spent on them. My guess is that this wisdom, if it ever arrives, will do so in the form of a generalization. My hope is that I am not dozing when it appears. Opportunity, to cite a generalization that is perhaps even more boring than it is false, knocks but once.

Meanwhile, I have an unrepentant fondness for authors who generalize. This would naturally include the great writers of aphorisms, many of them French (La Rochefoucauld, La Bruyère, Chamfort), a few German (G. C. Lichtenberg, Karl Kraus, Meister Eckhart), an occasional Englishman (Horace Walpole), and no Americans (Emerson, for me, does not qualify). Although novelists are supposed to show and not tell, I take particular pleasure in novelists who take a few moments off now and again to generalize. George Eliot goes in for this sort of thing, Proust does it rather more frequently, and, among living novelists, Anthony Powell, in his twelve-novel cycle, *A Dance to the Music of Time*, can almost be said to specialize in it. Not only does Powell himself, through his narrator Nicholas Jenkins, generalize, but so do other of his characters (the composer Moreland notably among them); and sometimes whole scenes will be given over to characters who generalize back and forth with one another. These generalizations are often a touch oblique, but unfailingly interesting.

"Nothing dates people more than the standards from which they have chosen to react," is a fair though modest sample of Anthony Powell's work in this line. But it can—and does—get much richer. Of a woman in one of the novels, the narrator asks, "Was she determined, in the habit of neurotics, to try to make things as bad for others as for herself?" Generalization, in Powell's hands, can be used even in the process of description. Walking into an apartment, for example, one of his characters smells "the fumes of unambitious cooking." Or he can create a general type and then go on to generalize upon his generalization. Such a general type, for Powell, is the "habitual role-sustainer," of whom he writes:

> Habitual role-sustainers fall, on the whole, into two main groups: those who have gauged to a nicety what shows them off to best advantage: others, more romantic if less fortunate in their fate, who hope to reproduce in themselves arbitrary personalities that have won their respect, met in life, read about in papers and books, or seen in films. These self-appointed players of a part often have little or no aptitude, are even notably ill equipped by appearance or demeanor, to wear the costume or speak the lines of the prototype. Indeed, the very unsuitability of the role is what fascinates.

The power of this, as of most generalizations, depends upon the experience one brings to it. I, in my experience, have known a number of Powellian habitual role-sustainers, not the least a contemporary who, though born in the Middle West, when in his early twenties became a kind of Englishman, a role he has sustained for more than a quarter of a century now. He is of the second type of Powell's habitual role-sustainers—that is, he is unsuitable for the role he has chosen. It doesn't come off. What is intended as elegance plays as pompous, even faintly comic. But it is too late to change roles. All one can hope for him now is knighthood or a plaque in Westminster Abbey.

Again, Anthony Powell notes of another of his characters that he spoke a number of foreign languages with facility, and that, as with all people who speak foreign languages easily, he was not quite to be trusted. Now here is an extraordinary generalization. So extraordinary is it that a reader needs to rub his eyes and read it again. To speak foreign languages easily, Mr. Powell is saying, is to be not altogether reliable. This seems wild, possibly a little mad. However, it presents a problem, at least for me, because almost everyone I have known who has had great facility in speaking foreign languages has been something less than reliable. Perhaps this gift of fluency is a form of linguistic adaptation: nature, in its inscrutable wisdom, has known that these men, because of their unreliability, will be asked to cross many borders and hence speak many languages and has equipped them accordingly, as in equipping certain tree-dwelling monkeys with prehensile tails.

As in the above instance, personal experience of the subject being generalized about is often essential to one's judgment of the quality of a particular generalization. Experience is the developing solution in which many of the most interesting generalizations are exposed, revealing some to be blurry, some botched, some perfectly precise. A quick call to the consulate may be enough to determine whether there are, say, any miniature golf courses in Mozambique, but only a certain longevity can help one to judge Proust when, generalizing, he writes, "After a certain age, from self-esteem and from sagacity, it is to the things we most desire that we pretend to attach no importance." A twenty-two-year-old student cannot hope to know if that statement is or is not true.

Sometimes one can have rather too much experience to judge a generalization. A few years ago, in the *New Yorker*, I read in a story by Cynthia Ozick about a character who was described, in a generalized detail, as the sort of man who carried in his pocket a Swiss

Army knife. Now, the author clearly did not think well of this character, and the Swiss Army knife was meant to be emblematic of his stuffiness and smugness, his superficiality and self-conceit. Did this generalized detail hold up? I thought about it, one hand scratching the back of my head, the other, in my pocket, fingering my two-blade Swiss Army knife.

"Women," I recently heard an acquaintance opine, "are able to eat enormous quantities of ice cream." Are women able to eat enormous quantities of ice cream? I have neither strong views nor ample data on the question, but I rather like the spirit of disinterested wonder behind the generalization. I also approve its fine undemonstrability. True, I have known a number of women who were not otherwise great (how to put it?) trencherpersons who could nevertheless dispatch large quantities of ice cream. But not to like ice cream, it seems to me, is to show oneself uninterested in food. I wish this generalization to apply indiscriminately to women and men both.

Women, I suspect, must provide the single greatest subject for generalizations, and I am much too cunning and cowardly to attempt to add here to the already vast stockpile of these generalizations. In a too-brief essay entitled "What a Lovely Generalization!" James Thurber claimed that women themselves go in heavily for generalization and that a woman's "average generalization is from three to five times as broad as a man's." That is a statement that fits fairly snugly into the category of highly dubious generalization, with some overlap into that of broad generalization. Highly dubious generalizations, in my view, are often more interesting than broad generalizations—or they tend, at least, to be more amusing. ("Often," "at least," "in my view," "tend,"—my, that is an uncharacteristically qualified statement; I shall try not to let it happen again.) Such an amusing, highly dubious generalization is to be found in the reason Evelyn Waugh offered for the worsened quality of proofreading in his lifetime: "I am told that printers' readers no longer exist because clergymen are no longer unfrocked for sodomy."

Broad generalizations, with their companions sweeping statements and comfortable conclusions, are almost always less felicitous. There is usually something lumpy about them, something intellectually indigestible; one cannot quite, as generalizations ask you to do, swallow them whole. Henry Adams went in for such generalizations. Edmund Wilson once said of Adams that he "esteemed him without being too crazy about him." Among living contemporaries, Malcolm Muggeridge, a writer I happen to be crazy about without much esteeming, has come more and more to specialize in the broad generalization, an example of which, from Muggeridge's diaries, *Like It Was*, follows:

> Civilizations grow weak because in them power becomes divorced from the mob in the form of wealth and hereditary privilege, or even constitutional authority. Its everlasting fount is the envy of the poor for the rich, the desire of the humble and meek that the mighty should be pulled down and they installed in their place. This is the essence of politics, and everything else is phoney.

The sentiments do not disgust me. I rather like the snap of the last sentence, with its authoritative air of cutting through intellectual frills and fustian. It is that *s*, that use of the plural in civilizations, that does it in. A single civilization ought, it seems to me, to be the legal limit of the scope of any generalization.

Clearly, a number of interesting issues, problems, questions arise in connection with generalizations. But if any of them is to be dealt with in a serious manner, codification will be required, and codification takes time and money. I have, therefore, put in for a grant from the National Endowment for the Humanities on behalf of a little not-for-profit organization I run, which I call The Center for Things on the Periphery and to which the codification of generalizations seems, as noted in my application, a perfect project. My grant, I have been given to understand, is still being processed, but the problem of codification of generalizations presses, and so, grantless, I beat on, boats against the current, borne back ceaselessly, et cetera, et cetera.

The first category is the most dangerous of generalizations and is called, fittingly, the dangerous generalization. Among dangerous generalizations, surely the most dangerous of all is the one that runs: "People who threaten suicide never do it." More common dangerous generalizations are those that have to do with racial and religious groups. To cite only a mild instance of such a generalization: in recent years I have more than once heard it said that "Orientals are terrible drivers." Can this be true? Generalizations have this extraordinary self-fulfilling propensity. Since hearing the generalization about Orientals being terrible drivers, I have duly noted a great deal of terrible driving by Orientals. Hence the danger of racial and religious generalizations. Minority groups have enough problems without them. Let us, then, adopt the policy of only positive generalizations about racial and religious groups, so that we shall have only intellectual Jews, dignified blacks, cultivated Orientals, and so on. The blandness of this will soon become so boring that in time perhaps these generalizations will die out altogether.

Generalizations that are close to racial and religious generalizations and that I hope will stay around are those about nations, their character and the conduct and quality of their citizens. There is something about the tone and tenor of these generalizations that I prize, even though they tend overwhelmingly to be malicious. At their most malicious, they run along the lines of the joke which has it that both the Hungarian and the Rumanian will sell you his grandmother, but the (I forget which) is worse because he cannot be trusted to deliver. Stendhal, who was a world-class generalizer, scarcely ever seems intellectually happier than when generalizing about a nation. Early in the pages of his *Life of Rossini*, Stendhal reports that the citizens of the nations of the southern part of Europe do not have the patience and perseverance to become first-rate violinists and flautists, and "instrumental music has wholly taken refuge among peaceful, patient folk beyond the Rhine." The reason that France has produced no great opera, according to Stendhal, is that French composers "have chosen blindly to imitate the Italian conception of *love*, whereas love, in France, is nothing but a feeble and second-rate emotion, entirely overwhelmed by *vanity* and stifled by the witty subtleties of *intellect*." Good old Stendhal, like a superior billiard player, he was not above kissing one generalization off against another. Thus, after writing about love being but a feeble and second-rate emotion in France—a generalization lovely both in its amplitude and its specificity—he rolls right on to write: "Now, whether or not there be any truth in this impertinent generalization, I think it will be universally acknowledged that music can achieve no effect at all save by appealing to the imagination."

The authority for Stendhal's generalizations was that he had visited the countries about which he had generalized so ex-cathedra-ly. He could answer in the affirmative the question "Vas you der, Henri?" One of the great pleasures of travel, surely, is the right it confers on the traveler to generalize about the places he has visited. Generalizations about a foreign country or strange city are a form of intellectual slideshow, and it is difficult not to bring these slides out to show to friends back home. One is, though, under an obligation not to bring back boring slides—not to show the intellectual equivalent of pictures of the kids atop the Eiffel Tower or of Ethel on a donkey in front of the pyramids. Generalizations about places must be fresh and neatly formulated. A friend, back from a week in Houston, recently remarked, "Everything vicious that has ever been said about Los Angeles is true of Houston."

The farther away the country or city about which one is generalizing, the more sweep and grandeur one may inject into one's generalizations. I much admire the travel essays of Jan Morris, but even in my admiration I am amused by the sheer width of her generalizations. She can write, "Indians, of course, love to reduce the prosaic to the mystic." That "of course" is, of course, a splendid touch. Again: "Delhi is a city of basic, spontaneous emotions: greed, hate, revenge, love, pity, kindness, the murderous shot, the touch of the hand." Couldn't that sentence, with just a bit of fine-tuning, be written about Chicago? It could, but Chicago is perhaps too close to home for one to dare it. Or yet again: "Iowans are marvelously free of grudge or rancor; violence is not really their style. . . ." If that generalization seems fairly sound to you, think again, for in its original form it was written not about Iowans at all but about Egyptians. As someone who himself goes in for generalizations, it's enough to take my breath away.

"There are two categories of people," wrote Kleist, "those who think in terms of metaphors and those who think in terms of formulas." I used to have a stronger taste for this kind of generalization than I now do. There is something appealing in the finitude of them. If there are only two types or categories or kinds—or even if there are four or five—then the world suddenly seems so much more intellectually manageable. Whole works have been built on such generalizations. The late Philip Rahv's most famous essay, "Paleface and Redskin," is one example; another is Isaiah Berlin's *The Hedgehog and the Fox*. Do people, I not long ago found myself saying to myself, divide between those who wish to survive life and those who wish to master it? Not bad, eh? Or so I thought, until it occurred to me that I fell into neither of my own two lovely categories. I wish neither to master life nor merely to survive it; I wish to understand it (more than I do) and to enjoy it (even more than I have).

Can it be that there are finally only two kinds of generalization: those that are true and those that aren't? Isn't it enough that a generalization be stately and finely formulated? Isn't it almost too much to ask that it also be true? Flannery O'Connor writes in a letter, "I have never met anyone with a stutter who was not nice." Now here is a generalization one wants to be true; something deep yet obscure makes one want to think that people put to the torture of the perpetual frustration of stuttering are, somehow or other, sainted. Alas, I have met people with stutters who are not nice, which for me does in that generalization. Other generalizations, especially those written in French, seem to call for assent; no language seems to me better suited for the flashy but false generalization than French. Thus, an anonymous Frenchman observes that translations are like beautiful women: "*Si elles sont fidèles elles ne sont pas belles; si elles sont belles elles ne sont pas fidèles.*" (If they are faithful, they aren't beautiful; if they are beautiful, they aren't faithful.) Sorry, but I have met a few beautiful and faithful translations and even more beautiful and faithful women. Ah, me, another generalization goes down the tubes.

Permit me now to suggest that there are not two but four basic kinds of generalization. In order of their popularity in the world, these are: generalizations that are (1) commonplace but false; (2) commonplace and true; (3) original but false; and (4) original and true. An original but false generalization, in my opinion, is E. M. Cioran's remark that "people who are in love agree to overestimate each other," while an example of an original and true generalization, again in my opinion, is Sir Herbert Grierson's remark that "witticisms are never quite true." As it happens, I adore witticisms, and it wounds me to acknowledge that I think Sir Herbert Grierson's remark both original and true. Yet true in my heart I know it is, and I take it as bad news.

But then so many of the best generalizations—that is, the original and true generalizations—seem to convey bad news. I take as bad news, for example, G. C. Lichtenberg's observation that "people who have read a great deal seldom make great discoveries." Of such discouraging generalizations, there is no shortage. Another term for a discouraging generalization is an aphorism. An aphorism need not be discouraging, but the best ones, again, usually are. Along with being assertive and aristocratic, aphorisms tend also to be world-weary. The Viennese writer Karl Kraus, who wrote some of the most devastating aphorisms, said of the form, "An aphorism need not be true, but it should surpass the truth. It must go beyond it with one leap." An example from Karl Kraus: "No ideas and the ability to express them—that's a journalist."

Do nations or cultures get the aphorists they deserve? Many of the aphorisms of Karl Kraus ("Social policy is the despairing decision to undertake a corn operation on a cancer patient") as well as many of those of Lichtenberg ("What they call 'heart' is located far lower than the fourth waistcoat button") are imbued with anger and disgust. Although Lichtenberg died in 1799 and Kraus in 1936, both men were raised and worked in Teutonic cultures. Can it, then, be that these men, though born more than a century apart, are expressing a similar cultural taste in generalization? If Teutons seem to go in for rage and loathing in their generalizations, the French seem to prefer an amused puncturing of pretensions, at least to judge from their aphorists—from La Rochefoucauld ("One would not know how to count up all the varieties of vanity"), to La Bruyère ("Favor places a man above his equals, the loss of it below them"), to Paul Valéry ("I introduce here a slight observation which I shall call 'philosophical,' meaning simply that we can do without it").

If a nation or a culture gets the kind of aphorists it deserves, why has the United States had no first-class aphorists? Instead we have supplied the fodder for fine generalizations by foreign visitors, from Tocqueville to Bryce to Santayana to Huizinga. But of ambitious aphorists we have chiefly Emerson. "Nothing great was ever achieved without enthusiasm," said Emerson, but perhaps he might have done better to temper his own. Emerson said everything. If he said one thing ("I hate quotations"), he could often be relied upon to have said the reverse ("By necessity, by proclivity—and by delight, we all quote"). Covering himself, he also said, "A foolish consistency is the hobgoblin of little minds. . . ." Emerson's generalizations are more like pronunciamentos. His tone is too vatic, his formulations are devoid of charm. As generalizations go, Emerson's are in many ways a model of how not to do it.

How, then, does one do it? How best does one fashion a generalization? The saying of it, when it comes to generalizations, is usually everything. Generalizations are of that body of knowledge known as unsystematic truths, and they may, as John Stuart Mill says, "be exhibited in the same unconnected state in which they were discovered." Still, it will not do to come on too high, or too sweepingly. Generalizations that begin "Man is . . ." or "Woman is . . ." seem almost to command dissent. Even for generalizations they are too general. "Nature" is another word I recommend pruning from all generalizations, and for largely the same reason: it is too vague, too ethereal, too much. Even God is more comprehensible than Nature. Man, Woman, Nature, God—these things, being general enough, stand in no need of further generalization.

"The most dangerous moment for a bad government is when it begins to reform itself." Now that generalization—it is by Tocqueville—seems to me splendid. It comes at things at a near perfect level of generality, neither too high nor too low. It calls up all those governments, from Roman to French to Russian, whose last-minute attempts at reform only made easier the way for the revolutions that toppled them. Its tone, authoritative and slightly ironic, seems to me near perfect as well, being neither dogmatic nor hesitant—dogmatism and hesitancy being the Scylla and Charybdis between which any seaworthy generalization must sail. If you can find objections or exceptions to Tocqueville's generalization, that is all right, too. Mill said of such propositions that "they are very seldom exactly true; but then this, unfortunately, is an objection to all human knowledge."

That most human knowledge is not exactly true I find rather comforting, as long as I keep in mind that some knowledge is a good deal more exact than other knowledge. The lesson in this for those of us who love generalizations and wish to keep on generalizing is fairly clear; it comes—no one, surely, will be surprised—in the form of a generalization: always seek the general and never quite trust it. If you don't think this makes any sense, just put another record on the stereo—make it something with a driving beat—and turn it up loud so that you don't have to think about it. We, I regret to say, have nothing further to discuss.

(1982)

Work and Its Contents

C omes another Depression," said my father, as he noted the patch of grass I missed in the center of our small back lawn, the weeds I forgot to pull up next to the fence, and the uneven edges I left along the pavement, "it's guys like you they fire first." I haven't yet been fired, but then neither have we had a major Depression. "If you work for a man for a dollar an hour," my father used to say, "always give that man at least a dollar and a quarter of effort." But my first job, at age thirteen, was that of a delivery and stock boy at Sanders Pharmacy and paid sixty cents an hour and was so excruciatingly boring—I mostly dusted bottles—that my problem was how to find a way to give Mr. Sanders even twenty cents an hour in honest effort.

When I was growing up my father gave me a good deal of advice about work that I could neither use nor quite shake off. But, then, what you have to know about my father is that he himself was a Herculean worker, a six-day-a-week, never-look-at-the-clock man until his retirement at seventy-five. Perhaps an anecdote will give you something of the flavor of his work habits. My father once told me, in complaint about a man who worked for him, that for fifteen years this man had come to work at 8:30 on the dot, which was the precise time his business opened. "You would think that once," my father said, "just once he would be early." "Dad," I said, "please don't tell that story to anyone else." But now I see that I have told it for him.

My father also used to say, over and over as it seemed to me then, "If you don't like your work, you're in real trouble." He began to tell me this when I was perhaps eleven or twelve, and I only came to know it was true when I was in my late twenties. Until then, work was work, a necessary evil, though not so evil as all that, something to fill the hours between sleeping and enjoying myself. "Work is the curse of the drinking classes," said Oscar Wilde, which is a remark I would once have found more amusing than I do now. Today I must own that I subscribe to the less witty, indeed not witty at all, but vaguely moralizing view of Thomas Carlyle, who in *Past and Present* wrote: "Blessed is he who has found his work; let him ask no other blessedness." If I did needlepoint, I should stitch that on my pillowcase and sleep on it, exhausted after a good day's work.

Not everyone, I realize, shares this taste for work. Far from it—so far that I sometimes think that the world is divided between those who work so they can live and those who live chiefly so they can work. I make this sound more black-and-white, either-or, one-way-or-the-other than it truly is. But the fact is, in my experience, some of the most forlorn people I know are those who haven't found their work: people of artistic temperament who have no art to practice, leaders without followers, serious men and women with nothing serious to do. On the other side, people who have found their work can seem, while at work, creatures of great dignity, even beauty. "A man blowing a trumpet successfully is a rousing spectacle," noted the Welsh writer Rhys Davies in one of his short stories. And so, too, is a man or woman working at anything he or she loves.

Contemporary novelists have tended to banish the subject of work from their books, though work, both in its dreary and in its glorious aspects, has been of great significance in so many novels of the past. One thinks of poor David Copperfield slaving away at the blacking factory; of Clyde Griffiths, his head full of dreams, working as a bellboy in Kansas City and on the assembly line at his uncle's shirt-collar factory in Lycurgus, New York; of the figure of Levin, in *Anna Karenina*, sweating joyously as he works in the fields with his peasants, stopping from time to time under the blazing sun for a swig of kvass; of the seamen in so many tales and novels of Melville and Conrad going about doing ship's work—scrubbing down the decks, lashing up the mast—and working together to fight off typhoons and other seagoing disasters. And finally one thinks of prisoner Ivan Denisovich, of his long day's work done under the worst possible conditions of cold, hunger, and fear, from which he emerges, in Solzhenitsyn's novel, with simple but hugely impressive dignity. In the novels of Solzhenitsyn a true sense of and love for work comes through, and part of Solzhenitsyn's distaste for politics is that it is the enemy of work. As the engineer Ilya Isakovich Arkhangorodsky says in *August 1914*:

"On one side—the Black Hundreds: on the other—the Red Hundreds! And in the middle"—he formed his hands into the shape of a ship's keel—"a dozen people who want to pass through to get on with a job of work! Impossible!" He opened his hands and clapped them together. "They are crushed—flattened!"

69

I was put in mind of the place of work in our lives, and in the general scheme of society, by an essay in *Harper's* (December 1982) entitled "Dirty Work Should Be Shared" by Michael Walzer. The argument of Professor Walzer's essay, though its general line is conveyed by its title, is a bit blurry. Professor Walzer wishes that there wasn't so much drudgery, so much hard, unpleasant, ungratifying, ill-rewarded work in the world. Like Oscar Wilde, from whose "The Soul of Man Under Socialism" he quotes, he would have "all unintellectual labor, all monotonous, dull labor, all labor that deals with dreadful things and involves unpleasant conditions . . . be done by machinery." Yet Professor Walzer knows this cannot be so, and that it is not soon likely to be so. But being an equalitarian, he yearns for a rearrangement of institutions, a readjustment of conditions, an alteration of names and attitudes whereby the burden of what he terms "dirty work" in society can be more equally shared than it is now. "Hence the question," he writes, "in a society of equals, who will do the dirty work? And the necessary answer is that, at least in some partial and symbolic sense, we all should do it." Exactly, or even roughly, how we should do it he does not say. Professor Walzer does, though, discuss such things as worker ownership of garbage collection firms, arrangements for work sharing in Israeli kibbutzim, the old French institution of the *corvée* (a form of labor for the state). But in the end he hasn't a solution and concludes not with a bang but with a whimper of exhortation: "Society's worst jobs should not be the exclusive business of a pariah class, powerless, dishonored, underpaid."

When one begins to talk about work in connection with power, honor, and payment, one steps onto a verdant field of quicksand. The world's work is, after all, only rarely paid for commensurately with its worth. This is a problem compounded by the fact that commensurability between work and wages is never an easy thing to determine, especially if one hopes to pay for work according to what one construes to be its social usefulness. If the job of determining such wages were mine, I should lower the wages paid for some work and raise those now paid for other, and some I should leave pretty much as they are. For example, I tend to doubt that the quality of policemen would become greatly improved if the job paid vastly more money, yet I have a hunch that the quality of doctors and lawyers might rise if they were paid less.

I used to hear the argument made fairly regularly that teachers are greatly underpaid, and at some point in this argument someone would inevitably say, "Why, even garbage collectors make more!" As someone in favor of better education—a courageous stand for me to take, don't you think?—this argument always made me a trifle edgy. I thought that garbage collectors deserved more. For one thing, teachers are usually teachers by choice, while garbage collectors collect garbage for want of anything better to do. For another, a good teacher is rather rare, but who knows a bad garbage collector? But if we are going to talk about the underpaid, what about that national treasure, that lonely yet proud figure, on whose shoulders so much of the quality of a country's culture depends—I speak of course of that splendid and stalwart chap, the essayist.

As an equalitarian, Professor Walzer, if I read him aright, would have teacher, garbage collector, and essayist earning roughly equal salaries (a true leg up, by the way, for the essayist). He would also like them, I gather, to be equally honored and equally powerful. He argues against the degradation of certain kinds of work—I am not sure anyone is arguing for it—and wants a society in which there will be "no more bowing and scraping, fawning and toadying, no more fearful trembling; no more high-and-mightiness." Somehow, I must here confess, I find myself not so much unsympathetic as uninterested in Professor Walzer's proposals. I am not sure, for example, that sycophancy is built into specific jobs. A duke can be more fawning to a powerful prince than a washroom attendant to a United States senator; some of the worst snobs I have ever seen in action have been waiters. Nor do the teacher, the garbage collector, and the essayist bow and scrape, fawn and toady before one another—or, for that matter, before anyone (unless it is in the nature of the individual to do so). I am not aware, either, that one causes fearful trembling in the others. No, it seems to me that they greet one another the way most people do who work at very different jobs—with a lively and only slightly muted incomprehension and indifference.

But, then, the difference in point of view between Professor Walzer and me is vast. As a social theorist of sorts, he likes to come at things at a fairly high level of generality, while the points he attempts to make seem to me of interest only when they are treated on a much lower level of generality. He feels he knows why certain social classes bog down in dreary work; I am more interested in how it is and what it took for so many members of these classes to have been able to climb out successfully. He is sure much modern work is degrading; I am more impressed with the competence, dignity, and ingenuity that people apply to difficult jobs. He begins his observations with a yearning for equality; I begin mine yearning to understand how even one person—I, for example—came to do what he does.

Professor Walzer feels that perhaps dirty work "should be done by society's only legitimate proletariat—the proletariat of the young."

There is, if I may say so, something a touch goofy about referring to the young generally as "proletariat"—Workers of the world unite! You have nothing to lose but your sneakers!—for it gives yet another abstract twist to a word that has by now almost completely lost its relation to reality. Still, it is true that the young do get a goodly share of society's worst jobs; or at least they used to. I know I had my share of these jobs when young, and each time I would set out on another one, my father would say, "It can't hurt you. It's good experience." It took me a while to understand that the term "good experience" was my father's artful euphemism for "bad job."

Of these bad jobs, as I say, I had my share. Most of the "good experience" of my youth served to convince me of my incompetence. I found that I grew bored quickly, and could not very well sustain, on my first job, a false interest in dusting drugstore stock for the duration of my two- or three-hour shifts at Sanders Pharmacy. I tried out as a golf caddy; this was during the time before golf carts and when clubs were not yet called by number but still had such names as mashie niblick—names that seemed to me more appropriate for canned vegetables. But one had to be out of the house by five in the morning to get in two full rounds, which, at age thirteen, I found difficult to do, so I quit, thus proving to myself that I was not a person of much perseverance. ("Quitters never win," said my father.) My first year in high school I worked as a food bagger in one of the first supermarkets in our neighborhood, a place called Hillman's. Milk still came in bottles, and the reason I recall this so vividly is that milk bottles seemed to break through so many of my bags before the women carrying them were able to get up the marble stairs leading out of the store. Although for some reason I wasn't fired, it wasn't long before I was out searching for fresh "good experience."

By now I was convinced that I had a short attention span, little perseverance (or, as the moralizers put it, "stick-to-it-iveness"), and wasn't very good with my hands. Yet onward, ever onward, substituting for a month for a classmate, I next worked as a busboy in a neighborhood Chinese restaurant. The neighborhood was predominantly Jewish, and the man who ran the restaurant, though Chinese, had begun to look a little Jewish himself, in the odd way that people have of absorbing into themselves their surrounding atmosphere. (The most notable example is that of people who begin to resemble their dogs.) I cleared dishes, poured the remains of tea over the Formica-topped tables, swabbing the mess up with a damp cloth, and scraped off the dishes in the tumult of chopping, frying, and Chinese language in the kitchen. After the restaurant closed—during the middle of the week, roughly at 8:30—the staff could eat, limitlessly, anything they wished, with the exception of shrimp dishes. At that time—I was then fourteen—it was Chinese shrimp dishes almost exclusively that I liked, and so I ate scarcely anything at all. Through the mechanism psychologists call "overcompensation," I continue to try to make up for this youthful folly.

But that summer I began the best job of my life—that of ball boy for a nearby university tennis coach and teaching professional. My job was to tote out a large box of used balls, which the pro would use to demonstrate strokes—backhand, forehand, volley, and three kinds of serve—to his pupils. During the lesson I would shag the loose balls and return them to the box. I would also sometimes throw balls to the pro, a great gruff but very gentle fat man, who would thwack them back across the net. On occasion I would demonstrate a stroke or a serve. Mostly, though, I shagged balls.

The pay was poor—it barely covered the expenses of my travel and courtside soda pop intake—but the benefits bountiful. These included unlimited free court time and a modest discount on equipment. I would hang around the courts all day long, working two, at most three, hours a day, the remainder of the time playing with people whose partners didn't show up or were late, or filling in as a fourth for doubles. The courts were clay, of a light copperish color, from which loose clay dust turned one's shoes and tennis balls lightly beige. The sun shone down, the days stretched out. A taut tennis net, a clean white ball, and pow—and life, as Mr. Khayyám's *Rubáiyát* has it, it was "paradise enow." The lesson this job taught, if on a very rudimentary level, was that work was best when it was combined with play.

This was a lesson reinforced by working with my father, which I began to do when I was sixteen years old and had acquired a driver's license. Although he then owned a business in partnership with another man, my father was this business's chief salesman, and my job was to drive him to cities anywhere from a hundred to four hundred miles away, where he would call on customers; I also lugged his sample cases, and sometimes wrote up his orders. My father, it occurs to me, was then exactly the age I am now as I write this.

I wish Arthur Miller had met my father before he wrote his lumpy and mawkish play about Willy Loman. My father was not only very good at what he did, but he seemed to enjoy it all immensely. "Now this is a very popular item," he would say to a customer. "I know a man who bought an enormous quantity of it—me!" Here was a man having a very good time while at work.

"What do you think," my father would ask, at six o'clock at the end of a day on which we had set out at four-thirty in the morning to drive two hundred miles. "What do you think—should we spend the night here or have a nice dinner and try to make it back home tonight?" For slow readers allow me to say that the correct answer was "Have a nice dinner and try to make it back home tonight." And this we would do. Some days we would put in eighteen or twenty hours. I would usually sleep long the following morning. My father would be down at (as he called it) "the place" well before it opened for business. I love my work now, but I think my father must have loved his even more.

Love is not something one reads much about in connection with work. Quite the reverse, in fact. Studs Terkel once assembled a book of interviews that he called *Working*, which turned out to be a clanging bestseller and which begins on this cheery note:

> This book, being about work, is, by its very nature, about violence—to the spirit as well as to the body. It is about ulcers as well as accidents, about shouting matches as well as fistfights, about nervous breakdowns as well as kicking the dog around. It is, above all (or beneath all), about daily humiliations. To survive the day is triumph enough for the walking wounded among the great many of us.

But then Studs Terkel's is the conventional anti-capitalist view of work. He is a man who sees capitalist conspiracies everywhere, the way the old John Birches used to see Communist conspiracies. He has a syndicated interview show on FM radio, and on this show his idea of a fine time is to interview someone who has written about some fresh piece of big-business skulduggery. It might be an interview with a man who has written a book about, say, IBM having recently acquired the Gerber baby food company, and he has discovered that the plumbing connected to the urinals in the executive washroom at IBM leads directly to the assembly line at the Gerber baby food factory, and . . . "That's right, Studs, it's as bad as you think."

Although there is much tough work in the world, some of it done under grueling and some of it under grinding conditions, I doubt that the picture of work conveyed by a tricked-up book like *Working* is anywhere near accurate as a picture of how most people regard their work. True, many people have been cornered by circumstances into work they would not have chosen if their freedom of choice had been wider; many people find themselves under bosses or supervisors who are stupid or petty tyrants; and many others long to work at something other than what they work at now. Yet many more people, my guess is, feel the need and the stimulus and the satisfaction of their work—and for these people not to work, quite apart from the money that work provides, is a kind of slow death. When on television one hears the unemployed interviewed, there is, naturally enough, much talk of bills piling up and of financial worry generally; but at another level one can grasp a deeper demoralization—their feeling, now that they are deprived of work, of uselessness.

Other people's work often looks fairly interesting to me, or seems to have oddly interesting virtues. Apart from jobs for which I am altogether unfitted—lion tamer, say, or brain surgeon, or ship's captain—there are only two jobs for which I feel a strong antipathy. One is working in a bank, which involves too much detail for my taste and the additional difficulty of spending my days handling other people's money, which would not exactly plant roses in my cheeks. The other job I should not like to have is that of clergyman, especially today when values are so scrumptiously scrambled and the prospects of making a dignified appeal for faith so slim. Yet T. S. Eliot, I note, much preferred working in the international department of Lloyds Bank in London to teaching; and many women in almost all the modern Western religions feel somewhat put down because they are not permitted to work at the job I wouldn't touch with a ten-foot pulpit.

When I was an adolescent I never had the best jobs: these included construction worker, which paid very well, built up muscles, and withal seemed very manly; or copyboy on a major metropolitan daily, which put one on the periphery of interesting events; or lifeguard, which, along with giving one an opportunity to acquire that most ephemeral of the world's possessions, a nice tan, put one in a fine position to meet girls. But neither did I have the worst jobs: these included setting pins in a bowling alley, which in those days paid ten cents a line and gave one an opportunity for so many uninteresting and extremely painful injuries; and selling shoes, especially women's shoes, which could try the patience of a glacier and often paid no commission, except one percent on polish and laces.

I had middling jobs. My last two years in high school I sold costume jewelry on Saturdays and during Christmas holidays downtown in what must have been one of the first of this country's discount stores. During the time I was there, two veterans of carnival life worked the costume jewelry concession with me. The first was Art, a man in his late forties, with pomaded black hair, who sweated heavily in all seasons. "Hold down the fort, kid," he would say, ducking out for ten or fifteen minutes, his breath, on return, areek with booze. He was a fumbling man who had confident views, particularly on contemporary sexual mores, which, though often amusing, seemed to me even then wildly erroneous. Then there was Fritz, an Englishman who referred to all other Englishmen as limeys. He had the accent of a man of some cultivation, and on the cheap cigarette lighters, lockets, and identification bracelets we sold he engraved names and initials with a grand artistic flourish. He was a fine companion, filled with stories of traveling round the world, in all a decent sort, though at the time very much down on his uppers. He would sometimes borrow a few dollars from me, which he always repaid. Fritz, too, was a boozer, not a nipper but a binger. He would miss work for two or three days, then come in as if nothing were amiss, his same good, gentle self. For reasons never known to me, and perhaps not to himself, he was not to be one of the world's winners.

By the time I had my first factory job, I was in college, which is to say that I knew for certain, if I hadn't already known it earlier, that I would not work at a labor job permanently. I was a visitor there, a tourist on the payroll. The factory made phonograph needles. It had no assembly line; instead most of the people, the majority of them women, worked at long tables. I worked in the receiving department. My job was to unload trucks, but not enough trucks came in to merit my working full-time at this, so I put in part of my time organizing and filing boxes of labels, which was heartily boring. But I also sat around a lot, schmoozing away with the head of the receiving room, a middle-aged man named Steve, who was extremely efficient at covering over the fact that he was exceedingly lazy. We were often joined by two brothers-in-law, Italians of fine high spirits, who were the factory's maintenance crew. Both were small men, and one of them might technically have been a dwarf. Well under five feet tall with a large head, long arms, and big hands, he was courageous in his mischief, sometimes ducking out to one of the factory's upper floors, where behind packing cases he might take a nap of two full hours' duration. The brothers-in-law appeared to use the factory as a place to hang out during the day. Their real life was elsewhere. Their true speciality was fixing up old cars, which they would sell for a few hundred bucks profit. Then they would buy another, and start fixing it up.

At the factory it was known that I was a college student, which was problematic. It was the first inkling I had of the separation between those whose lives revolve around books and those whose lives don't. I didn't want the separation made any greater than it needed to be, so instead of saying that I was studying such things as literature, history, and philosophy, I claimed I was thinking of going to medical school. This turned out to be a mistake. More than once the brothers-in-law wanted to know if I needed any dead cats for purposes of dissection, and I was sure that one day I would have to bring a dead cat home on the bus in a shopping bag. Worse still, Steve and other people round the plant came to me for medical advice, some of it, I fear, rather intimate in nature.

Many people at the factory told me to be sure to return to school, saying that they regretted not having had the opportunity to go themselves. Yet their lives did not seem to me either dreary or dreadful. On coffee breaks in the lunchroom their talk was what most talk is about: the economy, the previous day's no-hitter or the pennant race, the bowling league being formed for the fall, their kids. I recall each afternoon standing in line to punch out. The working day did some people in; others, indomitable, were not in the least done in. Not at all. Work, I thought then, is neither intrinsically dignified nor undignified; it is the people doing the work who give it its character. There are people who can make the creation of poetry or leadership of a large university or corporation seem loathsome, and then there are people who can make the job of porter or waitress seem a good and useful thing.

The most impressive man I encountered in the army was a training sergeant named Andrew Atherton, who in private life had been a soda jerk in St. Louis; the most intelligent person in many academic departments in universities is the secretary. Nothing, really, so surprising in this. Nearly a century ago Henry James noted the common occurrence of "imbeciles in great places, people of sense in small." Although few people actually work in Henry James novels, James knew a great deal about work and its special benefits. After the rude failure of his play *Guy Domville* on the London stage, James, it will be recalled, lapsed into a dark blue funk. The only way out of it, as he himself recognized, was work. Writing to his friend William Dean Howells, James recounted his depression and its antidote:

> The sense of being utterly out of it weighed me down, and I asked myself what the future would be. All these melancholies were qualified indeed by one redeeming reflection—the sense of how little, for a good while past (for reasons very logical, but accidental and temporary), I had been producing. I *did* say to myself, "Produce again—produce; produce better than ever, and all will yet be well."

And he did. And it was.

The restorative effects of work seem to be beyond doubt. Being out of work, for so many, is the surest path to self-loathing. The loss of work isn't only the loss of wages but the loss of an organizing principle in life. Blocked writers are but one example of the phenomenon. But one needn't turn to the arts for examples. Some years ago, when I had not yet produced enough work to be allowed to consider myself a writer, I underwent roughly a five-week period of unemployment. I was married and had children, and the sense of not producing for them diminished me in my own eyes, which is, I suppose, not surprising. What did surprise me, though, was that during this time jobs I would not formerly even have considered for myself suddenly came to seem highly possible, interesting, attractive even. Driving a bus, for one, or selling men's clothes, for another. Leisure enforced, I found, was no leisure at all, so I took no pleasure in my free time. At one point, just to be doing something, I attempted to sell newspaper subscriptions over the telephone; I rarely made more at this than seven or eight dollars for three hours' work—a figure so demoralizing that after less than a week of it, I quit. I walked around envying people who had jobs to go to. Unemployment had made me feel useless, utterly hopeless. I recognize that this doesn't compare with any sort of serious tragedy, or even with any sort of serious unemployment, but I nonetheless cannot recall when I felt quite so sorry for myself. At other difficult times in my life, at least I could throw myself into my work.

For a great many people TGIF (Thank God It's Friday) is a serious slogan, but then for a great many others so is TGIM (Thank God It's Monday). As a TGIM man, I think work has gotten a bad rep—and a bum rap—in recent years. Consider the word "workaholic," whose implicit meaning is drunk on work. Or consider the term "Protestant ethic," which began as an explanation for the economic behavior of a historical people but which today exists almost solely as a pejorative term applied to people who are thought to take their work too much in earnest. Those Protestants Max Weber described in his famous essay may or may not have been welcome in heaven for their hard work, but they surely could have spent their days worse—poolside, let us say, at Caesars Palace or at Esalen. I am neither Protestant nor quite a workaholic, but I have known many moments when work seemed to me a more pleasurable prospect than being with very good friends. Toward the end of two or three weeks of even a splendid vacation, I have longed to read my mail, to sit at my desk, to slip into harness.

Once one has acquired skills, it seems a waste not to use them. Strike, I say, even when the iron is merely warm. A career passes so quickly. ("Careerist" is another pejorative word.) Someone once said, cleverly in my view, that every career has five stages, which may be denoted thus: (1) Who is Joseph Epstein? (2) Get me Joseph Epstein. (3) We need someone like Joseph Epstein. (4) What we need is a young Joseph Epstein. (5) Who is Joseph Epstein? Am I now at stage 3, or getting close to stage 4? When I consider these stages, and how quickly one passes from one to the next, I think perhaps it is best to strike even before the iron is plugged in.

Life is short, and work life shorter. At many jobs, age works against one. Much work is, as the sociologists have it, age-specific. Certain jobs are more than a touch unseemly beyond a certain age: lifeguard, movie reviewer, gigolo, television anchorman or anchorwoman (unless you happen to have one of those granitic Cronkitic faces). The jobs I work at—writing, editing, teaching—though one can go at them for quite a spell, nonetheless all have about them a sense of a prime period, after which one does not figure to get better. Some writers, most famously Yeats, found their true prime in their old age, but most do not get better as they get older. Editors beyond a certain period tend to lose their touch and their passion. And teachers, perhaps from having been allowed to hold the floor for so long before a captive audience, not infrequently grow spiritually gaseous and mentally gaga. When I think of these possibilities, it occurs to me to strike even without an iron.

H. L. Mencken, himself a hard and highly efficient worker, says somewhere that it is probably a fine idea for a person to change jobs every ten or so years. Without consciously setting out to do so, I seem to have been following this plan. The last time I changed jobs was when, in my late thirties, I began teaching at a university. The chance to mold minds, the opportunity for lively exchanges of ideas, the pleasures of virtuous friendships with the young, all these are doubtless among the possible rewards of teaching. But what attracted me were the spacious margins of leisure—or, to put it less grandly, the time off seemed terrific. My view of the job then coincides with that held by my barber now. Often, in order to beat the rush of customers that gathers in his shop in the afternoon, I will go in for a haircut at nine or nine-thirty in the morning. Flapping the sheet over me, he will usually say, with a barely perceptible smile in which I think I have espied envy mingling with the faintest contempt, "Through for the day, Professor?"

I still think the leisure offered by university teaching is impressive. Yet while working at it, the job often seems oddly enervating. Perhaps it has to do with the pressures of intellectual performance—of being "on," in several of the complicated senses of that simple word. Perhaps it has to do with working too exclusively among the young, which can be a sharp reminder that young is, most clearly, what one no longer is. Perhaps it is the element of repetition, for teaching is one of those jobs in which, as one grows older, one's responsibilities do not increase. Perhaps it has to do with the fact that, in teaching, the sense of intellectual progress, in one's students and in oneself, is often unclear, and teaching is never more tiring than when the sense of intellectual progress is absent.

Still, teaching has its moments, and these come in various forms: exhilaration, surprising intellectual discovery, appreciation for things one felt confident went unnoticed. Yet of the jobs I do, teaching is the one I approach with a tinge of fear. I shall hold back on a quotation from Kierkegaard here, but even after several years on the job I often walk into classrooms slightly tremulous. Colleagues have told me that they continue to do so after thirty or more years of teaching. What is there to be fearful of? Of being boring? Of seeming boobish? Of, somehow, blowing it? I do, after all, know more than my students—at least most of the time I do. Yet the touch of fear is still usually there, and the troubling thing is that I tend to teach worse when it isn't.

I imagine fear has salubrious effects on other kinds of work. The stage fright of actors is of course well enough known. So, too, are those butterflies in the stomachs of even the most fearsome athletes before games. Do trial lawyers feel fear? I should hope that airline pilots feel a bit of it. I should hope, too, that surgeons feel fear, but fear, in their case, that stops well short of trembling. I don't mean to exaggerate the benefits of fear; a little of it, I have found, goes a long way.

So, in connection with work, does play. Good work often involves play, an element of fooling around even while doing the most serious things. Fortunate are those people in a position to transform their work into play. Artists are often able to do so. But I have seen fine waitresses and businessmen do it, too. The most fortunate people of all, though, are those for whom the line between work and play gets rubbed out, for whom work is pleasure and pleasure is in work. I may be one of those people. Strange. When I was a child I never dreamed of doing any particular kind of work, for none especially attracted me. I wished merely to be rich and respected, in a general way. Rich I am not; whether I am respected is not for me to say; but, because of the joy I am able to take in my work, I feel myself luckier than any child could have dreamed. Now if only I could shake this feeling that, comes another Depression, it's guys like me they fire first.

(1983)

This Sporting Life

Time, how do I waste thee? Let me count the ways: In lengthy telephone conversations with friends, chatting and laughing, schmoozing away the irreplaceable substance in fifteen-, thirty-, and forty-five-minute chunks. In reading bland and mostly biased accounts of terrible troubles in Gdańsk and Damascus, Beirut and Bombay, then watching it served up yet again, this time with audiovisual aids, by creamy-cheeked men and women whom we call anchorpersons, the English call newsreaders, and the French call *speakerines*—the news, which as soon as it is written or said isn't new anymore, much time dropped down the drink here. In dreaming while awake, casting my mind back over its increasingly lengthy past, sliding it forward over its increasingly shortened future, lolling about in time past and time future while effectively obliterating time present. In other innumerable small ways—the little detour into the used bookshop, the false start on yet another intellectual venture, the empty social evening—I have devised no shortage of efficient methods of smothering time. I am someone who knows very well what T. S. Eliot meant when he spoke of the "necessary laziness" of the poet. I only wish a person equally distinguished had come forth to speak on behalf of my condition—the unnecessary laziness of the non-poet.

But I seem to have left out my most impressive achievement in wasting time. Far and away my most serious work as a time-waster is in watching men—sometimes but less often women—in various costumes running or jumping or hitting each other, smacking, kicking, shooting, or stroking balls of different sizes into cylinders, goals, gloves, or nets. With the sole exception of auto racing, there is no game, match, contest, or race I will not watch. "Dear Boy," wrote Lord Chesterfield to his illegitimate son, Philip Stanhope, "There is nothing which I more wish that you should know, and which fewer people do know, than the true use and value of time. It is in everybody's mouth; but in few people's practice." In this same letter, Chesterfield tells the boy, "I knew a gentleman, who was so good a manager of his time, that he would not even lose that small portion of it, which the calls of nature obliged him to pass in the necessary-house; but gradually went through all the Latin poets, in those moments." I tremble to think what, were I Chesterfield's son, his reaction would be to his learning that I, over the past year, have spent time watching men with permanents and blow-dry hairdos bowling, other men in lavender and yellow trousers hitting golf balls, and stout women arm wrestling. "Dear Boy," I imagine him writing to me, "You seem to be making a necessary-house of your entire life."

From time to time I tell myself that I am going to stop, I am going to knock off watching all these games and useless competitions. Enough is enough, I say, quit now, while you're well behind; go cold turkey, put paid to it, be done, write finis, mutter kaput—enough is too much. The prospect dangling deliciously before me if I were to stop watching so much sports is that of regaining ample hunks of time that I might otherwise, and oh so much more wisely, spend. What might I do with the time not spent watching sports? Ah, what might I not do? Listen to opera, acquire a foreign language, learn to play the flute, go into the commodities market, actually play a sport. The possibilities, while not precisely limitless, are nonetheless very grand. Perhaps I shall one day do it. Wait, as loyal fans in cities with losing teams say, until next year.

If it were actually to come about, if next year I were to free myself of my bondage to watching sports, it would be a year like no other I can recall in my life. From earliest boyhood I have been a games man, passionately interested in playing games and in everything to do with them. In the neighborhoods in which I grew up, being a good athlete was the crowning achievement; not being good at sports was permitted, though not caring at all about sports, for a boy, was a certain road to unpopularity. Ours was strictly a meritocracy, with merit measured in coordination and agility and knowledge about sports.

The best-loved kid in our neighborhood was a boy named Marty Summerfield, whose father had pitched briefly for the Chicago White Sox. Marty was smallish, but he combined very high athletic prowess with absolutely astonishing physical courage. Still in grade school, I can recall him at least twice having to be carried off football fields with a concussion; in baseball, he would chase a foul pop-up off the playground into the street, where he would catch it to the screech of car brakes and the angry honking of horns; in later years I saw him refuse to back away from fights with young men six inches taller and fifty or so pounds heavier than he. There was no brag to him or any meanness. He had a smile that made *you* happy. He was our Billy Budd, but, thank goodness, there was never any need to hang him.

Although Marty Summerfield was very intelligent—he went off to college on a Westinghouse science scholarship—I do not recall his showing much interest in the statistics, lore, or other of the spectatorial aspects of sports; certainly not as much as I and others of us who were not anywhere near so good at sports as he. I have noted this phenomenon repeat itself in later years. Truly good athletes, men and women who can or once could really do it, seem not all that interested in talking about it. (Please allow for many exceptions here, chief among them the former athletes hired by television networks and stations to do "color" or to report sports news.) Ernest Hemingway's endless talk about sports—about baseball and boxing and hunting—has always made me think that he was merely passable as an athlete. As with sex, so with sports: too much talk about it tends to leave one a bit dubious.

Somehow it seems unlikely that a great writer would also be a very good athlete, almost as if the two forms of grace—verbal and physical—were in their nature necessarily contradictory. William Hazlitt was very earnest about the game called "fives," but how good he was at it I do not know. Orwell played a version of rugby football at Eton, though, unlike Hazlitt, never, as far as I know, wrote about sports. Vladimir Nabokov played soccer at Cambridge and is said to have been a very respectable tennis player, yet his pleasure in any game was greatly exceeded by his pleasure in lepidopterology. F. Scott Fitzgerald claimed that not playing football at Princeton was one of the great disappointments in his life. Evelyn Waugh played field hockey for his college (Hertford) at Oxford, noting of it, rather Waughfully, "There is a pleasant old world violence about the game which appeals to one strongly." This makes Waugh seem the possessor of greater athletic aplomb than he apparently had. A former student of Waugh's during his teaching days in the early 1920s remembers otherwise:

> In the matter of games he was in fact so undistinguished a performer that after a few humorous episodes it was thought better that he should not exercise with the senior boys. He was issued with a whistle and allowed to amble harmlessly around the football field with the ten-year-olds. In the summer term, still wearing his plus fours, he was a reluctant umpire at the cricket games of novices.

It would be a monumental surprise, not to say an outright astonishment, to learn that Henry James was a superior athlete, but the facts hold no such surprise in store. Yet throughout his adult life Henry James, in his ultimately losing battle against corpulence, had recourse to one or another athletic activity as a form of exercise. He rode horses in Rome, took fencing lessons in London, cycled round Sussex after he had moved to Rye; at one point he lifted dumbbells, difficult as it may be to picture Henry James, as we now say, "pumping iron." There is a lovely letter in the fourth volume of the *Henry James Letters* from James to his godson, Guy Hoyer Millar, in which he writes to the boy: "I learned from your mother, by pressing her hard, some time ago that it would be a convenience to you and a great help in your career to possess an Association football—whereupon, in my desire that you should receive the precious object from no hand but mine I cast about me for the proper place to procure it." In the course of the letter, in which James informs the boy that the football is on its way to him in a separate parcel, he allows that "I'm an awful muff, too, at games—except at times

I am not a bad cyclist, I think—and I fear I am only rather decent at playing at godfather."

As a boy, I was not an awful muff at games, but neither was I awfully good at them, either. I was quick and well coordinated, but insufficiently aggressive and too much concerned with form. I don't believe I was ever deceived, even as a small boy, about my being able to play a sport in college or professionally, although I should have loved to have been good enough to be able to do so. To attempt to take my own athletic measure, I would say that, for a writer, I am a fair athlete, while among serious athletes I am, as an athlete, a fair writer. I think here again of poor Hemingway, of self-deceived Hemingway, always quick with the inapposite sports metaphor, who, in a *New Yorker* profile written by Lillian Ross, talked about his quality as a writer in boxing terms:

> I started out very quiet and I beat Mr. Turgenev. Then I trained hard and I beat Mr. de Maupassant. I've fought two draws with Mr. Stendhal, and I think I had an edge in the last one. But nobody's going to get me in any ring with Mr. Tolstoy unless I'm crazy or I keep getting better.

This rather famous passage makes me want to talk, in something like the same terms, not of my writing but of my athletic abilities. Let me put it this way: I'm ready anytime to play Ping-Pong with Mr. Balzac. And if Mr. Dostoyevsky ever cares to go one-on-one half-court with me or to shoot a little game of "Horse," I'm ready to take him on, too. If either Miss Austen or Mrs. Woolf wishes to go head-to-head with me in an arm wrestling match, I think they both know where I can be reached. As for boxing, whenever he's ready to put on the gloves, tell Mr. Proust all he has to do is give me a jingle.

Until such time as any of these writers accepts my challenge, I can almost certainly be found seated on the south end of a couch, in a book-lined room, eight or so feet from a nineteen-inch Sony color television. There—you can count on it—I shall doubtless be watching exceedingly tall men slamming balls into baskets, or lumpily muscular men in helmets slamming themselves against one another. Then again I might be watching adolescent girls figure skating or doing gymnastics, or extremely wealthy young men and women thwacking fuzzy balls across a net, or slender men and women, almost any of whom might easily qualify as the centerfold for *Gray's Anatomy*, running distances far greater than the human body was ever intended to run. But if I were a betting man—which, as it happens, I am—I would bet that I would most likely be found watching a baseball game, for this game, which I never played very well as a boy, has become the game I more and more enjoy watching. Coaches speak of "benching" athletes, but I have been "couched." I don't want to know with any exactitude how much time I have spent over the years watching games from my couch, but my guess is that the amount of time would be—this is, as they say, a ballpark figure—roughly twice that which Penelope spent waiting for the return of Odysseus.

Booze and drugs, gambling and tobacco do not begin to exhaust the list of life's potential addictions. Some people cannot get through the day without a newspaper. Others take their fix in chocolate. I have been told that there are people who wig out on pasta. *The Concise Oxford Dictionary* defines *addict* colloquially as "enthusiastic devotee of sport or pastime." That's me—a colloquial addict. I don't require my fix every day, although I somehow feel rather cheerier if I know a game is coming up later in the day or during the evening. And if too many days pass without one, I do tend to get a touch edgy. I had my first serious intimation of this some eight or so years ago while on a two-week holiday in England, where, one evening in Bath, I realized that I hadn't watched a sports event for fully ten days and strongly felt the craving to do so. I turned on the television set in the hotel room to listen to the news. Then, suddenly, the BBC newsreader began to intone—it sounded like music to me—"East Birmingham 6, Brighton 4; Leeds 3, West Manchester 2; Bournemouth 4, Winchester 1." These were scores from soccer matches. I have almost no interest in soccer; I have certainly seen none of these teams. Yet I found the mere recitation of these scores soothing, and for the remainder of the holiday I looked forward to hearing soccer scores each evening. I believe this strange little anecdote establishes my bona fides as an addict—or, in the harsher term, "sports nut."

I have described some of the symptoms and labeled the disease, but you would be gravely mistaken if you are anticipating a cure. I have not found one and do not expect to. Instead of a cure, which is apparently unavailable, I seek a justification. What can be said on behalf of all the time I have put in watching games? Does it come to nothing more than—in the most literal sense of the word—a pastime, or passing time? Have my many hours spent watching games, either before my television or "live" (what a word!), been without any redeeming value? Am I doing nothing more than killing time? Enough questions. Stop stalling. Justify yourself or get off the couch. All right, since I have a few hours on my hands while awaiting a football game from the West Coast, let me try.

Although I scarcely watch sports for this reason, one of the benefits of watching them is that it keeps me in rather close touch with great numbers of my countrymen in a way that, without sports, I might otherwise have no hope to be. If you haven't a clue to what I mean here, please cast your eyes back over my previous sentence. What kind of person uses words such as *scarcely* or *rather* in the way that they are used in that sentence? Allow me to tell you what kind of person does—a bookish person. Without actually setting out to do so, I have become bookish. I am undeniably marked by the possession of general culture. I first noted this a few years ago when, after dining with a friend at an Italian restaurant in a lower-middle-class neighborhood, a woman waiting to be seated asked, "Where do you fellas teach?" "What do you mean 'teach'?" I asked. "My friend is the defensive line coach for the Miami Dolphins and I have a Buick agency in Terre Haute." This earned mild laughter, of the kind that follows enunciation of the phrase "Fat chance." In fact, my friend looked to me very much like a professor, which he is, but I had hoped I wasn't myself so readily identifiable. I guess I was still hopeful of passing for a not very successful lawyer, or perhaps a chemist, someone at any rate a little more in the world.

Not only do I apparently look to be what I am, but I also sound to be what I have become. A year or so ago, in connection with a book I had written, I agreed to do a radio interview. The interview was taped, and four or five weeks later, on a Saturday morning, I listened to it play over the local public radio station. As I did so, I thought, My God, I have somehow acquired one of those FM classical music station voices—a voice better adapted to saying words such as *Köchel*, *thematic*, *Hindemith*, and *motif* than to saying words such as "Yes, a hamburger sounds great to me." I sounded to myself a bit pretentious, not to say a mite snooty. Could it be locutions like "not to say" that did it? Or could I be imagining the entire thing? Any hope that I might be imagining it was ended when, last month, the six-year-old daughter of friends asked my wife about me, "Why does he speak English instead of American?"

The point of all this is that I believe there is a major division in this country between a small group composed of people who care a great deal about language and ideas and art, and another, vastly larger group for whom such concerns are considerably less than central. The problem, in my experience, is that this first group, even when it does not intend to, has a way of putting the second group off, making its members feel uncomfortable, slightly inferior, as if their lives were brutish and their pursuits trivial. It may well be that many members of the first group are truly contemptuous of the second group. Often, though, the contempt works the other way round. It isn't for no reason, after all, that piano players in whorehouses used to be called "professor." Anyone who has belonged to the first group must at one time have felt the sting of the division I have in mind. I recall being about four hours into a poker game with a number of printers, and, when the deal passed to me, I said, "OK, gents, ante up for five-card draw." At which point the guy sitting to my left, who was losing about eighty dollars, said, "Whaddya, some kind of goddamn Englishman?" Ah, me, as Turgenev's nihilist Bazarov says, "That's what comes of being educated people."

Not that I am displeased with being what I am—a man, that is, marked by the possession of general culture. I talk as I talk; I think as I think; I am what I am. My mind, such as it is, remains my greatest stay against boredom. Still, I find this division between the two groups sad. As a member of the first of these groups, I know I do not feel any contempt for the members of the second group. (Sorry to have to proclaim my own virtue here, but apparently no one else will come forth to proclaim it for me.) In fact, I tend to feel rather more contempt for members of my own group, the culturati, with whom I am more familiar—contempt, after all, being one of the items familiarity breeds.

Yet one of the things that make it possible to jump the barrier and cut across this division, at least in masculine society, is sports—more specifically, knowledge and talk about sports. (Here I must add that I have met many intellectuals, scholars, novelists, and poets whose addiction to sports is not less than my own. "Closet sports fans" is the way I think of them. Yet how easily they are flushed out of the closet. All one has to do is offer a strong opinion about one or another team or player in their presence and out they come.) For a bookish fellow in a democracy, knowledge about sports seems to me essential. But not for the bookish alone; not even for a fellow alone. A friend tells me about a woman he knows who operates at a fairly high level in the real estate business and who began to study the morning sports pages in the hope of making lunches with male colleagues and clients easier. The hope, as it turned out, was justified, for sports talk is the closest thing we have in this country to a lingua franca, though I wouldn't use that phrase in, say, a bowling alley or pool hall.

Sports talk is easier for me than for the woman in the real estate business, I suspect, for I have grown up with sports, played at them as a kid, know them, and love to talk about them. I also know how inexhaustible sports can be as a subject; it sometimes seems, in fact, that there is more to say about yesterday's baseball game than about *Hamlet*. Nor do I think there is anything the least phony about using sports this way. As a conversational icebreaker, sports is very useful. It can rub away artificial distinctions. While sports may well be the toy department of life, not of towering intrinsic importance in itself, it can lead in and on to other, more intrinsically important subjects.

Start with sports and before you know it you are talking economics, sociology, philosophy, personal hopes and fears. Socially, sports talk can be a fine lubricant.

I know I have often pressed sports into service, usually with decent results. I say "usually" and use the modest word "decent" because I think I may sometimes have gone too far. A few decades ago, for example, I found myself working in an urban renewal agency in the South. My fellow workers were mostly country boys. What they made of me I do not know. There was much to divide us: region, religion, politics. Asking them what they thought of the merits of the fiction of Jorge Luis Borges did not strike me as a happy way to glide over our differences. What did was sports. We talked Southwest Conference football, we talked baseball, we talked basketball. We got along.

I may have talked sports a little too well, for after a few weeks I was invited to play on the agency's basketball team in the local YMCA league. I showed up for the first game and learned that there were six members on the team, one of whom was in his early fifties. I was, in other words, a starter. Our opponents were made up of lean eighteen- and nineteen-year-olds of considerable height with, I remember thinking, rather menacing angularity of elbow. I had trained for this game by never smoking fewer than two packs of cigarettes daily for the previous ten years. Five or six times up and down the floor and I recall wondering if my life-insurance premiums were paid. Evidently time-outs had not yet been discovered in the South, for during the first ten minutes none was called. I had somehow managed to score three points, on a free throw and a crip layup. At the buzzer marking the end of the quarter, I walked over to the drinking fountain, into which I suavely vomited. Four or five games later, I went up for a rebound and, as good luck would have it, came down on my wrist, which was badly sprained. This excused me from further athletic combat. But the games I did play allowed me permanently to climb the barrier; in the eyes of the men I worked with I was OK and not a carpetbag intellectual.

But I don't want to push too hard the social advantages of knowing about sports. I don't watch them for social advantages. I watch them because most of the time they give pleasure. Nor do I believe that the reasons for my pleasure have much to do with personal psychology; I don't believe, in other words, that in watching sports I am attempting to regain my youth, or finding an outlet for violent emotions, or living vicariously through the physical exploits of others. No, part of the pleasure for me in watching sports is that of witnessing men and women do supremely well what may not be worth doing at all. It is the craft of superior athletes that is so impressive, and that seems all the more impressive at a time when standards of craftsmanship seem badly tattered. Literary awards, academic chairs, political power, journalistic eminence—all frequently seem to be awarded to people whose claims upon them appear so thin, and sometimes even actually fraudulent. But when a sixteen-year-old girl gymnast needs a perfect ten-point performance to win an Olympic gold medal, or a twenty-year-old college basketball player has to sink two free throws to win a game while fifteen thousand people are screaming at him and a few million more are watching him over television, or a golfer has to sink a tricky twelve-foot, slightly uphill putt—none of them, in these moments, can call on public relations, or social connections, or small corruptions, or fast talk. All they can call on is their craft, which they either have or don't have.

Sports also supply the pleasures of craft under pressure. I find I respond extremely well to pressure—to other people under pressure, that is. It excites me; I marvel at it. Much of sports is pressure organized. At any rate, the great moments in sports are those when athletes play through and win out under immense pressure. I am all the more admiring of people who are able to do this because, in the few moments of athletic pressure I felt as a boy, I have known something of its crushing weight. "Clutching," "choking," "the lump" are but a few of the descriptions for people whose athletic craft is reduced as a result of pressure. "Coming through," two of the loveliest words an athlete hopes to hear, is the phrase reserved for those whose craft is not impaired—is sometimes, in fact, heightened—by the presence of pressure. The grand spectacle of people coming through is one of the keenest pleasures of watching sports—and it is a spectacle not usually on display elsewhere with such shining clarity.

The spectacle of athletes not coming through, though not at all grand, is nonetheless much more moving. While we may admire the winners, most of us tend to side with the losers. Sports, it has been said, is about losing. There is a great deal to this, certainly when it comes to team sports. Coaches with preponderantly winning records exist in plenty, yet few are the teams that over the years seem to be able to repeat championship seasons. In professional sports, I can think of only three: the Montreal Canadiens, the New York Yankees, and the Boston Celtics. I have never cared enough about hockey to have passionate feelings about it, but I have liberally despised—"hated" is too passive a word—both the Yankees and the Celtics. What I have despised about them is that they won too frequently. I have discovered many people have similar feelings. Unless they happen to be one of your hometown teams, too-frequent winners in sports tend not to be appreciated. "Everybody loves a winner" is a truism that, in sports, doesn't hold up.

Of course, I speak as a fan, and a fan, it is well to remember, is short for a fanatic. Sports in America may well be the opiate of the people, but, as opiates go, it isn't a bad one. Often when watching a game on television, I will note the television camera focus on the crowd, whose members are to be found, index fingers raised aloft, screaming, "We're number one! We're number one!" and think how easily, in another country, similar faces might be screaming, "Perón! Perón!" or "Khomeini! Khomeini!" I have never seen an adequate explanation for the passion of the fan. Roger Angell, who writes about baseball for the *New Yorker*, has written that "belonging and caring" is what being a fan is about. But I have encountered too many instances of behavior on the part of fans that go beyond mere belonging and caring. I have a cousin with ulcers whose doctor advised him, unsuccessfully, to stop listening to Chicago Cubs games. Of fans of the same team, I recently read about a widow who each spring places a Cubs pennant on her husband's grave, and of a man, a Cubs fan for more than fifty years, whose deathbed words, his son claims, were "We gotta get rid of Kingman" (a high-salaried player notable for not coming through). A Chicago Cubs fan myself, when that team in 1984 lost its first chance to appear in a World Series in thirty-nine years by dropping its final playoff game to the San Diego Padres, I found I was mired in a slough of glumness that lasted fully a week. Fan-tastic. Such behavior cannot be explained to anyone who is not interested in sports; I cannot quite explain it to myself.

If we tend to idolize our athletes more than our politicians, I do not think that altogether a bad thing. I myself have not idolized an athlete since I was a small boy, but I have enjoyed the hell out of the really superior ones. *Dumb* appears before the word *jock* as frequently as *wily* before the name *Ho Chi Minh* and *untimely* before *death*, but I, for one, don't think athletes are unintelligent. They are unbookish, certainly; inarticulate, frequently; but dumb, scarcely ever, at least not at high levels of play. Instead their intelligence is concentrated upon their craft, and this they know in a way I can only hope I know mine. The only place I have ever seen the intelligence of athletes recognized is in the novel *Guard of Honor*, by James Gould Cozzens, where one of the book's protagonists assigns a military mission of importance to a young officer partly on the basis of his having played Big Ten football and thus being used to exerting his intelligence under real pressure.

While I do not idolize athletes, neither do I envy them. I consider them privileged human beings, men and women who have drawn lucky numbers in life's lottery. They are in the condition of someone born beautiful or to extremely wealthy parents. Lucky indeed. Professional athletes play games they love for salaries that take them effectively out of the financial wars that the rest of us must go on fighting our lives long. For a time the huge salaries that athletes have in recent years begun to earn bothered me. They are, in fact, immensely overpaid. Yet, as the economist Sherwin Rosen has explained, in an essay entitled "The Economics of Superstars," owing to television and now cable television revenues, the money is there, and I myself would just as soon that Julius Erving, or Dave Winfield, or Walter Payton have ample hunks of it than that even more of it go to some real estate or insurance millionaire who owns a sports franchise chiefly to soothe his own itch for publicity. Some say that athletes are too privileged, that they garner too many rewards too soon. I recall once watching an interview with Wayne Gretzky, the great young hockey player of the Edmonton Oilers. One of the television broadcasters pointed out to him that he, Gretzky, was at twenty-three already a millionaire many times over, that he had broken most of the records in his sport, that he would go down in history as one of the greatest hockey players the world has known. "Well, Wayne," the broadcaster said, "what can you possibly have to look forward to?" Gretzky, not a fiercely articulate fellow, paused, then said, "Tonight's game."

Addict and fanatic that I am, I must also confess that few of the supposed "issues" having to do with sports in its contemporary settings greatly trouble me. Amateurism, for one, is an issue upon which much false piety has been expended. In college athletics, violations having to do with recruiting athletes do occur, and are punished when discovered. But everyone—excepting perhaps the officials of the National Collegiate Athletic Association—assumes that a great many others go undiscovered. I once heard a radio announcer, a former pro football player covering a Chicago Bears–Detroit Lions game, ask where a tackle on the Lions had gone to college. "Notre Dame," said his companion in the broadcast booth. "He went from Notre Dame to Detroit?" the first announcer responded. "Hmm. He must have taken quite a cut in pay." The next week the announcer himself took quite a cut in pay, for he was fired. Perhaps rightly. Violations in amateur sports are like adultery: everyone knows it goes on; still, it will not do to talk about it too openly.

Tennis has now all but dispensed with amateurism, and nearly all involved in the sport feel better for having done so. Track and field looks as if it might be the next sport to do so. In Eastern European and other Communist countries there is no hypocrisy about amateurism because there isn't any amateurism; in this regard one may say about them what Randall Jarrell said about the college president in his novel *Pictures from an Institution*: "He had not evolved to the stage of moral development at which hypocrisy is possible." Most universities and colleges that have big-time football and basketball programs have arrived at that requisite stage of moral development—and, hence, at hypocrisy, too. With millions and millions of dollars involved in gate receipts and television revenues and millions more for those teams that get to bowl games and postseason tournaments, college athletics aren't what they used to be.

But, then, neither is college. And because it is not, because so much of the prestige of college has been dissipated and the quality of education degraded, it becomes more and more difficult to think of the majority of college athletes at schools with big-time programs as anything other than young men serving out their athletic apprenticeships in the hope of one day becoming professionals. When such basketball players as Magic Johnson and Isaiah Thomas leave school at the end of their second or third year, or when a young man skips college altogether to make a run at a baseball career, one no longer exclaims sadly, "But their education! What a shame!" Education is good, after all, only if it is really education. What is impressive to me is a young man who plays a major sport at a major school and is still able to find time to devote himself to serious studies, let alone excel in them. My guess is that the number of such young men is not legion.

At this point I believe I am scheduled to deliver a political rant, bemoaning the rise of the power of money and the fall of the prestige of education. But sports fans, when it comes to sports, are curiously apolitical. They tend to take the world of sports pretty much as they find it. Within the realm of sports itself, they tend to be purist conservative—that is, they want the sports world forever to remain as they found it. Innovation is anathema. Apart from improvements in equipment, almost all changes that affect the games themselves are regarded as regrettable. This, at any rate, is my view. I dislike the advent of Astroturf in baseball and football; I dislike both the three-point play in pro and the shot clock in college basketball and the new dominance of the slam dunk in both; I dislike the designated hitter in baseball; I dislike the tiebreaker in tennis. . . . Some sports seem less sacrosanct than others: gradual changes in the game of pro football are permissible, yet alter baseball and you are fooling with the liturgy. To paraphrase the old and long-dead Chicago alderman Paddy Bauler, "Sports ain't ready for reform."

As much pleasure as sports have given me over the years, I am sure I do not want to have more to do with them than I now do. True, before I hang up my couch, I should like to see, in person, "live," a few World Series games, a Super Bowl, a Kentucky Derby, a Wimbledon final. But I shouldn't want to be a sportswriter or broadcaster. I once wrote an article about an elegant pro basketball player named Bob Love; in preparation for it I went to eight or ten of his team's practice sessions; I interviewed him and his coach and his teammates. Along with the fee for the article, I was given a press pass for a full season's games. It was good fun, superior jock-sniffing, in the locker room phrase. Somehow, though, I felt too much like a camp follower, which is the true relation of the press to the actions they cover. One such article is all I ever care to write. Visiting the toy department is nice, but who wants to live there?

In watching sports, I seek not so much a golden mean or even a silver one, but will settle for something akin to a tarnished bronze mean. Achieving anything like real moderation here is now well beyond me. If I never watch another game, I have already seen many more than my share. But I fully intend to watch another game, and another and another and another. My justification is that doing so gives me great delight; my defense is that it causes no known harm, and, on occasion, I learn a thing or two from it. Yet, a number of years ago I recall hearing that Eric Sevareid, who was then reading the Sunday evening news on CBS, complained that it was demeaning to as serious a man as he to have to give the day's sports scores on his news show. I hope that this is true, for if it isn't I owe Mr. Sevareid an apology for thinking of him, ever after, as a starter on my All-American Pomposity team, along with William Jennings Bryan, Daniel Ellsberg, Barbara Walters, and the older Orson Welles. I don't know about anyone else, but I would rather have those sports scores than Eric Sevareid's opinions about NATO, the Sino-Soviet dispute, and the balance of payments. Not that I don't think about such things. I do, but I can't say that I look forward to them. What do I look forward to? Among other things, along with Wayne Gretzky, to tonight's game.

(1985)

A Former Good Guy
and His Friends

I recently saw a copy of the high school newspaper that appeared the week of my class's graduation and found myself a bit miffed to discover that I was not voted Most Popular or Best Liked or Most Friendly or Best Personality or any other of the categories that speak to the ideal, vivid in the days of my youth, of being a Good Guy. It may seem immodest of me to talk about myself in this way, and normally I should refrain from doing so, but the plain fact is that I worked sedulously at being thought not merely a Good Guy but an extraordinarily Good Guy and felt that I had greatly succeeded. Whence this interest on my part in being such a devilishly Good Guy, you may ask. I suppose it came about as a matter of elimination. Since I was neither a first-rate athlete, nor a notably successful Lothario, nor even a half-serious student, all that was left on the buffet of roles for me to choose from was Good Guy or thug, and since I hadn't the wardrobe for thug I went for Good Guy—and I went for it in a big way. Almost anyone who attended Nicholas Senn High School in Chicago when I did will, I feel confident, tell you, "Sure, I remember Epstein. He was a Good Guy."

What a Good Guy is turns out not to be so simple a question. If Aristotle had gone to Nicholas Senn High School—a notion it gives me much delight to contemplate—he would doubtless have been able to posit no fewer than eleven kinds of Good Guy and compose an ample disquisition on the nature of the Good Guy, or Good-Guyness. Perhaps a disquisition is required, for there is apparently some disagreement about what constitutes a Good Guy. Not long ago, for example, when I remarked to a friend from my high school days that I thought I used to be a fine specimen of the type known as Good Guy, he replied that he thought I had not quite made it. I was very popular, he allowed, but I wasn't bland enough. The pure Good Guy, he argued, should be very bland. Your true Good Guy should never give offense, or even hint at the potentiality for giving offense, and I, who was locally famous for an above-average sharpness of tongue, was considered verbally too dangerous to qualify as a pure Good Guy. Very well. I can accept that. Let me, then, revise my earlier statement: Almost anyone who attended Nicholas Senn High School when I did will, I feel confident, tell you, "Sure, I remember Epstein. He was a Good Guy—only don't cross him."

Does the ideal of the Good Guy still exist? For all I know, it may have gone the way of the Cute Girl, which, I gather, no self-respecting female above the age of ten nowadays cares to be thought. But as I construed it then, a Good Guy was someone whom vast numbers of people felt to be a Good Guy. I thus set out to convince vast numbers of people. It proved no very complex task. Ben Franklin, whom I did not read until years later, remarks in his autobiography that, if you wish to insinuate yourself in the good graces of another person, the trick is not to do that person a favor but to have him do one for you. So the trick of making many friends, at least on the superficial level on which the Good Guy operates, is not to charm them but to let them charm you.

Many friends is what I wanted: multitudes, large assemblages, whole hordes. To acquire them I was ready to turn off the charm. I was, in those days, the reverse of a snob; I looked up my nose at everyone. No one was too lowly for me to court. I became a boredom-proof listener, a full-time dispenser of bonhomie. Sashaying through the halls of our high school, greeting my innumerable conquests in the Good Guy sweepstakes, I uttered a stream of babblesome salutations not to be equaled for inanity outside a major league infield: "Hi, babes," "What say," "How're you makin' it," "Take it easy," "Hang in there," "How's it goin'," "Be good," "Yo!" and fifteen or twenty other utterances of equal profundity that I have since forgotten.

In cultivating friends, I was calculating, but not altogether insincere. If one way to make friends is to show a great interest in other people, showing such an interest, however artificial it might be at the outset, can before long issue in genuine interest. Besides, I not only collected but liked people; I liked their oddness and idiosyncrasy. As a good listener, I was taken into many a confidence and vouchsafed many a glance into secret desires, passions, fears—all of which the incipient if still quite unknown writer in me found fascinating. As a Good Guy, I knew how to keep a secret, never to betray a trust, and was, withal, a ready and reliable confidant. "Kids say the darndest things," a smarmy radio "personality" named Art Linkletter used to remark. They do indeed, and I liked their saying many of them to me, which was one of the minor fringe benefits of being thought such a corking Good Guy. A larger benefit was the small number of people who, initially captured by my Good Guy maneuvers, have thus far remained lifelong friends.

Still, I may have exulted too much, albeit secretly, in this knack I had for making friends easily. Sometimes I would try this knack out, like a professional tenor singing in the shower at home, for the sheer pleasure of exercising it. I would choose a young thug ("hoods" we then called them), or a shy girl, or someone whose background was utterly different from my own, and set out to win him or her over to my ever-enlarging stable of friends. Almost always I succeeded. It was pure art, really—friends for friends' sake. In those days, had I had a reasonable grasp of grammar and syntax, I could have written a book entitled *How to Win Friends Without Caring in the Least About Influencing People.*

I merely wished to be liked, and only by everybody I met. To be thought a Good Guy by all—this didn't seem too much to ask. Occasionally it would get back to me that someone or other didn't understand what lay behind my considerable popularity. I felt my appeal ought to have been self-evident to him; I was, self-evidently, a Good Guy. Then there was a small band of people around whom I stepped gingerly. They were insensate to my blandishments, these people—most of them boys, but also a few girls—whom I thought of, even in high school, as "in business for themselves." In a rough sense, each of us is in business for himself—each of us, that is, is preeminently concerned about his own preservation and rise in the world and has a necessary and probably sensible selfishness—but these people were rather more selfish than was either necessary or sensible. They were generally rather intense and (no rather about it) humorless. The very notion of the Good Guy, with all his airy friendliness, was alien to them, and so, consequently, was I. It only now occurs to me that I was also possibly in business for myself in those days. My business was being popular. It was a pleasant enough line of work, requiring no character whatsoever.

I can write all this now chiefly because I am—as a great many people will tell you—no longer a Good Guy. I may not even be, to shift at last to lowercase spelling, a nice fellow. I have not yet arrived at the stage of Evelyn Waugh's character Gilbert Pinfold, who of himself asks, "Why does everyone except me find it so easy to be nice?" but I find I do not much mind making enemies. Some enemies seem to me eminently worth having. This is something that the old Good Guy in me failed to understand. Chiefly through writing a good deal of journalism and literary criticism, I have by now acquired, I feel certain, an ample supply of enemies. If the people I have written critically about feel as I do about the people who have written critically about me, my guess is that they have not altogether forgotten me and that, should my name ever crop up in their presence, it is cause for them to murmur a brief Bulgarian curse or a stirring undeleted epithet.

Perhaps because, as a former Good Guy, it has taken me so long to acquire enemies, I like to dwell upon them and on occasion I have even dreamed of them. In one such dream the people I have written harshly about are gathered together in a large room in a Manhattan hotel to throw a party for me. There they stand, as in a drawing out of *Esquire*: Joseph Heller, John Updike, Norman Mailer, William F. Buckley Jr., Gore Vidal, Renata Adler, Philip Roth, Ann Beattie, Gabriel García Márquez, and others too numerous to mention. In this dream I sit alone, in white tie and tails, at a long dais. Everyone in the room is standing, champagne glasses raised in my direction, waiting for me to speak. "Sorry, gang," I announce at last, a wide smile plastered across my face, "but no more Mr. Good Guy."

If early life taught me how to gather a wide acquaintanceship, and later life how not to fear enemies, the great mystery remains friendship. Aristotle, who devotes fully two books of the *Nicomachean*

Ethics to the subject of friendship, begins by remarking that "without friends no one would choose to live," which seems to me quite true. Yet the quality and variety of friendship are nearly inexhaustible, and, as Aristotle says, "not a few things about friendship are matters of debate." The first matter for debate, perhaps, is one's own interest in friendship—or, more precisely, one's own devotion to friendship. "The only way to have friends," writes Joubert, "is to throw everything out the window, to keep your door unlocked, and never to know where you will be sleeping at night. You will tell me there are few people mad enough to act like this. Well then, they shouldn't complain about not having any friends. They don't want any." I suspect Joubert is correct about this, even though it means that I, who value my friends, do not qualify as someone absolutely devoted to friendship. I want to have friends, but on my terms—and, as I grow older, these terms grow more and more strict.

Although not usually at its center, friendship plays a part in many of the greatest literary works. Straightaway there is the friendship of Achilles and Patroclus. Cervantes presents, in Don Quixote and Sancho Panza, a lovely instance of a friendship between unequals and opposites. Dickens provides many of his young heroes with charming, self-effacing friends—Tommy Traddles, Herbert Pocket, etc.—of a kind we could all use in our corner. The friendship that develops between Huck Finn and Jim is of course one of Mark Twain's great touches—perhaps his greatest touch. The delicacy and subtlety required in friendship—almost always referred to as "personal relations"—is nearly the entire subject of E. M. Forster. In Henry James it is not so much friendship as the betrayal of friendship that looms so large. But the novelist of friendlessness is Joseph Conrad, whose heroes are among the loneliest figures in literature and among the most moving in part because of their solitariness, which gives them their tragic dimension.

Possibly the greatest literary friendship on record, and the most literarily consequential, was that between Montaigne and the poet and magistrate Étienne de La Boétie. The two men met when Montaigne was thirty, La Boétie thirty-three. Their rapport was immediate and perfect; each was able, in letters and in person, to reveal his soul to the other. In 1563, four years after they met, La Boétie came down with an intestinal ailment from which he died, with Montaigne at his bedside. Montaigne was permanently bereft. Donald M. Frame, Montaigne's biographer and translator, believes that "there is much to show that the *Essays* themselves are—among other things—a compensation for the loss of La Boétie." With Étienne de La Boétie gone, Montaigne had no one to speak with and write for but himself—and the world. La Boétie is the friend, and theirs the single dominant friendship, referred to when, in his essay "Of Friendship," Montaigne writes: "In the friendship I speak of, our souls mingle and blend with each other so completely that they efface the seam that joined them, and cannot find it again. If you press me to tell why I loved him, I feel that this cannot be expressed, except by answering: Because it was he, because it was I." The void left by the death of La Boétie was never to be filled by Montaigne; references to him in the *Essays* are frequent; eighteen years after his friend's death, Montaigne can still be troubled by thoughts about him. Which is greater, having known such a friendship or its loss, is a question that troubled Montaigne his life long.

Such a friend is rare at any time, in any life. I have never known such a friend in my own life, and I am not at all sure I should want one. (I exclude my wife, whom I consider to be in the realm above that of friendship.) As a boy, I recall how important it seemed to have a best friend; and I, as someone who had made friends rather easily, had, seriatim, several best friends. I might have a best friend for a summer, or a school term, but gradually we would drift not quite apart but to a friendship of lesser intensity. In a best friend I desired someone to pal around with, someone to rely on, someone occasionally to confide in. I required no full communion of souls, not being myself a very soulful character. The notion of the best friend carries over into adulthood with marriage, where, traditionally, the groom appoints a best man, who is presumably his best friend. I have been married twice—I believe I got it right the second time—but the combined total attendance at both my weddings was two; I had witnesses in place of best men. Even now I do not feel the want of a best friend, but I do have a number of good friends whom I cherish.

Was it Plutarch who said that one didn't need more than seven friends? Until this moment I have never counted mine, but—dead on, Plutarch—it turns out I can think of exactly seven friends, very good friends, whose death or disappearance from my life would devastate me. I can think of a second tier of ten or so friends who enrich my life but with whom the same degree of easy intimacy and depth of feeling does not quite exist. I can think of a third tier of twenty or so people whom I am always pleased to see or hear from, in whose company I feel perfectly comfortable, and with whom I believe I share a reciprocal regard. (Although they are more than acquaintances, are the people in this third tier truly friends? There ought to be a word to denote relationships that fall between that of acquaintance and friend, but there is not; the language—as Flaubert once remarked in attempting to express his love for his mistress—is inept.) After this third tier, in the stadium of my social life, we next move up to the

grandstand of acquaintances and the bleachers of business associ-
ates. The first tier has not changed, and some members of it I have
known for forty years. Some come down from the third tier to sit
in the second; and a few from both the second and third tiers have
departed, either through death or disagreement, before the game
(my game) is done.

"How many intelligent people do you know in this city?" Saul
Bellow once asked me. Ours is a city of roughly seven million people,
of whom he said he had discovered three who were intelligent. High
standards, these, and behind these standards was the clear implication
that he valued intelligence above all else in friends. I hope I don't
insult my friends when I say that it is not chiefly for their intelligence
that I value them, even though all are intelligent. Some I value for
their point of view; some for their loyalty and steadfastness; some for
their seriousness and integrity; and two or three for their goodness,
by which morally freighted word I mean to imply a combination of
all these qualities.

When I think of the qualities that might unite the first tier of my
friends, I am hard-pressed to come up with any persuasive pattern.
I share interests with all of them, but they are not the same interests.
Three of the seven are not bookish; four of them have politics different from mine. These same four are my exact contemporaries and
indeed were high school classmates; the other three are older than
I, one of them more than twenty-five years older. Sexist swine that
I am, all seven are men. (About women as friends, more presently.)
None is Orthodox in his religious views, and from two of them I have
never heard any talk of religion at all; and although one would think
one ought to know this about good friends, for all I know these two
are atheists. (Must make a mental note to ask.) Two—not the same

two—do not live in the same city as I do. Some among these seven good friends of mine have never even heard the names of the others. All seven are united in two things: first, none is what I think of as a high-maintenance friend—someone, that is, who requires regular ministering to in the form of visits, daily telephone calls, or lengthy letters; and, second, all have agreed to appreciate me.

Along with appreciation of me, we also, my close friends and I, do not disagree strongly on any important subject. I am not certain how much disagreement a close friendship can bear. I don't think I could have a close friend who is a racist or an anti-Semite. I am not sure I could have a close friend who despised my politics; yet agreement on politics, though pleasing in a friend, is not for me, I like to think, decisive. I have found myself among fairly large groups in which nearly everyone agreed with my political views, and a most comforting feeling such an atmosphere can provide. But I have always been impressed by Tocqueville's remark, made in his *Recollections*, that in politics "shared hatreds are almost always the basis for friendship." Hatreds, even cozily shared ones, are not a good basis for friendship; they too soon lead to one's having to accept the enemy of one's enemy as one's friend. The enemy of one's enemy, after all, can turn out to be himself a terrible character. Politics may make strange bedfellows, but finally not very good friends, as witness John Reed, he of *Ten Days That Shook the World*, writing to H. J. Whigham, his editor on the *Metropolitan Magazine*: "You and I call ourselves friends, but we are not really friends, because we don't believe in the same things, and the time will come when we won't speak to each other."

Perhaps the reason the number of people I currently call friend seems so large has to do with my age, which is pretty near smack-dab middle age. Being middle-aged, I am able to have friends chronologically on either side of my own age: friends ten or twenty or even thirty years older than I and friends ten or now even twenty years younger. Meanwhile I retain my contemporaries, upon whom death has thus far made no inroads. With older friends, my age sometimes seems to dissolve, and in some cases I have felt something akin to experiential seniority to people twenty or so years older. I have been lucky in having some of the most interesting older people I have met take me seriously.

I had a friend whom I much admired, a man in his middle-eighties, whom I never met but knew only through correspondence. He first wrote to me about something I had written in the *American Scholar*; I answered his letter; and each time I wrote anything in this or any other magazine he would write to comment upon it and to dilate upon the same subject, usually turning out something much more interesting than I had written. In his business life he had been in advertising, and as the editor of the leading trade publication for the advertising industry, he told me he saw it as his job to try to make advertising less vulgar. "You have only to look about you to see how successful I have been," he added. He had delicious irony and, being of an advanced age, he felt no need to dawdle over clichés or empty pieties. He seemed to read all the intellectual magazines, loved Trollope, closed out each evening with a page or two of Burton's *Anatomy of Melancholy* "because I find a page or two of his magnificent prose gives me a fitting way to end the day," and he even took the icy plunge into contemporary philosophy. He described himself to me as a compulsive reader, and once, before a national election, noted:

Are you inflicted these days with fervid pleas to save the country? I get at least one in every mail. I will, for the sake of something to read, read an invitation to attend the opening of a new cleaning establishment but I will not punish myself by reading campaign letters. After all, even a compulsive reader has limits.

I soon found that part of the pleasing afterglow of publication was receiving a letter from him. Thinking to deepen our relationship, I once wrote to him when I was planning a visit to a large city near his own smaller one to invite him and his wife to lunch. He wrote back to say that his eyesight was no longer good enough for him to drive on freeways, his hearing was all but shot, and, since he went out less and less, he really didn't have any fit clothes for dining out. He thanked me for my invitation but would have to refuse. Besides, he said, nowadays he was much at his best in his letters. I never made another such invitation and we continued to exchange letters for a year or so more, when, one early summer's day, I received a letter from his daughter that began, "My father . . . died June 15th after a three-day illness. I know how much his correspondence with you meant to him. When he came home from the hospital last fall, the first thing he did was to have me sit down and type a letter to you on the horrors of modern baseball." A friend unmet but still missed.

Friendships with the young are very different. I have a number of such friendships, almost all of which have derived from my work as a teacher and a writer. I never set out to make them. But over a decade as a university teacher I have found eight or ten students to whom my heart has gone out. All of them wish to be writers or to do one or another kind of literary work, and they, I assume, have found my acquaintance useful. I am a touch flattered by these friendships, for they function in the way that Aristotle prescribed for friendships between the young and the older—that is, these young friends honor me and I in my turn try to be helpful to them. With one exception, I do not have what Aristotle termed "friendship of the complete type with them." This is in part because we do not share a common past; in part because they, being young, live largely in the future, while I try to live in the present; but in greatest part because, for now, we are not equals. I hope I do not treat them with condescension, yet the fact is that thus far along I have achieved more in the line of work to which they aspire, and it is this, achievement, that makes us unequal. (As they grow older and achieve more, this inequality will narrow.) I have been on the other side of such relationships, the younger man who pays homage to the older, who repays him in the coin of utility: by advice, by helping through his connections, by permitting conversational intimacies. Perhaps because I have benefited from such relationships, I feel gratified to enter into similar ones myself, now in the role of senior man. I feel as if I am passing on the baton that had earlier been passed on to me.

I have found the most delightful of such unequal friendships to be the most unequal of all—that between a parent and his children. Here, again, Aristotle is my guide; he notes that the inequality derives from the fact that a parent may disown a son or daughter for dishonorable behavior but, because his or her debt is too great, a son or daughter may not disown a parent. Is it possible, though, to declare one's child one's friend? Is blood thicker than friendship? I have felt something very akin to friendship with both my sons, and felt it fairly early in their lives. I remember an autumn afternoon on which I went with my eldest son, then fourteen, to Sears, Roebuck to get new tires for my car. I thought the job could be done in an hour; it turned out to take four. We had lunch in a Chinese restaurant. We walked the streets of the neighborhood. We babbled away to each other on all sorts of subjects. Because the car was still not ready, we sojourned to the appliance section of the Sears store to watch a bit of the U.S. Open tennis tournament while we sat on rolled-up rugs. *What a boon companion this kid is*, I thought. *If he weren't my son, I can imagine him, when grown older, as my friend.*

There have been times in my life when I felt I required no further friends; I said to myself, as one says when dealt a set hand in draw poker, *I'll play with these*. But this hasn't been so, and I am pleased that it hasn't. Even now, in middle life, I continue to gain friendships while I watch other friendships lapse or otherwise fall away. I am not quite up to the ratio of Evelyn Waugh, who in this connection reported: "In the first ten years of adult life I made a large number of friends. Now [Waugh was forty-three when he wrote this] on the average I make one new one a year and lose two." My own efficiency is not so high. I say "efficiency" because there are times when those of us who are promiscuous in our choice of friends feel we could do with many fewer. These are the times when the duties of friendship seem greatly to outweigh its pleasures. Lunches to attend, phone calls to return, letters to answer, obligations to repay—sometimes the duties of friendship (and these are the lighter duties) seem all too much. And they are often too much, unless, of course, one is friendless, in which case one pines for lunches to attend, phone calls to return, letters to answer, and obligations to repay. Friendship may know no happy medium.

Not everyone has the same appetite for friendship. P. G. Wodehouse once claimed that he required few friends. But then, he was happily married and happy in his work, and this combination of good fortune doubtless lessens the need for friends. Friends are more important to the unmarried or the less-than-happily married, I think.

That very social being, Henry James, who was a good friend to so many people and who always took the obligations of friendship with the utmost seriousness, nonetheless seemed, for much of his later life, a friendless man; and toward the end he remarked, plaintively, that he felt himself quite without contemporaries. Mencken claimed not to care much for the company of writers, yet for a long stretch he befriended, and championed, that otherwise lonely figure, Theodore Dreiser. Max Brod was a supremely good friend to Kafka. One senses that Melville did not get anywhere near the spiritual sustenance he had hoped for from his friendship with Hawthorne. The friendship award in American literature, however, ought to go to William Dean Howells, who proved so good a friend to Henry James and Mark Twain, two writers who had very little use for each other.

Howells never had to introduce James to Twain, luckily enough for him, for introducing two of one's friends to each other can produce a tense moment. How delightful when they turn out to appreciate each other! How dreadful when they don't! Then there is the tricky terrain when one of your friends attacks another of your friends to you. Obviously, one must stage a defense; just as obviously, it must be a careful one, so that in defending your attacked friend you do not seem to attack the attacker. I have a close friend many of whose own friends I heartily despise and at whom, in lulls in our conversation, I sometimes like to toss verbal darts. I sympathize with my friend—I have been placed in this position myself—but not enough to let up on him. Why does it bother me that a man I like so much has friends I so dislike? Do I see it as a judgment on me? How, after all, can I have so good a friend who has such miserable taste in choosing friends?

What kind of friend am I? I try to be good but know I am not great. Perhaps it is that I am able to live very comfortably within my family, that my work fills up larger and larger portions of my days, including weekends; but I think it is accurate to say that I do not so much depend upon as enjoy my friends. Certainly, I am less and less aggressive in friendship; increasingly, I hang back and wait for friends to get in touch with me. I allow long stretches to pass in which I do not see people I care a good deal about. More and more I feel at greater ease as a guest than as a host. Apart from a small circle of very dear friends, the effort required of friendship seems to me harder and harder to make. Not long ago I let a close friendship die because I had heard that this friend had said things behind my back that were painful to me; more recently, I informed a friend who had moved to another, distant country that I could not keep up my end of our correspondence; since then a business associate with whom I was on my way to forming a friendship accused me of sharp dealing in a publishing matter, and so I suggested to him that, if he really believed what he said, we cease to speak to each other for a period of five years (we still have two years to go). Fifteen or twenty years ago I would have acted differently in each case: confronted my friend with what he said, kept up my end of the correspondence, argued my innocence with meticulous care. No longer.

As one grows older, one realizes better the limits of friendship. In my case, I have begun to realize how far I wish to go with my friendships, which is to differing limits with different friends. At the lowest end of the scale, I have false friends: I deem them false not because of any hypocrisy on their part or mine but because our friendship is made up of pretense on both sides, and it is the taste for cordiality that makes this pretense possible. As a former Good Guy, I retain a special weakness for entering into this kind of friendship, which is, like a magician's trunk, hollow at bottom.

Next on the scale are casual friendships, such as the one I have with the salesman at the shop where over the years I have bought my suits. This man and I have never addressed each other by any but our last names. Since I sometimes go two or three years without buying a new suit or jacket, the time between our meetings is ample. Yet when we do meet, a fine feeling prevails, and I believe that this feeling is not owing to salesmanship alone. We have a certain regard for each other; we enjoy talking together about nothing in particular: my work, his travels, the city in which we both live. The last time I was in the shop I learned that, within the same month, his wife had died of cancer and he had had a stroke. People I have known better than he have died or suffered affliction, and yet their troubles have affected me less—or at least I have thought less about them. In friendship "casual" can be a tricky term.

I have other friends whom I don't think of as casual at all, whom I genuinely like, yet whom I am perfectly content to see on the most limited basis. I have a friend from college days with whom I go to one, sometimes two baseball games a year; we do not meet in winter. I have some friends I see only for lunch (and one or two with whom I am always planning to meet but never do meet for lunch). I have friends whom I see only when their wives are along; I have other friends whose husbands or wives I have never met. I have a friend who lives a mere two miles from where I do and whom I generally meet but once a year and sometimes less frequently than that. I have a category of friends whom I am pleased to run into but do not wish necessarily to see again soon; there is always a slightly embarrassed silence when we part without either of us saying, "We must get together again soon."

At a high school reunion I attended—this was for the school at which I was not voted Most Popular, Best Liked, Most Friendly, etc.—I felt an odd mixture of elation and sadness, for such events, I realized, are really graveyards of dead friendships. It was lovely to see all these friends from my past. As Logan Pearsall Smith once put it, "The mere process of growing old together will make the slightest acquaintance seem a bosom friend." Hence the elation. The sadness came from the knowledge that there was no real hope of renewing any of these relationships, that at such meetings we jump back to our youth for this one night, but that by morning we shall recall why we haven't stayed friends through the years—because, that is, life has dragged us elsewhere and there is no point in pretending that we can drag ourselves back.

I number more than a few women in the second and third tiers of my friends, and yet I must add that I think of women as belonging in a different category of friends. Montaigne thought women incapable of friendship: "Besides, to tell the truth, the ordinary capacity of women is inadequate for that communion and fellowship which is the nurse of this sacred bond; nor does their soul seem firm enough to endure the strain of so tight and durable a knot." From such remarks are movements such as Women's Liberation made. One of the nicest consequences of the current Women's Liberation movement, I should say, is that it has brought out the fellowship (Flaubert is correct; the language is frequently inept) between women, making friendships between women seem, to pick up Montaigne's phrase, "tight and durable" indeed. But friendships between men and women are something else again. La Bruyère speaks interestingly to this point:

Friendship may exist between a man and a woman, quite apart from any influence of sex. Yet a woman always looks upon man as a man, and so a man regards a woman. This intimacy is neither pure friendship nor pure love. It is a sentiment which stands alone.

I once asked Lillian Hellman about Edmund Wilson, a writer I much admired but never met and who, from his letters and diaries, seemed damned unpleasant. "You have to realize," she said, "that there were really two Edmund Wilsons: the man's and the woman's Edmund Wilson. If you were a man, Edmund had to prove his superiority to you by demonstrating that he was smarter than you. He was the intellectual equivalent of the playground bully. But if you were a woman, he could be very gentle, sweet, *gallant*, even, when he had no sexual interest in you. I of course knew him as a woman, and so have nothing but nice thoughts about him."

This seems to me very penetrating, and not alone about Edmund Wilson. I suspect we are all a bit two-faced in this regard, depending upon which sex we are facing. In discussing friendship, the moralists almost invariably contrast it with erotic love, holding friendship to be on a different level because of its disinterestedness, a quality to which erotic love can never lay claim. Too often when even the most decorous men and women are together the sound of flutes can be heard off in the forest, albeit neither party is prepared to gambol to them. Still, the gentlest wind of Eros can give an odd twist to a friendship between a man and a woman. Is it correct to say that when men and women are together they find it difficult to be themselves? Or is it more correct to say instead that they are most like themselves?

Let the flutes resound, let the winds of Eros blow the roof down, I know I am not ready to give up any of my female friends. I am not, in fact, ready to give up any of my friends. Aristotle says that a happy man has need of friends; I am not sure I qualify as his happy man, but I know I have need of mine: for the delight and support and affection they give. He also says that "it would seem actually impossible to be a great friend to many people," adding later, when considering the question of whether we need friends more in good fortune or in bad, that "the presence of friends . . . seems desirable in all circumstances." I agree on both points, while recognizing that I for one may have more friends than the philosophical limit allows. Still, this comes under a category that Aristotle, for all his marvelous comprehensibility, does not consider—that which I think of as the Happy Problem. For now I am fully prepared to live with mine.

(1985)

A Fat Man
Struggles to Get Out

How do things stand with you and the seven deadly sins? Here is my scorecard: Sloth I fight—to a draw. I surrendered to Pride long ago. Anger I tend to give in to so often that it makes me angry. Lust I'd rather not discuss. I haven't thus far done well enough in the world to claim Avarice as anything more than a theoretical sin. I appear to be making some headway against Envy, though I realize that it's touch-and-go. Of the seven deadly sins, the only one that has a continuing interest for me is Gluttony. But "continuing interest" is a euphemism; by it I mean that Gluttony is the last deadly sin that excites me in a big way—so much so that, though I am prepared to admit that Gluttony can be deadly, I am not all that prepared to say it is a sin. As soon as I pop this chocolate chip cookie in my mouth, I shall attempt to explain what I mean.

I am not beautiful and I am probably not very fit, but I am, at least in a rough geometrical sense, in shape. I weigh what the charts say I ought to weigh. To some people I may seem slender. For the most part, I am not displeased with my physique. Certainly I have no wish to be fat; flabby I should heartily dislike; portly is a touch more than I should prefer—but, let me confess it, stout, solid dignified stout, doesn't sound that bad to me. Was it Cyril Connolly who said that within every fat man a thin man struggles to get out? With me the reverse condition obtains: I am a relatively thin man in whom a fat man struggles, sometimes quite desperately, to get out.

That fat man is no gourmet. He cannot claim to be a gourmand, which A. J. Liebling, a fat man who did get out, once defined as someone who loves delicacies and plenty of 'em. My fat man is less discriminating. He longs for quantities of sandwiches and great mounds of rather greasy french fried potatoes followed by great hunks of cake, a little snack washed down with tankards of soda pop (with Pepsi-Cola, to be specific, and not the no-calorie, caffeine-free, unleaded kind, either). Ribs, pizza, raw oysters, servings of ice cream that cover the entire surface of dinner plates—these are the names of some of my fat man's desires. He is always on the lookout for inexpensive restaurants that serve in impressive tonnage—restaurants out of which he dreams of walking, a toothpick clamped in his mouth, remarking to himself, "Yes, indeed, a slap-up meal; they did me very well in there."

You can see why this fat man cannot be turned loose. I do on occasion let him out for a weekend or a holiday, in what I suppose is the gastronomical equivalent of a work-release program. But set scot-free, left to forage full-time for himself, this man would kill me with his teeth and bury me with a fork. Clearly a dangerous character, he must be held under lock and key and, when let out, kept under the strictest surveillance. Moderation is a principle he does not recognize, deferred gratification is a phrase of whose meaning he remains ignorant, compromise he won't even consider. All this being the case,

I can only say to him, as I frequently do, "Sorry, Tons-of-Fun, it's the slammer for you."

Perhaps I would be better off in the condition of a friend who one day told me that, as the result of a boyhood fistfight in which his nose was so badly smashed it had to be remade, he had lost roughly eighty percent of his sense of taste. To him food was now almost sheerly a matter of fuel. I greeted this announcement with a mixture of envy for his release from a troubling passion and sadness at his deprivation. I have known others who could eat until the cows come home, and then slaughter the cows for a steak sandwich—all without the least effect on girth or chin or limb. These, in my view, are among the favorites of the gods. To me the gods have dealt differently, bestowing upon me an appetite that is matched only by my vanity. I wish to live fat but be thin.

I was not bred for the kind of careful abstinence that is the admired eating standard of our day. A finicky child, I was catered to in my extreme fussiness. (Freud says that a man who as a child feels assured of his mother's love is likely to think himself a conqueror; I say this same conqueror is likely to have a weight problem.) Whatever Joseph wanted, Joseph got—in my mother's kitchen, Lola had nothing on me. In adolescence, my tastes in food broadened and my appetite deepened. Ours was always an impressive larder. I can recall many a night, before settling in to sleep, fixing myself a little snack that might consist of, say, a dozen or so cookies, a pint of butter pecan ice cream, a gross or so of grapes, and four fingers of salmi. Nor was sleep after such a repast in any way a problem. Today, of course, this kind of snack, attempted at my age, could only be construed as a suicide attempt.

My mother knew I ate huge portions at home, but she could not know that the ample meals she served me were perhaps half my daily ration. She could not know because I did not tell her. As a serious eater I hadn't, you might say, come out of the pantry. But out of the pantry I surely emerged. After a breakfast at home of orange juice, eggs, and toast, I would, upon arrival at high school, generally plunge into a smoke-filled school store called Harry's, where, to fortify myself for the strenuous mental effort that lay ahead, I engorged something known as a chocolate square (approximate weight: one-third pound), a small stein of root beer, and the smoke of two Lucky Strike cigarettes. Often with friends I would take lunch at a nearby Jewish delicatessen called Ashkenaz; the meal usually consisted of soup, corned beef sandwiches, and other of those Jewish foods that, as one sour-stomached Jewish gentleman I know has put it, have caused more difficulties for the Jews than Pharaoh himself. After lunch it was back to the classroom, where, on a full stomach, I was easily able to ignore what should have been the rudiments of my education. After school, a *flâneur du gastronomique*, I might knock back a small bag of french fries liberally slathered with ketchup, which, most afternoons, along with perhaps a banana and six or seven cookies, would see me through to dinner.

Proust famously used food—his little fluted madeleine cake—to beckon memory; working at things the other way round, I beckon memory to recall food. I remember a Rumanian Jewish restaurant to which my parents used to take us where the waiters seemed to have stepped out of Jewish jokes. Once, as a small boy, when I asked one of them if the restaurant had any soda pop, he, towel over his shoulder, pencil poised over his order pad, sourly replied, "Yeh, ve gots two kinds. Ve gots red and ve gots brown." I remember when a small chain of rather deluxe hamburger restaurants named Peter Pan was caught serving its customers horse meat and, in a gesture to return to the public's good graces, gave away free hamburgers for a day, thus creating a living fantasy in which every boy could be his own Wimpy. In the autumn of 1952, Dwight David Eisenhower was elected president, elaborate peace negotiations were under way in Korea, François Mauriac won the Nobel Prize for literature, and I, a freshman in high school, tasted pizza for the first time and thought I had died and gone to heaven.

That same year, in an episode of shame, I recall walking along the avenue with my faithful companion, Robert Ginsburg, who, always the tempter, suggested we buy and share and dispatch a cake. Dispatch it we did, but I cannot say neatly. As in so many of our combined enterprises, an element of planning was missing. In this instance, the cake now purchased, we noted the absence of utensils for cutting it—a large chocolate affair with a combined chocolate and pistachio frosting—and, once cut, for conveying it to our mouths. We could have brought the cake home, there to have an ample slice in his or my mother's kitchen. But we did not want a slice of cake, however ample—we wanted an entire cake. So we ate it, walking along side streets, prying great fistfuls away from the cake and stuffing them into our mouths in the style we designated "one billion BC." We are talking about two reasonably well-brought-up middle-class boys here, you understand, but true hunger, to the truly craving, will turn even a middle-class lad into a savage.

Middle-class and Middle Western, I should have added, for when I think of the ideal middle-class meal of my youth, eaten in a restaurant, it comprises the following plain but to me, then as now, quite pleasing Middle Western menu: it begins with a shrimp cocktail; followed by a wedge of iceberg lettuce with Thousand Island dressing; followed by a rather thick slab of medium-rare prime rib of beef, with a baked potato (not cooked in aluminum foil) lavished with butter and sour cream with chives; and concluded with strawberry shortcake and coffee. This is, you will recognize, almost an entirely prelapsarian meal; it could only have been eaten in good conscience before the vile knowledge that certain foods can clog arteries, set tumors growing, send up blood pressure. If you are someone who would like to get to ninety-six or ninety-seven, and hence someone attentive to death by cancer, heart attack, or stroke, what you are permitted from that meal I have described, once the calories, the cholesterol, and the caffeine are removed, is a plain baked potato on a bed of undressed lettuce with a few strawberries atop it nicely garnished with chives. Dig in.

I mock such curtailment of pleasure—I hate it, truth to tell—yet I am myself victim to it. Far from always, but still all too often, I look down at the plate set before me to find potential death through possible heart disease or cancer lurking there—and if not death, social disgrace through being overweight. Until roughly twenty-five years ago, those of us born into industrially developed countries, though we may not have known it, were all living in the kitchen of Eden. The snake responsible for casting us out is named Diet: today few are the people who are not dieting for health, for beauty, for longevity. *Eat to Win* is the title of a recent bestseller that supplies diets and menus for people who wish to stay young and athletically competitive. The well-named *Self* magazine calls it "the eating wave of the future." *Eat to Win?* Whatever happened to eat to enjoy?

Not that I am above diet. I spend a serious portion of my life attempting to lose the extra four or five pounds that clearly wishes to adhere to me. I gain it, I drop it off, I gain it, I drop it off—we are, those four or five pounds and I, like a couple who cannot agree to live peaceably together, but who refuse to separate permanently.

I need no reminder when they have returned: when the press of my flesh rubs the waist of my trousers, it is time to miss a meal, hold the fries, play strong defense generally. Aggravation makes the best diet, in my view, and once, in a troubled time in my life, I dropped off fifteen pounds without consciously attempting to do so. Another time I set out to lose twenty pounds; I did it, and I wish to report that the feeling upon having succeeded in doing so is one I describe as "fatness of soul." One is so splendidly well pleased with oneself. An element of fanaticism slides in. One has lost twenty pounds—why not twenty-five? A friend described my play on the racquetball court as quicker than a sperm. I thought I looked wonderfully well when I had lost all that weight: so lithe, so elegant, so youthful. Apparently this was not the effect I everywhere conveyed, for more than one person, during this period, asked my wife straight-out if I were suffering from a wasting disease.

Because of this little experience I believe I can understand something of what goes on in the mind of the anorexic. The anorexic is the reverse of the glutton, but it is well to remember that the anorexic is the other side of the same coin. (The currently accepted definition of anorexia nervosa is "a serious illness of deliberate self-starvation with profound psychiatric and physical components.") As food excites the glutton, so does it repel the anorexic (most of whom are adolescent girls or youngish women). The glutton's idea of a jolly fine time is precisely the anorexic's idea of hell. As the glutton in extreme cases will have to have his jaw wired to prevent him from eating, the anorexic will in equally extreme cases have to be hospitalized and force-fed through tubes.

For the true glutton, as for the true anorexic, food may well not be the real problem; the love and hatred of food, when they take on such obsessive energy, doubtless mask deeper problems, distinctive in individual cases. But it is interesting that reactions to food can be a significant symptom in serious psychological disorders. Freud, that suspicious Viennese, thought that a great deal more was going on at the table than met the fork. Unquestionably there sometimes is. But I prefer to stand on this question with Cyril Connolly, who put into the mouth of a character in his story *Shade Those Laurels* the lines: "They say that food is a substitute for love. Well, it's certainly a bloody good one."

I like my gluttons mildly obsessive but not compulsive. I prefer to think that in their pursuit of food they are not crying out for attention never given them by a thoughtless mother, but instead are trying to duplicate the lovely meals given to them by a thoughtful mother; or, if not that, then I prefer to think they are simply hungry—most of the time. Consider Falstaff, about whose childhood and parentage Shakespeare supplies us with no helpful information. He is perhaps a bit more of a soak than a pure glutton ought to be, but he is otherwise an ideal type, and one who oughtn't to be made to lie still for psychoanalysis. Friar Tuck, Robin Hood's man, is another in the line of delightful fat boys. Let us not neglect, in toting up our serious trenchermen, the monks in Rabelais, whose merest snack could render any forest full of endangered species. The great gluttons of the movies of my boyhood were an Austro-Hapsburgian character actor named S. Z. ("Cuddles") Sakall and Sydney Greenstreet; Sakall played his fat man sweet, as if he were a walking piece of very creamy pastry, while Greenstreet played his menacing, as if he were a hard dumpling that, should it roll over you, could cause serious damage.

The literary hall of avoirdupois has no shortage of tenants. Those two butterballs, G. K. Chesterton and Hilaire Belloc, gain admittance without question. Balzac, who was a bit of a pudge, deserves a place. So, too, does Henry James, who fought weight all his life and, as photographs from his later years reveal, was finally defeated. Mustn't forget Edward Gibbon, that chubby, inelegantly formed little man who wrote only streamlined, elegantly formed sentences. The nineteenth-century French writers Sainte-Beuve, Gautier, Flaubert, and Edmond de Goncourt, while not quite Keystone Kops, were nonetheless all nice-sized boys, the result no doubt of those elaborate meals at Magny and other Parisian restaurants. E. R. Curtius has commented on the corpulence of Friedrich Schlegel. Among American writers William Dean Howells and Wallace Stevens were, to put it softly, heavyset. Poor Oscar Wilde emitted such pointed wit from a rather pasty, lumpy body. Evelyn Waugh ended his days with his trousers let all the way out. Edmund Wilson was no flyweight. No shortage of embonpoint among the literati.

But then there are those anorexics of culture who seemed to exist on aperçus and orchids: Ronald Firbank, Aubrey Beardsley, Lytton Strachey, and Proust. As anyone who has read Céleste Albaret's memoir of her employer, dear M. Proust, can tell you, that Marcel could be a very picky eater. Still, I believe I should rather have Proust over for dinner than Kafka, who doesn't seem a man easily fed. Yet it may well be that it would be more pleasant to have Kafka for dinner than to go out oneself for dinner at the home of Leonard and Virginia Woolf, whose gaunt looks scarcely suggest that they set a very handsome table. Judging now from their girths and from what is known of their appetites, I shouldn't mind dining, at a table for five, with Samuel Johnson, H. L. Mencken, A. J. Liebling, and Jean Anthelme Brillat-Savarin. How fine the talk would be! Separate checks, of course.

When an adolescent I used to lunch from time to time with a man who, I estimate, weighed in at roughly 350 pounds. He worked for the father of my friend Robert Ginsburg. He had all one would expect in the way of jollity from a large and gluttonous man. He called himself the Fat Man. How fat was he? A single detail will suffice for description. In his car he kept an old towel—his *shmatte*, he called it—which, when driving, he laid across his belly to prevent the steering wheel from wearing away his trousers.

The Fat Man was Robert's and my Falstaff, though it is fairly certain that neither of us will go on to become the king of England. Like Falstaff, he commanded a highly colorful vocabulary. When a driver in a car behind him honked, his standard riposte was "Blow it out your duffel bag, fathead." He introduced us to various of the gaieties of the flesh, overeating not least among them. He knew the best inexpensive restaurants in every neighborhood in Chicago. He enjoyed his vittles and piled them high upon his plate. He was once described as eating corned beef sandwiches as if they were cornflakes. He seemed to take minor offense if his luncheon companions failed to eat heartily. Robert and I did our best never to give offense. "Have another piece of cheesecake, boys," the Fat Man would say, "you owe it to yourself." *You owe it to yourself*—a finer glutton's motto cannot be devised. A philosophy of life is contained in those five short words.

The Fat Man died before the advent of nouvelle cuisine, but I feel confident in my belief that he would have found it, as a serious feeder, laughable. I have eaten perhaps a dozen such meals, all very expensive, and the majority of them, I am pleased to report as a partial excuse, on other people's expense accounts. The dishes to be had in such restaurants, as the carefully coiffed waiters who tell you about them like to say, "make a very nice presentation." I suppose a lot depends upon how hungry one is for a very nice presentation. I have eaten dishes in such restaurants wherein, at moments, I thought I was devouring a Kandinsky or a Frank Stella painting. Then there are those bloodless specials to deal with. "May I tell you about our specials?" the waiter will ask. ("Of course not," an acquaintance with more social courage than I has taken to retorting.) "Chef Yoshie has prepared tonight a delicate terrine made up of twenty-six pâtés and a sausage composed of the spare parts of a 1973 Ford Pinto. We also have medallions of pigeons' heels in a savory hot fudge sauce, with just a hint of tarragon." Something there is about the announcement of those specials that makes a genuinely crapulous man yearn for a bowl of chili and a large side order of mashed potatoes.

Worse news: it's spreading. An informed source, as they call them at the *New York Times*, informs me that there is now a nouvelle Mexican restaurant in Dallas. One morning a few years back I was hit by specials at breakfast in San Diego. In my own city, Chicago, theme restaurants have had a long run, and so we have beaneries with such names as Jonathan Livingston Seafood and Lawrence of Oregano. We also have nostalgia dining, with one popular joint got up as a 1950s diner, with waitresses who chew gum, fifties tunes on the jukebox, the whole bit. I am told that the food isn't bad, though I haven't visited it because I fear the place must be chiefly frequented by what I think of as "fun couples."

I prefer my restaurants shorn of fun couples. I don't like restaurants where status is the true entrée. Nor do I want too many vegetarians on the premises. "Vegetarianism is harmless enough," said Sir Robert Hutchison, a former president of the Royal College of Physicians, "though it is apt to fill a man with wind and self-righteousness." I like some burly guys around—eight or ten size 48 suits in the place. I like a restaurant where you can get a virile BLT club sandwich ("one of those complicated American sandwiches, with lots of layers," as an English friend once described it), where they know the meaning of creamy coleslaw, where they serve a significant hamburger. I don't wish to seem more Philistine than I am, but I'm talking about that disappearing commodity—plain but serious grub.

I prefer women, too, to be of hearty appetite, though a gluttonous woman seems to me less than appealing. Samuel Johnson took this thought a step further: "If you once find a woman gluttonous, expect from her very little virtue." The strumpets in *Tom Jones*, in corroboration of Johnson's point, were powerful trencherwomen. Although slender herself, Edith Wharton was a woman with an eye always out for the main course. Certainly in her novels she was attentive to the food her hostesses served, and described food very well. In *The Age of Innocence*, in the character of Mrs. Manson Mingott (oddly enough, herself a stingy hostess), Edith Wharton provided the one hugely fat female character I can think of in American literature:

The immense accretion of flesh which had descended on her in middle life like a flood of lava on a doomed city had changed her from a plump active little woman with a neatly-turned foot and ankle into something as vast and august as a natural phenomenon. She had accepted this submergence as philosophically as all her other trials, and now, in extreme old age, was rewarded by presenting to her mirror an almost unwrinkled expanse of firm pink and white flesh, in the center of which the traces of a small face survived as if awaiting excavation. A flight of smooth double chins led down to the dizzy depths of a still-snowy bosom veiled in snowy muslins that were held in place by a miniature portrait of the late Mr. Mingott; and around and below, wave after wave of black silk surged away over the edges of a capacious armchair, with two tiny white hands poised like gulls on the surface of the billows.

The really fat woman has never been an ideal in Western history, though the zaftig or appealingly buxom woman à la Rubens or Renoir of course has. The past fifteen or twenty years have been hard on women in this regard, for they have been years that, despite all the new freedoms attained, have left women hostage to the look that Tom Wolfe has called "starved to perfection." I have known more than one woman who has sacrificed her good looks through the kind of carrot-and-celery-stick dieting that is required to achieve this look of upper-middle-class emaciation. It was Proust, I believe, who said that, beyond a certain age, most women can retain either the beauty of their figure or the beauty of their face—but they cannot retain both.

This was no very great problem for the wives and mistresses of Louis XIV, who, portraiture makes plain, liked his women zaftig. Dining with Louis, they could scarcely have been otherwise. Although not a fat man himself—he was fortunate in being tall—he was one of history's profound feeders. "His appetite," writes Nancy Mitford in *The Sun King*, "astounded the onlookers and frightened the doctors." Dinners at Versailles, one must allow, were impressive. The king ate, again according to Miss Mitford, "a meal composed of four plates of different soups, a whole pheasant and a whole partridge or chicken or duck (according to what game or poultry was in season) stuffed with truffles, a huge quantity of salad, some mutton, two good slices of ham, a dish of pastry, raw fruit, compotes and preserves." In Louis XIV, divine right was reinforced by divine gastronomical might, for he was beautifully equipped for adventures of the table: at his autopsy he was discovered to have a much larger than average stomach and bowels double the normal length.

The Romans were not famous for being dainty feeders; no people who had thought to devise the institution of the vomitorium could have been. The towering glutton among the Roman emperors was Vitellius, who, even on campaign, Suetonius tells us, "always kept a lavish supply of delicacies within reach of his hand." At home he did not dine but banqueted—three and often four times a day. If Vitellius invited himself out, such were his expectations that it rarely cost his hosts fewer than four thousand gold pieces to set out a table for him. Suetonius notes: "Vitellius paid no attention to place or time in satisfying his remarkable appetite. While a sacrifice was in progress, he thought nothing of snatching lumps of meat or cake off the altar, almost out of the sacred fire, and bolting them down; and on his travels would devour cuts of meat fetched smoking hot from wayside cookshops, and even yesterday's half-eaten scraps." Talk about fast food.

Suetonius cites gluttony and cruelty as Vitellius's two reigning vices. Is there a connection between the two? Many a cruel ruler has been a fat boy—Nero and Henry VIII leap to mind. Unfortunately, the data are missing for even a wild generalization. Yet this much can be risked: the possession of power appears not in the least to slake other appetites, food among them. King Farouk of Egypt was a complete tub. Mao Tse-tung was clearly a man who could make his chopsticks fly. The grandfather of the current Aga Khan carried pro football weight without pro football muscle. William Howard Taft, our twenty-seventh president, was built like two walruses with a single head. After Lenin and until Gorbachev, the Soviet Union has not known a leader of normal girth, which has doubtless contributed to the just fame of Soviet tailoring in the fashion capitals of the world. Attaining power, then, seems to be no satisfactory substitute for the passionate craving for food; it merely gives one a chance to sit down to some real meals.

But I see that I have progressed thus far into this essay without rolling out the sweets trolley. The time has arrived. The sweet tooth is an affliction that leaves some people quite untouched. I am not among these people; neither was Evelyn Waugh, who once called gluttony "the master-passion of boyhood" and who knew that many a glutton sets out on his unappeasable path through a childhood craving for sweets. Writing of his fifth-form visits to the Grub Shop near his public school, Waugh wrote: "No subsequent experience of the haute-cuisine or the vintage can rival the gross, innocent delight in the commonplace confections that now began to reappear." The shop offered cakes and buns and ices and chocolates and various whipped-cream contrivances. This sounds quite superior to the sweet fare of my boyhood— about which more directly—but then the English is so much more a tea and tiffin culture than the American. In *A Passage to India* E. M. Forster writes that Aziz "had been warned that English people never stop eating, and that he had better nourish them every two hours until a solid meal was ready." Aziz was well-advised, I think, for the English remain, even after the sun has long set on their empire, the world's greatest nation of noshers. What else is an English tea but the nosh regularized and turned into an institution?

The shop across from our grammar school was called Miller's, after its owner, a Jewish immigrant who lived upstairs from it with his wife and daughter. The shop sold a few groceries, some sandwich makings, detergents, school supplies. But its main attraction and, my guess is, its main source of revenue was a glass cabinet three feet high and perhaps ten feet across that sold the most delightful small poisons and tooth destroyers, which went by the name of penny candy. Gums, waxes, licorices, gelatinous and sticky substances in every color and shape were available in that glass cabinet. Before school, at recess, during lunchtime, after school, children pressed up against it, calling out, "Gimme a wax lips, two machine-gun belts, a jujubes, and three Fleers bubble gum." But before Mr. Miller, bending to the cabinet with noticeable effort, could get these things, another kid would demand, "A pack of Bazooka, three jawbreakers, a mustache, and four cents' worth of red licorice whips." Running that shop required the patience of a saint. Mr. Miller, I regret to have to report, didn't have such patience, and so would regularly break down, crying out to the heavens, yelling at a child, occasionally chasing an older boy out into the street. Those sessions could not have lengthened Mr. Miller's life, but I do know that my regular visits to his shop as a boy have continued to enrich an impressive line of my own dental specialists.

An habitué of Miller's I shall not soon forget was a boy of my own age whom I shall call Mick Stone—a name that rhymes with his own true name and that speaks to his considerable bulk, for at the age of thirteen he already weighed in at roughly 190 pounds, or some fourteen stone. He was the first true glutton I had met. A slow-moving and somewhat morose lad, as free from malice as he was from wit, he must have concentrated all his mental energies on thoughts of food. He was no mere theoretician. At recess, over at Miller's, he sprang into action. A cash outlay of a quarter at Miller's in those years—a time when a bottle of soda pop cost a nickel—identified one as a high roller. Mick Stone must have spent nearly a dollar daily. He was a boy who unfailingly put his mouth where his money was. There on the playground he would wolf down a box of twelve doughnuts, or five or six packages of Twinkies and as many Mounds bars, or four Dreamsicles, a full jelly roll, and a simple Butterfinger. Recess, it is important to understand, was only fifteen minutes. Thus fortified, he would return to class, refreshed and free to turn his full attention to thoughts of lunch.

My reaction to the gluttonous Mick Stone was one that combined amazement with vague envy. I knew that as a feeder he was way out of my class; I knew that I didn't want the encumbrance of vast flesh that was only the most evident wage of his particular sin. Still, I envied the fact that he was someone who would have no traffic with moderation. Food is not a thing that easily allows for moderation. Consider ice cream. I know of only two conditions in which I have ever existed with regard to ice cream: I leave the table either not having had enough, or I leave having had too much. Sometimes a single spoonful can make the difference between not enough and too much. Enoughness, in relation to ice cream, is not a state I have known; I am inclined to think it may not exist.

It may be a mistake to attempt moderation in eating. Instead one must make a choice: either to eat away, let 'er rip, and suffer the consequences; or hold back, bail out well before fullness, and also suffer the consequences. I have decided on the latter course, with occasional forays into gluttonous feeding. It seems to me the wiser way, allowing for a longer life, provided I do not go down in an airplane crash, or under the wheels of a truck, or through an arbitrary disease. Meanwhile, the consequences are a persistent hunger nibbling away at the edge of my consciousness. I suffer from a condition that not Freud but I have named Entrée Envy: a certain sign of the potential glutton, Entrée Envy involves a quick check at restaurants to make sure that no one at my table has ordered better than I and a feeling of sadness upon discovering that someone else has a fuller and more interesting plate. I also tend to hear the following lines from an old Negro blues tune, which I have rewritten slightly to read:

I may be beautiful but I'm goin' to die some day,
So how's about a little feeding before I pass away.

Somerset Maugham, at the beginning of a story entitled "Virtue," tells that, when he was young and poor, he resolved that, if he were to become rich, he would smoke a good cigar every day of his life after lunch and dinner. It is, he claims, the only resolution of his youth that he ever kept. It was also "the only ambition I have achieved that has never been embittered by disillusion." (Freud, that connoisseur of disillusion, was another regular cigar smoker.) Does food bring disillusion? In the same paragraph Maugham talks about oysters and lamb cutlets; and the thought of evolution and the "millions upon millions of years [these] creatures [have taken to] come into existence to end upon a plate of crushed ice or a silver grill," he says, leaves him sad. I must say that the fat man inside me has never had such solemn thoughts. For him life is strictly man eat cutlet and, so to say, no bones about it. And yet . . . and but . . . and still . . . and however . . . disillusion remains after the dessert dishes are cleared. There was all that happiness upon the plate and now it is gone.

I had planned to end this essay with a chronicle of a day in which I let my fat man loose upon the countryside. It was to be a story whose cast included German pancakes and French pastry, pizza and ribs, corn and potato salad, steaks and rich fowl, a small tub or two of sweet butter. I thought I might order two entrées, a thing I have never done.

But I find I cannot bring myself to do any of it. The flesh is willing, but the spirit is weak. I have been living carefully too long. After such a day, I fear belly vengeance; I see a picture of my wife driving up to an emergency room with me stretched across the backseat, a cool compress across my brow, groaning and pledging repentance.

There is, then, a deep fraudulence at the heart of this essay. While writing it I ate a fruit salad, munched on salt-free crackers, drank the abysmal brew known as diet soda, kept a post-card-size picture of the obese Orson Welles taped to my refrigerator. More shocking to report yet, while writing this essay I actually lost two pounds. Oh civilization! Oh bloody discontents!

(1985)

Tea and Antipathy

Imagine my chagrin at learning, as I not long ago did, that a writer whom I rather blithely despised for what I take to be his fraudulent self-righteousness and utterly self-assured hypocrisy, had cancer. Until then I had so enjoyed loathing him, my distaste for everything about him had seemed so complete, so pure, so uncomplicatedly pleasant, and now it was incomplete, alloyed by his misfortune, complicated by my own sympathy for his illness. This was a real setback. I had counted on being able to continue disliking him for another decade or two. It was as if someone had removed a wall against which I had happily grown accustomed to banging my head.

"You know," I explained to a very dear friend, "while I dislike quite a few people, I do not really wish them to undergo physical pain and certainly not death." "I understand," she said, "you merely wish those you despise to feel more stress." That was it precisely. More stress is exactly what I wished for those whom I consider my enemies. By stress I mean I wish that their children will grow up to dislike them; I wish them trouble with the IRS, sharp reductions in the status that is so vital to their well-being, perhaps a bit of public humiliation—all the little things that cause, as my friend so delicately put it, "more stress."

I suppose this makes me a pretty good but not a great hater. I should rather not be a hater at all, of course. I respect people who struggle against permitting themselves the indulgence of hating. Much grander, I realize, to be above such mean feelings. Lofty amusement leading on to generalizations about the flaws in human nature seems to me a finer response to people whom one finds repugnant. How much better to accept people as we find them! Yet I find that to love one's neighbor often involves an effort of will, whereas to hate one's enemy seems to come so naturally. What does not come naturally to me is ready forgiveness for injuries suffered. On those occasions when I have made an earnest attempt to turn the other cheek, in that other cheek I have inevitably discovered my tongue inserted. Hating exacts such a strong feeling that it can be a serious distraction; indulged in a concentrated way, it can even diminish one's own high opinion of oneself. Hating can skew the judgment, furrow the brow, take the bloom off one's complexion. Getting one's knickers in a twist, as the English used to call being in an agitated state, tends to remove the crease from one's trousers. It ain't, kiddo, good.

I have never been fond of the prospect of myself hating someone, and early in life I tried my best to avoid doing so. Like everyone else, I encountered people I did not like. Usually I was able to register my distaste for their selfishness or their cruelty or their crudity and then avoid them whenever possible; as with sand traps and water holes on a golf course, I shot around them and played on through. But all this changed when, in my late twenties, I became enmeshed in intellectual life. Something there is about the nature of intellectual life that seems to encourage rivalrous and rancorous feelings. Edward Shils, a thinker who does not fall back regularly on psychological labels, has said that paranoia is the reigning psychological condition of the intellectual, and I believe he is absolutely correct. Anyone who has worked among scholars knows that, in the humanities and social sciences, there is no academic subject, from numismatics on up, that does not have its politics, and these politics can sometimes be internecine. Such politics do not discourage paranoia. "Even paranoids have real enemies," famously said Delmore Schwartz, who was himself certifiably paranoid. Not every intellectual is a paranoid, but I have yet to meet one who did not claim to have real enemies. And this is especially so among literary intellectuals. "I don't know how it is in other professions," says a character in George Gissing's *New Grub Street*, "but I hope there is less envy, hatred and malice than in this of ours."

In intellectual life sticks and stones are not thrown, but well-aimed words can pierce the skin. By now the intellectual insult has acquired nearly the status of a genre. It has been going on long enough for Penguin Books to bring out not one but two collections of famous literary insults. Pride of place in this line perhaps ought to go to Alexander Pope, who in *The Dunciad* set down 1,670 ten-syllable lines, not a false rhyme among them, blasting away at his contemporaries for "dullness," a comprehensive term Pope meant to include shoddy reasoning, bad taste, and general stupidity. Much of the time Pope felt he was returning insult for injury; and no target was too minor for him to knock off, for, as he put it, "It would vex one more to be knocked on the head with a piss-pot than by a thunderbolt."

William Hazlitt—"pimpl'd Hazlitt" to his enemies—is another English writer who gave rather better than he got. Perhaps it is more accurate to say, when he got, he gored, for he had a lovely knack of combining fury with precise formulation, with which he could rip an opponent wide open. When Hazlitt's book on Shakespeare was attacked by William Gifford, the editor of the *Quarterly Review*, Hazlitt replied in a forty-page "A Letter to William Gifford, Esquire," in which he described the *Quarterly Review* as the "receptacle for the scum and sediment of all the prejudice, bigotry, ill-will, ignorance, and rancour afloat in the kingdom." The Goncourt brothers made a specialty of dining out in Paris and returning home to put down—in both senses of the phrase—the behavior of their dinner companions in their famous journal. Chekhov claimed to be "physically repelled by abuse no matter at whom it is aimed," and wondered why journalistic critics "write in a tone fit for judging criminals rather than artists and writers." Yet even Chekhov, for all his vaunted "gentle humanity," could be savage when confronting a point of view or an intellectual position he thought spurious.

In our day some of the most vicious insults seem to have been made by the intellectuals gathered around the magazine *Partisan Review*. Their best shots were all fired behind one another's backs in the form of comments that somehow always found their way to their targets. The paranoia of Delmore Schwartz, who was an associate editor of *Partisan Review*, was in this sense planted in fertile soil. Schwartz himself is supposed to have said of Lionel Trilling that of course he was very intelligent, but he wished Trilling didn't say even the most obvious things in a tone of voice more appropriate for announcing a cure for cancer. Philip Rahv, one of the principal editors of *Partisan Review*, was especially brutal at the behind-the-back intellectual insult, and, when asked why he went in for it with such vehemence, chalked it up to what he called "analytical exuberance." In *The Truants*, William Barrett's splendid memoir of the *Partisan Review* crowd, Barrett recalls Delmore Schwartz remarking, " 'Analytic exuberance'—Philip Rahv's euphemism for putting a knife in your back." William Phillips, the magazine's other principal editor, used to refer to Rahv's various wives and women friends as his "alter-Iagos." Nobody escaped this kind of maiming remark. When some years ago I asked another member of the *Partisan Review* crowd how Harold Rosenberg (who was then still alive) was doing, he said, "You know Harold, still acquiring every expensive painting he can lay his hands on while waiting for Marxism to get its third wind." And they say words can't kill.

Do people say such horrendous things about me behind my back? In his essay "On the Pleasures of Hating," Hazlitt remarks, "I care little what any one says of me, particularly behind my back, and in the way of critical and analytical discussion: it is looks of dislike and scorn that I answer with the worst venom of my pen." I care rather more, but I suppose I must count myself lucky in having very few rough things that were said about me behind my back reported to me. When I was much younger I had a friend who used to say terrible things to my face, and then go and praise me behind my back—a strange reversal of normal procedure. Such insults made about me behind my back that have been reported to me have tended not to be well formulated but merely sincere expressions of heartfelt hatred. No one thus far has thought to say of me, "He writes very nicely. Do you suppose English is his first language?" Or: "He appears to have such confidence in his views. Looking at him, and given those views, I cannot for the life of me imagine whence this confidence derives."

I have been called some charming things in print, among them a "cultural terrorist" and a "Stalinist." I was once called a "racist" for writing that my own children, before they had developed table manners, ate like Apaches. A vastly overheated third-line literary critic once led off an essay about me and two other writers who share some of my views with an epigraph from Hemingway that made reference to "yellow bastards." On more than one occasion people have asked, publicly, that I be fired from my job. In every one of these instances I believe I understood the motives behind such behavior, but for me, I am sorry to report, to understand all is not to pardon all. I shall doubtless forget many of these insults, yet I have not truly forgiven any that I can remember. *Dieu les pardonnera*, to paraphrase Heine. *C'est son métier.*

I prefer not to meet the people I dislike. Perhaps this is because, being an intellectual, I tend to dislike them for their ideas, and to discover, upon meeting them, the ideas made flesh can be disconcerting. One is likely to discover some quality in them, even some defect, that curbs one's distaste. I not long ago attended a conference at which I met an editor whose magazine encourages just about everything I find lamentable in public life. If the ideas promoted in his magazine were to win through, this country would become an exceedingly unpleasant place for me. At a session of the conference at which I spoke I had no trepidation about attacking these ideas. But at the break for lunch I found myself walking ten or fifteen yards behind this editor, from which perspective I noticed that he had bad feet. He walked funnily; he wore special shoes; he lived with real discomfort, possibly persistent pain; he became more human for me. I could no longer dislike him with the same cheerful gusto. Making enemies is easy, William Dean Howells once noted, but keeping them is not.

I am reminded of a letter George Orwell wrote to Stephen Spender in which he explains how he had once been able to attack Spender, but had changed his mind after meeting him. Orwell tells Spender that he regarded him as a poet whose verse meant very little to him as

well as a Communist sympathizer—the letter was written in 1938—
to whose views Orwell himself was hostile. He was able to think of
Spender, as he puts it, "as a type & also an abstraction. Even if when
I met you I had not happened to like you, I should still have been
bound to change my attitude, because when you meet anyone in the
flesh you realise immediately that he is a human being & not a sort of
caricature embodying certain ideas." Orwell concludes: "It is partly
for this reason that I don't mix much in literary circles, because I
know from experience that once I have met & spoken to anyone I
shall never again be able to show any intellectual brutality towards
him, even when I feel I ought to."

Since reading that letter many years ago, I have had a few
opportunities to meet Stephen Spender, but have gone a bit out of
my way to avoid doing so. I have never treated him to the intellectual brutality that Orwell speaks about, yet the fact is that I
prefer to hang on to my strong dislike of his writing, and do not
wish to jeopardize it through personal encounter. I prefer to keep
the possibility of intellectual brutality in reserve, for I find I cannot
meet someone, pretend to like him, and then attack him in print—I
cannot do so, that is, without a strong sense of acting hypocriti-
cally. On the other hand, I note a number of people who have not
allowed personal meetings with me to keep them from treating me
with intellectual brutality afterward. (Can it be that my personal
charm is not quite foolproof?) On the third hand—we complicated
thinkers sometimes require four or five hands to make our point—I
greatly admire those few writers I know who can go on the attack,
or take an attack, no-holds-barred, and have drinks afterward with
the very people with whom they have just engaged in intellectual
combat. Such writers seem to be able to hate certain intellectual

positions without hating the people who hold them—to hate, that is, the sin but not the sinner.

Nature, remarks Hazlitt, seems "made up of antipathies: without something to hate, we should lose the very spring of thought and action." Hating, it is discouraging to report, may be more interesting than loving. Certainly the range of emotions associated with hatred is much greater than that associated with love, and its language is correspondingly richer. Indignation, rage, scorn, disgust, loathing, fury, vengeance, grudge, contempt, jealousy, contumely, malice, wrath, embitterment, and let us not forget our old friend Schaden-freude—now here is a vocabulary a fellow can work with. Think of the writers who, were it not for hating, would be out of business. Swift comes immediately to mind, for all strong satire begins in hatred. Dostoyevsky hated in the name of Christianity. Strindberg and Ibsen blew a cold wind of hatred down from the north. None of these, I must confess, is among my favorite authors. But other authors whom I adore hated, so to speak, selectively. The English critic D. W. Harding wrote an essay on Jane Austen entitled "Regulated Hatred," in which he argues that Jane Austen had very mixed feelings about the society in which she lived. Dickens believed in evil and despised it wherever he described it. Max Beerbohm, who once said that anger was "a rare feeling for me," nonetheless deeply disliked, if he did not actively despise, George Bernard Shaw. And Karl Kraus, whose satirical lashings appeared in his own Viennese journal *Die Fackel*, to which he eventually became the sole contributor, said, "I no longer have any collaborators. I used to be envious of them. They repel those readers whom I want to lose myself."

Things worth hating in the world are never in short supply: hypoc-risy, cowardice, cruelty, disloyalty. Then there are world-class villains, among whom Stalin and Hitler remain permanently hateful. Hatred between nations is far from scarce: the Greeks hate the Turks, the Koreans hate the Japanese, the Irish hate the English, and there is no love lost between the Pakistanis and the Indians. Nirad C. Chaudhuri, the gifted Indian writer, has written about what he calls "the real East-West conflict," the hatred of the Third World for the West, which, "arising from historical experience, has bitten into the subconscious to become a self-propagating emotion capable of discovering ever new grievances to feed itself." Chaudhuri wrote that in 1957, and I should like to show anyone who believes that things have improved since that time some choice real estate in downtown Managua.

Politics provides the clearest channel for hatred. Tell me your politics and I shall tell you whom you despise: Qaddafi or Botha, Arafat (Yasser, that's my baby) or Pinochet. Yet impersonal hatred is sometimes difficult to sustain. The larger the object of hatred, the less concentrated the emotion one can bring to it. There are of course men and women who can hate entire peoples. Anti-Semites are an ugly example. ("He who hates the Jews," Eugen Weber has written, "hates mankind.") But I know a woman, a Polish Jew from Lodz who was in Auschwitz, who not only hates the Germans but also hates the Poles; and, when the Russians were bearing down on the Poles during the rise of Solidarity, I recall her remarking that, remembering how cruel the Poles were to the Jews during the Nazi era, she could feel no sympathy for them now as victims of the Russians. Yet her hatred was not impersonal—far from it. There are hatreds one doesn't approve but has to respect.

Easily the most hated American political figures of my lifetime have been Franklin Delano Roosevelt and Richard Nixon. I was eight years old when Roosevelt died, and never felt any special animosity toward him, then or since. To this day, though, I run into old-line Republicans whose fuse goes off at the mere mention of his initials. Nixon, for me, was a different story. As a youthful reader of the *New Republic*—weekly strolling, as S. J. Perelman once put it, down "the *couloirs* of the House and Senate, aghast at legislative folly"—I early decided that Richard Nixon was the villain of villains. (I am now a middle-aged reader of the *New Republic*, but one who, as my next paragraph will make plain, appears to have run out of aghast.) Nixon's political victories left me sullen, his setbacks brought me a refreshed belief in the progress of humankind. I detested him deeply and comprehensively.

When Richard Nixon lost the gubernatorial race in California in 1962, I greeted the news in the manner in which the Hasidim greet the Jewish holiday known as Simchas Torah—with dancing in the streets. After he announced his retirement from politics, however, telling journalists assembled for a news conference that they would no longer have Dick Nixon to kick around, I became nervous. Without Richard Nixon to despise, what would I now do with my spare time? As history shows, I need not have worried. Another decade of reverse ecstasy awaited me. Yet at Richard Nixon's greatest defeat, Watergate, I discovered that, somehow, my scorn had flown, my fury had grown flaccid. The events surrounding Watergate brought other Nixon haters paroxysms of pleasure; one sensed that, during the Watergate hearings, they could scarcely wait to pop out of bed in the mornings to watch these hearings on television and, baby, let the good times roll. I found I could not join them. I should have felt the delight associated with consummation, but instead felt only sadness. Unrequited love may be a bore, but hatred, I suspect, may never allow for a satisfying conclusion.

Richard Nixon is a man who did not wish to be hated, but more interesting to me are those people who do not seem to care whether they are hated or not. Some among them seem not merely unconcerned about having enemies but appear actively to seek them out, and usually have no difficulty in finding them. F. R. Leavis was evidently such a man. Always kind to his students, he could be crushing to colleagues or to anyone else who didn't agree with his views. Simon Gray, the playwright, who was a student of Leavis's at Cambridge, has recalled another of his teachers asking him what he thought of Leavis. Gray reports: " 'Yes,' he said fretfully, when I'd nearly got into my stride, 'I do wish he'd hurry up and die.' " Yvor Winters, the American poet and critic, lived out his days in roughly the same combative condition as F. R. Leavis. In an essay about his friend the poet J. V. Cunningham, Winters wrote about "the doctrine of hatred, or anger," arguing that "it is no accident that so many great writers have sooner or later retreated from society," from which they feel excluded. Hating and being the object of hatred is not the gentlest way to live, a fact that Winters knew well enough to write a lovely poem on the subject entitled "Hymn to Dispel Hatred at Midnight," whose final lines run:

> Hence unto God, unsought,
> My anguish sets. Oh, vain
> The heart that hates! Oh, naught
> So drenched in pain!
> Grief will not turn again.

Although Leavis and Winters clearly had what used to be called "a natural cussedness," it is more important to note that both men lived against the intellectual spirit of their times. So, too, did William Hazlitt and Karl Kraus live against the spirits of their respective times. To say no, to go against the flow, is a most efficient way to accumulate enemies. I fancy myself a man who in some respects sails against the Zeitgeist, yet I do not fancy myself someone who hungers for intellectual combat or derives real delight from having enemies (though I do have a few enemies that I am rather proud of). When I used to get a piece of hate mail, or find myself saying something that I knew would bring me the enmity of other people in the room, it would cause my stomach to churn. Nothing much for it, however. An intellectual is finally the sum of his opinions, especially if these opinions add up to a point of view; and he cannot change them to suit the company he happens to be with at the moment. But I had better stop before I begin to sound like Lillian Hellman in trousers.

Bandying about a variety of strongly held opinions may in some ways influence people, but it is not the surest way to make friends. Where possible I try to keep my own opinions in check. Difficulties arise when others come forth with confidently put opinions opposed to my own. Along with reflexes, muscle tone, and a few other items, tact departs with age; and in such situations I find it increasingly difficult to hold back from saying precisely what I think. I was not long ago in the company of an editor of a journal of opinion who was in the habit of using such introductory phrases to his sentences as "On balance" or "To be fair," after which usually followed statements that were neither particularly balanced nor fair. I found I could not resist pointing out to him his little tic of using falsely impartial phrases, and thereby made, I feel confident, another lifelong friend.

Certain subjects make for natural enmity and can turn polite society into impolite society—fast. If one is looking to save on fuel bills, politics is likely to heat up a room quicker than just about anything else. In certain circles, the subject of educational reform will turn the trick. In recent years, discussion of the women's movement can be depended upon to send the thermostat up thirty or so degrees. (In Barbara Pym's novel *Some Tame Gazelle*, I find this lovely line: " 'I shall never understand women,' said Dr. Parnell complacently.") Similarly, certain names have acquired a built-in explosive quality. In this connection, the name of Henry Kissinger is an almost foolproof land mine. In intellectual quarters mention of the name of Norman Podhoretz, Susan Sontag, or George Steiner is guaranteed to get the conversation off small talk. When he was alive the conductor George Szell, famous for his autocratic behavior, could inflame anyone he worked with. Once, when Szell stormed out of the Metropolitan Opera, someone said that he was his own worst enemy. To which Rudolf Bing responded, "Not while I'm alive." But one doesn't have to be alive for one's name to continue carrying the power to raise blood pressure. I was seated some years ago at a dinner with nine people, most of us strangers to one another, when someone brought up the name Robert Hutchins. A mild-looking, bespectacled man queried gently, "May I ask, is there anyone at this table who is Robert Hutchins's son-in-law or niece or anything of that sort?" When no one allowed having any such relation to Hutchins, the man leaned in and hissed, "I hate everything about that SOB."

A distinguished university president, upon retiring from his job, is said to have remarked about the people with whom he worked, "I don't hate anyone, but I must admit that I despise a great many people." That very precise formulation reminds me that I have been using the word "hate" in rather a baggy-pants fashion—that is, so loosely that almost any unpleasant feelings can be fit into it. Yet the range of distaste of a healthy hater is vast, subtle, and topographically intricate. It is, for instance, perfectly possible to like someone without in the least respecting him, and just as possible to respect enormously someone one doesn't in the least like. Then there is that rather ample body of people whom one neither likes nor respects but who do not come near qualifying for one's hatred. The university president is correct; one can despise a person for acts of cowardice or duplicity or shameless self-promotion—I restrict myself to standard despicable academic behavior—without hating him. Despising is much to be preferred; hating takes up too much psychic energy.

Many other things in life are not worth despising but instead simply tick one off. Some among them are obvious: inefficiency, incompetence in high places, empty language, vandalism, waste, and so forth. Where things that tick one off become interesting, though, is where the rational gives way to the quirky and the quirky to the slightly mad. In one of the essays in *The Crack-Up*, F. Scott Fitzgerald drew up a list of things that, during a bad time in his life, he could not bear: "I couldn't stand the sight of Celts, English, Politicians, Strangers, Virginians, Negroes (light or dark), Hunting People, or retail clerks, and middlemen in general, all writers (I avoided writers very carefully because they can perpetuate trouble as no one else can)—and all the classes as classes and most of them as members of their class." Even for someone in the throes of a nervous breakdown, that is an impressively comprehensive list of antipathies. I have never put together such a list of my own, but if I did, one of the items on it would be people who make too great a fuss about the stylishness of F. Scott Fitzgerald.

Unlike Fitzgerald's antipathies, which tend to fall into categories, my own are almost exclusively particular. Too fancily cut beards, for example, will set me off, but so will unkempt ones. I was not long ago pleased to see this antipathy shared by the late George Balanchine, who noted that beards, which were authentic in his father's generation, today are the essence of stylelessness: "All right, somebody wants to look like Christ, you know—the hair and all. But it's silly, it looks silly on people. It's all a fake." Vanity license plates on cars can get me worked up. And people who have installed telephones in their cars "tick me to the max," as the kids say nowadays. When, in my own car, I see someone driving alongside me talking into a car telephone, it is all I can do to refrain from asking him if he would mind terribly calling my wife to tell her that I shall be late for dinner.

Parents who express their own pitiful yearnings for elegance and give their children a poor start in life by awarding them pretentious names—Ashley or Brandon, Fairfax or Tiffany—seem to me blinkin' awful. Although it is probably the sheerest economic jealousy on my part, it lifts my spirits to discover that someone driving a Rolls-Royce looks sad. In traffic I never give such people a break; nor do I give a break to people who drive Cadillacs, Mercedeses, Jaguars, or BMWs; I figure that they have already had their breaks in life. I secretly hope that people who militantly pursue culture never find it. All the world loves a winner, it is said, but I find myself regularly pulling against too-consistent winners: the Boston Celtics in basketball, the Los Angeles Dodgers in baseball, the Dallas Cowboys in football. Such is the complexity of these matters that I sometimes find my antipathies deeply divided: when, for example, Gore Vidal and Norman Mailer argue, or Barbara Walters interviews Lauren Bacall, or General Westmoreland sues Mike Wallace and CBS. As you can see, a man with strong antipathies is seldom bored.

Shared antipathies can sometimes be the basis for friendship, especially when the antipathies give one the feeling of belonging to a select minority. This has happened to me on more than one occasion. Living in the South in the late 1950s and early 1960s, I found myself falling in with a social set whose single defining characteristic was its strong anti-segregationist sentiment. More recently, as a contemner of much of the new literary criticism and social theory now rampantly fashionable in universities, I have found myself warming immediately to those who share my strong views. "Of course I loathe all that garbage," said a young teacher, a new acquaintance, over a Chinese lunch. Here was a sentence that added great flavor to my Mongolian beef and tea. Tea and sympathy is nice, but tea and shared antipathy is even better. But behind shared antipathies even greater sympathies must lie.

When antipathy replaces what was once sympathy, sadness results. The hatred for each other of parties to a divorce is perhaps the most obvious example. "Of all the objects of hatred," wrote Max Beerbohm in *Zuleika Dobson*, "a woman once loved is the most hateful." One has first truly to have loved another person to be able to hate him or her in the way that divorcing couples are often able to hate each other. In a divorce all the weapons for effective hatred are nicely in place: knowledge of each other's desires, fears, and unpleasant little secrets, all of which can be brought into play for vengeance or betrayal. At a lower level of intensity are friendships that have been sharply broken off or have been allowed to go sour. When this occurs the chain of emotion runs, or at least it has in my experience, from anger, to sadness, to regret, to antipathy, to apathy, to cold indifference, to no longer giving a damn. I recently learned that a former friend was to undergo a divorce in a marriage that was crucial to him; and what I felt at learning this sad fact was—almost nothing at all. Even

Schadenfreude, the malicious enjoyment of another's misfortune, would have been preferable. In some situations hatred seems much more human than simple indifference.

In half a century of middle-class living, I believe I have felt a fairly full range of the feelings, grand and petty, that are usually subsumed under the category of hatred. I have felt jealousy, envy, and rage; I have felt petulance, distaste, and irrational prejudice. But I do not believe that I have ever felt that emotional condition known as self-hatred. ("Why should he feel self-hatred," I can hear someone about whom I have written wounding things say as he reads that last sentence, "when my hatred for him is surely enough for both of us.") I have been angry with myself for committing foolish errors, ashamed of myself for insensitive behavior, disgusted at myself on those occasions when I have failed to meet other people's quite reasonable expectations for me—but sustained and pervasive hatred of myself, this I have come nowhere close to feeling. The conventional wisdom about self-hatred is that it is the hatred internalized by those people—minority groups, deviants, etc.—who feel themselves despised as outsiders in their own societies. Yet I wonder how true this is. I have known people with a talent for self-destruction; I have known people who were ashamed of their backgrounds; I have known people who have attempted suicide, but I am far from certain that any of them qualifies as a true self-hater. Then there are those people who seem to spew up so much hatred that one assumes that it must derive from a volcano of hatred for themselves. It would be gratifying if this were so, but I am not convinced that it is.

When I think of the strong haters I have known, the ugly, the really lethal haters, they have almost always been sorely disappointed people. Life, they somehow feel, has let them down. They are not where they want to be, not doing what they want to do. Things have gone awry, things are askew, all's wrong with the world—and everyone else is to blame. Their argument is with Fate, but they quarrel with you and me. Disappointment embitters, and embitterment sups comfortably with hatred.

Although I have said more than a few kind words for hating in this essay, I hope I do not qualify as a serious hater. I know I have not been disappointed by life—quite the contrary. As Philip Rahv assigned his propensity for poisonous remarks about his colleagues to analytic exuberance, so do I assign my manifold antipathies to what I prefer to think of as "nice discrimination." ("You are, sir," says Sydney Greenstreet to Humphrey Bogart in *The Maltese Falcon*, "a man of nice discrimination.") Sometimes I fear my discrimination has become too nice. Recently, for example, a friend offered to put forward my name for a club whose membership is made up of men who work in the arts, publishing, journalism, and government. Reading down the club's membership roll, I discovered that, among those whose names I knew, there were more members I disliked than liked—and thus I declined the generous offer to join this club. I believe this qualifies me as distinctly unclubbable, something I had never intended to become.

As I grow older, my guess is that my antipathies, dislikes, peeves, and prejudices (rational and irrational) will not grow fewer. Shall I gradually become a curmudgeon—am I one already?—and end my days as a full-blown crank? It is not, I confess, quite what I had in mind for my old age. Yet I must also confess that I have never worked so well until I learned what it was I detested in life. "Hate must make a person productive," Karl Kraus wrote, "otherwise one might as well love." And Chekhov has a character, in his story "Gooseberries," who exclaims, "I am old and not fit for the struggle; I am not even capable of hatred." For myself, it was only when I came to know what I hated that I came to love intensely those things that matter most to me in life. Hatred is finally only productive in the name of love. That, I recognize, comes near to being a paradox, which is unfortunate, because, as it happens, I hate paradoxes.

(1986)

An Older Dude

Five-O. Roman numeral L. Half a century. Five big ones, baby. I refer to my age. This year I turn fifty, with no hope of turning back. It is a bit of an amazement to me. Him Tarzan, me boy, or so I used to think, except that now I am decades older than the inarticulate ape-man himself and a good deal less agile even than Jane. I, a stripling, a mere lad, only yesterday a fine broth of a boy, shall soon have fifty winters under my belt. The evidence for my age is there. I look in the mirror and, like an actor in a long-running play, I know my lines; also my wrinkles, pouches, and circles. Recently, filling out a bureaucratic form, I was able to supply my birth date, height, weight, and eye color readily enough, but when asked the color of my hair I instinctively lifted my cap to let the clerk decide for herself on brown or gray. On a good day, when the light is right, I do not look a week over forty-eight, though where I live there are not that many good days. But enough of these little self-deceptions. I am fifty, and, realist that I am, I must now conclude that my life is at least a third over.

St. Augustine says that "we should not underestimate the significance of number, since in many passages of sacred scripture numbers have meaning for the conscientious interpreter." In my own life, I have paid little attention to the number of my years. The supposedly great decade markers—twenty, thirty, forty—whirred past, and I paid them no more heed than as a boy I did to the Burma-Shave signs along the highway: I noted them, smiled, and drove on. Owing perhaps to my having become a father fairly young—I had charge of four sons by the age of twenty-six—I was unable to linger overlong on the glories of youth, except in fantasy. I tended to be precocious in other, less important ways. Perhaps it was the era into which I was born, but I never looked upon youth as an occupation or religion or social class. It was instead something one enjoyed—if one was lucky—while passing through it.

"Act your age," mothers would say to their children when I was a boy. "Be a man," fathers would exhort their sons. "Aw, grow up," older sisters and teenage girlfriends would exclaim. In fact, growing up didn't seem like a bad idea. A goodly number of grown-ups walked the streets in those days. Think only of the movies. Edward G. Robinson, Humphrey Bogart, Cary Grant, James Cagney—these were men who appeared on-screen in suits and ties, hats, black shoes. Grown-ups. Robert Redford, Dustin Hoffman, Robert De Niro, Harrison Ford—these are men who, at the same age as Robinson, Bogart, & Co., one thinks of as characteristically in jeans, sneakers or boots, loose collars. Graduate students. One could make a similar comparison of actresses. Compare Bette Davis and Jane Fonda, Ingrid Bergman and Meryl Streep. All are fine actresses, but the former are women, the latter girls who continue to grow older. Nowadays there aren't so many grown-ups—just a lot of older dudes. It is, apparently, what the culture calls for just now. I happen to be writing this in a short-sleeve rugby shirt, chino pants, and tasseled loafers. I'm an older dude myself.

Just as I have never been able to think of Hugh Hefner as a play-boy—he has always looked to me like an insurance salesman—so neither can I quite think of myself as an older dude, all physical evidence to the contrary notwithstanding. Not that I wish to remain forever young. Unlike Philip Larkin, who once declared that not having to get mixed up with children more than compensated for having to start earning a living, I rather enjoyed my childhood and adolescence. But enough was enough. Becoming grown-up, with its promise of freedom, was always more alluring to me than anything youth could promise. The allure was there when I was very young. At the age of seven, at most eight, I used to watch a man named Sid Carter play softball in my neighborhood, and he represented, at least for me, some of the promise of growing up. Sid Carter must have been only in his early twenties, but from the perspective of age seven or eight, that was plenty old. A marvelous athlete, he could hit a softball from Farwell Beach in Chicago roughly to Bessarabia. Tall, slender, tanned, his sandy-colored hair brushed straight back, he was dapper even in softball duds. In street clothes he was never less than perfectly turned out; elegance and flair came naturally to him. He drove a cream-colored Plymouth convertible. I recall thinking that, when I grew up, I, too, would own a convertible.

I never have. I suppose I never shall. My eldest son does, though. Not long ago he traded in his car for a high-powered British sports car. He called to report this to me, with what I sensed was a slight trepidation in his voice lest his square old man think him frivolous. "Dear boy," I said, "I'm glad that you have a sports car. I want you to have all the things I never had: sports cars, a beautiful Chinese girlfriend, lots of foreign languages." If you sense some yearning here, you are probably correct. If you sense serious regret, you are mistaken. I shall muddle through all right if I never drive down the Pacific Highway, the top down on my Porsche, gently teasing the lovely Dai-yu in Persian. Yet growing older does remind one of all the things one is now unlikely to do, or have, or be. I believe I have come to grips with the distinct possibility that I will never be a United States senator, or own a horse in the Kentucky Derby, or write a novel as long and as good as Proust's. I can live with these deprivations. I don't want your pity.

What I would prefer is that you find a way to stop the clock from running. When one is young, one lives as if one had a thousand years to go. Once one hits fifty, as E. B. White, a considerable hypochondriac, once said, one feels one has about twenty minutes to live. One is humming the damn "September Song" all the time. In this morning's paper I read that Robert A. Comfort, one of the five men who robbed the Hotel Pierre in 1972, died at age fifty-three. Alexis de Tocqueville—Mr. T. himself—was taken out of the game at the same age. Philip Larkin, a man who seemed to have had the gift of perpetual middle age, while in his fifties (he died at sixty-three) once remarked: "If you assume you're going to live to be seventy, seven decades, and think of each decade as a day of the week, starting with Sunday, then I'm on Friday afternoon now. Rather a shock, isn't it?" It is. It also forces one to place a whole new interpretation on the notion of TGIF.

As I turn fifty, it occurs to me that, unlike Tocqueville or Robert A. Comfort, I shall never write a great book or take part in an adventure such as a three-million-dollar heist. Neither shall I slam-dunk a basketball nor publish a translation of Horace. Some of these things are technically possible—the robbery and the Latin translation—but more and more unlikely. I recently met a man who all his life wished to fly a plane; at sixty-four, upon his retirement, he learned to do so; and now, nearing seventy, he is about to fly solo to Europe. Impressive. I should love to learn to play the harpsichord, and with the injection of large sums of money in lessons and even larger sums of time given over to practice, my guess is that I could learn to play "Clair de lune" with a proficiency that, should a person with good manners be listening to me, would doubtless bring on in him a hemorrhage owing to violently suppressed laughter. But I am certain not to attempt to learn to play the harpsichord. There are too many other items on my agenda that are more pressing. Reaching the age of fifty may not confer wisdom—that honorary degree is given to few and never at commencement time—but it does allow one to understand rather better the poet Joseph Brodsky's remark that "every choice is essentially a flight from freedom."

The fact is that I am a man on a schedule. Some people are and some people aren't on a schedule, and the people who aren't are probably luckier. Those people who are on a schedule—who plan to be millionaires by the age of thirty, publish ten books by the age of forty, or hold serious economic or political power by the age of fifty—always hear the clock ticking, feel the light breeze caused by the turning of calendar pages, sense footsteps (whose?) following them. My own schedule is far from clear, though in some loose way I have always kept one. Its chief purpose appears to be to convince me that I am, inevitably, a bit behind. In college, not long after I somewhat inchoately decided I should like to become a writer, I met a classmate who, at the age of sixteen, had already published a short story in *New*

World Writing, a magazine with a paperback book format that included among its contributors Federico García Lorca, William Carlos Williams, and Ignazio Silone. Not yet out of the starting gate, I already felt myself several furlongs off the pace. Henceforth I carefully noted the birth dates of published writers younger than I, and, while I did not wish them ill, I did hope they would slow down.

My classmate who published a story in *New World Writing* at sixteen has not, so far as I know, published anything since. What happened to him? Having opened so grandly, did he then draw bad cards: a fatal illness, an automobile accident, alcoholism? Or did he instead forego life lived on a schedule? Did he come across the advice of Lambert Strether? In Henry James's *The Ambassadors*, Lambert Strether tells the character little Bilham, "Live all you can; it's a mistake not to. It doesn't matter so much what you do in particular, so long as you have your life." When issuing that sound advice, Strether was fifty-five, or five years older than I—and Henry James, when putting the advice in Strether's mouth, was himself fifty-eight. Good advice though it is, is it available to one who is on a schedule? The question is, of course, one that occurred to Henry James—what serious question didn't?—for James himself was on a schedule, piling up book after book, so that in later years he wondered if he had allowed himself to live as fully as he might have done. As Strether goes on to tell little Bilham, "Still, one has the illusion of freedom; therefore don't be, like me, without the memory of that illusion. I was either, at the right time, too stupid or too intelligent to have it; I don't quite know which. Of course, at present, I'm a case of reaction against the mistake; and the voice of reaction should, no doubt, as always be taken with an allowance."

The only other American writer as good on the subject of middle age as Henry James is that great klutzy genius Theodore Dreiser.

After Dreiser lost a decade of his writing life to a mental collapse and to regaining his confidence following the failure of *Sister Carrie*, he wrote like a man on a very strict if often confused schedule. Dreiser created the most powerful portraits of middle-aged men in American literature: Lester Kane in *Jennie Gerhardt*, Frank Cowperwood in the so-called *Trilogy of Desire*, and, most memorably, George Hurstwood in *Sister Carrie*. What is astonishing is that Dreiser created Hurstwood, the quintessence of the middle-aged man in crisis, while he, Dreiser, was still in his twenties. It was Dreiser who, in Hurstwood, depicted the midlife crisis fully seventy years before it became a cliché in the thick-fingered hands of the popular psychologists, thus confirming Freud's famous statement that psychology has most to learn from the poets.

I am pleased to report that I myself have not yet had anything resembling a midlife crisis, at least as such episodes are advertised in popular culture, and I plan to go to my grave without one. Merely because the label is there doesn't mean everyone has to paste it upon his forehead. Besides, with the span of life increasing, it is no longer quite so clear where midlife is. *Life Begins at Forty* was the title of Walter B. Pitkin's bestseller of 1932, a book written in cheerful reaction to the then-prevailing notion that senescence first began to set in at forty. Nowadays it more often seems that not life but adulthood begins at forty—sometimes between obtaining an MBA and acquiring a condominium. A great deal in contemporary culture permits one to indulge the delusion that one is still youthful well into one's thirties and even one's forties.

The moment of truth will arrive. However young one may feel, one is no longer young when in the eyes of the young one is not young. Somerset Maugham tells, in *A Writer's Notebook*, that the moment of truth came for him when, one day in his early forties, he got into a cab with a woman and her niece, and the niece took the strapontin, or tip seat, leaving the more comfortable seats for her aunt and him. (If you can recall tip seats in cabs, you are no longer so young yourself, darling.) A bachelor friend of mine noted that the moment of truth came for him when a younger woman he was out with suggested that they repair to a bar that had "a really knockout sound system." Another friend marked the moment when, after a day spent outdoors, he returned home to discover that, owing to thinning hair, the top of his head was sunburned. My own moment came when, delivering a lecture on Theodore Dreiser to a class of college freshmen, I began by saying that "Dreiser was the first major American writer from the other side of the tracks." No sooner was the sentence out of my mouth than it occurred to me that my class could have no notion about what tracks I was talking about. I was thirty-seven, and obviously old well before my time.

My time was part of the problem. I was born in 1937, which means that in 1965 I was twenty-eight years old. I mention 1965 because that was the year that the era known—with chronological inexactitude— as the "sixties" got under way in earnest, with the prominence of the Free Speech Movement at the University of California in Berkeley. Virginia Woolf famously (and rather dubiously) declared that human nature changed in 1910; I am quite certain that human nature did not change in 1965, either, but one of the things that did begin to change in that year was the way people thought about age. Suddenly to be young was everything, and even not very young people became aggressively, even militantly, youthful. The ground for the apotheosis of youth was prepared by the election of John F. Kennedy and the orgy of publicity given our young president and his youthful staff.

By the middle 1960s this apotheosis of youth had taken a rivalrous, slightly nasty turn. Old geezers among us will recall one of many slogans of the day: "Don't trust anyone over thirty."

I was not yet thirty, and hence technically trustworthy, but exceedingly ill-prepared to join the kiddie corps. I had a family and a well-paying job; I had, for crying out loud, a mortgage. Wearing my hair in the style of George Eliot or pulled back in a ponytail like Debbie Reynolds did not seem to be, as people said at the time, "my thing." I prefer to think that I had too much irony—and, I hope, iron—in my makeup to smoke pot with either a straight or a laughing face. I rather liked to wear a necktie; had I wished to wear bell-bottoms, I should have joined the navy. Allen Ginsberg was not my idea of a serious writer, nor Timothy Leary of a clear thinker, nor Herbert Marcuse of a profound philosopher. The sixties, when you got right down to it, was not my idea of a good time.

With the arrival of the sixties it was as if a curtain—I believe a man named Churchill has already used up the metaphor of an "iron curtain"—had descended that divided the young from those who chose not to be young. Age had less to do with it than temperament and condition: John Lennon, the head Beatle, for example, was only three years younger than I and a year or two older than George Will, the conservative columnist and a grown-up. Natural predilections of temperament put me on the side of the not-young—E. T. A. Hoffmann, not Abbie Hoffman, was my idea of a hero—but, temperament aside, having a family clinched it. Experiments with high-powered drugs of the kind that went on in the sixties may have been interesting, but psychological interest was not the first thing to come to mind when I learned that a friend of my adolescent stepson had killed himself with an overdose of LSD. The sexual freedom of the sixties was also enticing, but, such are the limitations of human nature, it, too, did not come without cost. If I found myself on the not-young side of the curtain, others my age and older chose the young side, and many of them have remained there, living out their days as post-hippie Dorian Grays.

At fifty you can no longer claim that you are young, the way you might, say, at forty-five, and get away with it. At fifty, however young, even immature, you may feel, you have to begin regarding yourself as middle-aged, early middle-aged, if that adjective makes you feel any better, but middle-aged nonetheless. At fifty you can look much younger than you are, if that is important to you (and if it was not important to lots of people, health clubs and plastic surgeons would be out of business). At fifty you can, with training, run a marathon, play serious tennis, swim the English Channel. At fifty, again with training, you can have a lover of twenty-four. (I once knew a man in his early fifties who was married to a woman of twenty-three, but this same man also kept a mistress of forty-five. When I remarked on this unusual reversal of procedure, and asked him why, with so young a wife, he needed an older mistress, he put out his hands, palms to the heavens, and replied that he had to have someone to talk to.) At fifty you can still be in pretty good shape—*for fifty.*

Middle-aged—the English language contains jollier words, surely. Middle-aged has something of the ring of the end of the party about it. It suggests loss of hair and gains in flesh, stiffening of joints and loosening of teeth; it suggests a dimming of vision and memory, of diminishing physical and mental powers generally. It is a Bosporus, a Golden Horn, of the life span, where not east and west but age and youth meet; and like Istanbul, the city on the banks of the Bosporus, middle age can be filled with not always charming surprises: you make it through fewer and fewer nights without arising to inspect the plumbing; in winter the hair departs your shins; the clerk at the hardware store, with irony you could live without, refers to you as "young feller"; you cannot remember what you had for dinner on Tuesday, but you can remember the lyrics to Vaughn Monroe's hit songs. You don't recall having booked passage, but you appear to be, very slowly, sailing to Byzantium, which, as Yeats seems to imply, is the country of timelessness.

On the positive side, at fifty, if life has been kind, leaving you with no serious illnesses or permanent disappointments, you begin to get the feeling that you are playing, as the sports announcers say, "in control." You see more going on around you. Setbacks are easier to take; victories are no less pleasant, but you know that the sweet taste they bring does not last long. Baggier and saggier though your skin may grow, you feel more comfortable in it. Things that used to outrage you can now sometimes amuse you. You do not expect so much from other people, or from yourself. You care less about what other people think of you. This last point is similar to one made by Somerset Maugham, who was always a rigorous registrar of his own age. In *A Writer's Notebook* Maugham wrote: "That is what makes youth unhappy, the vehement anxiety to be like other people, and that is what makes middle age tolerable, the reconciliation with oneself." I hesitate to use the word, lest I be thought to be claiming it for myself, but middle age does sometimes give one the faintest suggestion that one may be acquiring "perspective."

Yet is it perspective that explains what I can only describe as my loss of awe for the living? When I was younger, it seemed that giants walked the earth: Churchill, Gandhi, de Gaulle in politics; Matisse, Stravinsky, Thomas Mann in art; Einstein, Fermi, Planck in science.

The last figure for whom I felt a similar reverence was George Balanchine. The only living figure for whom I feel anything approaching such regard is Solzhenitsyn. Still, I wonder: Have I grown larger, smarter, surer in my perspective, or have men and women grown smaller in some indefinable way? I continue to respect what I take to be solid achievement in art and scholarship, but age has brought with it a loss of the capacity for adulation.

It was Evelyn Waugh who, having submitted himself to a painful and less than altogether necessary operation for hemorrhoids, claimed that his motive for doing so was perfectionism. I cannot claim to have had any serious standing as a perfectionist, but, now at middle age, any tendency in that direction has departed (gone perhaps to the same place to which the hair on my shins departs in winter). I am also through with self-improvement programs. But I do note around my apartment the presence of a plastic jump rope, two ten-pound barbells, and racquetball equipment—all there to testify to my hopes for one day getting into shape. What shape? At fifty, I suppose an oval is most likely. Intellectual self-improvement programs, too, are over for me. All I wish now is to become a little less stupid in the years left and to become more than a little better at my craft. As people close to me will tell you, I was never much good at self-improvement anyway.

From the perspective of fifty, I can now see that I have been extremely lucky. Lucky not to have been seriously ill, lucky to have been born in an interesting and free country, lucky even in my generation. Mine has been a generation that has missed having to go to war, which, in the present century, is like having lived out of doors in the rain and somehow avoided getting wet. My generation was much too young for World War II, still too young for Korea, and then too old for Vietnam. Having come of age in the United States in the 1950s, we missed the excitement of generations that came of age before ours—excitement, however, that carried certain penalties with it. The twenties, for example, when Prohibition was in force, produced an inordinately large number of alcoholics, largely because, as a man of that generation once explained it to me, drinking was inseparable from the idea of the illicit, and hence inseparable, too, from excitement. The thirties, with its crunching Depression, left a great many people hostage to anxiety over money all their lives, while a great many other people lapsed into the swamp of sectarian politics, from which they, too, never quite reemerged. To have come of age in the forties was to have one's maturity marked indelibly by World War II. But to have come of age in the fifties was to miss being swamped by public events, to be a little out of it, and, when you came right down to it, to be a little out of it was not a bad place to be. To be absolutely in it, to be altogether with-it, brought its own disadvantages, not least among them the loss of perspective. (Must remember to supply the antecedents for all those *it*s at a later date.)

Tolstoy had no problem with the antecedent for *it*. In *The Death of Ivan Ilych*, *it* is death, impure and unsimple. "It alone was true," Tolstoy has Ivan Ilych reflect. "Face to face with *It*," Tolstoy later writes. "And nothing to be done with *It*. Only look and shudder." I recently reread Tolstoy's terrifying story, and not the least terrifying thing about it, to someone who is about to turn fifty, is that poor Ivan Ilych, in the story, is only forty-five. And "the thought had suddenly come into his head: 'What if in reality my whole life has been wrong?' " Ivan Ilych's whole life, as Tolstoy leaves no doubt, has indeed been wrong, wasted on the inessential and the irrelevant, which is what makes his death so bitter. The power of Tolstoy's story is of course in making every reader above a certain age—forty, let us say—ask that same question of his own life: "What if in reality my whole life has been wrong?"

There really is no way around asking that question, though there are endless ways of providing elusive answers to it. I do not so much ask the question of myself directly as consider it indirectly through the yearning to change my life, or at least my work, which comes upon me periodically. A few years ago, for example, I felt a powerful urge to drop all intellectual work—to continue reading, to continue writing (though much less than I now do), but to take a job that would put me more in the stream of daily life. One day I confided this to a graduate student, who, I rather insensitively failed to consider, longed to do exactly the kind of work I was contemplating leaving. "My God," she said, "if you are not happy, I may just commit suicide." I tried to explain, but am fairly certain that I did not succeed. You live, an old saying has it, and you learn. You live, I myself find, and you yearn.

If you are anything like me, you yearn above all to go on living. Unlike Ponce de León, I have never searched for the fountain of youth, but I should be heartily pleased if I could find a way to freeze time. Unlike, too, Mr. John McSorley, the founder of McSorley's Old Ale House (written about so splendidly by Joseph Mitchell), who, upon ceasing to drink at age fifty-five, was supposed to have announced, "I've had my share," I feel nothing of the kind about life. "If you're fifty-five and retired," runs the beginning of a commercial for an insurance company, and every time I hear it I think, *Wait a minute, I am fifty and have only begun.* It's a fine age, fifty, an age when one begins to feel a certain ease in the world and mastery over one's environment, and I should like to remain at fifty for another twenty or thirty years. Somehow I have the sense that this will not be permitted.

At fifty one begins to be comfortable with oneself, but the more comfortable one feels, the more uncomfortably one feels time running out. The minutes, the hours, the days go as slowly as ever; it is those damn weeks, months, and years that now speed past. While I remain as youthful and beautiful as always, why, I cannot help ask, have so many of my contemporaries grown to look so old? It feels as if I have just arrived at the table, and they are already bringing out dessert; I have just stepped out onto the dance floor, and the band is getting ready to play "The Party's Over." Hold the waiters! Stop the music! I like it here. I don't want to leave.

And yet am I ready to do everything possible to stay? It is not always easy to distinguish between the love of life and the fear of death. ("It" again.) Nor are love of life and greed for it quite the same thing. I have acquaintances who—out of a love of life? a fear of death?—are slowly but rather systematically eliminating life's little physical pleasures: cutting out tobacco, alcohol, caffeine, red meat, cholesterol-laden food, all sugar. Soon their meals will be reduced to three dandelions and a nice cup of boiled water. These same people also generally torture themselves with exercise. (I like very much the saying that jogging extends one's life—but only by exactly the amount of time that one spends jogging.) Why do I find all this mildly upsetting, if not slightly obscene? It strikes me as greed for life, as opposed to love of life; it is a demonstration of people whose greed makes them willing to do any-thing for duration; and greed, even for good things, is not very pretty.

When I think of the distinction between the love of life and the greed for duration, I think of the writer A. J. Liebling. With the aid of his fork, Liebling had early joined the ranks of the obese, an army he was never to leave. Like many of the Frenchmen he knew of the generation before World War I—"the heroic age" of dining, he called it—Liebling never developed "the ulcers that come from worrying about a balanced diet." He did what he wanted to do; went where he wanted to go; wrote extremely well on those subjects he wished to write about; and lived with the throttle full-out—though a more appropriate metaphor would be "the plate always heaped up." Doubtless he would have lived longer had he lived more carefully. But had he lived more carefully—eaten less, drunk less—he would not have been A. J. Liebling. He had his fill and enjoyed the show, paying the check and leaving the table in his fifty-ninth year. Between the dandelion-and-boiled-water set and A. J. Liebling, a compromise position is possible. My own preference would be to live like Liebling and last until age ninety-seven. There is a contradiction here, I realize, but then, fortunately, the law of contradiction is not enforced, lest the jails overflow.

I can't supply a drumroll to go with this cliché, but the fact is that we human beings are the only species born with the painful foreknowledge of our death. Should this foreknowledge slip our minds, age is there as a perpetual crib, or pony, to remind us that life itself is a terminal illness. That at any rate is one way of looking at it. Another is to disregard age, as did Johnny Nikanov, aka King Cockeye Johnny, the gypsy who also appears in Joseph Mitchell's *McSorley's Wonderful Saloon* and who, when asked about his age, answered, "Between forty-five and seventy-five, somewhere in there. My hair's been white for years and years, and I got seventeen grandchildren, and I bet I'm an old, old man." There is something immensely appealing about that—about, more specifically, living outside age.

Most of us, I suspect, live our lives between these two possibilities, recalling that life is a terminal illness while at the same time forgetting our age. Our age seems incidental, something that has happened to us that we hadn't a great deal to do with, or that happened while we weren't looking. Sometimes our age frankly astonishes us; it is as if it were a strange country we suddenly find ourselves in. *Fifty,* one says. *How the devil did I get here?* If one thinks of age as a phonograph record, for many people the needle of their spirit seems to have stuck well before their actual age. I know a woman in her eighties who carries herself as if she were, tops, thirty-four. Despite the depredations of time and the ravages of illness, she is still, somehow, in spirit, sexy. I knew a man in his seventies in whom the mischievous eyes of a boy of eleven shone. My problem, if problem it be, is that I am and feel and look—fifty.

As ages go, and as long as one has to have some age, I am rather fond of fifty. It has a nice middling sound to it. It qualifies for the French phrase *d'un certain âge,* which I render, idiomatically, as "not so young." Yet neither is it all that old. It is roughly two-thirds up the mountain, not a bad place to view those thirty years below as well as those thirty or more years above. Fifty is an age old enough for one to have suffered serious disappointments, yet young enough not to be completely out of hope. Proust, who died at age fifty-one, wished to recapture time, and came as close in his great novel as anyone is likely to get; I, at fifty, will settle for allowing time to continue to run. "Miles to go before I sleep," the poet wrote, and I hope his words apply to me. Even now I am planning on being a colorful elderly dude, filled with rich and dubious stories. Should I achieve eighty years, I just may claim to have played ball with Jackie Robinson, to have danced for Diaghilev, to have been Anton Chekhov's gin rummy partner. At that time, feel free to call me a liar, an outrageous old codger, even gaga. But call me a senior citizen and you had better carry dental insurance.

(1986)

You Probably
Don't Know Me

I used occasionally to play racquetball with Saul Bellow, the Nobel Prize—winning novelist. I was then in my late thirties, Bellow in his late fifties. To offer an athletic as distinct from an aesthetic criticism, if a Nobel Prize were offered for racquetball, Saul Bellow would not have won it. He was a middling player, I a bit above middling, but the difference in our ages made our games, to me at any rate, a touch frightening. The problem was that Bellow knew only one way to play, and that was full-out, which at his age was dangerous. To be "in the pink" is thought to be a fine thing; but on the racquetball court it didn't take Saul Bellow long to be somewhere in between the vermilion and the magenta. Sometimes, after a particularly vigorous point, I would inquire the score from my place at the service line and hear it come back to me in the piping, rather quavering voice of a man physically in extremis. *My God*, I thought, *what if he drops dead right here on this racquetball court!* And then, tenderheartedly, near bursting with compassion, I proceeded to think—of myself.

In particular, I began to imagine how I might be treated by the press in the event of such an unpleasant happenstance. Suddenly I saw a headline that read "Nobel Novelist Goes Down for Final Count as Essayist Looks On." I imagined a grainy photograph taken inside the racquetball court, in whose caption I am mentioned as "Man at left in shorts unidentified." Spinning an unascertainable number of years forward into the future, I espied my own two-inch-long obituary, in the dolorous typeface of the *New York Times*, carrying the small-type headline "Man Who Served Death to Nobel Writer Dies Out of Court." Whew! A damn near thing and luckily avoided, not only for Saul Bellow but for me.

I am not certain why I seem naturally to identify with men and women who in newspaper photographs are themselves unidentified, but I do. I find my heart also going out to those who are given brief obituaries for playing cameo roles in history through their relation to the lives of the truly famous: the ex-wife of the third son of an American president, a lawyer who represented celebrities, a half sister to a shah, a brother-in-law to a well-known comedian, a violinist who toured with Caruso, a Hollywood voice coach, the owner of an umbrella and cane shop that catered to politicians, the widow of a cellist, the father of an all-American basketball player, the great-grandson of Karl Marx. So, too, am I taken by people who have limited, if not to say severely restricted, claims to fame, such as the man who took the famous photograph of the raising of the American flag on Iwo Jima, one partner of a famous bridge team, the first black federal bankruptcy judge, a prominent hand surgeon, an expert on jaw malfunctions, the lyricist for "If You Knew Susie," or the creator of the first Orange Julius. The late M. Doug Wood, a name unknown to almost everyone, provides a perfect example of what I have in mind. His obituary in the *New York Times* of May 7, 1987, reads in toto:

M. Doug Wood

Salt Lake City, May 5 (AP)—M. Doug Wood,
a co-founder of Evelyn Wood Reading Dynamics,
died Saturday at the age of 83.

Besides his wife, his survivors include his daughter, Carol
Davis Evans of Tucson, Ariz., and four grandchildren.

The briefest possible obituary for one of the founders of speed-reading—has the punishment ever more snugly fit the crime? *Well,* I recall thinking, reading this pared-down obit on the day it appeared, *at least it won't take anyone too long to read about his demise.* Doubtless, Doug would have wanted it that way.

I wonder, too, if when alive, Mr. M. Doug Wood did not feel a slight but fairly frequent twinge of resentment over the greater fame enjoyed by Evelyn Wood, his wife, whose name has become synonymous with the dubious invention of reading so fast that one ignores style, nuance, and irony. Did Ira Gershwin, who wrote all those lovely lyrics, feel a similar resentment at the greater fame of his brother George? Doug Wood and Ira Gershwin, though they may have shared naught else, share the status, at least so far as the public knew, of being sidekicks, right-hand men, secondo dons. Of honorable sidekicks, there has been no paucity: the Lone Ranger had Tonto, Roy Rogers had the untidy Gabby Hayes, Wonder Woman had a pudgy, bonbon-chomping pal named Tootsie. At a higher literary level, Sancho Panza and Falstaff are second bananas, packing as much if not more potassium as the first bananas with whom their creators bunched them.

To play the role of sidekick, to accept the status of second banana, however substantial the rewards, nonetheless requires certain gifts of temperament: one must be prepared to subsume one's interest to those of another, to settle for less in the way of attention and glory and other of those prizes that men and women, in their well-advertised vanity, have always striven for. One must, in short, be ready to let go of one's ego.

Many jobs—in fact, most jobs—demand the submergence of one's own interests. In literary life, an editor, a biographer, a translator, an anthologist, a bibliographer—all are indispensable, yet all are second, some even third, bananas. Journalists used to be third, possibly fourth, bananas, but no longer. Journalists, especially television journalists, are usually among the best-known local people in any city; and my guess is that most of us can name our local anchorman much more readily than our congressman. Any good Marxist would take all this as self-evidently true; after all, journalists control the means of production—and what is being produced is, of course, fame.

Ah, fame, which Milton (neither Berle nor Friedman) called "that last infirmity of noble mind," is far from afflicting only the noble-minded. The desire for fame was once thought to be, along with the love of truth, a sign of great character. But today everyone knows that a proper attitude toward fame requires that one disregard it, or at least look askance at it. Fame, it is understood, is as ephemeral as a suntan—perhaps more so. Fame is tinny, fame is bogus, fame is ultimately empty. In the future everyone will be famous for fifteen minutes, or so said a man so famous that I think I shall not even bother to give his name. Fame is a shuck and a crock, humbug and poppycock. Who needs it?

Sorry to have to report, I believe I do. If needing fame is perhaps putting it a bit strongly, let me revise that statement and say that, at a minimum, I know I should rather like it. As a general rule, I would add that, unless you happen to be cheating on your husband or wife, or are employed as a spy, it is usually nicer to be known than not. One of the few ways that I failed to misspend my youth was sitting in bars, but I clearly recall, in my early twenties, the glow of appreciation I felt when, awaiting a table in a popular Italian restaurant I had been to the week before, the bartender, a middle-aged man of grave mien (he was probably ten years younger than I am now), remembered what I drank. "It's scotch and water, isn't it, sir?" he said. My heart leapt the bar and landed in his pocket. In remembering what I drank, he seemed to discern that I was not of the mass, to lift me above the ruck of ordinary suckers, and to make plain that I was a young man of rare quality whose very drinking habits were worth noting. Had we been in France, I should have grasped the lapels of his short red bartender's jacket and kissed him on both cheeks. Instead, in my more measured Midwestern manner, I merely lavishly overtipped him.

If it is nice to be known, it is even nicer, for one who has a taste for fame, to be talked about. In contemporary life, being famous may be no more complicated than being talked about. Of course, the way one is talked about is decisive. My own first small bout of fame—that is to say, of arranging to have myself talked about—came in high school when I turned down membership in a senior boys' honorary society for students who had been on the school's athletic teams or active in extracurricular activities. I was passed over the first time new members were taken in, as was a friend of mine, who was also a likely candidate for membership. One day, talking about it, we resolved that, should we be asked to join on the second round of invitations, we would tell the members of this honorary society to stow it in Ashtabula.

The morning I was informed that I had been elected, I told the two boys who had come to break the happy news to me that I was sorry but I must refuse membership, owing to my having so many other activities. Later that morning my friend, who had also been elected, asked, in a worried voice, if I would mind greatly if he went back on his pledge, broke our compact, and accepted membership. I told him that of course it was fine with me, that I quite understood his position, that he was not to worry about it in the slightest. What I really felt was delight to be doing this alone, so that I wouldn't have to share the distinction of being the first boy in the school's history to refuse membership in this generally admired society. The limelight, such as it was, would be mine and mine alone. It would be I, and I alone, who would be talked about. And so I was—for about two or three days, after which everyone lost interest. But while it lasted, I have to add, I enjoyed it immensely.

No doubt about it, fame was jolly, but as with many another of the jolly items on life's menu—food and sex jump to mind—it didn't last very long. As with food and sex, so with fame: one couldn't subsist very long on the mere memory of it. Himself no stranger to fame, Freud once said that the artist gives up fame, money, and the love of beautiful women for his art, through which he hopes to win fame, money, and the love of beautiful women. His subject was sublimation, a point on which I have never been quite convinced: Is Aleksandr Solzhenitsyn, for example, sublimating through his writing? To ask the question is to ridicule it. Although fame is one of those things one is not supposed to want, most people nonetheless seem to. "I'm really a very private person," many a starlet has told ten or twenty million people on many a talk show. Even quite bashful people, when it is available to them, do not altogether shun fame; they merely prefer that people talk about them when they are not present.

A desire for fame, and of a quite crude kind, was certainly among the motives of my own incipient urge to become a writer. When, at roughly the age of twenty, I thought I might one day be able to write, I did not wish to do so because I felt I possessed powerful truths that only I was capable of formulating for the world. Nor was I driven to work free, as the boys in the head trades might put it, from a terrible childhood that left me many a ghost to bury in one or another kind of writing. True, I adored the sound, shape, and feel of words and was much taken with the superior game of lining them up in sentences and paragraphs, but I cannot really say that I was impelled to write out of aesthetic necessity. Something far simpler and rather more embarrassing to report was at work; this was that I felt a tremendous desire, ardor, make that sheer heat, to see my name in print. I would dreamily imagine it in different typefaces: in the Caslon Old Face of the *New Yorker*, in the all-caps Bembo of *Poetry*, in the Times Roman of the *Times Literary Supplement*. Just my name, you understand; what appeared under or over it mattered scarcely at all. Bodoni Bold of me to admit to this coarse vanity, but I tell you, sans serif, that I would have willingly exchanged a toe or an appendix to find my name in any of those or many another magazine. In listing the motives for writing that Orwell set down in his famous essay "Why I Write," he put first, "Sheer egotism." No dope that George.

"You remind me of a famous actor," said the young man checking me out in the express lane at the supermarket on a steamy Sunday evening, "but I can't remember his name." "How can you be sure I'm not that famous actor?" I asked. "Because you wouldn't be here," he replied—quite rightly, too. He never was able to recall the actor's name, and I left hoping that the actor wasn't, say, Ernest Borgnine. Looking like someone famous can carry its own comic ironies. One summer I saw a man at the Ravinia Music Festival outside Chicago wearing a bright red T-shirt across whose front large white letters proclaimed, "I Am Not Cesar Romero." Of course, he looked exactly like Cesar Romero, a condition he must have enjoyed hugely; for if he didn't, why was he wearing a mustache and hairdo altogether similar to "the old Latin lover's," as the gutter press might describe him. Which reminds me that it was in the gutter press—the *National Enquirer*? the *Star*?—that I noted an item about the actress Farrah Fawcett wishing to make a movie in which she plays Fawn Hall, Colonel Oliver North's assistant, who rather looks like Farrah Fawcett and may even have been consciously imitating the actress's looks. What we have here, then, is an actress wanting to play the part of someone who, in so-called real life, may have been modeling herself on that actress to begin with. Rich stuff. Where did you say you wanted that mirror put up, Señor Borges?

To look like someone who is famous is one thing; to be the child of someone who is famous is quite another, much more difficult thing. There is an amusing story about the son of Arnold Schoenberg reprimanding his father for scolding him, arguing that he is after all the son of a great composer and hence someone rather better born than Schoenberg himself. But most stories about the children of the famous, especially the artistically famous, are stories of sadness, squalor, and defeat. Nathan Asch, the son of the once world-famous novelist Sholem Asch, in a heartbreaking memoir, "My Father and

I," wrote: "There is more apostasy, suicide, homosexuality, fraud, and lying as well as plain ne'er-do-wellism among [the children of famous artists] than among the children of other kinds of people." Without knowing the first fact of their actual lives, one's sympathies immediately go out to the daughter of Rita Hayworth and Orson Welles, the son of Mary McCarthy and Edmund Wilson, all the children of Picasso. And one silently thanks one's own parents for the unconscious kindness implied in their remaining, outside their circle of friends and business acquaintances, happily obscure.

Once, when working as a publisher's editor, I was told that a man with a manuscript wished to see me. Small, red-haired, with refined features, he set his manuscript upon my desk before introducing himself. On a white card pasted to a black plastic manuscript cover was typed an academic-sounding title and under it the name, followed by the suffix "Jr.," of the most famous producer in the history of Hollywood. "Are you . . ." I began, about to ask the question he had doubtless been asked hundreds, perhaps thousands of times already. His eyelids drooped over his eyes, he nodded his head slightly, and there was no need to finish my question. In the brief droop of those eyelids I saw a life haunted by the ghost of a famous father, Irving Thalberg.

If one has drawn a ticket in life's lottery as the son or daughter of someone famous, it is probably a good idea to go into a line of work other than that of one's famous parent. This is so because the competition against a famous parent is so unfair, the odds so stacked against the child, the chill of constant comparison so likely to freeze him up. Some, true enough, win through. But for every Pliny and Pitt the Younger there must be uncounted Plinys and Pitts the Worse and the Sadder. Some of us take a not-so-secret pleasure in learning about the failures of the children of the famous. When we hear that the great writer's daughter has had a nervous breakdown, or that the famous actress's son is a drug addict, we do a half gainer, double somersault into the dark pool of our souls. Such is the cost of fame, we conclude about these family tragedies, and it isn't worth it. And for the nonce we feel justified in our own obscurity.

Better luck, perhaps, to have been born more distantly related to someone famous. In my time I have known a nephew of the Notre Dame football coach Frank Leahy, a cousin of the television comedian Morey Amsterdam, a sister of the boxer Barney Ross—as an exercise in name-dropping, I must confess, this is pitiful—and all seemed quite pleased with their connections with the famous in their families. Their relatives' fame didn't weigh down on them, but, on the contrary, seemed to buoy them up a bit. Even remote association with the famous tends to do that for people. This is a lesson I learned fairly early in life, and I put it to use as an adolescent attempting, almost always vainly, to pick up girls in a large and now long-defunct amusement park in Chicago called Riverview. My modus operandi in those days was to ask any gaggle of girls—on behalf of my pals and myself—if they went, say, to Schurz High School. When they replied, usually rather curtly, that in fact they went to Roosevelt, I would jump in with "Ah, then you must know my cousin, Louie Landt," who just happened to be the star of the Roosevelt High basketball team. Whatever school a group of girls claimed to go to, I claimed cousinage with that school's current basketball or football star. It generally worked, at least to break the ice. I accumulated a lot of broken ice, those summers of my adolescence. Such is the strange power of fame.

And such is the oddity of fame that the first thing most people who

191

achieve it try to do with it is avoid it or, at any rate, complain about its encumbrances. One tends to think of fame in this connection with dark glasses, darting into limousines, screaming at press photographers who have gone too far, hiding away in villas on the Dalmatian coast to which the pestering bloody public cannot gain entry. Fame, in this reading, is a bed of thorns in which no one can hope to get any rest. In extreme cases, such as that of J. D. Salinger or Howard Hughes or Greta Garbo, reclusiveness is the usually unsatisfactory answer. Carried out on a grand or zany enough scale, one is only likely to become—as did Salinger, Hughes, Garbo—even more famous for wishing to avoid fame. Perhaps the desire for fame is one of those tricky wishes that one does best not to mention to your local djinn.

Others toss and roll in their fame, lapping it up, loving every minute of it. The interview, the press conference, the talk show—bring 'em on! The woman from the *New York Times* on the phone, the photographer from *People* setting up in the living room, the dork with the minicam from the local television station ringing the doorbell—hey, as they say in the beer ads, go for it! The best tables in the best restaurants, mail filled with offers and invitations, the feeling that the world really is at one's feet, such can be among the high, heady delights that accompany fame. "Where to?" a cabdriver in Paris is said once to have asked Herbert von Karajan. "It doesn't matter," the famous conductor is said to have replied. "They want me everywhere."

I have never come near to having been wanted everywhere, but I have from time to time been permitted to potter a bit about the purlieus where contemporary fame is manufactured. Usually in connection with books I have published, I have been interviewed by *Vogue* and *W,* I have been the subject of three dreary pages in *People,* and

I was once a solo guest on *The Phil Donahue Show* (surely you remember, it was the same splendid week that he had the transsexuals and Kareem Abdul-Jabbar). I tell you this to establish that I am a man who has had his foot past the bordello door. Didn't much like it in there, I have to confess. The air was fetid with fraudulence. Taking part in an exercise so essentially phony depressed me.

As for the exercise itself, it might be called Killing Time and Filling Space. Or so at least I thought of my job a number of years ago when, on a tour to promote a book, I visited seven cities in six days, gassing away on various radio and television talk shows and lending the details of my private life for eight or nine newspaper feature stories all about me. Not long afterward, on television before an audience of I don't know how many millions, I gazed deep into the blue eyes of Phil Donahue to discover that they resembled the city of Oakland in Gertrude Stein's youth in that there was "no there there." Did I, as a result of these efforts at self-promotion, become famous? Not very. Did I at least sell vast quantities of my book? Not many. Still, I like to look fondly back upon that time and think of all the friendships I didn't make.

"Do you know me?" ran the tagline from an American Express television commercial. Whenever it played on my television set, I found myself muttering in response, "No, sir, nor do I wish to." I always thought that the advertising agency that staged those commercials missed a fine opportunity by not having the man who says, "Do you know me?" turn out to be Martin Bormann, or Josef Mengele, or some still-at-large mad serial killer in California, but then those ad boys do tend to play it safe.

If I were in such a commercial, I should like my own tagline to be "You probably don't know me, and, if it is all the same to you, why don't we just leave it that way." By which I mean that, however passionate the hunger for fame on the part of writers, it is doubtless best that they not be too well-known. Although there have been writers of great celebrity in America, from Mark Twain through Ernest Hemingway to Truman Capote, and although toward the end of his life Leo Tolstoy may have been the most famous man in Russia, as a general rule it is better that writers be observers but not observed, as close to ringside as they can get but not themselves in the ring. Yet writers may hunger more for fame than other artists do because, first, people do not see them performing their art, as they do dancers and actors and musicians; and, second, writers do not see their audience actually enjoying their work, as do painters and playwrights and composers. Only once have I seen a stranger reading something I had written; this happened on a New York subway where a woman standing alongside me was reading an essay I had in the current month's issue of *Harper's*. It was all that I could do not to tell her that I was the author of the essay she was reading. I surely would have done so had she not read with so clearly disapproving a look upon her face that my taking a bow just then seemed a serious error.

"You probably don't know me, and it is driving me nuts" is another view of fame, and one that tends to be held by people who have had fame, took much delight in it, and now sense it is leaving them. I have a friend who until recently was a member of the city council in Chicago; he is a man with strong opinions, which he expresses well. Because for the better part of his time on the council he was in opposition to the faction in power, he was frequently called upon to criticize the mayor on the six and ten o'clock news shows. This has made him locally famous; in Chicago his had become a household face. I hope he will not mind my saying that he rather enjoys this fame.

I note that whenever we enter a restaurant or other public place, he checks the room to see if he is recognized. He usually is. A waiter or the owners of the restaurant or a customer will ask him if he isn't the fellow they suspect he is. Although he is not made rapturously happy by this, it is plain that he is pleased to be recognized. He has not made anywhere near as much money in politics as he could have made as a lawyer, and he may well view such fame as he has earned as a sufficient substitute (psychic) income, which seems to me fair enough.

But should he stay out of politics, and hence out of television camera range, his local fame—the political consultants, I believe, call it his "recognition factor"—will no doubt quickly diminish. In a year, people will strain to recall his name; in eighteen months he may well be taken for a weekend weatherman; in two years—oblivion. I remember reading a journalist's account of going into the Sans Souci restaurant in Washington, D.C., with a man who had only a few years before he left a job as a chief political correspondent with one of the major networks. The Sans Souci was then said to be the favorite restaurant of Henry Kissinger—this was late in the second Nixon administration—and hence a politically potent place. The former network correspondent checked the room and, the journalist recounted, no one in the joint recognized him—and it was as if someone had poured machine oil over the food. Those who live by the kind of large, lumpish fame made possible only by the television camera often die without it.

Not everyone is so piggish in his appetite for fame as to require it in the heavy portions dispensed by television. I not long ago visited an old friend awaiting surgery in a once grand but now slightly dilapidated Jewish hospital—"Kings have lain here," wrote Karl Shapiro of such an institution, "and fabulous small Jews /

And actresses whose legs were always news"—and noted countless memorial plaques. Every wing, section, surgical theater, waiting room, patient room, elevator—everything, in short, but the ashtrays, urinals, and toilets was dedicated to the memory of someone or other. Some donated money to memorialize parents or dead children; others doubtless left money behind in their wills to memorialize themselves. You can't take your money with you into death, but you can leave enough behind to allow the memory of yourself to linger awhile. In his autobiography, Irving Howe reports that Abram Sachar, then president of Brandeis, used to tell potential donors to the university the story of the Widener family giving money to Harvard to honor the memory of their son Harry, who went down with the *Titanic*, so that today students at Harvard rarely say, "Let's go to the library," but instead say, "Let's go to Widener." Howe writes: "A hush fell across the room. One could almost see quivers of emotion journeying from soul to soul, as if the assembled manufacturers and real estate men were ruminating, 'Someday maybe they'll say, "Let's go to Shapiro!" ' "

To have a major university library named after you, to be recognized in a fashionable restaurant, to have a plaque bearing your name in the elevator of a fading hospital, to have a local bartender know your drink—obviously, there are degrees of fame, yet no clear measure to gauge it. When the bill was presented from Père-Lachaise cemetery for burying Balzac, whose entire life was a struggle for fame, the great writer's name was spelled "Balsaque." (Surely there is a moral there somewhere.) I have always been partial to the definition of fame that holds you are only famous when someone who is crazy imagines he is you. I tried to remember who said that, and when I finally found it in *The Viking Book of Aphorisms*, I discovered that it was that prolific author who goes by the name of Anonymous. (Can there be a moral here, too?)

Thirty or so years ago, one might have argued that fame was being on the cover of *Time*, but now that is no longer true, nor does being on the cover of any magazine, or the subject of an ornate scandal, or the winner of honors and prizes. All these things, it is now commonly understood, render one a celebrity, and celebrity, it is also understood, is seasonal. In medicine, in fashion, in art, Proust once remarked, "there must be new names." That one of the new names this week, or month, or year happens to be yours shouldn't be taken too seriously.

Yet, as is not quite the case with money and power, the only people who can authoritatively dismiss fame are those who either have it or have walked away from a solid opportunity for attaining it. As coolheaded a man as Spinoza said he thought that those who cried out most loudly against fame were probably themselves most desirous of it. In order to despise fame properly one really must have it, and being in the superior position of despising it may even be worth the effort of achieving it. I wouldn't know; I would, however, like to know.

Everyone who writes, I have no doubt, would like to be famous, and not only famous now, while on this earth, but, embarrassing enough to admit given the odds, famous after he has departed the earth. And this, I believe, is true of serious and frivolous writers alike. All of us would like to have said about us what I heard a eulogist say of the songwriter Yip Harburg: "He is survived by his words." A certain absurdity is built into this desire, to be sure, and this is that death presents at least three distinct possibilities—heaven, hell, or sheer oblivion—none of which is a condition likely to be improved upon by posthumous fame. Still, every writer likes to think that posterity will take his proper measure, which also means that he hopes posterity will esteem him as he wishes to be esteemed. Given the general level of vanity among writers, it is fair to say that contemporary society has not arrived at the stage of development where this is possible.

Yet there is a serious distinction between wanting fame and wanting recognition for one's accomplishments. Edward Gibbon, for example, upon completion of his great history, noted: "I will not dissemble the firm emotions of joy on the recovery of my freedom, and, perhaps, the establishment of my fame." As is now known, about Gibbons's fame there was no "perhaps" whatsoever. Gibbons's fame arrived on schedule, remained, lived after him, endures today more than two centuries later, and, based on solid achievement as it is, is entirely deserved. Without such fame, based on true accomplishment, there can be no tradition, no worthy models, no passing on of high achievement across generations and down through centuries. In this sense fame is no trivial matter.

Yet it sometimes seems as if fame is all a writer can think about—his reputation, his ranking among other writers, and the rest of it—and yet it is probably the worst thing for him to think about. To think about posthumous fame is still worse. As soon as he begins to direct his writing to future generations, it is almost certain to become portentous and empty. As soon as he begins to think of his own fame in comparison with that of his contemporaries, his mood figures to turn rivalrous and mean. Fame, for a writer, is very difficult to control. If he writes too little, his fame is endangered; if he writes too much, it is also endangered. The appetite for money or power can be slaked; I at any rate have seen people once quite mad for money or power be calmed after they had achieved an ample portion of either. I cannot say the same for those with a strong taste for fame. "*La gloire et le repos sont choses qui ne peuvent loger en même gîte,*" wrote Montaigne, which I should loosely translate, "You want fame, kid, kiss tranquility goodbye."

In a certain kind of stupid, falsely sincere television interview, there comes a moment toward the end when the interviewer leans in and, in a serious and intimate tone of voice, asks, "How do you wish to be remembered?" To which the person being interviewed usually responds, "As a person who always cared deeply for quality," or "As a good parent to my children," or "For my work with animal shelters," or some such self-congratulatory lie. To the question "How do you wish to be remembered?" my own, simpler answer is "For as long as possible."

(1987)

Short Subject

S hould you urgently need to reach me, here, to save time, are a few places you are almost certain *not* to find me: browsing happily in the grain section of a health food store, sitting under a dryer reading *Popular Mechanics* during the final stages of a male permanent at Vidal Sassoon, pasting up "Thank You for Not Smoking" signs on firing-squad walls, shopping for a cabana suit at the M. Hyman & Son Big & Tall Men Store. Unless you happen to live in Chicago, there is every likelihood that you have never heard of M. Hyman & Son, where they claim to "suit the big guy at discount prices." I have no doubt that they do just that, but, reading the store's advertising copy, it occurred to me that no one has ever called me "big guy." Nor has anyone ever referred to me, as I seem to recall their female costars in the movies used regularly to refer to Clark Gable and John Wayne, as "you big galoot." Not even the very plainest woman, let alone Marlene Dietrich, has ever slung an arm around my neck, drawn me closer to her, and exclaimed, "Kiss me, big boy."

If you begin to gain the impression that I am not one of M. Hyman

& Son's ideal customers, you are onto something. Although I have been called many things, I have never been in the least danger of being called Moose, Big Daddy, or Bubba. Quite the reverse; I have always considered myself fortunate to have evaded being called Pee-Wee, or Half-Pint, or Shorty. In a grammar school skit for an assembly on Lincoln's birthday, I, at age eleven or twelve, as the shortest boy in the class, played Stephen Douglas, the Little Giant, opposite the Abe Lincoln of Jack Sheasby, the tallest boy in the class, in a sensibly abridged version of the Lincoln-Douglas debates. This feels like the place in the paragraph where I should insert something like the following sentence: "However, in the summer between my junior and senior years of high school I grew eleven inches to my present height of 6'2"." That summer I may in fact have grown three-quarters of an inch. I kept waiting to "shoot up," in the phrase popular at the time, but never did. Today, in my early fifties, I am beginning to believe it may never happen.

Just how small is this guy anyhow? you may by now be asking. *Have I all these years*, you are perhaps wondering, *been reading a dwarf?* I shall set out some figures presently, but first I think it mildly interesting that most curiosity about male height seems to be not about how tall but about how short certain men are—and by certain men, I chiefly mean certain movie actors. When I was a boy there was much guessing about the exact height of Alan Ladd. Figures as low as 5'2" were bruited about. It was said that Ladd had to stand on a box to kiss his leading ladies. Edward G. Robinson, James Cagney, John Garfield, George Raft, Spencer Tracy were scarcely suited to be power forwards in the National Basketball Association; Humphrey bloody Bogart is said to have been no more than 5'5½" or 5'6", sweetheart.

Now it is the height of Robert Redford and Paul Newman that is in the flux of controversy. Evidently neither man will divulge his exact height. One would think that the science of investigative reporting could find a solution to this problem—have Bob Woodward or Carl Bernstein stand next to them and make some elementary deductions. Thus far neither Butch nor Sundance will apparently measure up. Estimates on their respective heights run from 5'5" to a respectable 5'10". Both actors are said to be rather touchy on the subject. Upon meeting either of them, it is probably wise not to begin your conversation by saying, "Loved your last flick, little guy."

I am nowhere near so touchy about my own height, though it, too, is in that same controversial flux. Nothing pleases a fat man more, said A. J. Liebling (himself a very fat man), than to be called muscular. What, similarly, pleases a short man is to be asked, "What're you, about 5'10"?" I was once asked, "What're you, about 5'9"?" and I glowed for a full week. I think of myself as 5'7", but I can't seem to get a clear consensus on it. I not long ago wrote an essay about living in Little Rock, Arkansas, where I have lived at two different times in my life, and in the course of the essay mentioned getting a letter from a Southern journalist who remarked that I was a small legend in Little Rock. In the essay, I noted this and my answer, which was to say that I didn't know about the legend but, being 5'7", I would accept the small part. The editor of the magazine in which the essay appeared, a friend of many years, changed my copy to read "but being *under* 5'7"" (italics mine, vicious tactlessness his), which is what I would call heavy editing.

Unfortunately, he turns out to have been factually correct. A few months later, I had a physical examination, during which I weighed in at 135 pounds and measured 66½ inches. When the physician wrote these figures down, he asked, rather perfunctorily, "What did

I say, 67½ inches?" I nodded, lying, and added, "I believe so." I am now down in my own medical records at 5'7½". But what will happen when I next go in for a physical and it is discovered that I am in fact only 5'6½"? Will my physician feel that I am too young to be losing height so rapidly? Will he order various CAT scans and other tests to be run in search of the cause of my lost inch? Will I be sent off to the Mayo Clinic? Or perhaps to Zurich, where there is doubtless a lost-height specialist, a man I imagine to be 4'11" with thick glasses and an impenetrable German accent? Complicated stuff, height, and not merely, as the sports announcers are wont to say about baseball, football, golf, and other sports, a game of inches.

Somerset Maugham, who was 5'7" and none too pleased about it, says somewhere that the world is an entirely different place to a man of 5'7" from what it is to a man of 6'2". Maugham's is a telling and true point, so long as one does not push it over into the chief psychological cliché about shortness. I refer to the notion that short people, in particular short men, tend to overcompensate for their size through outsized aggression and ambition. In this reading, T. E. Lawrence, had he been five or six inches taller than his 5'4", could have devoted all his time to his wretched translation of Homer and let the Turks and the Arabs fight it out on their own. Ambition, ample and aggressive ambition, turns up in every shoe size. In literature, for example, Ivan Turgenev and George Orwell were nice-sized boys; so, in politics, were Franklin Delano Roosevelt and Charles de Gaulle. The theory of compensation, as an explanation for the behavior of small men, comes up way short. (Good old language, it never lets you down.) One of the nice things about having been Napoleon (at 5'2") is that at least no one could ever accuse you of having a Napoleonic complex.

203

Not that size doesn't have multitudinous influences on one's life. Although there have been witty big men—Oscar Wilde comes first to mind—wit and humor seem more in the province of the smaller man. Chaplin, Keaton, the Marx Brothers were all small men. We expect a comedian to be small. He may also be fat. W. C. Fields was fat; so was Oliver Hardy. Fat is funny, small is funny. Lou Costello, of Abbott and Costello, was small and fat—a winning comic combination. Tall isn't funny, perhaps owing to its being too imposing, even slightly menacing. Tall and handsome conjoined are, with rare exceptions, especially unfunny. One can always fall back on being the tall and silent type, of whom, in the movies, Gary Cooper was the apotheosis. But if one is small and silent, one is likely merely to be counted shy. Small men are under an obligation to do more talking; perhaps this is why so many among them are always joking.

We all have certain expectations about the physical size of the writers we read—expectations that are often wildly mistaken. One of the nicest compliments I ever received came from a man who, upon meeting me after having read my work for many years, remarked that he expected a fatter man. "You are too slender to be so funny," he said. So delighted was I by the remark that at my next meal I had two desserts. Along the same line, I always thought Chekhov short, possibly for so doltish a reason as his mastery of the short story. (He turns out to have been a bit taller than average and, when young, movie star handsome.) Tolstoy, whom I should have thought tall, was smallish though sinewy; I have seen him described as a giant dwarf. William James had the elongated head of a tall man, but was rather short; his body, after that fine head, rather disappoints. I tend on the other hand to think of Shakespeare, about whose height

I know nothing, as having the large head of a short man. I recently read that Freud was 5'8", though he looks smaller, as do all his early followers. No one who has ever seen a photograph of Freud and his circle would mistake it for a photograph of the Los Angeles Lakers.

I should have guessed that Jane Austen was small, chiefly because of the delicacy of her charmingly oblique observations. Wrong again. According to J. E. Austen-Leigh's memoir of his aunt Jane, "in person she was very attractive; her figure was rather tall and slender, her step light and firm, and her whole appearance expressive of health and animation." In her novels Jane Austen frequently describes the figure and carriage of her characters, and it will scarcely come as a surprise that she held some extremely interesting views about size. Reading along in her novel *Persuasion*, I discovered Miss Austen writing of a tertiary character that her amplitude made the expression of sorrow appear unseemly: "Mrs. Musgrove was of a comfortable substantial size, infinitely more fitted by nature to express good cheer and good humor than tenderness and sentiment. . . ." Then, to reinforce her point, Miss Austen adds:

> Personal size and mental sorrow have certainly no necessary proportions. A large bulky figure has as good a right to be in deep affliction as the most graceful set of limbs in the world. But, fair or not fair, there are unbecoming conjunctions, which reason will patronize in vain, which taste cannot tolerate, which ridicule will seize.

The point is quite indefensible, even a little crazy, yet absolutely true: there is something slightly appalling about the spectacle of a large person expressing sorrow. When a small woman cries, she weeps; a large woman, doing the same thing, is more likely to be described as blubbering.

Dorothy Parker, herself a small woman, caught the same point in "Big Blonde," her best story. Her heroine, a former model named Hazel Morse, is a large sensual woman prevented by her nature from introspection and by her many men friends from giving vent to the sadness that so often swamps her. Big babes are not permitted to give way to depression, and Dorothy Parker emphasizes that women of Hazel's kind, who don't mind having a fellow who buys them clothes and maybe pays the rent, all tend to be large:

> They were all big women and stout, broad of shoulder and abundantly breasted, with faces thickly clothed in soft, high-colored flesh. They laughed loud and often, showing opaque and lustreless teeth like squares of crockery. There was about them the health of the big, yet a slight, unwholesome suggestion of stubborn preservation. They might have been thirty-six or forty-five or anywhere between.

The largeness of such women as Hazel Morse seems only to add to their vulnerability. When Hazel fails at an attempt at suicide through an overdose of veronal tablets, a physician, looking down upon her large rumpled body, pronounces, "You couldn't kill her with an ax." There is a line whose jolt could drop a rhino.

If large men and women are nearly condemned to being robust, sporty, and full of high spirits, small men and women, however naturally full of bonhomie they may be, are often thought devious. In literature, treachery is frequently assigned to small people. Many of Robert Louis Stevenson's villainous characters turn out to be small; when Dr. Jekyll transmogrifies into Mr. Hyde, for example, he becomes shorter. I don't recall if Shakespeare ever refers to Iago's size, but no one, surely, would put him above 5'8". Cassius, of course, is "lean and hungry," but was he also short? An economist with whom I discussed this felt that Cassius is best thought of as having the head of John Kenneth Galbraith, though not quite his 6'8" frame.

"It's not what you have here," my father used to say, pointing to his flexed biceps, "it's what you have here," he added, pointing now to the right temple of his forehead. At 5'4" no Kareem Abdul-Jabbar himself, my father was fond of telling me the story of David and Goliath, with its salutary reminder of what a good little man can do. I have just reread the David and Goliath story, and, in retrospect, I'm not at all certain that it offers much in the way of consolation. To be sure, it took real courage to go up against this champion of Gath, "whose height was six cubits and a span"—by my reckoning 9'9", which makes him likely to have gone early in the NBA draft. David, a youngest son, is described as a "stripling"; he refuses armor, saying he hasn't earned the right to it. All very impressive. But the fact is that David got in the first and only shot—"And David put his hands in his bag, and took thence a stone, and slang *it*, and smote the Philistine in his forehead, that the stone sunk into his forehead; and he fell upon his face to the earth"—and scored something of a lucky punch; some might even compare it to a quick kick in the groin. I never raised this objection to my father. Nor, when he pointed to his biceps and then to his forehead, announcing that it was better to have it in the latter location than in the former, did I suggest, as it occurred to me often to do, that it might be best of all to have it in both places.

By the time I was seven or eight, I suspect I must have known that I was destined to be small and that, consequently, certain adjustments had to be made. Although I was a fairly good grammar school athlete, being small, I knew I was precluded from playing certain positions—first base in baseball, fullback in football—that called for being tall or powerful; I knew that it made no sense to swing for home runs or to attempt to knock the next guy off his feet through clean brutality. Violence as a mode of settling boyhood arguments was closed off to me, except with boys roughly my own size; in argument I would have to rely on cleverness and cunning. No point, either, in developing crushes on the taller girls in the class, no matter how pretty or sweet-natured they might be. By the time I was twelve, it was perfectly evident to me that central casting had not sent me to earth to be a tough guy, or the sort of boy girls would swoon over, or a hero generally. Central casting was a bit unclear about what role I was to play; I would have, over time, to develop my own.

I hope I have not given the impression that being smallish was painful. It wasn't. I had enough up here—see figure 1, not shown, short man pointing to right temple—to avoid ever being tormented or even teased about being small. Besides, I wasn't as small as all that; I was even rather tall for a short fellow. Yet, given a choice, I should much have preferred to have been the toughest kid in the class and the boy all the girls were daffy about. Being small did, however, teach early the lesson that life has its unalterable conditions and limitations. Size, or more precisely height, could not be changed through diet or calisthenics, pills or surgery, or psychological self-improvement programs. Your height is the one card you cannot toss in in exchange for another.

The genius of Sir Laurence Olivier, I have heard it said, included his ability to act much taller than he was, and to do so absolutely convincingly. I find this most impressive. I do not think myself an altogether unimaginative person; I can imagine myself a woman, a member of other races, all ethnic groups, tremendously rich, completely broke, a Medal of Honor winner, on the run from the police. But what I cannot successfully imagine myself is a foot taller than my actual height. On many occasions I have attempted to do so. The most recent of these was on a sunny afternoon while watching a baseball game at Wrigley Field in Chicago.

Four empty seats to my right sat a man, in his early forties I should guess, shirtless, in cutoff jeans, gym shoes, a dark beard, aviator sunglasses. Well soaked with beer, he was regaling four youngish women, who looked to be office workers out for an afternoon in the sun, with loud accounts of his sexual daring and astonishing virility. Had I been a foot taller—6'7", let us say, if you will permit me to round off that odd half inch in my favor—I do believe I should have spoken to the fellow. Standing well above him, I might have said:

"Sir, I won't trouble you more than a moment. Your charm, I am sorry to report, has worn a little thin, and I must ask you to remain silent for the remainder of the game, with the exception of cheering for the team of your choice and singing 'Take Me Out to the Ball Game' during the seventh-inning stretch. If these conditions seem to you too stringent, don't hesitate to say so, for I am sure another seat elsewhere in the ballpark can be found for you—and one I shall be delighted to carry you to, in a state of consciousness or unconsciousness, as you prefer. Do think about it."

A foot taller, might I not develop into a quiet, somewhat well-spoken bully? Would I not suddenly find myself acting to rectify the many little rudenesses in life I find so wearying? I see myself, in a traffic jam, uncoiling my considerable length from behind the wheel of my car, stepping out into the street, my head high above the ruck, the calm enforcer, the man who straightens things out by speaking in the voice of true reason with just a hint in it of real menace. No, the more I think of it, the more I am inclined to believe my physique is nicely mated to my temperament, given my many passions, impatience, and strong opinions. It is probably best that I am not in a position to do much about these things except express them through talk and writing.

This same physique also neatly fits me for intellectual work. Not many university teachers, editorial workers, artists, my guess is, are on the select mailing list of M. Hyman & Son. Only among artists and journalists could Ernest Hemingway have got away with his bogus tough-guy act; the same act, attempted at the construction site or on the assembly line, would have had the old boy in the dentist's chair before lunch break. At most universities, however, it would have gone over beautifully. Outside the physical education department, faculties are not notable for their Olympic muscularity. If a university teacher is not short, there is every chance that he is underweight, overweight, has a slouch, is hiding a weak chin behind an unkempt beard, or is otherwise misfitted or mildly deformed. To walk around a university is to realize that natural selection never takes a day off.

Along with being a university teacher, an editorial worker, a bit of an artist—in sum, a member in good standing of the shorter classes—I am also Jewish. The notion of Jews as puny has been put to rout and final rest by the efficient ferocity of the Israeli army, or at least ought to have been. (Whenever he sees soldiers of the Israeli army on television, the comedian Jackie Mason reports, his first reaction is to think they are Puerto Ricans.) Yet I continue to think of Jews as characteristically short. Despite the notable Jewish boxers, power hitters, football and basketball players, I still think of a good-sized

Jewish man as about 5'9". ("I'm a Jewish six-footer," someone once told me, "you know, about 5'10½.") A Jew much above six feet tall has always seemed to me overdoing it; he looks out of character, more than a touch odd, somehow slightly out of proper proportion. I think of such people falling into a category I call "Too Tall Jews," which has the same cheerful rhythm as the name of the 6'9 Dallas Cowboy defensive lineman Ed "Too Tall" Jones. If the late Harold Rosenberg, the art critic of the *New Yorker*, had not been 6'5 or so, would his criticism perhaps have seemed less cloudy? If Arthur Miller were not 6'2 or 6'3, would his plays have been more grounded in reality? Maybe so.

Forgive me for having dwelt so long on Jews and height, but being both Jewish and short I feel as if I belong to two ethnic groups simultaneously. When I learn, say, that Nijinsky was short, I feel an emotion akin to learning that Walter Lippmann was Jewish: "Ah," I say to myself in both cases, "one of our boys." Is there something similar to ethnic pride that might be called short pride? Not that I am about to begin wearing T-shirts that carry the message "Short Is Beautiful," or "When You're in Love, the Whole World's Smallish." Yet I am not, apparently, alone in feeling short pride. A friend, who is also short and a baseball fan, recently revealed to me that he has assembled an All-Time All-Star Short Players team, composed of players all of whom are under 5'8. Some of his selections are not surprising: "Wee Willie" Keeler at 5'4 was a cinch to make the team. But I didn't know that the great Cub slugger Hack Wilson was only 5'6. Sure'n' it's a great day for the Shortish.

The short have not exactly got long shrift in literature. There is the pathetic Tiny Tim, of course, and Walter de la Mare wrote a novel about a young girl's growing up—or, more precisely, not having grown up—titled *Memoirs of a Midget.* But most writers do not bother to describe their characters' height, unless it is extraordinary. Nor do most autobiographers mention how tall they are. How tall was Rousseau? He tells us everything else about himself, but not, to the best of my memory, his height. I have always imagined Ben Franklin short and John Stuart Mill tall, but I don't think either refers to his height in his classic autobiography. Nor do I remember Henry Adams anywhere remarking that he is quite short—no more than 5'4 or 5'5, I'd say, judging from photographs. Would he have been less sour, I wonder, at 5'11? Would the country have looked different to him at 6'1?

Montaigne informs us that "I am a little below medium height" and that, frankly, it bugs him. It is not only a serious defect, he says, but a "disadvantage, especially for men in command or office; for the authority given by a fine presence and bodily majesty is lacking." He quotes Aristotle saying that little men may be pretty but not handsome. Warming to his subject, Montaigne adds:

> Where smallness dwells, neither breadth and roundness of forehead, nor clarity and softness of eyes, nor the moderate form of the nose, nor small size of ears and mouth, nor regularity and whiteness of teeth, nor the smooth thickness of a beard brown as the husk of a chestnut, nor curly hair [Montaigne was bald], nor proper roundness of head, nor freshness of color, nor a pleasant facial expression, nor an odorless body, nor just proportion of limbs, can make a handsome man.

It's almost enough to cause a man under six feet to send off for elevator shoes.

Henry James, whom no one is likely to have described as rangy, occasionally mentions the height of his characters, but chiefly, in my recollection, when they are especially small. A secondary character in *The Ambassadors* named John Little Bilham is referred to everywhere in the book as "little Bilham" because of his diminutive size. In *The Princess Casamassima*, the novel's tragic hero Hyacinth Robinson is time and again described as "little Hyacinth," even when he grows to adulthood. I once asked a class to whom I was teaching the novel why James seemed continually to emphasize Hyacinth's smallness. I was able to convince them, through the usual strong-arm tactics, that the answer might be because, given Hyacinth's relation to two women in the novel, James, by stressing his character's littleness, wished to take him out of sexual contention. One of the two women, the working-class Millicent Henning, for example, is always described as large and robust, and therefore any notion of Hyacinth being her lover is disqualified. "How small, exactly, do you think Hyacinth is?" I asked, hoping someone would answer five feet, perhaps 5'2 at the maximum. "Well, how small is he, Miss Palmer?" I asked, when no one cared to hazard a guess. "I don't know," she said. "I suppose about your size." Ah, another magical moment in teaching.

"Stand tall, soldier," I can recall our elegant, whippet-lean 6'2 training sergeant Andrew Atherton bellowing, generally as a prelude to chewing out a recruit. Tall, for him as for most people, clearly was an approbative. In bygone movie days, tall was linked up with dark and handsome to describe, say, Cary Grant. Short, dark, and handsome somehow isn't the same. Splendid to be bighearted, but you don't want to be thought small-minded. You want to be careful, too, about coming up short. *Petty* derives from *petite*, which is of course French for "small." Small fry, small change, small beer—all convey the notion of triviality. The word *little* has become an intensifier, applied to people who are not themselves necessarily small, chiefly to add a dollop of contempt or to suggest insignificance, as in "that little fool," or even "what a little monster he has turned out to be." In short (so to speak), the language is loaded against us.

Still, I can recall a time when being tall seemed to have its own drawbacks. A tall young girl was usually a shy young girl, and often today, most touchingly, still is. Tall boys came in two varieties: thin and gangly or thick and oafish. To have been more than, say, 6'3 in high school and even college was an almost certain guarantee of being ill-coordinated. With occasional exceptions, in sports the very tall seemed to convey an aura of hopelessness. (To be very tall and not compete in sports was, worse, to convey an aura of freakishness.) In basketball, where great height was an obvious advantage, the very tall were instructed to hang around near the baskets in the hope that the ball would fall into their hands, whereupon they could pass it along to someone shorter who would know what to do with it. At a side gym at the University of Illinois sometime in the middle 1950s, I recall watching no fewer than three coaches attempt to teach a 6'7, rather thickset sophomore basketball player how to jump. I felt as if I were watching three trainers working with a bear.

As if to underscore the fundamental difference between the tall and the small, in the Chicago high school system of my boyhood, two basketball divisions were created: junior basketball was for boys 5'8" and under; senior basketball for boys 5'8" and above. Connoisseurs tended to feel that junior basketball was superior; the players were better coordinated, size couldn't replace skill, the game was quicker and more sophisticatedly played. Junior basketball in Chicago may have been one of the few occasions in all Western history when a substantial number of young males lied about their height—lied, that is, downwardly. Each year there was an official measuring-in for junior basketball, and many boys who were 5'9" or 5'10", preferring to play junior ball, slumped and slouched up to the measuring standard, trying to lose an inch or two through poor posture. Many were the stories about boys staying up all through the night before in the hope that lack of sleep would diminish their already modest size. Of an older kid in our school named Harry Shadian, who was very kind to me when I was a freshman, it was said that, in the attempt to "measure in" for juniors, he stayed up for two full nights drinking coffee and smoking cigarettes while carrying another boy named Dick Burkholder on his shoulders. The picture of the two of them continues to exert its fascination. While Harry Shadian was smoking and drinking coffee, what, I have wondered, was Dick Burkholder, perched upon his shoulders, doing? Not, I suspect, eating watercress sandwiches and reading La Bruyère.

Not only was junior basketball abolished in Chicago in my sophomore year in high school—providing one of the few serious disappointments in my otherwise agreeable youth—but then, ten or so years later, as if the needle of evolution had jumped eight or ten grooves, suddenly large boys and men became normally, in fact beautifully, coordinated. Earlier such extraordinary professional basketball players as Bob Pettit and Dolph Schayes, both well above 6'5", had moved with splendid fluidity, and one was occasionally treated to the spectacle of a quick and graceful fatboy on the football field, but all at once it seemed as if there were hundreds and hundreds of such athletes. Now one regularly saw men of 6'6", 6'9", 7', 7'2", who with an antelope-like bound could spear a fly ball just as it was about to leave a ballpark, or catch up with a man a foot or so shorter who had a twenty-yard lead, or pop into the air with the clarity and tautness of Massine, except that Massine, at the end of such an effort, never bothered to finish off with a three-sixty, double-pump, in-your-face, slam diddle-do dunk. Such men had names like Winfield, Bird, Strawberry, Magic, and Julius Erving (a name at whose close I always await either the name Horowitz or Shapiro, though it never arrives). These are men who regularly manage feats of coordination that men more than a foot shorter never even thought to attempt. In sports, it has made the old concept of "the good little man" rather obsolete. If one can't at least be more graceful than larger people, what, one has to ask, is the point of being small?

Or, to put it even more blatantly, who needs small men? Certainly one doesn't find much call for them in the classified section. When once briefly unemployed and hence a powerfully close reader of all employment ads, I do recall reading an ad asking specifically for small men—to clean out heating ducts in large office buildings in Manhattan. I regret having failed to apply; it could have been my one chance to have been turned away for being too tall. To return to sports, horse racing requires that jockeys be small, or at least light in weight, and diving, gymnastics, and figure skating favor smaller competitors, who have less body to control in the difficult physical configurations these sports all require. I tend to think of great mathematicians—Einstein and Ramanujan are two examples—as smallish men, and so, too, musicians: Beethoven, though stocky, cannot have been tall; Toscanini was distinctly short, and the contemporary composer and conductor Nicolas Slonimsky, in his recent autobiography, gives his height as 5'5¾" (only a short man will take every quarter inch he can get). Psychoanalysts I have met tend to be short, and so, too, violinists. The shortest audiences I know are those that attend chamber-music concerts. Pope, Keats, and Swinburne were all exceedingly short, and so was Dylan Thomas, though, when fully sauced, his height was not the first thing most folks generally noticed about him. Disraeli and Churchill, the greatest English politicians, of the nineteenth and twentieth centuries, were both fairly short. . . . But surely you can feel me struggling here, thrashing around, seeking a pattern.

Character, Heraclitus famously says, is fate, but how does one's size affect both character and fate? Had Pushkin been taller—and he was quite small—might he not more easily have walked away from the foolish duel over his honor as a husband that ended his life when he was only thirty-seven? Taller, would Evelyn Waugh still have been, as Cecil Beaton recalls him from school days, "a tiny but fierce ringleader of bullies"? For in some sense Waugh remained a small bully all his days. Not all the short tough guys were in the movies. Edmund Wilson, another short man on the stocky model, despite his deceptively friendly and furry nickname of Bunny, often played the intellectual bully. At 5'4" or so, Milton Friedman quickly makes it plain that he is not a man to be fooled with, at least in economic argument, where he could take your scalp off quicker than you can say Joan Robinson.

Height, if I may go off on a gender bender, is no very big deal for women. To be a woman above six feet carries, I am sure, its complications, but small women don't seem to operate under some of the same constraints, compulsions, pressures that small men sometimes do. The petite, moreover, is a category of feminine refinement. Women don't, when young, have to worry about being called Pip-Squeak, Twerp, or Half-Pint. ("Lay off the 'Shorty,' " says a petulant Spencer Tracy to Clark Gable at one point in the movie *Boom Town*.) Outside the duct-cleaning business, short men have never constituted an ideal type, but for a time in American life short women did. In the late 1940s and through the 1950s, the female type of the cheerleader—short, bosomy, full-calved, energetic—was much admired. Debbie Reynolds and, at a steamier level, Elizabeth Taylor represent the type in its Hollywood version. At my high school, they abounded; a few were named Mary Lou, but more than half seemed to be named Bobbie. "They may not be all that elegant," a wag with whom I went to school once remarked, "but they sure hold the road."

For a long while now the day of the Mary Lous and Bobbies has been over. Clothes have long since ceased to be designed with such women in mind, and they have no current representative in the movies. Tall and slender is nowadays the winning ticket, for both women and men. One sees this everywhere, and not least prominently in the elaborately mounted fantasies that are the magazine advertisements of the 5'6" clothing designer Ralph Lauren (né Lifschitz), which are populated exclusively with lithe and lanky WASPs lounging about in cowboy, tennis, or boating duds. Any man even roughly Ralph Lauren's own size showing up in any one of these fantastical ads is as unlikely as the appearance of the Modern Jazz Quartet at a Hasidic picnic.

Height may be one of the few departments in life where the best break comes with being average. Extremes to either side can be a serious nuisance: to be either 4'10" or 6'10" carries its own bedeviling inconveniences—from finding shoes small enough to finding beds big enough. What today is average height is not altogether clear. Like the poverty line, the average height line, one assumes, is going up all the time. When I was a kid, 5'8" or 5'9" seemed average height for a man; now 5'10" appears closer to the average. The higher the average rises, the lower I fall beneath it. It could get worse. As some people grow elderly, their faces become blurry, as if someone had fooled with their contrast button; while others, usually those who are small to begin with, tend to shrink in size. I believe I am going to be one of the shrinkers. I could one day look back at 5'6½" as my dinosaur age.

Although I have said that I cannot imagine myself truly tall, and although I have gone on about height at such (oops, sorry) length, neither do I tend to think of myself as small, at least not most of the time. Usually I think of myself as I appear to myself in my dreams: a man of average height, neutral looks, and medium build. And so in my workaday life do I think of myself until I stand next to someone quite large—as when I discovered myself, in the Los Angeles airport, standing alongside the 7'1" Wilt Chamberlain, into whose belt atop immense chocolate-colored velour trousers I found myself staring. At such moments I am brought up (sorry again) short. Yet otherwise I do not think overlong (*oy!*) about my physique and go about heightless and fancy-free.

Despite these disclaimers, I do feel there was something strongly formative about growing up on the short side. I cannot say why, exactly, but I sense that, had I been four or five inches taller, I should have been a radically different person than I am now. Discussing an acquaintance at lunch one day, a friend said to me, "He's the most underconfident tall man I know"—and then he paused, and added—"just as you are the most confident short man I know." That is an interesting distinction, and a compliment with lots of slack in it for interpretation. Does it mean that I am extraordinarily confident *for* a short man? Or does it mean that, given my shortness, it is remarkable that I am so confident? Life, like me, is too short to worry about such ambiguities—and besides, with my confidence, who cares? Yet I do have the distinct sense that my confidence and size, too, are somehow linked. As Émile Zola, Teddy Roosevelt, Lenin, Lord Beaverbrook, Fiorello La Guardia, Picasso, and a few other shortish fellows would be pleased to testify, there has never been a big demand for small underconfident men. Besides, as a man once told me, it isn't what you have here but what you have someplace else that counts. And that, Bubba, is about the size of it.

(1988)

Smoke Gets in Your Eyes

Just now the five most menacing words in the English language may well be: "Thank You for Not Smoking." One feels about these five words that a sixth word is missing but strongly implied, and it could be any of the following: *chump, creep, pig, scum, leper.* The war on smoking, in other words, appears to be going extremely well. Smokers are being nicely segregated in the vast number of restaurants that provide smoking and non-smoking sections. Smokers can no longer indulge in their pleasure during flights in the United States. Smoking is being increasingly restricted in public places, and in many offices and factories it is altogether outlawed. A European couple of my acquaintance, smokers both of Gauloises, *sans filtres*, report that in a Colorado hotel they were asked if they wanted a smoking or non-smoking room. "Towards a Smoke-Free New York" runs the title of a *New York Times* editorial, urging state legislators to turn up the screws on tougher restrictions against smoking. "No Smoking Except in Designated Areas" is a sign one is likely to see more and more in the years ahead, and those designated areas figure to become more and more out of the way. Perhaps one day there will be a sign that reads "No Smoking Except in the Andes."

I am myself a former smoker. As J. Alfred Prufrock measured out his life in coffee spoons, I measured out mine in Kools, filtered and mentholated, generally not many fewer than forty a day. Like Mark Twain, I found quitting smoking easy—I had done it hundreds of times. But the last time I quit was on a cruise ship in the Mediterranean under a cloudless, sublimely blue Greek sky, and that was more than a decade ago. Still, I must confess that every so often a cigarette looks good to me, though a cigar, which I smoked only infrequently even during my smoking days, can look even better. Temptation is stayed, however, because I have come to believe almost every terrible thing that is said about smoking—that it causes cancer, heart attacks, emphysema, and just about everything else except bad citizenship. And now, of course, to smoke qualifies one for being a bad citizen, too, at least to hear some people tell it.

I quit smoking for the same reasons that many people turn to religion: out of fear and hope. I fear leaving the earth any earlier than need be, for I greatly like it here; and I hope to outlive my enemies, which forces me to stay in excellent physical shape. I cannot say that I felt all that poorly when I smoked, but then, as someone who has been blessed with almost continuous good health his life long, I haven't a clear comparison to go by. As the hypochondriacal Oscar Levant might have put it, after quitting cigarettes I suppose I felt a little less lousy. I coughed less, I ate more heartily, I breathed more easily at the top of the stairs. Where I really felt fine, though, was spiritually. Stopping smoking filled me with what I can only call fatness of soul. I thought myself in control of my own life, no longer hostage to a strong habit, now calm and in command, a beautiful human being—in all, rather a superior mother-grabber. I retained this belief for longer than was seemly. Nowadays, when I see someone obviously as addicted to cigarettes as I was, something of this feeling of superiority returns, at any rate until I remember to despise myself for harboring it.

Yet most smokers I know have a conscience in worse shape than mine. Many among them are smoking scared, and I note that even the most case-hardened smokers among my acquaintances have reverted to the more sissified brands of cigarettes: Merit, True, Carlton. When death doesn't worry them, social ostracism does. They light up guiltily, and puff away apologetically. They have come to be thought, and now think themselves, walking engines of pollution. A dear friend of mine used to turn her head so abruptly to the side when exhaling smoke, lest any float under the nostrils from her companions, that I worried she would sooner die from a broken neck than from lung cancer. "Nelly," I once said to her, "why don't you simply slip under the table and finish your cigarette in peace?" One of the saddest questions one can hear these days is "Do you mind if I smoke?" for it is at once an admission of weakness and a request for what has come to be taken as a grave imposition. I should not be surprised to learn that the question "Do you mind if I smoke?" is today fairly often answered, "Yes, actually, I do mind—very much."

Yet for decades we all lived comfortably enough with smokers and smoking and the smell of smoke. Now, suddenly—presto chango!—smokers have become the most hounded and perhaps detested minority group in America. Because of this, when I do not feel superior to them I feel sorry for them. People complain peevishly about the smell of smoke. They tend to cough around smokers, making plain their protest against smokers ruining not only their own health but the health of everyone around them. Smokers nowadays tend to be treated generally as if they have a distinctly antisocial affliction, like continuous belching, except that, unlike the belchers, they have brought it upon themselves, filthy weaklings. No single bit of etiquette in my lifetime has changed so radically and so rapidly as that connected with smoking.

Except for the odd case of the asthmatic or those specifically allergic to smoke, nonsmokers in the past rarely seemed to complain about smoking, or if it disturbed them they kept it to themselves. Of course, today some of those who are most puritanically unpleasant about smoking are ex-smokers. Beware of converts; they carry stakes and fagots and matches. But the real turning point for the weakening of the social position of smokers has been the increasing evidence that smoking is bad for one's health—downright dangerous, in fact. Where smoking was once a convivial part of social life, it has now become an edgy if not slightly closeted activity. I should not be surprised to learn that many candidates for public office find it politic to conceal their smoking from the voters. Smoking, in the current health-minded atmosphere, may even be thought to show bad character.

"*Midnight Run,*" writes Stanley Kauffmann in the *New Republic*, "has more cigarette smoking in it than any American film I can remember since the era of cigarette-danger consciousness began." Before this time the movies provided some interesting smokers. Humphrey Bogart was an almost perpetual cigarette smoker in the movies in which he appeared, and very much an unfiltered type generally. Edward G. Robinson smoked cigars in his movies, as did Sydney Greenstreet. Peter Lorre smoked in the Continental style, the cigarette perched perpendicularly upward between his thumb and index finger. Among women, Lizabeth Scott and Marlene Dietrich had rich, raspy cigarette voices, thought by some—myself among them—to be very sexy. Miss Dietrich wielding a cigarette holder could make an adolescent boy quickly forget any baton twirler he might ever have admired. But easily the most impressive female smoker was Bette Davis; she could make the simple act of smoking a cigarette into a high dramatic gesture, like falling off a cliff.

Miss Davis has the female lead in what must be the smokiest movie ever produced, *Now, Voyager* (1942). The male lead is Paul Henreid, who is perhaps best remembered for playing Victor Laszlo, the French freedom fighter who is Ingrid Bergman's husband in *Casablanca*. Although I don't know Paul Henreid's nationality, in his movies he seemed to represent gentle European masculine elegance to the highest possible power. The plot of *Now, Voyager* is too sentimental to bear recapitulation. The movie deserves to be seen, however, purely for its smoking, which is nothing short of *exquisito*. *Now, Voyager* is the movie in which Henreid regularly places two cigarettes in his mouth, lights both, and deftly hands one to Miss Davis, who inhales from it dramatically. Through the better part of the movie Miss Davis and M. Henreid speak to each other through cumulus clouds of smoke. The movie ends not on a passionate kiss but on a languid smoke, and a fine sexy smoke it is. Miss Davis and M. Henreid smoking in evening clothes over the rail of an ocean liner are, somehow, sexier than any two contemporary actors I can think of who, clean lungs and all, are going at it on-screen hammer and tongs in the buff.

When actors now smoke in movies it is generally to underscore that they are villainous or weaklings or death-defying. Smokers in the movies are no longer elegant, in the style of Louis Hayward or George Sanders, who seemed not so much to smoke as to wear their cigarettes. Nor do they avail themselves of such dashing appurtenances as slender silver cigarette cases, of the kind Fred Astaire was wont to slide out from the inner breast pocket of his dinner jackets, or initialed gold cigarette lighters, of the kind that Adolphe Menjou or Noël Coward used blithely to flick under their own cigarettes. So common was smoking in the movies of the thirties, forties, and fifties that, my guess is, an actor, even if he didn't smoke, even if smoking made him ill, probably had to learn to handle a cigarette, the way he might have had to learn to handle a horse, because a great many roles required it. Today such an actor could protest having to smoke in a movie and in a trice have the surgeon general, the PTA, the EPA, the environmentalists, and the full forces of (to adopt a phrase used in the Spartacist League newspaper *Workers Vanguard*) "health fascism" on his side.

Novels of the same vintage tended to be heavily nicotinified. In them, characters were often "inhaling deeply," or "exhaling the smoke slowly," or "flipping away the butt disgustedly." It gave a character something to do at the close of a line of dialogue. Most writers of that day—the twenties through the fifties—seemed themselves to be smokers, at least if one goes by dust-jacket photographs, and a lot of smoke seems to have seeped into their books. "Slowly, without turning his head," writes John O'Hara in *Appointment in Samarra*, "he pulled himself up to a half sitting position and reached out for the package of Lucky Strikes on the table between his bed and Caroline's bed." Later: "He turned. It was Father Creedon. 'Oh, Father. Good evening. Cigarette?' 'No, thank you. Cigar for me.' The priest took a cigar from a worn, black leather case." And later still: "There was no newspaper on the table, but he did not want to speak to Mrs. Grady, so he sat there without it, not knowing whether the damn paper had come, with nothing to read, no one to talk to, nothing to do but smoke a cigarette." I didn't make a count, but *Appointment in Samarra* may well be a sixty-cigarette novel.

In those days a cigarette, plainly, was a novelist's friend. When nothing was happening, he could let his characters knock off for a smoke. In the current day, if a character in a novel smokes, it is likely to be merely another of his or her problems. "She takes a drag on her cigarette," a line in a contemporary story reads, "and inspects her varicose veins. . . ." In a novel by a young writer named Michael Chabon entitled *The Mysteries of Pittsburgh*, rather more marijuana than tobacco is inhaled, but when a cigarette is smoked it is not identified by brand. (In O'Hara, whether a man smokes Lucky Strikes or Camels tells an informed reader a little something about the man.) And sometimes the facts of smoking are got wrong. "I smoked a cigarette in the rain," writes Michael Chabon, "which is the best way to smoke a cigarette." This, in my experience, is not true.

My first cigarette was smoked in the rain; make that my first five or six cigarettes. The brand was Herbert Tareyton, cork-tipped but unfiltered, rather loosely packed, so that filaments of tobacco stuck to one's tongue. I and my friend Norm Brodsky, who was puffing away along with me, were twelve. Tareytons were Norm's father's brand of cigarettes; my father smoked cigars, though on the rare occasion when he bought a pack of cigarettes it was usually Tareytons, too. We bought the cigarettes at Simon's Drugstore one rainy school day afternoon. Lighting them in the rain wasn't easy, and smoking them, when raindrops first blotched, then dampened the paper was no cinch, either. My recollection is that we each smoked five or six cigarettes, and then, lest it provide incriminating evidence, tossed the rest of the pack in the bushes. We can scarcely be said to have enjoyed the cigarettes we did smoke, though neither of us became the least bit sick, as young boys, toward the end of being taught a lesson, are supposed to become the first time they smoke. Norman and I both went on, as it turned out, to distinguished smoking careers.

I cannot recall the exact moment when I decided to become a regular smoker. Doubtless it was linked to the realization that I was not destined to win glory as a high school athlete. The seal was set on this realization late one afternoon deep in the autumn of my fifteenth year. A fairly lowly sub on our school's frosh-soph basketball team, I was seated at my accustomed place toward the end of the bench next to a boy named Les Handler in the drafty gym of Kelvyn Park High School on the West Side of Chicago. Les and I only rarely got into games, a situation to which I had become sadly resigned but to which Les could not quite reconcile himself. Sitting there on the bench, he had become a gonfalonier of grievance, of a not highly witty order I am bound to report, and as each game progressed he provided me with a running commentary in which he didn't mind remarking that many of the boys who played ahead of us on our own team were really quite (I euphemize) excrementitious.

Les was going on in this vein at Kelvyn Park that dark autumn afternoon when, with four and a half minutes left to play and our team well ahead, Coach Eugene Fricker called out, "Epstein, Handler." We left our places on the end of the bench to take up a position of readiness, on one knee, awaiting a time-out or a foul so that we could go into the game. Four and a half minutes, for us, was a substantial block of time—substantial and potentially delightful; it stretched out before us luxuriously, like the promise of a weekend with, say, Rita Hayworth. Except that no time-out was called nor any foul committed, and as the buzzer sounded for the end of the game, Les Handler and I were still in empty readiness on one knee alongside Coach Fricker.

Dressing in the dank Kelvyn Park locker room, neither of us spoke. I, sunk in despondency, had nothing to say. Les had already used up all his profanity in his game-time commentary; besides, the English language was deficient in that it failed to provide words adequate to his anger. Now dressed, we went off together, not wishing to ride home with the other team members. All that was left to us by way of giving vent to our extreme frustration was to break training. Not that anyone cared if we did, you understand, but it seemed the least we could do. We were too youthful to buy liquor; drugs had not yet come on the scene. Instead, wearing leather jackets and carrying our gym bags, we walked into a corner mom-and-pop grocery store and emerged with two Pepsi-Colas, a box of Dolly Madison chocolate-covered doughnuts, and a pack of Lucky Strikes. It would not be the last time that a cigarette would present itself as a consolation.

Ours was a high school in which, I would guess, roughly half the kids smoked, with boys, I would guess again, more active in this line than girls. Smoking was an emblem of adulthood, the most readily and cheapest available (cigarettes were then twenty-five cents a pack), and the ideal had not yet become to remain youthful into old age but to act as grown-up as possible when one was young. Many of my classmates—not all of whom would go on to college—appeared to have attained a quite astonishing simulacrum of maturity; they dressed, looked, and took themselves for adults. So it seemed the most natural thing in the world, when they briefly interrupted a heavy conversation about cars, pro football, or the mysteries of sex, to slide a pack of Chesterfields or Old Golds out of their shirt pocket, tamp down a butt, light it with a Zippo or Ronson, and release a thin but authoritative stream of smoke.

Many though by no means all of my closest friends smoked. I

229

cannot make out a clear pattern among those who did and those who didn't. Odd, is it not, the way some people are never in the least tempted by those habits that keep life jumpy if not always jumping for others of us: smoking, drinking, gambling, promiscuity. In the case of "the tenacious weed," as I have recently seen tobacco described, some people were instantly repulsed by it; some others failed to see the point of it; and a fortunate few could take it or leave it. I took to it straightaway, and by the age of sixteen was a full-time and altogether serious smoker. By a serious smoker I mean someone who begins and closes and otherwise punctuates his day with cigarettes.

Although my parents knew I smoked, I did not, in high school, like to smoke my first cigarette of the day at home, lest they think their charming boy already addicted to cigarettes, which of course I was. I waited instead until I was picked up for school by Ronald Harris in his 1949 blue four-door Plymouth. I was one of five passengers in that Plymouth, along with Ronnie Harris, who made six, all of us smokers. On wintry mornings, the Plymouth's windows shut against the cold, however sunny it may have been outside, inside that car it was like London on a particularly foggy night. Hams and loxes, I suspect, have been smoked in clearer air. I remember once, just after the Plymouth had been parked and we departed from it, looking back to note smoke curling out of it as if it had earlier been on fire. That I survived more than a year of morning rides in Ronnie Harris's mobile smokehouse leads me to doubt the claims of the anti-smoking campaigners about the dangers of what they call "secondhand smoke." Were these claims true, I should be writing this essay in a room in a Swiss sanatorium.

Emerging from Ronnie Harris's Plymouth, we all strode into a cavern with a long marble-topped bar known as Harry's School Store.

It was at Harry's that I ate my first bacon-lettuce-tomato sandwich, which, with baseball and the light bulb, I number among the three greatest American inventions. Along with excellent BLTs, Harry's, at all hours, provided a heavy haze of smoke, which I added to before class, at lunch, and then again after school. I could apparently still go three- or four-hour stretches without requiring a cigarette, for, though I cut more than my share of classes, I cannot recall ever doing so because I was desperately in need of a cigarette. Instead I smoked when I could, in a jolly and by my lights sporty way, drawing smoke deep down, belching it out in perfect smoke rings, French inhaling, learning to light a matchbook match with one hand, exhaling smoke through my nose like an angry bull in a comic book.

Although it was not the chief reason I went to school there, the University of Chicago permitted smoking in classrooms, which I thought a fine thing. Students and professors both smoked away—so much so that, in the context of the seriousness of the university, smoking almost came to seem an intellectual gesture. (French intellectuals were evidently also heavy smokers; Camus and Malraux, both of whom I then took for culture heroes, seem invariably to be photographed with cigarettes pendant from their lips.) Some of my instructors at the university were nervous smokers; several unattractively so, with nicotine-stained fingers and ashes dribbling down their rumpled lapels; a few, though, could make smoking seem an elegant tic and were able to use their cigarettes to underscore points the way other people used italics. Cigarette smoke itself came to seem part of the atmosphere of intellectual discourse.

My own smoking must have increased in intensity during these years. I chose not to study in beautiful old William Rainey Harper Library because I couldn't smoke there, and smoking concentrated my intellectual powers, or so I told myself. Hyde Park, the neighborhood in which the University of Chicago is located, is an enclave, then as now locked between two tough slum neighborhoods, but I found that if I ran out of cigarettes after, say, nine or ten at night, I was still ready, after much hesitation and more trepidation, to run (I use the word here in its literal meaning) out for more. I was not yet ready to kill for a smoke, but evidently quite prepared to be mugged for one.

An army is said to march on its stomach, but when it isn't marching, it is, at least in my peacetime experience of the military, smoking on its duff. The army hour, like the psychotherapeutic hour and the academic hour, is composed of fifty minutes, with the last ten minutes given over to smoking a cigarette. Cigarettes were cheap—fifteen cents a pack at the PX—and therefore plentiful. Every barracks, orderly room, latrine was decorated with red cans (known as butt cans) filled with sand for cigarette ashes and stubs. No reading matter was permitted the first eight weeks in the army, not even a newspaper, but the men who designed the extremely effective exercise in the breakdown in civilian personality known as basic training were not so crazy as to try to stop young troopers from smoking. "OK, men, the smoking lamp is lit," one or another sergeant was regularly barking out during basic training. "Light 'em if you got 'em." I had 'em, I lit 'em.

Of the time I spent in the army, I should have to say that I liked the time spent smoking best, which was roughly a sixth. As a serious smoker, I tried in civilian life to keep to a military budget of one cigarette for every waking hour. This, though, proved difficult to keep, for so many of life's activities seemed to call for accompaniment by a cigarette. Coffee without a cigarette seemed unnatural; booze without a cigarette, impossible. A meal required capping off with a smoke, a fine meal with two or three. Emerging from the subway or completing any little trip or errand called for a nicotine reward. Picking up a cigarette while on the telephone came especially easy. In a minor crisis—a deadline looming up, an argument, tension of one kind or another—all cigarette budgetary bets were off, and I smoked whenever the nicotine twitch beckoned. I began to do things like drink more coffee to heighten the pleasure of smoking. ("It was never the sex, my dear, it was the cigarettes afterward" would make a good crack in a comic novel of the kind no one writes anymore.) King-size cigarettes had long since been on the market, but the genius had not yet arisen to invent what many a serious smoker among us really required: the all-day cigarette.

During this period, I became greatly enamored of the accouterments of smoking. Had I been a cigar smoker, I should no doubt have carried around a little gold cutter and kept a humidor box on my desk. Had I been a pipe smoker, the possibilities would have been endless; from pouches to racks to tampers to humidor jars to special lighters to little holsters—one could almost build a life around smoking a pipe. For a cigarette smoker the possibilities were much narrower. A cigarette holder seemed to work well for Franklin Delano Roosevelt, but if one wasn't actually president of the United States it seemed, for a man, a mite pretentious. Cigarette cases, very slender ones, monogrammed, of gold for women and of silver for men, best received as a gift from someone of the opposite sex, always struck me as a handsome touch. Offering a cigarette to a companion from one's cigarette case, then taking one out for oneself, tamping it down a time or two atop the closed case—here was a gesture fit for white tie, tails, and Fred Astaire. (Whether Fred Astaire really smoked I do not know, but in movies he handled a cigarette wonderfully well;

no one was better at flipping a cigarette away.) By the time I could afford a silver cigarette case, cigarettes of differing lengths were being produced—one cigarette, it will be recalled, claimed to be "a silly millimeter longer"—which made it difficult to purchase a case, for one didn't know what length cigarette one might next be smoking. Somehow the cigarette case had already seemed a part of a permanently bygone era, an accessory fit only for drawing-room comedies, Somerset Maugham stories set in the Malay states, and smart New York supper clubs.

Which left cigarette lighters. At one time or another, I must have owned nearly every kind made. I have owned cigarette lighters that, in retrospect, have given more pleasure than the cigarettes they lit. I once owned a gold-filled Dunhill—purchased for forty-five dollars in 1965, a great extravagance—that increased my smoking by the simple delight that feeling its heft in my hand and lighting it gave; I was always playing with it, and as long as I had it out, I would, before putting it back in my pocket, use it to light a cigarette. As a wayward youth on a visit to New Orleans, I once watched the performance of a redheaded striptease artist named Reddi Flame, and of course it is precisely a ready flame that an efficient cigarette lighter confers. To reach over to light a woman's cigarette with an elegant lighter seemed a grand thing—still does. In *Lifemanship*, Stephen Potter mentions a man he names William Staines, who won the devotion of women sheerly through the perfection with which he wielded a cigarette lighter:

> He had a rack of a dozen lighters, which he cleaned and put in order once a week. Before making for his girl, he would select one, fuel it, put in a new flint, taking care to choose a large

and manly one for the tiny, frightened girl, or one, for instance, with cigarette case and pencil attached for the slightly oopsy girl. At precisely the right moment in the cigarette manoeuvre, fire would dart from his hand. He had trained himself to see a pretty girl feel for a cigarette across three platforms of Waterloo Station, as it were, and to be behind her, flame ready, before the cigarette was at her lips.

Potter claims that Staines's real genius was that "by concentrating on *one part*, he was able to suggest *the whole*." Staines was so elegant with his lighter that most women went on to believe that everything he did must be an expression of beautiful manners—"even," Potter writes, "if she found herself left with the two heaviest bags to carry, and was asked to stand over them while Staines himself went into the refreshment room for a cup of tea."

I should not like to go on the road now selling cigarette lighters, especially table lighters, which used to adorn the coffee table in most middle-class homes but which have now all been removed. Owning a tobacco shop also strikes me as a difficult way to become wealthy, though I can remember when tobacco shops were almost as common as gas stations. The ultimate tobacco shop was Dunhill's; today, alas, it is more and more given over to selling clothes and costly kitsch. I used to go into Dunhill's near an office I once worked in, usually to buy a pack of their cigarettes or a cigar. The chief clerk in the tobacco section was a lower-middle-class Englishman who was immensely knowledgeable and not in the least snobbish. He was able to discuss the arcana of pipe tobacco mixtures in a manner that excited the interest of connoisseurs; he could tell you about the exact quality of the most recent shipment of cigars, which had such promising names as Dunhill Monte Cristo Colorado Maduro No. 1. In the humidor room, where boxes of cigars were kept in vast quantities, powerful men rented small lockers in which they stored their own expensive cigars (including occasional importations from Cuba that came by way of Canada) under ideal conditions. The names on these lockers—those of the mayor, a gossip columnist, judges, wealthy merchants, the conductor of the symphony orchestra, a cardinal—represented a healthy chunk of what once used to be called "the power structure." Cigars and power seemed to go together.

Cigar smokers were a different breed from cigarette smokers; they appeared more substantial, less nervous. While cigarettes seemed a habit, cigars seemed part of a man's character. One thinks of Winston Churchill, characteristically, with a tumbler of scotch in one hand, a good-sized cigar in the other. A photograph of H. L. Mencken on the wall above my desk shows him in a silk striped shirt, typing away, a cigar jammed into the corner of his mouth—and the cigar looks right. Groucho Marx used his cigar the way Charlie Chaplin used his cane: as a baton with which to conduct his madcap comedy. Although political cartoonists are fond of using the cigar as a symbol of the big-time capitalist, Bertolt Brecht, both an anti-capitalist and an anti-American, adored Virginia cigars. A cigar suggests prosperity, and, sometimes, corruption. The smoke in the infamous smoke-filled rooms in which political deals were made was, presumably, cigar smoke. Fight managers smoked cigars (usually chewing on the stubs); so, too, did gangsters who arrived at the upper echelons of their trade. Carmine Galante, an alleged Mafia guy, was killed in Brooklyn with a cigar actually in his mouth.

But the gentlemanly tradition in cigar smoking is richer than that of the thug and plug-ugly tradition. This tradition, largely though not wholly English, is one in which cigars were smoked in clubs and at table with port after the ladies had left the room. In this tradition a cigar becomes a gentleman's accessory, an appurtenance, like a walking stick or a fine pocket watch. Unlike these items, a cigar gave delight beyond that of mere possession. Arthur Rubinstein, who lived to the age of ninety-five, was turned on to cigars at thirty and claimed they gave him "untiring pleasure." Untiring pleasure is what Ernest Newman (1868–1959), the splendid music critic of the *Times* (of London), appears to be taking from the cigar he is smoking on the cover of the first volume of his *Essays from the World of Music*. A bald man in thick spectacles, sitting in a deep, heavily stuffed armchair, wearing a loose-fitting lounge suit, listening, one gathers, to music being played upon a phonograph, Newman holds a cigar, smoked about halfway down, in his right hand, a cigar that seems almost animate, rather like a pet, an object in any case most companionable. This, you feel looking at the photograph, is cigar smoking at a high level.

There is something not merely masculine about cigars, but something that seems positively to exclude women. Cigarettes are androgynous, and can be shared between men and women. They have often been construed as an accessory to romance: "Here we are," runs a line from a love song from my youth, "Out of cigarettes / Holding hands and yawning / Look how late it gets . . . ," and so forth. None of this is true about cigars. Cigars are emblems of male celebration, used to mark the closing of a deal or the birth of a child. Lighting up a Macanudo, a Royal Jamaica, a Thompson Tampa, one feels a bit of a man of the world; and two men lighting up cigars together often feel a wholly masculine sense of intimacy. Unless they happen to be George Sand, women do not smoke cigars; most women, in fact, detest and protest against them, claiming it is their stench they abhor. The number of women who have made romance with a man conditional on his giving up cigars cannot be known. Kipling, in a poem of twenty-five rhyming couplets entitled "The Betrothed," wrote about a man whose fiancée asks him to choose between her and his cigar smoking. The poem's famous penultimate couplet runs:

> A million surplus Maggies are willing to bear the yoke;
> And a woman is only a woman, but a good Cigar is a
> Smoke.

My father smoked cigars, not very costly ones, at the rate of six or seven a day. Cigar smoke was one of the smells, a halfway-smoked cigar in an ashtray one of the sights, of my youth. I used to smoke an occasional cigar, but their chief effect upon me was to quicken my hunger for cigarettes. Pipes, which I also tried, were worse. I always liked the smell of burning pipe tobacco, unless I was the man burning it, in which case I scarcely smelled it, but had to concentrate my full attention on keeping the pipe from going out, my tongue from swelling, my clothes from being set aflame by errant ash, and my face from looking hopelessly smug and perhaps eminently punchable. Pipes were permanently out, but roughly a year ago I smoked a cigar, a cheapy Antonio y Cleopatra Grenadier (light wrapper), which I nursed through a nine-inning baseball game and which I enjoyed immensely, though I worried a bit about whether it would help put me back on the road to that dread Irish seducer, Nick O'Teen. My father, on the other hand, after smoking for more than half a century, one day in his seventy-fifth year stopped cold, without fuss or bother, and never looked back.

"Life is a sum of habits disturbed by a few thoughts," wrote Valéry, and of these few thoughts perhaps none is more disturbing than that having to do with giving up one of those habits. I don't remember exactly when it first occurred to me to stop smoking—I may have had a bad cold, or a case of flu—but, even though I did not succeed in quitting, life was never quite the same afterward. I now inhaled smoke and exhaled guilt. I could no longer enjoy smoking nor, since I found it very difficult to quit, could I enjoy not smoking.

Few things can more quickly reduce one's generous estimate of one's own character than attempting to quit smoking cigarettes. To know oneself thoroughly hostage to those little white tubes of tobacco damages one's sense of self-grandeur, not to speak of putting a frightful crimp into one's utopian politics. (In *Darkness at Noon*, Arthur Koestler is very good at showing how important cigarettes are to Rubashov, his defeated revolutionary hero.) During lost bouts with quitting smoking, I was not above going up to friendly-looking strangers who were smoking to ask, in a parody of Bogart in *The Treasure of the Sierra Madre*, "Excuse me, but do you happen to have a cigarette for an ex-serviceman?" Late in the afternoon of a day on which I had not smoked, my mind might vaguely drift off to imagining a personal tragedy of a kind that would permit me to return to cigarettes: "Oh, yes, his entire family has been wiped out in a flood. It's no wonder he's returned to cigarettes, poor man." Even now, a decade after no longer smoking regularly, I appear in one of my own dreams with a cigarette in my hand, disappointed with myself for having gone back to smoking.

When I failed at quitting smoking, I thought it certain proof of my weakness of character. Now that I have quit smoking, am I entitled to think myself a man of strong character? Life offers its tests of character, but I strenuously doubt that quitting cigarettes is among them. Besides, I didn't quit smoking to improve my character, or to help clean up the environment, or to close in on physical perfection. I quit smoking because I was afraid of dying, or at least of dying any sooner than is absolutely necessary. I have no wish to give up my room in this comfortable and amusing resort even a minute before actual checkout time.

What I think quitting smoking may be about is the comedy of human resolution. The Virgil of this subject is the Triestine novelist Ettore Schmitz (1861–1928), who wrote fiction under the name Italo Svevo. The first chapter of Svevo's novel *Confessions of Zeno* is entitled "The Last Cigarette." In it Zeno Cosini, a Trieste businessman, undergoes medical and electrical treatments and finally psychoanalysis in the effort to give up cigarettes. All are abortive, despite his endless resolutions to quit smoking. No cigarette, after all, tastes quite so good as the last cigarette. What better, then, than to make every cigarette one's last? Or, when one has resisted smoking for several hours, the clean feeling in one's mouth, as every smoker and former smoker will verify, only makes one long all the more for another cigarette. "Directly I had smoked it," Zeno notes, "I felt remorse and again began making the very resolution I had tried to repress." With the making of fresh resolutions, the remorse felt at breaking them, and the remaking of renewed resolutions, the days pass agreeably enough for Zeno. So seem they to have done in Svevo's own life, for he was fairly clearly writing out of personal experience in *Confessions of Zeno*. Most photographs of Svevo show him cigarette in hand, and P. N. Furbank, one of his biographers, tells that, on his deathbed, Svevo, seeing his physician-nephew light up a smoke, asked for a truly last cigarette. Sad to have to report, he was denied it.

Do they, I sometimes wonder, order these things better in Europe?

When I was last there, no maître d' asked me if I wished to sit in the smoking or non-smoking section of his restaurant. People in the streets of Florence and Ravenna smoked away, near as I could make out, quite guiltlessly. A friend, a physician who is not himself a smoker, reports that on a TWA flight to Stockholm he and his fellow passengers were treated to a quite menacing lecturette about not smoking on the plane, except in designated areas, and especially about not smoking in the lavatories, where there were smoke detectors—and fooling with them, everyone aboard should know, was a federal crime. "Returning on SAS we found the Scandinavians much more humane," he writes. "They didn't mention any of this." On a flight I took from San Francisco to Chicago, before smoking was banned on most domestic flights, the chief stewardess announced that, owing to the crowdedness of the flight, there would be no smoking section at all on the plane, and hence no smoking, except in the first two rows of first class. A large number of people applauded, as if to say, "Good, let those smoking dogs suffer." When the writer Raymond Carver recently died, at the age of fifty, of lung cancer, the *New York Times*, in its obituary, saw fit to note that Carver was "a heavy cigarette smoker until he became ill," thus using the occasion of a man's death to deliver a little health sermon.

The time has long passed when Americans have looked to Europe as the font of all wisdom on living the good life; if anything, the traffic here appears to be running the other way, especially among the young in Europe, who glom on to almost all things American with real excitement. But Europeans have been sensible in thus far taking a pass on the new American health fascism, in which everything is subservient—not to the state, as under political fascism—but to the ideal of extending sheer biological life. I am myself someone who is not only immensely greedy for life but who, if the truth be known, lives pretty much according to most of the tenets of health fascism: pledged to the shining if utterly unheroic goals of clean lungs, clear arteries, tidy intestines, and a glowing carcass generally.

Although I appear to live with equanimity under this regime of health fascism, within me, still very much underground, a timid resistance fighter lurks. This is the fellow who, when he learns that a middle-aged man has bitten the dust while jogging, smiles inwardly and knowingly at the futility of efforts at human perfection; who is secretly pleased to hear that an obviously alcoholic woman has died, peacefully in her sleep, at the age of ninety-six; who is always delighted to know about any man or woman who beats the health odds by simply ignoring them. This same fellow is always advising me, when confronted by a temptation that might be hazardous to my health, to let 'er rip. Sometimes I listen to him; more often I do not. On smoking we have reached a compromise, which is that, if I make it to eighty, I shall begin smoking again. It's fewer than thirty years away. If you are around then, too, try not to act surprised if I ask for a light.

(1989)

The Man in
the Green Hat

Unlike every other paragraph I have written in my life, this one
I am writing while wearing a red fez. It is a serious fez, too,
quality goods, purchased more than twenty years ago in Cairo and
lent to me by its owner, a dear friend. I do not know whether I am
wearing it correctly, but there it sits on top of my head, its black fringes
dangling just above my right ear. In this fez I look like a man who
has seen his share of the world's corruption and who is prepared to
respond, strictly as a middleman you understand, to the most complicated murmurous suggestions. "A jeroboam of absinthe, a jade anklet,
a male llama that understands Croatian, and a heavy-duty dry-cell
battery?" I can hear myself saying. "Is not a problem, *effendi*. All four
items will await you back in your room at the hotel within the hour."

I begin this paragraph in a green velour hat, a cross between a
fedora and a trilby, its brim snapped down back and front. It is a
handsome hat, in my opinion, but I am not in the least handsome in
it. "Country Gentleman" is marked inside its crown. Wearing it, however, I look more like a city dog. Specifically, in this fine hat my face

rather resembles the face of an oversized spaniel in a compromising position—apologetic, half embarrassed, distinctly mournful. This is not quite the fashion statement I wish to make. Yet I do require a hat, especially in Chicago, where from December through March the city usually does a nice imitation of Moscow on Lake Michigan. I grow old, I grow old, the top of my size 7½ long oval head grows cold. It also begins to grow a bit silly looking in the caps I have taken to wearing in recent years as protection against the weather.

That I have gone through thirty-odd years of adult life in a cold climate without regularly wearing what I think of as an adult hat is a mildly interesting social fact. I have owned the green velour hat that gives me the fetching spaniel effect—in his memoirs, the musician Nicolas Slonimsky tells that, when still struggling with the English language, he once introduced Pablo Casals to an audience as a great cellist and "distinguished Spaniel"—I have owned this hat for better than fifteen years, and never once have I worn it out-of-doors. At one point, I gave it to my father, who shares my large head size. He did not look the least like a spaniel in it, but in time grew tired of the green hat, and I have since reclaimed it. I continued to admire the hat, so long as it didn't have my head in it. Then the other day I clapped it on while I happened to be wearing glasses—I also have grown a good crop of gray hair that now shows underneath the brim—and it looked rather better, or at any rate less ridiculous, on me. I may one day before too long wear the hat in public, I thought to myself, perhaps trying it out late at night in some quiet nearby suburb that doesn't have a leash law.

Mine is the first generation to give up wearing serious men's hats. Ours is the first generation for whom wearing a hat is no longer de rigueur, which, as the boys in the back room at *Webster's* will tell you, precisely means no longer "prescribed or required by fashion, etiquette, or custom: proper." Such hats as we wear tend to be slightly comic ones, parodistic versions of serious hats: little snap-brim jobs, or floppy Irish tweed numbers, or checkered lids of the kind to which the late Bear Bryant, football coach of Alabama, was partial. Early in the 1960s, men who worked for advertising agencies used to wear a short-brimmed hat known among themselves as the Madison Avenue crash helmet, but in no other line of work that I can recall did a serious hat seem, as they say in the army, "standard issue." Today a man walking the streets of an American city in a homburg, with its curled brim and high crown, is likely to attract more attention for his oddity than another man dancing a boogaloo in a deep-sea diving suit.

Not long ago I found myself seated at a small lunch party next to a man who had only recently retired as president and principal owner of a successful manufacturing company. We appeared to have nothing in common yet got on quite well. I don't recall any of the subjects we talked about, but our conversation flowed nicely, each of us establishing with the other that he was a man of gravity, good humor, and superior perspective—establishing that we were both, in short, men of the world. When at the end of the lunch we rose from the table, my companion told me that he much enjoyed our talk and asked for my card so that he might call me to arrange another meeting. I had only to admit that I had no card to feel the breeze from my fall in his estimation. I wrote out my telephone number for him, but it wasn't the same. A man without a business card was not, in his view, somehow a substantial fellow. He never called. In retrospect, I am glad that he didn't see the hat I wore that day, a herringbone eight-section cap that, even though carried by all the Anglophiliac men's stores with names like the Shropshire Lad, was worn by workers fresh off the boat and newsboys in Horatio Alger novels.

This man was of my father's generation, the generation of men for whom hatlessness was roughly equivalent to shoelessness. For these men, to go out meant to go out in a hat. When I was growing up, I cannot recall my father being out-of-doors without his hat. The least errand—down to the drugstore at the corner for a newspaper, for example—required putting on his hat. To this day he seems, out-of-doors, a bit undressed when hatless, which in any case he rarely is, though he no longer wears felt hats made by such firms as Dobbs or Stetson but instead dons the jauntier, more relaxed chapeaux of the kind befitting a man now retired from the business wars ("seamed all over with the scars of the marketplace," as Henry James once characteristically put it).

Men of that generation early formed their style, their conception of how a man ought to look, and not only went with it, as we should nowadays say, but stuck with it throughout their lives. Edmund Wilson's getup for socializing at the Wellfleet beach at Cape Cod, ably described by Alfred Kazin ("the too elegant cane, the stains so carefully preserved on the Panama hat, the absurdly formal long white shirts sometimes flopping over the bulky stomach in Bermuda shorts") is a reminder that men of a certain era had a fixed manner of dress. "I have only one way of dressing," Wilson told Kazin, and he apparently never felt the need of another.

I myself have several ways of dressing. I am at this moment wearing a high and weighty fur hat, purchased for me in the Soviet Union for roughly seventy dollars. The hat stands some six inches high; it has earflaps that tie together across its top; its fur is luxuriantly dark. I am very fond of this hat, though I tend to wear it only three or four days a year—on those days in Chicago when it is so cold that running a Jiffy Lube franchise on the equator seems immensely attractive. I would wear my Russian hat more than I now do but for the inconvenient fact that when people see me in it they tend to laugh. As they pass me, adults smile, as if to say, "Look at that clown." Kids, especially little kids, point and giggle. I think the problem is that the hat makes me appear top-heavy, so that I seem a pair of galoshes walking under a fur hat. Handsome and splendidly warm though it is, perhaps this hat is not the best headgear for anyone who is not very tall, very Russian, or very unselfconscious.

Hats have long been a stock prop for comedians. One thinks of Chaplin's and Laurel and Hardy's little bowlers, Keaton's pancake boater, the broken-down top hat of Harpo Marx worn at the back of his curly blond wig—props and trademarks all. Gangsters, according to the old movies, never went hatless; and I gather the fact that so many gangsters in the 1920s were photographed wearing costly hats, usually with extravagantly broad brims, drastically hurt the hat business. A cowboy without a hat is suitable only for bartending. A spy ought to wear a hat; so ought a detective, and an insurance man, and anyone whose job carries the title of commissioner. I would go a step further and say that all jobs that carry the title commissioner ought to come with a hat.

A number of other jobs should require a hat, and I mean a serious hat: a pinched-front, gray-felt, small-feather-in-a-black-band, I-kid-you-not, grown-up man's hat. As many jobs are nowadays referred to as "hard hat" jobs, so ought there to be "serious hat" jobs. A bank officer should wear a serious hat, and so should a chief of police and all judges (circuit court on up). No man should be hired for a university presidency until he is seen in such a hat; and if he looks ridiculous in one, then perhaps search committees would do best to find another man for the job. Perhaps something of the grandeur of the United States would be restored if senators volunteered to wear serious hats. Let's face it, there have to be some adults around here someplace.

Heads of state once wore crowns, but today they ought at least to wear, as Mikhail Gorbachev, I note, did when he showed up in New York City, a gray-felt, two-inch-brim, suede-finish job. No American president has regularly worn a hat since Lyndon Johnson, and then he wore a Texas special (about six and a half gallons, by my rough reckoning). John F. Kennedy wore a top hat to his inaugural and a serious hat on rare occasions; Richard M. Nixon sometimes wore a hat. Ronald Reagan wore no hat, except a cowboy number when riding on his ranch in California, and the mere idea of a hat on Jimmy Carter—who brought the first hot comb and blow-dryer into the White House—is laughable. President Carter was too carefully coiffed to wear a hat, and hats are hell on ambitious male hairdos.

Hat or hairdo, a man cannot have both, and thirty or so years ago, before the advent of male hairstyling, most men chose hats. A man's hat was, moreover, a thing to which he could easily become strongly attached. After all, it traveled with him day after day; it underwent the same heavy weather; it was part of his style and manner of addressing the world. If in time a man's hat came to look a little the worse for wear, so, probably, did he. Frank Sullivan, author of *The Night the Old Nostalgia Burned Down* and other works, in a piece entitled "A Man Never Drops a Hat," wrote about a twelve-year-old hat he was forced to relinquish: "I should never have deserted the faithful friend if there had been enough left of it to be true to." Sullivan recounts how hatcheck girls handled his hat "with disdain and tongs," while others made jokes about it. Still, he writes: "I grew to love that hat as only a man can love an old hat, and perhaps in its mute hatlike way it grew fond of me." Frank Sullivan was what is technically known as a humorist, but I am not altogether certain that he is kidding here.

Two ways to view an old hat: one is that it is beat-up and misshapen; the other is that it is nicely broken in. In the World War II movies of my childhood, the ace American fighter pilots—frequently played by Dana Andrews, Van Johnson, Robert Taylor, among others—always wore leather-billed service caps with what was known as "the fifty-mission crush," meaning that they had survived a great many dangerous missions and, like their owners, had been through a lot. These hats always had a comfortable, marvelously natural look, especially when their wearers pushed them slightly to the backs of their heads. My own somewhat similar hat, worn while serving in the peacetime army in the late 1950s, had a no-mission non-crush, and its rigid leather headband invariably left a welt-like red mark across my forehead. Wearing that hat, which I did as seldom as I could, I always felt uncomfortable and unnatural, as if I were missing something large and important. Missing, I came to conclude, was a bus, for in that hat I felt less like a soldier than a bus driver.

The late Arnaldo Momigliano, the distinguished historian of the ancient world, wore hats that had the civilian equivalent of the fifty-mission crush, except that in Arnaldo's case the hat looked as if he had been shot down over enemy territory on each mission and had managed his various escapes through a series of swamps, bogs, deserts, and avalanches. Arnaldo dressed with that disregard for the niceties of haberdashery permitted only to the world's greatest thinkers and scholars. (Recall Einstein, who always dressed to the nines, negative integer.) Arnaldo simply did not care about clothes, except for the warmth they gave, and this showed nowhere more than in his treatment of his hats. Small, dark gray, not inexpensive—they were in fact Borsalinos—after being in his possession for only a few months they looked, as befitted an ancient historian, as if they had been on winter campaign with Hannibal. Traveling with Arnaldo by plane, I have seen him stuff his hat into an already fully crammed overhead compartment as if it were a scarf, or perhaps an envelope, then slam the compartment door shut without giving it another thought. Those hats paid a heavy price for riding on top of so interesting a head.

Arnaldo Momigliano knew very well the comic condition of his own hats. He once gave me a brief account of shopping at a rather swank Borsalino store in Milan, at a time when it had become plain even to him that another of his gravely mutilated hats must be retired. The Borsalino salesman evidently knew, if not precisely who Arnaldo Momigliano was, that he was a man of great distinction, and his respect for men of distinction easily eclipsed any contempt he may have felt for the professor's unpressed, only approximately fitted clothes. Great care was devoted to waiting on him, to making certain that this new hat—*il povero cappello*, what brutal treatment awaited it—was a proper fit. When the sale had been concluded, Arnaldo asked about his old hat. "Ah, *professore*," said the salesman with a slight bow, "not to worry. We have already taken care of it." Momigliano's wonderfully expressive eyebrows jumped slightly over his glasses, he smiled with his head bent slightly to the right, and the index finger on his right hand was extended to make an undotted exclamation point to close the unspoken sentence, "What exquisite tact!"

The earliest photograph I have of myself taken while wearing a hat shows a boy of three or four, in a tweed fingertip coat, clutching a bag of penny candy, standing on the balcony of an apartment in New York, ample cheeks puffed out by a forced-for-the-camera smile, sandy-colored bangs showing under a leather flier's cap that buttons under the chin and has goggles attached. One can read much into this uncandid snapshot. Here is a little boy who has had much love. He will require vast quantities of attention later in life. He will not be easily pleased. Figures to have dental troubles. May just develop a thing about hats.

When I was a boy, it occurs to me now, I always had one or another kind of hat. I recall a not very impressive Indian headdress and, later, a more impressive Daniel Boone coonskin cap with a real raccoon tail. I had a number of brightly colored stocking caps, some that trailed down my back with a tassel at the end. There was a white navy gob's cap and several dark blue watch caps. A thick wool red-and-black-checked cap with earflaps that I lost, maybe on purpose. Various baseball caps came my way, especially in grammar school days, and I broke in the bills of all of them, shaping them tentlike, as soon as I acquired them, in imitation of big-league ballplayers of the day. I remember in particular a red hat, an amalgam of a baseball and a hunting cap, that gave me pleasure every time I wore it. At ten years old, I thought I looked terrific in that hat; wearing it lifted my spirits, which were not low to begin with, and made me feel I was (in the phrase of the day) an astonishingly neat guy. Odd, is it not, how a piece of clothing—a hat, a shirt, a necktie, or a jacket—can induce one to take the most generous view of oneself and can bring one more sustained happiness than a good idea.

A hat that brought me no happiness at all was the maroon baseball cap I wore for nine or ten weeks during the sixth grade when I had a bout of—even now the word brings back the smells and sensation of shame—ringworm. A certain amount of it was then, as they say, "going around." Children of my generation were told not to put their heads on the backs of their seats at the movies, for this was supposed to be the main cause for the spread of the infection. I don't know if I caught mine at the movies or elsewhere, but one night I began scratching my scalp fiercely, and the next day my mother took me to the dermatologist with the most powerful reputation in Chicago. With large, confident hands, he held my head firmly under an ultraviolet light. "Yep," he said, unmoved, "he's got it."

The consequences following from that "Yep" were that I had to have my head shaved and that each night my mother washed my scalp in some special solution that smelled like every hospital corridor I have since walked, after which she spread a vile-smelling purplish salve over the infection. I had to wear a gruesome stocking cap made out of an old nylon stocking, over which I wore my maroon baseball cap. Having ringworm seemed like having what we kids used to call "cooties," but to the highest power. It seemed to me at the time a humiliation and a damnation and a bloody embarrassment. I brought a note to school that told of my infection and explained that I would have to wear my hat in class. No one, as I recall, teased me, no one made me feel any more leperish than I already felt. But one morning, walking along the halls between classes, our principal, a little man in an invariably gray suit whose name was Herman Ritow, snatched the hat off my head, exclaiming angrily, "Young gentlemen do not wear hats indoors." I stood there, my nylon-stocking cap over my shaved head, feeling exposed and utterly ashamed. Realizing that he had made a mistake, he apologized, but I felt unmasked as I never have since and hope never to be again.

To contradict the estimable Mr. Ritow, young gentlemen nowadays do wear hats indoors. Occasionally, a male student will show up in one of my classes wearing a hat, which puts it up to me to decide whether or not to call him on it. Often, I do, though usually not directly, preferring the sly-dog to the head-on confrontational approach in such matters. "That hat, Mr. Swenson," I recall once asking a young man wearing in class the black-and-orange cap of the San Francisco Giants, "are you wearing it for religious reasons?" When—shocking to report—he allowed that he wasn't, I gently signaled that he remove it, which he did without fuss. In a larger class, on another occasion, I noticed a student sitting toward the back of the room wearing a tight wool watch cap. He was a superior student, and so I decided to say nothing about his hat until after class, when, stopping him at the door, I asked, "Mr. Weiner, why are you wearing that hat?" "I was late this morning," he replied, "and didn't have time to shampoo." He then removed his hat, which released a small violence of curly, kinky, and spiky hair, a live and mobile bramble patch. "Mr. Weiner," said I, "please put your hat back on before you put out someone's eye."

But it is not the young alone who ignore the etiquette of wearing hats. On an airplane to New York, I not long ago sat a few rows behind a professor from the University of Chicago who wore his hat—a suede sports-car cap—for nearly the entire flight. Men wear hats of all kinds in supermarkets and in department stores and on buses. A man who regularly tipped or even touched the brim of his hat when passing women or acquaintances would likely today be thought to have a tic. Baseball players still take off their hats when the national anthem is played, but I'm not sure many other men do. The seasonal rhythm of changing men's hats must by now be almost lost, so that a passage such as the following from Eudora Welty's *The Optimist's Daughter* will one day seem—if it does not seem so already—as obscure as an Aztec rite for killing poultry: "Back home, Judge

McKelva had always set the example for Mount Salus in putting aside his winter hat on Straw Hat Day, and he stood here now in his creamy panama." What a charming detail! Here's mud in your eye, Judge, and none on that creamy panama.

As the etiquette associated with wearing hats has all but disappeared, the institutions once in existence to deal with the care and maintenance of men's hats have disappeared completely. Establishments that cleaned and blocked men's hats, once ubiquitous on the cityscape, are now quite as difficult to find as new castanet or phylactery repair shops. Presumably, nowadays when a hat becomes dirty or begins to lose its shape, one pitches it out, even though it is not uncommon for a good man's hat to go for more than a hundred dollars. Leather hatboxes, of the kind I imagine Proust, the Duke of Windsor, and other serious wearers of serious hats must have had, are simply no longer available outside of antique shops. Hatcheck concessions in nightclubs and good restaurants, manned (make that womanned, you sexist dog) by hatcheck girls (always called girls no matter how old they were), are distinctly a thing of the past, with the consequence that the care of one's hat when on the town is pretty much one's own lookout. Even such a reliable old figure of speech as "If I'm wrong about that, I'll eat my hat" no longer has any grip, since the chances are great that the man who has said it isn't wearing a hat.

"If you're right about that," men used to say in the heat of argument, "I'll buy you a new hat." I don't say it, nor does anyone say it to me, but that doesn't stop me from buying myself a new hat whenever I come upon one that strikes me as amusing or that might make me as suavely dashing a figure as I secretly have always felt myself to be. I haven't thus far found the latter hat, but I have acquired a fair number of the former. I have owned a deerstalker cap (à la Sherlock

Holmes) in a material of bold checks; a wide-brimmed soft white hat fit for a deeply tanned Davis Cup official in the glory days of amateur tennis; a World War II tanker helmet (which I used to play football when I was in grammar school); a dark blue cap, with lots of what in the military used to be called scrambled eggs across its bill, of the kind worn by astronauts aboard battleships after they have completed successful celestial cruises; and authentic replicas of the caps—the most chastely elegant in all of baseball, in my view—of the Boston Red Sox and the St. Louis Cardinals. I no longer own any of these chapeaux. I have given some away to people who expressed admiration for them, misplaced others, allowed all somehow to get away from me.

A hat I still own, one that even as I write this sentence sits on my skull, is a rich blue baseball-style cap with the interlocking letters N and D in gold thread woven across its front, which stands for Notre Dame. It cost fourteen dollars and is a fine piece of goods but for one flaw: it has a small piece of plastic belting at the back that allows one to adjust it to fit different head sizes. It is, in other dreary words, what is known as "one size fits all." One-size-fits-all must be a boon to cap makers, who no longer have to worry about sizing hats to the eighth inch, but it does take the notion of individuality away from one's hat. Would Henry James have worn a one-size-fits-all hat? Would Oscar Wilde? Or either of the Brothers Goncourt? Seems doubtful. Among literary men, perhaps only Tolstoy, who late in life fancied a floppy peasant's hat, and Walt Whitman, who affected a high-crowned, broad-brimmed hat for the frontispiece of *Leaves of Grass*, would have gone for it. Whitman might even have written a poem, one of those democratic dithyrambs he specialized in, entitled "One Size Fits All":

Send me your fat-, your large-, and your lumpy-
     headed,
Your crania quite narrow, most pointy, and small.
America, where the shape of a head need not be
     regretted,
Great Democratic land where one size fits any and all.

Max Beerbohm once wrote rather a better poem about his old man-about-town top hat, which he abandoned when he left England to live permanently in Italy:

Once I used to perch on Max Beerbohm's pate,
But now he's become Italianate;
So here in contempt and disregard
I moulder for ever at Appletree Yard.

A photograph of the Italianate and quite aged Max Beerbohm hangs on my wall, and in it he, the dear old dandy, is sitting upon a wicker chair on the balcony of his villa at Rapallo. At the time this photograph was taken, he must have arrived at his eighties, which did not impair his fastidiousness. In the photograph he is nicely turned out in a cream-colored soft flannel suit with white waistcoat and dark tie and dark socks. But the crown on this jewel of a man is his hat, a straw boater worn at what I believe used to be called a rakish angle. It is a fine finishing touch. My guess is that Max would wear this hat when alone, standing on his balcony staring out at the limpid blue Mediterranean. Many a deliciously impish, interestingly charming thought must have floated beneath that old straw boater.

I was myself last seen in Italy in a hat altogether un-Italianate. It is a cotton khaki number, with a soft crown and a narrow red-and-blue headband and widish brim that I usually wear pulled down all the way round. I try to wear it with panache, but I am fairly sure it doesn't come off; the general effect is a bit suburban, not to say public golf course. I was last seen donning this hat in Florence, in the Piazza Signoria, near the Palazzo Vecchio, a plaid short-sleeve shirt on my back, copies of Christopher Hibbert's book on the Medicis and Montaigne's *Travel Journal* in my hand, cleverly disguised as a simple, rather unworldly American tourist.

Among Europeans, the English were traditionally a notably well-lidded people. The Victorians and Edwardians had splendid hats in rich assortment. Winston Churchill was a hat man, and his hats, worn either on state occasions or in leisure, never disappointed; on him they all seemed very Churchillian. Rex Harrison made popular the soft checkered hat he wore as Professor Henry Higgins in *My Fair Lady*. Before his disgrace, Jeremy Thorpe, then leader of the Liberal Party, brought back the low-crowned, narrow-brimmed hat known as the trilby (named after the chief character in George du Maurier's novel *Trilby*). Bowler hats, which every Englishman who worked in the City used to wear, are nowadays much less in evidence in London. I'm not sure that today there is a characteristic English hat. A pity, I feel, though I am not exactly sure why I feel that it is. Room here for a theory? When a nation loses its empire, I wonder, does it also lose its hats?

The male beret, like the baguette, may seem a staple of French life, but one doesn't think of Frenchman as behatted. Charles de Gaulle is most readily recalled in his kepi, but recent French premiers—Giscard d'Estaing, Mitterrand—balding though they are, have sought their own versions of *la gloire* pretty much bareheaded.

Camus, Malraux, Sartre, the most famous French literary men of the past half century, were almost always photographed, outdoors as well as in, hatless. André Gide was sometimes photographed in his library wearing over his starkly bald pate a largish skullcap—Sainte-Beuve, a century earlier, wore a plainer version of the same cap—of the kind favored by the Sephardic Jews of North Africa.

Which brings me to my good friends the Jews—"Some of my best Jews," a rabbi who, during the 1960s, lost many of his congregants to Quakerism is supposed to have exclaimed, "are Friends"—whose males, according to Orthodox tradition, are supposed to keep their heads covered in the sight of God. Oddly, apart from the small skull-cap called the yarmulke, the Jews have not invented any particular headgear that I know about. True, the Hasidic Jews of Eastern Europe wore, or at least the wealthier among them did, an extravagantly fur-trimmed circular hat. But otherwise Jews have worn the hats of the countries in which they live. Among the ultra-Orthodox, one comes upon small boys wearing black versions of what I have been calling serious men's hats, which adultifies them, and it always takes me slightly aback. Normally observant Jewish boys of college age, dressed in every other way quite as their contemporaries are, will wear doily-sized yarmulkes held in place toward the back of their heads with bobby pins. Coming out of the Princeton Club in New York a few months ago, I saw such a young man walking in. *Ah*, thought I, *F. Scott Teitelbaum.*

Having established by these remarks what in our touchy times will pass as my bona fides as a Jewish anti-Semite, let me double down, as they say in Vegas, and see if I can't win some points for being a racist by asserting that, for some while now, black men have worn hats with more flair than anyone else in America. Sidney Poitier looks

the newest, resembling Nehru's Congress Party cap, but rounded, a cross between a cantor's hat and a bloated yarmulke; or perhaps like a French judge's in Rouault, or a working doctor's in a Daumier print"). Gogol, of course, wrote "The Overcoat"; a shame he didn't write "The Hat" to go with it. John O'Hara published a collection of stories entitled *The Hat on the Bed*, and one of his stories in another collection, *Assembly*, is about a man whose most salient characteristic, at the outset of the story, is that he wears a plastic rain cover for his hat. When, in Flaubert's novel, Bouvard and Pécuchet meet for the first time on the Boulevard Bourdon, they fall into conversation only because they discover that each has taken the precaution to write his own name into his hat. And what, in *Alice's Adventures in Wonderland*, drove the Mad Hatter mad, exactly? Clearly, we have here a rich subject: hats in literature. Perhaps we ought to open the canon, as they nowadays say in university English departments, where they always have plenty of loose cannons around, and let in Hat Lit.

I have recently had lunches with two men who wore serious hats and had serious titles to go with them: one a gray-pinched-front-wearing federal judge, the other a mellow-copper-shading-into-brown-trilby-wearing former ambassador. Both lunches gave me much pleasure. But more to my oblique point is how correct these gents—one of whom is younger than I, the other older—seemed in their hats. Caps wouldn't have done for either of them, and to have gone bareheaded on the wintry days on which we met would have seemed foolhardy for men who had impressive responsibilities. How is it, I ask myself now, that they wore their hats, while my green hat seems to wear me, leaving me standing there with the earlier-mentioned mien of an indisposed spaniel?

I think it is that though my hair grows grayer and thinner, my eyes pouchier and dimmer, though I realize that I shall never sing at the Carlisle, live in Paris, or be adored for my divine physical grace, though I rely heavily on my age and experience in teaching the young and am pleased to have lived through an interesting half century of history, even though and despite and notwithstanding all of this, I, in some part of my decreasingly agile mind, continue to think myself, if not exactly a youth, then nevertheless a young fella. "There's nobody too old to be young," Saul Bellow wrote in *The Dean's December.* "That's the present outlook." I wish it weren't mine. One afternoon not long ago, the more I thought about it, the more disappointed in myself I became.

I strode to the closet, put on a raincoat and scarf, and clapped the green hat on my head. It was late afternoon, but still light, and I had a few errands to run. I looked at myself in the mirror before I left and the effect, despite my determination, was still pure spaniel. So be it. I walked into the downtown section of the town in which I live, attempting to appear nonchalant while keeping an eye peeled for anyone who might be giggling at me in my hat. I walked two blocks at a brisk pace, looking at reflections of myself in store windows whenever I passed them. The green hat still seemed strange sitting there atop my head. But no one, near as I could make out, was laughing or gazing upon me with a look that implied, "Catch the turkey in the green hat!"

A young woman asked me for directions to the local YWCA, which in my green hat I gave and she took with a perfectly straight face. In the stores where I shopped, and in the library where I picked up a book, I removed my hat, but no one seemed to think it odd that I was carrying such a hat. True, I met no friends or acquaintances, who might have remarked witheringly on my new headgear, but I kept moving through that cold and drizzly Midwestern afternoon, eager to return to my apartment without being jolted by odd or hilarious looks.

When I was back in the apartment, I left my hat on, with its now single-mission crush, to see if I looked any different in it. In the mirror I looked not like a spaniel but like a boxer—not a prizefighter, that is, but the breed of dog: my eyes under the hat were red-rimmed and a touch rheumy from the cold and I seemed to myself rather jowly. Well, a boxer is not yet an adult male of mature years, but it does beat a spaniel, at least in my view. It's a start. I intend to make further outings in my hat. If you happen to see a smallish man in a green velour hat, stroke his back, scratch him behind the ears, give him a biscuit if you have one on you, but whatever you do, please don't laugh at him. He's only trying to act his age.

(1989)

A Few Kind Words for Envy

Well, though many an arraigned mortal has in hopes of mitigated penalty pleaded guilty to horrible actions, did ever anybody seriously confess to envy? Something there is in it universally felt to be more shameful than even felonious crime.

—Herman Melville

You may as well know the worst about me, Doctor: I have not coveted my neighbor's wife in years, and I certainly do not want his Rolls-Royce, his duplex, or his shiny new fax machine. The young walk by, with their lithe limbs and clear minds, the years and years stretching out leisurely before them, and I feel no longing to change places with them. Neither do I desire to be a United States senator, a university president, the benevolent dictator of a small, mineral-rich country nestled in a lush setting in a lovely mild climate. I have no longing to enjoy the emoluments of the editor of the *New York Times*, the president of L'Académie Française, or Magic Johnson. Please do not understand me too quickly here, Doctor. I am not, I assure you, expressing complacency, smug (isn't *smug* the inevitable adjective here?) self-satisfaction with my own lot in life. No, something deeper, more mysterious, is going on. I am, not to put too fine a point on it, losing my capacity for envy, and I wonder, Doc, what can it mean?

I suppose none of this would worry me if, for so many years, I hadn't envied so widely, so thoroughly, so energetically. Many were the mornings I woke envying and many the nights I retired to envy, with time off for several little breaks for envy during the day. I read somewhere that one of the few benefits of growing older is that, in one's psychic economy, envy is replaced by admiration. I am not sure what I currently do with the time I once lavished upon envy, but I am quite sure that I do not pay it out in admiration. Can it be, too, that, now that I envy less, I shall grow fatter, for Horace, in the *Epistles*, remarks that "those who envy others grows thin despite vast wealth" (of envy, he adds, "Sicilian tyrants could never have contrived a better torture"). Is my loss of envy, then, likely to result in substantial weight gain? Am I, by envying insufficiently, endangering my health, Doc?

To begin my life not quite with the beginning of my life, the first thing I can remember envying was the parents of two boys I grew up with named Sammy and Billy Cowling. I loved my parents a very great deal, you understand, but on paper they just didn't stack up next to the Cowlings' parents. For openers, their father, Sam Cowling Sr., was on the radio; he was the comedian on a then immensely popular radio show called *The Breakfast Club*, where, among other things, he did a bit known as Fiction and Fact from Sam's Almanac. Even at five years old, I knew that being on the radio was pretty hot stuff. He also happened to be a friendly man, kindly and thoughtful to children, and a good athlete. Sam Cowling Sr. owned baseball spikes. I knew of no other father but the Cowlings' who owned spikes. Mrs. Cowling was feminine, beautifully so, and named (are you quite ready for this?) Dale, which was the name of Roy Rogers's wife. The Cowlings seemed so wondrous to me as a child that, in those days, I shouldn't have been surprised to learn that they kept a flowing-maned palomino in the dining room of their two-bedroom apartment. I don't want anyone to think that I envied the Cowling kids their parents so much that I would have traded my own for them. I would never finally have done that, but before deciding not to do it, I believe I would have had to give it considerable thought.

The second thing I remember envying was Catholics. For a time, from roughly age four to seven, I thought the United States was a Catholic country. This was owing partly to there being a preponderance of Catholic families on our block and partly to the movies of those years, a large number of which seemed to feature Bing Crosby, Barry Fitzgerald, Spencer Tracy, and Pat O'Brien playing priests. I envied the rigmarole of the Catholic Church, at least as it came across to me in the movies and in the bits and pieces of it I was able to pick up from families such as the Cowlings. Nothing theological or even religious about this, for I was in fact rather like Valéry, who felt that the Protestants had made a big mistake and should have gotten rid of God and kept the pope. I liked the lighting of candles, the confessional, the prohibition against meat on Fridays, the clothes of priests and the extraordinary getups of nuns. "May I offer you my seat, Sister?" I used to say whenever the opportunity presented itself on Chicago streetcars or el trains. "Excuse me, Father, but would you care to have my seat?" I would announce with just a slight hint of an Irish brogue. Any fisher of souls who knew his business could have had me in the net in those days in fewer than thirty seconds.

I keenly envied friends who had hair of a kind that could be combed to resemble the hairdos of Gary Cooper, Cary Grant, Clark Gable, John Wayne, Errol Flynn, and other movie stars of the day. My own hair was thick, curly, thoroughly disobedient. It resisted pompadours, widow's peaks, and wouldn't even tolerate a simple part. "My goodness," I remember my mother once saying to me, "that part in your hair looks like Milwaukee Avenue," a reference to a lengthy diagonal street in Chicago that every so often juts sharply to the left or right or takes a surprising turn. I longed for precisely the kind of hair I didn't have—for lank hair that bopped up and down rhythmically when I ran and that I would frequently have to brush back out of my eyes with my hand. When crew cuts became the haircut of choice for Midwestern boys between twelve and eighteen, my hair wouldn't allow a serious flattop crew cut, either. All my attempts to obtain a crew cut ended in my coming away with an extremely short haircut that, mocking the power of prayer and pomade, would not stand up. Wishing to look like a brutish Big Ten athlete, I merely looked, as I am told an immigrant woman in Princeton once put it, like "a nice boy clean and cut from the Ivory League."

None of this, I realize, quite sounds like the envy that has had such a poor historical press. I refer to the envy that Balzac, in *Lost Illusions*, described as "an ignoble accumulation of disappointed hope, frustrated talents, failures, and wounded pretensions"; that Orwell called "a horrible thing," which "is unlike all other kinds of suffering in that there is no disguising it"; that the Austrian novelist Marie von Ebner-Eschenbach rated beneath hatred, noting that "hatred is a fertile, envy a sterile vice"; and that Gore Vidal, a writer scarcely known for specializing in the goodness of humankind, cites as "the only credible emotion, isn't it?" The motive for Cain's slaying of Abel was envy. Melville's splendid *Billy Budd* shows the horror that envy acted upon can achieve. "The vilest affection," Francis Bacon called envy, "and the most depraved," and in cataloguing by type those frequently obsessed by envy, he writes: "Deformed persons, and eunuchs, and old men, and bastards, are envious." Not, as I say, a good historical press.

Envy is apparently more easily felt than defined. Semantically, the word provides a thicket out of which only a philologist in a pith helmet and carrying a magnifying glass is likely to emerge with his spirits intact. Envy and jealousy, envy and emulation, envy and invidiousness, envy and ambition, envy and desire, the distinctions, the connections, the shades of meaning, the contextual nuances, all these things, if tracked down and carefully considered, could keep a fellow off the streets till well after the turn of the century. As there are some faces only a mother could love, so are there some books only a German scholar could write, and just such a book, *Envy: A Theory of Social Behaviour*, has been written by a Professor Helmut Schoeck, but it, on the matter of definition, plunges one back into the thicket. The standard dictionaries, I fear, are not very helpful on this troublesome word, either. I have, therefore, decided to supply my own definition: envy, I say, is desiring what someone else has—a desire usually heightened by the knowledge that one is unlikely to attain it. This definition nicely accommodates my feelings about Sam and Billy Cowling's parents, the Catholic Church, and tractable hair.

My homemade definition leaves out the dark elements of spite, hostility, ill will, and begrudgment that most definitions of envy usually include. These elements cause the Parson, in *The Canterbury Tales*, to call envy "that foul sin . . . the worst sin there is"; these elements give envy its unenviable status as one of the seven deadly sins. Yet there is also a milder, even approbative sense of envy that is free from all malice, as when the Reverend Sydney Smith, writing to Francis Jeffrey, remarks: "I envy your sense, your style, and the good temper with which you attack prejudices that drive me almost to the limits of sanity." I don't think that Sydney Smith, who chose his words punctiliously, misused *envy* here and that he really meant *admire*—he not only admired these qualities in Jeffrey but wished he had them himself.

Along the same line, I recall several years ago, awaiting a table in a restaurant, sitting in a bar in which a man was hired to play, on a small electric organ, such sappy songs as "I Left My Heart in San Francisco," "The Way We Were," and "Raindrops Keep Fallin' on My Head." The unspoken consensus in the bar was that plainly this man loved his work too much, for he was banging away at his instrument with a fervor almost religious in intensity, making conversation just about impossible. Then, during a brief pause between numbers, a smallish, well-dressed man, a customer sitting only a few seats away from my own, walked over to him, handed him a hundred-dollar bill, and told him to take the rest of the night off. How I not only admired but envied that gesture, the rightness and not least the largeness of it! The fellow seemed pleased with the money, which was probably more than his regular night's wages; the room settled down into calm talk; and I felt a tinge of envy for what I had just witnessed, knowing that, had the notion even occurred to me, I probably would have offered the man a mere twenty bucks to knock off for an hour or so.

Not that I haven't felt my share of rich purple envy, the kind mixed with lots of malice and generally grudging feeling. But I don't recall feeling much envy of this kind when young. Such envy as I did feel was instead rather impersonal. I envied the freedom and wider experience of kids older than I; I envied boys who had the knack of winning the affection of beautiful girls; finally I envied those who had the unfailing ability to make themselves enviable. Being born to parents of middling wealth and being oneself of middling talent is surely to know envy more comprehensively than otherwise, for it permits envy of those both above and beneath you. From my earliest adolescence, I recognized that there were families who lived better than mine—in larger houses, with more expensive cars, and more capacious habits generally—and felt them, somehow, luckier than I. But I also felt envy for those born without my advantages, and the constraints that went along with them, and I remember reading, in high school, a series of novels with slum settings—*A Stone for Danny Fisher*, *The Amboy Dukes*, *The Hoods*—that made me feel that people who grew up in slums grew up more interestingly, sexier, luckier than I. Envy perhaps begins with the attribution of luck to the next fellow, for it seems that people with a real flair for envy—of whom I was clearly one—almost always sees the next fellow as, somehow, luckier than themselves.

Very little about my youthful envy was subtle, and this, I believe, was owing to my having grown up in a family in which snobbery was almost nonexistent. Delicate, and even rather bulky, calibrations in status were of no concern to my parents, who did not bother to make many social distinctions beyond noting that some people were pleasant and some nasty, some rich and some poor, some Gentile and some Jewish. Not at our dinner table were you likely to hear discussions about the fine distinctions between Williams and Amherst colleges, a Brooks Brothers and a J. Press suit, the Budapest and the Juilliard string quartets. The Midwest was my milieu, and Midwestern the outer limits of my view. In both my own high school graduating class and in the class that preceded mine, only two students went to Ivy League schools—both, as it happened, to Harvard—and neither was a boy it would have occurred to me to envy. For envy to take on interesting twists, shadings, and dark refinements, a little knowledge—always, as the old maxim has it, a dangerous thing—is required.

Three writers who did, I think, know a good deal about envy, young and at first hand, were F. Scott Fitzgerald, John O'Hara, and the journalist George Frazier. Fitzgerald, who lived in the poorest house on a very good block in St. Paul, Minnesota, learned about envy as a boy and had this knowledge honed as a young man who ran the gauntlet of snobbery at Princeton. The great event of John O'Hara's life turned out to be a nonevent, his not going to Yale, which, wise though O'Hara was in so many other ways, he appears never to have gotten over. George Frazier, who came from the Irish neighborhood in Boston known as Southie, went to Harvard but with the certainty that, as an Irishman in the early 1930s, he could never hope to make the best clubs or quite cut it with students who came from the best families and prep schools. Frazier was an admirer of the fiction of Fitzgerald and O'Hara, and all three men were immensely, intensely interested not only in style but in stylishness. Frazier even wrote a column in *Esquire* under the rubric "Style," which tended to be about people who had it and people who didn't. The three men also shared Irishness, at a time in our history when being Irish did not carry the comfortable, vaguely comical connotations it does today. I think they never got over the feeling of being boys and young men with their noses pressed to the glass, outsiders looking enviously in. Too keen an interest in style, I have come to suspect, betrays an early life of longing and envy.

The best-known method for combating envy is to arrange to acquire everything you want in life. Unfortunately, it often takes the better part of a lifetime to decide what, precisely, it is that you do want, which leaves damnably little time to acquire it. "I suppose you must be well," wrote Virgil Thomson to Paul Bowles, "you had everything there was when you were young; nothing left to have, I suppose." An odd error, in so worldly-wise a man as Virgil Thomson, to think that wanting ever ceases. So long as avarice, lust, the appetite for glory, and snobbery continue to play as main attractions in the human heart, there is unlikely to be any serious shortage of wanting.

The sorting out of one's wants, especially when one is young, can be nearly a full-time job. I believe it was so for me, for, as I look back upon my young manhood, there was scarcely anything I didn't want and hence didn't vaguely find myself resenting in those who had it. I had only to see a beautiful woman with another man for my mind to jump to the question—the injustice, really—of why she was not instead with me. I would drive by suburban estates, walk past plush Park Avenue apartment buildings, and readily imagine myself happily ensconced therein. A Rolls-Royce convertible would tool by and, the resentment string in my heart plucking discordantly, I would not wish its owner well. (Not long ago, being driven in heavy traffic in a flashy raspberry-colored Cadillac Seville, I suggested to the car's owner, an intelligent woman who takes the world as it is, that she put out her arm to request a break in the traffic so that she could get into the next lane. "I'm afraid," she said, "that in a car like this people tend not to give you many breaks.") When I was young all I really wanted from the world was money, power, and fame—and, naturally, the little perks that went along with them.

The problem, I have long since concluded, is that I spread my desire too thin. I merely wanted everything—but nothing, evidently, greatly enough. I also hit a lengthy detour in my desirousness—I am, apparently, still on it—when I developed this strange passion for acquiring the knack of writing interesting sentences. Although this passion freed me from the comprehensive generality of my desires, it concentrated my envy. For the first time, my envy lost its character of general longing and took a turn toward the particular, where envy usually gets unpleasant. What I now envied, with some intensity, was people of my own generation—I was then in my early twenties—who wrote better than I. Since I did not write all that well, my envy was given a wide berth and a fine chance for regular workouts. Around this time I can recall reading, in a biographical note, that a contributor to *Poetry*, a magazine I much admired, was born in 1940, which was three years later than I, a fact that registered like a rabbit punch to the kidneys. I didn't write poetry, you understand; nevertheless it seemed to me offensive for this young woman, three years my junior, to publish in a place in which I should have loved to publish had I written poetry. If this sounds a little crazy to you, not to worry; it only sounds crazy because it is.

The first of my contemporaries of whom I felt envious was a fellow undergraduate at the University of Chicago who had published a short story at the unconscionable age of sixteen. He had published it, moreover, not in some vulgar popular rag such as the *Saturday Evening Post* or *Redbook*, but in a then immitigably highbrow journal called *New World Writing*, where it appeared alongside work by the likes of Federico García Lorca and Wallace Stevens. I, who dreamed of publication, of seeing my name not in lights but in very small type, and who knew that publication, with luck, was still several years off, looked upon this boy and felt the sting of the world's terrible injustice. I also felt toward him a simple desire to exchange lives. I do not say that I despised him—he was very amiable, without the least air of superiority—but I should have preferred he matriculate elsewhere, so that his presence not remind me of my own drearily slow progress. Strangely, so far as I know, he never published another thing. Did some personal tragedy intervene, I wonder, or was his petering out owing to his own lack of sufficient envy?

Writers and musicians tend to be rivalrous, which means, inevitably, envious and jealous. (Jealousy, Professor Schoeck holds, "remains the passionate endeavor to keep something that is one's own by right," whereas envy has to do with wanting something belonging to another.) Painters, for some reason, seem less envious of one another, or at least I, with limited knowledge, can think of more genuinely comradely behavior among painters than among musicians and writers. (All exceptions granted: John Morley, for example, said that Matthew Arnold "had not a spark of envy or jealousy.") Envy figures to be deepest at the top. Isaac Stern is famously generous to young musicians, but is he, I wonder, sound on the subject of Jascha Heifetz? At a dinner party in heaven, I think it probably a good idea not to invite, on the same evening, Shakespeare, Goethe, and Tolstoy; nor would I recommend seating Leonardo and Michelangelo next to each other. Having achieved great fame, having garnered all the world's great prizes, does not necessarily slake envy. Nor are scientists free from envy. "Don't call X this morning," a friend once advised of a scientific acquaintance of ours. "The Nobel Prize was announced, and since he didn't win it again this year, he's likely to be in a foul mood." The joke here is that, a few years earlier, X had already won it.

But then artists and scientists have no monopoly on envy; it is merely that their often monstrous egotism tends to display it in high comic relief. Academics are very good at envy, too, and it takes so little to get their envy into gear: the slightest advantage or advancement gained by a colleague will usually turn the trick. Modern corporations, sociologists and journalists have been claiming for years, are scarcely more than envy organized. Freud contended that all women, to a lesser or greater degree, were envious, because of the absence in their own anatomy of a certain male appendage—as sweeping a generalization as our century has to offer. And as long as we're talking appendages, Melanie Klein, the Freudian psychoanalyst, maintained that envy is learned, literally, at the breast, and in a paper entitled "Envy and Gratitude" she rattles on at depressing length about "the primary envy of the mother's breast." As a member of a generation whose parents felt breastfeeding was bad form—we, so to speak, dined on takeout—I feel disqualified from commenting on the persuasiveness of Dr. Klein's argument. I suppose, as the saying is, you had to be there.

Such theories—and I, for one, do not envy anyone who subscribes to them—gain currency chiefly because envy appears to be so universal a phenomenon that an equally universal theory seems to be required to account for it. No known society, from simple tribes organized around a belief in magic to large industrial nations organized around a belief in communist equality, has ever been entirely free from envy, and in many societies—those that are fearful of the evil eye of envy, those that through competition encourage envy—it has been dominant. Envy has long been considered a theological problem, with its power of sowing discord, especially where it abuts its sister sin of pride, for even among saints it is possible to imagine one envying the other's greater spirituality. Spiritual envy is often the subject of the novels and stories of J. F. Powers. The great political (Churchill, de Gaulle), spiritual (Gandhi, Martin Luther King Jr.), and scientific (Freud, Einstein) figures of our century were none of them without envy in their lives. The pope, I am prepared to believe, is without envy, but was he before he became pope? Mother Teresa of Calcutta is the only person alive today that I can think of who appears to be utterly free from envy. Doubtless there are others, but if they were to meet in a convention, I don't think one would need to reserve all the rooms in the Helmsley Palace to accommodate them.

I hope no one thinks that because I began this essay by saying I was running out of envy, I imagine myself approaching the spiritual trim of Mother Teresa. "I have never known life without desire," remarks the hero of Italo Svevo's *Confessions of Zeno*, and neither, I must report, have I. And where there is desire, be assured, nearby envy lurks. I thought, for example, that I had long ago made my peace with money and material possessions. The terms of the treaty, set by me, were entirely in my favor. I liked having money, respected money, had not the least doubt of the importance of money in human affairs. Yet I long ago decided that I would never knowingly truckle for money, or, if I could help it, expend great energy on projects whose sole result was pecuniary gain. Insofar as possible, I felt, everything I did should either amuse me or contribute to my intellectual progress—preferably both. My mind, in this scheme, would dwell in the clouds, my bottom never rest for long on the bottom line.

In exchange, I agreed to surrender all fantasies of real wealth: the country estate, the Paris apartment, the limousine, the staff of unobtrusive but absolutely reliable servants. Such fantasies ought to have been easily enough surrendered, for fairly early in life it became evident to me that I should never be rich. Part of my problem is less an antipathy than an inability to concentrate for long on money. It isn't that my mind is too fine to be violated by money matters, but instead that I haven't the attention span to learn the fundamentals of the stock, commodities, options, and other markets, or even to learn how to get the best out of the smallish sums I am able to save. Part of the problem, too, is that I could never quite imagine myself rich, with all the world's objects within my grasp. You are rich, says

Henry James in *The Portrait of a Lady*, when you can meet the demands of your imagination. My imagination, that nag, would never allow surcease in its demands, so that even with billions I could not, by Jamesian prescription, qualify as rich anyhow.

Do I, I ask myself, envy the very wealthy their riches and what they have brought them? I like to think not, and yet I do find myself taking a perhaps uncommon delight in hearing stories about burglar alarm systems going off in homes with serious art collections and spoiling otherwise gracious meals. Why does my spirit jump a notch when I see a large Mercedes being towed ignominiously off to Rolfe's Auto Repair? Can it be that we have a case here of Schadenfreude, that little subdivision of envy that *Webster's* allows itself the rare luxury of going alliterative to define as "malicious merriment at someone else's misfortune"? La Rochefoucauld gives Schadenfreude a genuinely hideous twist when he turns it very personal and remarks that "we always find something which is not displeasing to us in the misfortunes of our best friends." That is not envy, though—it is merely pure human viciousness. But there is, I think, a national Schadenfreude that is excited by revelations about the ostensibly very fortunate—the rich, the beautiful, the immensely talented—living in great emotional squalor. Howard Hughes supplied the country with Schadenfreudic titillation that lasted for months when it came out that his having a fortune in the billions of dollars did not prevent his living, poor devil, at the emotional level of a rodent. On its dark side, a democracy enjoys few things more than the spectacle of the rich undone, the beautiful besmirched, the talented penalized. See any issue of the *National Enquirer, People,* or *Vanity Fair* for confirmation.

Whatever their other deprivations, academics, intellectuals, and artists find no shortage of occasions for Schadenfreude or straightforward envy. The promotion denied, the manuscript rejected, or the dead-on devastating review can put the ugly little curl into the sympathetic smile of the colleague one had thought, until now, civil enough and not displeased with your success. "The Book of My Enemy Has Been Remaindered" is the title of a poem by Clive James whose refrain lines run: "And I am pleased." "And I rejoice." "And I am glad." Attend the honest Schadenfreude note amusingly played by Mr. James exulting at the defeat of a book by a rival poet:

> What avail him now his awards and prizes,
> The praise expended upon his meticulous technique,
> His individual new voice?
> Knocked into the middle of the next week
> His brainchild now consorts with the bad buys,
> The sinkers, clinkers, dogs and dregs,
> The Edsels of the world of movable type,
> The bummers that no amount of hype could shift,
> The unbudgeable turkeys.

In intellectual life, awards and prizes are no longer quite the efficient swizzle sticks for stirring envy that they once were. Pulitzers, Guggenheims, NEHs, NEAs, honorary degrees—too many of all of these have by now been given out, and to too many mediocre people, for them any longer to carry much prestige, and hence to excite much envy. One award, though, can still do the job—narrow the eyes, quicken the pulse, dry the palms, send a little black cloud across the heart—and this is a MacArthur Fellowship. "It isn't the principle of the thing," my father used to say when attempting to collect bad business debts, "it's the money." And so with "Big Macs," as they are known in the trade, it isn't the prestige—too many not very impressive MacArthur Fellows already walk the earth—it, too, is the money. To win a MacArthur Fellowship is to go on a five-year ride at as much as $75,000 a year, for a total score of nearly four hundred grand. Nowhere near the kind of money that a switch-hitting second baseman can bring down these days, true, but still a nice piece of change.

My own carefully considered view of the MacArthur Fellowships was, I believe, similar to that held by most intellectuals, artists, scientists, performers, and inventors: sheer resentment for just about every nickel that did not go to me. I could understand the foundation's need to come across for a Navajo underwater architect or a woman weight lifter who is making a series of documentary films based on the Talmud; there are, after all, political reasons for such awards. But I failed entirely to understand the reasoning behind all the awards to literary men and women, none of whom, when you came right down to it (which I did rather quickly), seemed nearly so fit for a MacArthur as I. I won't go into my qualifications here, except to say that they seemed to me damn near perfect: my work was unusual and various; from the outside, I must appear overworked; and, like 99 percent of my countrymen, I could use the dough. What was more, a MacArthur Fellowship was one of the few such awards I had any hope of winning, for I had long ago determined never to apply for a grant or prize. If people wished to give me these things, splendid, but I was raised to believe that you didn't ask strangers for money.

So I went along from year to year, happy enough in my mild resentment, gaily mocking each year's fresh crop of MacArthur Fellows, until it was revealed to me that I had myself been nominated for a MacArthur. Good friends even sent me thoughtfully inflated letters of recommendation they had been asked to send in on my behalf.

The envy in my soul now had to make room for its first cousin, greed. I thought a goodly amount in an unconcentrated way about what I might do with the money such a fellowship would bring in. If I had long ago agreed to forgo the large luxurious things, I had a decided taste for the small luxurious things: the German fountain pen, the Italian loafers, the dish of raspberries in midwinter. With my MacArthur Fellowship, there would be more of these things, much more. And, while at it, I ought to acquire some really good luggage. Most of the money, I thought, I would pocket away in some high-yield bank account, perhaps with an eye, at the end of the fellowship's five years, to plunking it all down on a modest house on Fiesole overlooking the red roofs of the city of Florence. The Big Macs were announced, I knew, sometime in the summer, and so about June first I began opening my mailbox in anticipation of finding that envelope from the John D. and Catherine T. MacArthur Foundation informing me that I had won a fellowship and might now, baby, let the good times roll. I thought, too, with some glee, how discouraging my winning a MacArthur Fellowship would be to my enemies. Alas, no letter arrived; it was not to be; and now, with the printing of these last few paragraphs, it isn't ever likely to be.

Had I won a MacArthur Fellowship, of course, I should have stepped across from the shady to the sunny side of the street—from being an envier to being envied. Even without a MacArthur, I might, it occurs to me, already have crossed that street. In the eyes of many, I am among the world's lucky people. And so—I knock wood here, lest the evil eye fall upon me—do I generally think myself. I have all the essential things: work that amuses me, excellent health, freedom, the love of a good-hearted and intelligent woman. Ought not that be sufficient? It ought, except that, human nature being human nature—or is it instead my nature being my nature?—it hasn't been sufficient to diminish envy; or at least it hasn't been until recently.

Within the past few years, two acquaintances, roughly my contemporaries, have written books that have made them millions of dollars. Despite the fact that my most recent royalty check was for $2.49, I found that I did not feel the least wisp of envy for either of these fellows; nor do I now. Not long ago I went to dinner with a political columnist who appears regularly on television, and our meal was interrupted by a request for his autograph; on the way out of the restaurant he was twice stopped by strangers and congratulated for recent work. I thought this fascinating, but my envy gland, usually so sensitive, gave not a twitch. True, for my own writing, posterity and not prosperity is the name of my (slightly embarrassing to admit) desire; and rather than widespread fame, I prefer to have a good name among a select audience of the genuinely thoughtful. But none of this is a convincing reason not to have felt envious. What good is longing, after all, if you can't long for contradictory things: the pleasures that riches bring and a life of simplicity, fame and privacy both? If you are going to force envy to be consistent, you're likely to put it out of business.

Many people would, of course, prefer to see envy go permanently out of business. Arthur Rubinstein, in his memoirs, remarked that at bottom anti-Semitism was owed chiefly to envy, and that the anti-Semite's "real hatred is concentrated on the Jews who possess the highest standards of ethics, intelligence, and talents, on those who, whenever allowed to compete, become prominent in all possible fields like science, art, or economy." On the other side of the ledger, envy is a foe of drab leveling. L. P. Hartley has written an anti-utopian novel entitled *Facial Justice* in which equality is known as Good E and envy as Bad E; what makes envy Bad E is that it arouses people's passions, for discrimination, degree, difference, all the things that give life variety and make it interesting. Without these differences, Hartley's novel argues, life is scarcely worth living.

Perhaps the problem lies in the word *envy* itself. There is a good envy, of the kind that encourages dreams and aspiration, and a bad envy, based on disappointment and hatred. Perhaps a new word is needed, one that falls between envy and admiration, to describe the positive qualities of the former and strip it of traditional pejorative meanings. But the language, as Flaubert remarked in a very different connection—he was trying to convince his mistress of his love for her by describing its intensity—is inept.

Meanwhile, my own problem, I begin to realize, is that I am becoming more discriminating in my envy. What I am discriminating against is the world's larger, more obvious prizes: wealth, fame, power. Glittering though these prizes are, and as they once were to me, I now find them mainly glaring, and in my own life even a little beside the point. I still envy large things, among them genuine achievement, true religious faith, real erudition. I justify envy of these things on the ground that surely there is no point in envying things you can actually have and that it is only the unattainable that is worth a serious person's envy.

The only expensive item I continue to envy is a small, well-made house with a fine view of water and of a naturally elegant landscape. For the rest, I envy things on which a price tag cannot be put, many but not all of them fairly trivial. Permit me to list them. I envy anyone who can do a backward somersault in midair from a standing position. I envy men who have fought a war and survived it. I envy people who speak foreign languages easily. I envy performing artists who have the power to move and amuse audiences to the point where the audience wants the performance never to end. I envy people who can travel abroad with a single piece of carry-on luggage. I envy people who have good posture. Above all, I envy those few people who truly understand that life is a fragile bargain, rescindable at any time, and live their lives accordingly.

(1989)

Waiter, There's a Paragraph in My Soup!

Do not read, as children do, to amuse yourself, or, like the ambitious, for instruction. No, read in order to live.

—Flaubert

George Bernard Shaw, who in a long life said so many things, said that "[I] could remember no time at which a page of print was not intelligible to me, and can only suppose I was born literate." I wish I could suppose the same—I wish, now that I am at it, that I could have called Shaw "Bernie," which might have taken a bit of the helium out of him—but I cannot. I can recall, quite precisely, the excitement of learning to sound out words on the page and that the page in question was one from the Sunday comics, or what used to be called "the funny papers." I can recall as well the time when it began to be clear that reading would be not only a source of heightened pleasure for me but indubitably the central experience in my life. In fact, I tend to spend something on the order of five hours each day reading. By my rough calculations, this means that if I live on to my middle seventies, I shall have spent something like eleven and a half years, of twenty-four-hour days, with a book or magazine in my hands.

It would be more if I hadn't come to books rather late in life.

When I did I was already twenty and precocious in the ways of the world, while retarded in those of the mind. Reading reports about the shameful condition of our schools, I smile the furtive smug little smile of the man who has gotten away with something. When I learn that only a very small percentage of seventeen-year-olds in America have read *Tess of the D'Urbervilles*, or know why *The Federalist* was written, or can locate Yugoslavia, Greece, and France on a blank map, I confess that I neither read nor knew how to do any of those things at seventeen, and I am none too confident about other such items that appear in these reports now that I am in my fifties. An extremely happy childhood in which books played almost no part and an indolent adulthood of the most desultory reading have made this possible.

My passion for reading showed up in the dark winter of my junior year at the University of Chicago. That winter, because all my classes met in the morning hours, I decided to sleep days and stay up nights, on the model, I subsequently learned, of George Sand. I would return from class at eleven in the morning and sleep until dinner at six or so. After dinner I played poker or gin, watched television, went to the movies, schmoozed, and engaged in other such character-building activities until nearly midnight. Then, when everyone else had turned in, I spent three or so hours doing my various school assignments. That left four or five utterly quiet, altogether solitary, absolutely delicious hours for reading exactly what I pleased.

What I pleased to read was not all that elevated. Elevation to heights where oxygen equipment would come in handy was already available in the classroom, for the curriculum of the University of Chicago offered only great books for study. I had no argument with that; I still don't. But I, for my own personal reasons, had a simultaneous hunger for merely good books and even for a few rubbishy ones. So there I sat, in a small but immensely comfortable armchair purchased for five bucks from the Salvation Army, in my robe, a blanket over my lap, smoking cigarettes and drinking coffee or Pepsi-Cola, reading the novels of John O'Hara, Christopher Isherwood, Aldous Huxley, Henry Miller (in the plain green paperback covers provided by the Olympia Press), J. D. Salinger, Truman Capote, and I forget what others, awaiting the sunrise, feeling flat-out, deliriously, pig-heaven happy.

The hook was in, deep down, permanently planted. Henceforth one of my life's perennial problems was how to clear a decent bit of time for that lovely, antisocial, splendidly selfish habit known as reading. In *The Principles of Psychology*, William James remarks that "the period between twenty and thirty is the critical one in the formation of intellectual and professional habits," which certainly proved true in my case. I was fortunate in being able to indulge my newfound habit in a big-time way by being drafted for two years into the peacetime army, where reading, in the fastnesses of army posts in Texas and Arkansas, seemed far and away the best if not the only game in town. Early in my time in the army—in, specifically, basic training—no books, magazines, even newspapers were allowed, and, though this lasted only eight weeks, I can distinctly recall feeling it as a genuine deprivation, like withdrawal from cigarettes or sweets. Later in the army I found myself living alone with occasional stretches of seventy-two hours with no responsibilities and no money for sporting diversions and nothing else to do but read, which I did, at three- and four-hour uninterrupted clips. Too much of a good thing? William James, in his chapter on habit in *The Principles of Psychology*, suggests that "even the habit of excessive indulgence in music, for those who are neither performers themselves nor musically gifted enough to take it in a purely intellectual way, has probably a relaxing [by which James meant a *bad*] effect upon the character." But I took care of this little problem by determining to become a writer. No other occupation, after all, would begin to justify such a voracious appetite for reading.

Not long after this decision, I moved to New York, which, say whatever you like against it, is a fine town for reading. What makes it so fine is that New York has the best bookstores; better yet, the best used book stores; the greatest availability of serious magazines and journals—and all of this in the most generous abundance. Shortly after I arrived in New York, I found a shop near the public library that sold back issues of *Commentary* and *Partisan Review*, and some days, rather than look for a job, I took five or six such back issues to the park and read the day away. Later, when I found a job, it turned out to be near lower Fourth Avenue, which in those days had an impressive array of used book stores. Walking along Fourth Avenue, I always felt like a sailor in port at Macao; temptation lurked everywhere, and so, prudent fellow that I was, I often left my wallet in my desk back at work, lest I blow money meant for telephone and electric bills on, say, a complete set of John Ruskin. A hazardous city for an innocent reader, New York.

While living in New York I acquired the habit of rarely going out without tucking a book or magazine under my arm. Vibrant and fascinating though New York can be, it has so many parts and patches that are best read through: riding subways, standing in bank lines, arranging any sort of bureaucratic business, sitting through traffic jams. New York probably offers more good reasons to avert one's eyes than any other city in America, and where better to avert them than into a book? To this day, though long removed from New York,

I still usually walk about with a book in hand, and I keep a book or two in my car, often getting in a quick paragraph at a stoplight. If you happen to be behind me, please don't honk when the light turns green, for I could be coming to the end of a paragraph.

Sometime in my middle twenties I began to review books, which, as a reader, I looked upon as the equivalent in sports of turning pro. The notion of being paid for reading was exhilarating. To be sure, the money was poor, but the hours were long and the fame quite fleeting. As a youthful book reviewer, I was apparently able to do a convincing impression of an intelligent and cultivated fellow, and so I was soon asked to review books intrinsically much more serious than I was. Would I care to review the most recent volume of Bertrand Russell's autobiography? Yes, I rather should. An English translation of Thomas Mann's letters is about to be published, and would I be interested in writing about it? Actually, I would. The memoirs in four volumes of Alexander Herzen have appeared, and did I have time to read and write about them? Not, I allowed, a problem. (Who, exactly, was Alexander Herzen, I recall thinking after agreeing to write about him, and I rushed to an encyclopedia to find out.) Yet I worked hard on these reviews, reading lots of other books in connection with them, in no small measure because I was fearful of making a jackass of myself by committing some horrendous error. This, I believe, is what is known as getting one's education in public. Whether it is also known as fraud is a question I prefer to let pass.

As a reviewer, I took notes on my reading and made light vertical pencil markings alongside pertinent passages that I wanted either to quote or to reread. It was all a bit like being a student again, which was not my idea of a jolly good time. One of the reasons I was so eager to be out of school—and knew with a certainty that graduate school was not for me—was my ardor to read what I wished and in precisely the way I wished to read it: not to read for examination or to acquire someone else's sense of a book. My temperament led me away from concentrated study. An expert—on anything—was the last thing I wished to become. If not in life then at least among books, I was a born roamer. Boswell reports that Samuel Johnson's mind was "more enriched by roaming at large in the fields of literature, than if it had been confined to any single spot," adding that "the flesh of animals who feed excursively, is allowed to have a higher flavour than that of those who are cooped up." If desultory reading was good enough for the Doc, I figure it is plenty good enough for me.

But to read desultorily, to be an intellectual roamer and grazer, luxurious though the freedom of it is, carries its own complications. Certain reading habits require a commensurate reading habitat. Multiple have been the definitions of the intellectual, that professional dilettante, but any realistic definition should include the unfailing identifying mark of his living amidst a vast welter of paper. In the abode of the intellectual, books, magazines, newspapers are everywhere. The splendidly sensible Sydney Smith, in composing a sketch for a cheerful room, suggests that tables "should be strewn with books and pamphlets," but he elsewhere warned that, to preserve oneself from becoming completely swamped by books, one should never "suffer a single shelf to be placed in [a room]; for they will creep round you like an erysipelas till they have covered the whole."

In my own apartment, books and magazines are currently in every room, including the kitchen. I am married to a woman whose tolerant love for her husband has caused her to repress her natural (and quite reasonable) penchant for order, which I try, with uneven success, to respect. I shiver at the thought of what my apartment would resemble if I lived alone. Harry Wolfson, the great Harvard scholar, who was a bachelor and a man of wide interests, is said to have kept books in his refrigerator. A pity microwave ovens weren't in wide use in Wolfson's day—he died in 1974—for one would have perfectly accommodated his Loeb Classics.

The home of any serious desultory reader has to be a shambles of odd reading matter, chiefly because such a reader has no useful principle of exclusion. By the very nature of his reading, his interests tend to widen not to narrow, to exfoliate endlessly, like a magical rose. Ten or so years ago I could have confidently said that I had no interest, as a reader, in space travel. I have since taken a very elementary course in astronomy, and so books on space and astronomy come into our apartment, as does a subscription to *Astronomy* magazine. A recent trip to Italy has brought modern Italy into the already crowded list of subjects I now read about regularly. An essay in the British magazine *Encounter* on a writer I had not hitherto heard of named Julian Jaynes caused me to acquire a copy of Jaynes's book *The Origin of Consciousness in the Breakdown of the Bicameral Mind.* It begins brilliantly. Another bookmark in yet another book; another book atop yet another pile of books—one of several—with bookmarks in them. It is endless, absolutely endless—and I must confess that I wouldn't have it any other way.

Having too much to read isn't the worry; having too little to read has been on occasion. In paucity, never profligacy, lies fear. Sir James Mackintosh, the journalist and jurist who wrote for the *Edinburgh Review,* used to travel around the country with so many books in his carriage that he couldn't pull down the windows. S. N. Behrman, the American playwright and memoirist, used to travel with a portable library, a smallish leather case that contained twenty-five or thirty books. To people who do not require ample dosages of print, taken daily, this will seem excessive, even foolish. I myself think it shows eminent good sense. Abroad, in the town of Ravenna, I had read my way through the books in English that I had brought along. Sheer panic set in. I discovered a shop off the Piazza del Popolo that sold British paperbacks. I bought two novels of the insufficiently amusing British novelist Simon Raven, at the scandalous price of ten dollars a shot, which at least calmed me down until I returned home.

I don't mean to imply that anything at all will satisfy my hunger for reading. I have never, for example, been able to read detective stories or spy thrillers, no matter how elegantly composed, though I enjoy both kinds of story in the movies or on television (which I often watch with a book or magazine in hand). Wherever possible I prefer books that amuse me; this comes down to meaning books that were written with style. I would rather read a stylish book than a styleless more scholarly book on the same subject. I have of late been reading Sacheverell Sitwell's *Liszt*. Doubtless more serious books on Liszt have been written. Yet Sachie, as Sitwell's friends called him, seems to me to have written a fine book because he knew what was interesting in life, knew how to tell an anecdote well, knew how to put a lot of spin on his sentences. He was, in two words, no dope. I prefer not to read dopes. I prefer to read writers who know more about the world than I do, and to steer clear of those who know less. I discover more of the latter as I grow older, but the growth of my own wisdom is not proceeding at so alarming a rate that I fear running out of things to read.

Although reading is a solitary act, it need not be done in isolation from other acts. In his chapter on habit, William James cites a man named Robert Houdin who could read while juggling four balls. (I assume he wasn't reading Immanuel Kant.) A husband and wife conversing behind their separate sections of the newspaper over breakfast is an old cartoon set piece. Lots of people—I am among them—read while watching television, sometimes during commercials or through the more trivial news items or awaiting a weather report or sports scores. Reading while watching baseball on television is especially fine and, given light reading, is easily brought off with the help of instant replay. Why do one thing at a time when you can do two? And between the two done simultaneously, light reading and watching television, the former almost always wins out.

People commonly read while bathing and sunbathing. In my time I have done a good bit of both, but I may have been pushing it when in my early twenties I brought a copy of the *New Yorker* to read in a steam bath. It was in fact my first visit to a steam bath, and once inside I proceeded to clamber to the topmost bench, nearest the ceiling, whence the heat exuded. I must have been sitting there reading the *New Yorker*'s racing writer Audax Minor no longer than three or four minutes when I felt an odd pulsating in my forehead. I touched my hand to it and discovered a good-sized vein. I next looked down to find that one of the pages of the magazine had raveled itself round my wrist, the humidity in the room causing it to cling to my forearm. Head pulsating, arm now wrapped in dampened slick paper, body wound in a sheet, in panic I fled, never again to make the mistake of treating a *shvitzbud* as a substitute for the Reading Room of the British Museum.

Reading not in the bath but in the bathroom is a subject that, in any earnest survey of reading habits, cannot be avoided. ("It's alimentary, my dear Watson.") Recently asked for permission to reprint an essay I had written, I in turn, never shy of the vulgar question, asked if there was a reprint fee provided. There was none, I was told by the editor, but he hastened to add that his journal was ardently read by its subscribers. "Really," he said, "they take it to the john." I had not hitherto thought of that as a standard, but it is unquestionably true that one tends to take only reading matter that one is genuinely interested in to the bathroom. (The same goes for the hospital.) Whether an author thinks it beyond the dignity of his work to have it read in the bathroom is another question. As a bathroom reader myself, I should feel honored to have others read me in the room that the English, in a notable euphemism, used to call "the House of Commons."

Books for bathroom reading oughtn't be too heavy, in any sense of the word—neither too large nor too densely argued. What is wanted is writing that can be read in short takes, easily abandoned and returned to at a later time without losing the thread. Diaries and journals and collections of letters fill the bill nicely; so do wittily written novels of modest length. I read a volume of Tocqueville's letters in the bathroom; I am currently reading selections from James Agate's amusing diary (*The Selective Ego*); and some years ago, over a two-year stretch, I read through the twelve slender novels that comprise Anthony Powell's *A Dance to the Music of Time*. More recently, I read three volumes of Frank Sullivan's humorous writings, and I continue to read, intermittently, two books by Arthur Koestler on scientific subjects: *The Case of the Midwife Toad* and *The Watershed*, a biography of Johannes Kepler. But then everyone will have his own notions about what makes for the most commodious reading.

Reading while eating has its own complexities. Eating alone, especially in a restaurant, one's solitude seems redoubled. One notices, as one rarely does when dining in company, the lengthiness and noisiness of one's chewing, the slight awkwardness with which one handles one's cutlery, one's ineptitude with lettuce. Dining in solitude renews one's sense of the necessity of company to the enjoyment of food. A book at the side or in front of one's plate takes one's mind off all that, serving as a screen against the public when dining out, as a companion when dining alone in one's own home. I do not like to eat in restaurants when I am alone, and avoid it whenever I can, but when I cannot I always come armed with a book or magazine. I eat most of my lunches alone, at home, and automatically pick up something to read while eating lunch.

Here the problem is never what to read but what to eat—more specifically, what kind of food can be efficiently eaten while reading. (Taking the opposite tack, Edmund Wilson once remarked that the Marquis de Sade was the only writer he couldn't read along with his breakfast.) Soup, for example, is very poor stuff while reading. Not only does it require concentration on its own, not only is it potentially messy, but it doesn't allow one much pause between spoonfuls to read a paragraph or so. Of more solid foods, pastas, stews, club and other sandwiches that require two hands to manipulate are rather more than is wanted. A plain cutlet is nice, or a cold breast of chicken; so is cheese (if you can afford the cholesterol) and fruit—one takes a bite of food, chews deliberately, reads a paragraph, returns to the plate, and then returns to the page, which sets up a nice little rhythm of reading and eating, reading and eating. Certain sandwiches can be quite good, too, a cold turkey sandwich, say, or a ham sandwich, or any other cold cuts that are without greasiness, which will inevitably find its way onto the page, as the jelly from a peanut butter and jelly sandwich inevitably will. It's a deep problem, and Reading Lunches, on the model of TV Dinners, may be the solution. I hope to get around to packaging such lunches for mass consumption once I complete the proposal I have been writing to Ted Turner about my idea for turning some of the great Hollywood Technicolor extravaganzas—*The Ten Commandments, Gone with the Wind, Fantasia*—into black and white.

I hope nobody is gaining the impression that, merely because I seem to be reading all the time, I get much reading done. I don't, or at least it doesn't feel as if I do. Perhaps the chief reason I don't is that, apart from being an unmethodical reader, I am also a fairly slow reader and have been ever since I made the decision, in my early twenties, to become a writer. As a writer, I don't claim to read more penetratingly than others, but I do find that I ask certain questions while reading that non-writers need not ask. Anyone reading an interesting passage in a book asks, if often only subconsciously, Is what I have just read formally correct? Is it beautiful? What does it mean? Do I believe it? Along with these questions, a writer asks two others: How technically, did the author bring it off? and Is there anything here that I can appropriate (why bring in a word like *steal* when it isn't absolutely required) for my own writing? Reading not alone for meaning and pleasure but also for style, in which further meaning and pleasure are usually to be found, can surely keep a fellow from being able, as the speed-reading schools all promise, to sit down early of a Saturday afternoon to read through the collected works of Werner Sombart and still have plenty of time left over to enjoy oneself at the big dance.

If I were a fast reader, I have sometimes thought, it might only be the worse for me. My reading ambitions might have doubled. I might have been unhappy—felt guilty—if I didn't read at least a book a day, as the literary critic Stanley Edgar Hyman once told me that he did.

As a fast reader, too, I should have often been tempted to stay up all night to finish a stirring book—a thing I have done only twice in my life, both times with novels: once, in my adolescence, with Willard Motley's *Knock on Any Door*, and a second time, in my twenties, with I. J. Singer's *The Brothers Ashkenazi*. H. L. Mencken is said to have been a blazingly fast reader. Samuel Johnson may have been, if not faster, more efficient, for according to Adam Smith's account as retold through James Boswell, Johnson "had a peculiar facility in seizing at once what was valuable in any book, without submitting to the labour of perusing it from beginning to end." It was Johnson who thought Henry Fielding's novels a waste of time, who said that no one ever wished *Paradise Lost* longer, and extended this remark by once asking Mrs. Piozzi, "Was there ever yet any thing written by mere man that was wished longer by its readers, excepting *Don Quixote*, *Robinson Crusoe*, and the *Pilgrim's Progress*?" Johnson's own method was to begin a book in the middle and if he felt the inclination to read more to go back to the beginning.

My own present modus operandi is to begin a book at the beginning and, for one reason or another, often to bog down somewhere near the middle. On a quick search of our apartment, I find twenty-three books with bookmarks in them, and this does not count books I am reading for professional reasons. Jumping from one book to another, reading lots of magazines in between, sometimes I go a week or two without actually finishing a book. Every once in a while, out of sheer frustration, I sit down and finish reading two or three books, if only to get some minor sensation of completion in my life. All these half-read books, taken together, form no pattern, show no evidence of anything resembling coherence. Here, for example, currently resting half-read on the coffee table in our living room is the following pile of books: *Max Weber*, a biography by his wife, Marianne Weber; *Words in Commotion and Other Stories* by Tommaso Landolfi; *Collected Poems, 1919–1976* by Allen Tate; *Fast Company: How Six Master Gamblers Defy the Odds—and Always Win* by Jon Bradshaw; *A Part of Myself*, the autobiography of the German playwright Carl Zuckmayer; *A Distant Episode: The Selected Stories* by Paul Bowles; and *Conducted Tour: A Journey Through Twelve Music Festivals of Europe and Australia* by Bernard Levin. One distinctly feels the want, in this brief list, of a slender volume of instruction on needlepoint for left-handers and a Rumanian cookbook for heterosexual men who like to entertain at home, which would round things off nicely.

What admirable catholicity of taste! I can imagine some people saying in response to this confusing little pile of books. But then I can as readily imagine others saying, What a mushbrain the man must be! Myself, I incline toward the latter camp. If I had to extrapolate the personality of the man from this pile of his half-read books, I would posit a man without much discipline, an intellectual clearly, but also a hedonist of the intellect, who gives way to his every whimsical interest. He may be a man who has come to feel that not only is reading a significant form of experience but in some respects is rather more efficient and pleasurable than actual experience. He is a man—no *may* about it—who was much taken with the following brief passage, in a review by Mark Amory, in the British *Spectator*:

Reading about bridge has several advantages over playing it: no waiting, no cross partners, you do not lose money, you can stop when you want to, it can be done in the bath, every hand has a point. Best of all, you can visit above your station, and at least appreciate the skill of others.

Each of us will have his or her own list of words or phrases that can readily be substituted for *bridge* in that passage. Mine would include *boxing, Third World travel, complicated love affairs*.

As widespread and central an experience as reading is, seldom is reading mentioned in novels. We are told that Don Quixote's imagination was inflamed by reading too many trashy novels; so, too, was Emma Bovary's, much to her ultimate chagrin; and Jane Austen occasionally makes plain that one of her characters is victimized by his or her reading. But the only novel in which a character actually appears sitting down in a chair reading, at least to my knowledge, is Somerset Maugham's *The Razor's Edge*. The narrator of the novel comes upon the young American Larry Darrell, sitting in his club reading William James's *The Principles of Psychology*, and at the end of the day he is still there, having finished reading James's nearly fourteen-hundred-page tome in a single sitting. This small bit of reporting has always seemed to me to place in peril Maugham's reputation as a writer in the realist tradition.

Visual artists have done better by the subject of reading. Renaissance painters would occasionally paint a monk or saint at study. Persians would paint a caliph or scholar in a garden with a volume of verse in his hand. A pity, I have always thought, that Rodin didn't put a book in the other hand of *The Thinker*. The nineteenth-century painter Gustave Caillebotte, who was much interested in the life of the mind, has at least three paintings that I know of in which people are reading: in one, a man in a high straw hat, a loose white blouse, and espadrilles is reading with his back to the viewer, while his wife pauses in their lovely garden; in another, three women are doing needlework while a fourth reads from a small book, perhaps containing poems; and in the third, a man is reading a newspaper as his wife, whose back is to us, nevertheless expresses forlornness as she looks out a heavily draped window onto a Parisian street. I thought Edward Hopper might have painted people reading, but, on further thought, given Hopper's penchant for the subject of loneliness, it is unlikely, for no one absorbed in a book is really lonely.

On Reading is a charming little book of photographs, chiefly taken in Paris and New York, by the Hungarian photographer André Kertész (1894–1985). Many of these show people reading in public places: parks, churches, libraries, fire escapes, standing on city streets. However public the setting, a person reading, these beautiful photographs make plain, is engaged in a private act. One also grasps that reading, though far from a passive act, is nonetheless a reposeful one. Reading may provide most of us all the repose we obtain outside of sleep. Whether he is photographing an elderly vagrant reading a newspaper just fished out of a trash can or a well-set-up gentleman in his book-lined, wood-paneled study in Paris, people out of motion, at rest, in repose, are Kertész's true subject in this book. Repose ought, in some part, to be the intention of all readers.

Some reading, of course, is more reposeful than others. The least reposeful for me is that provided by the newspapers. Many people make a meal out of a newspaper, chewing and swallowing every morsel; I can't find the makings for the lightest of snacks. I read only one, the *New York Times*, and that only six days a week, and, like the prostitutes of Athens, never, never on Sunday. A wise man whose name I cannot recall said that one picks up newspapers in anticipation and inevitably sets them down in disappointment. I no longer feel the anticipation. I chiefly consult the newspaper to get a feeling for the heft and slant of current political opinion and to discover—the only real news—who has died. I scan the letters column in the (usually) vain hope of finding a man or woman after my own heart. I take a pass on the editorials, unless they promise to be especially cowardly, and quickly check the sports. I glance at the reviews and absurdities on display in the pages given over to the arts. I merely glimpse the general news, and read only to the end articles about scandal. I prefer to have the whole deal out of the way in something under twenty minutes, and generally do.

I suppose I justify being so cavalier about reading newspapers because I put in so much time reading magazines, which provide me with a vast quantity of information about current events, social trends, and what is the going thing in art and much else. Something like twenty-five magazines come into this apartment, all but four of them American. I love magazines, and shall never forget the excitement when in my last year of college I discovered such intellectual magazines as *Commentary, Partisan Review,* and *Encounter.* Around the same time I began reading the *New Yorker,* which I have continued to do for more than thirty years, and other magazines—the *New Republic, Harper's,* the *Atlantic*—for nearly as long. There are times when it feels as if *all* I read is magazines, other times when the backlog of unread magazines rises perilously high and getting through them seems an impossibility. At such times, I hope that the magazines that continue to arrive will have nothing in them of interest to me: that the *New Republic* will give an issue over to a symposium on arms control, that the *Atlantic* will run a thirty-two-page essay on global soil erosion, that the *New Yorker* will begin a seven-article series on growing surprisingly large radishes in canoes in southwest Canada by John McPhee. I earlier mentioned not reading the *New York Times* on Sunday, but a friend saves the *New York Times Book Review* and the *New York Times Magazine* for me, and I pick them up from him in clumps of eight or ten copies of each. Having all these copies there before me all at once is a wonderfully effective way of warding off any chance of my reading, say, a review of the memoirs of a woman who grew up in the home of a reform rabbi in Las Vegas or a lengthy account of industrial development along the banks of the Gogra in Nepal.

But lest anyone get the mistaken notion that I have become even mildly discriminating in my reading habits in my middle years, let it be known that I am a subscriber to *Vanity Fair*. There is nothing about *Vanity Fair* I like, but I find myself reading a large amount of each issue, doubtless with a stricken look upon my face, for it is filled with articles written by people, about other people, all whose ideas on what constitutes the good life are so far distant from my own as to make it almost seem as if we are of different species. I also alternate subscribing to *Esquire*, *Gentlemen's Quarterly*, and a newer, more malicious magazine called *Spy*. Any one of the three is quite sufficient, for their main purpose, at least in my personal reading diet, is to remind me how far behind the times I am falling—and, given the times, how pleasant is the fall. As if to underscore this, *Spy*, to which I currently subscribe, prints a good deal of material in a minuscule type that I cannot read without strain. Continual reading, surely, has contributed to the fact that I now wear glasses almost full-time. "Professor," a student said to me the other day, "I didn't recognize you not wearing your glasses." "Ah, my dear," I wanted to answer, "I do not recognize myself wearing them."

My eyesight does not figure to improve, nor does my appetite for reading figure to diminish. I wish I could settle down into fixed reading habits—like the man I know who reads a chapter of *The Pickwick Papers* every evening—or begin now to devote myself to rereading many of the important books I read badly because I read them too early in life the first time around. But I think this is unlikely. If anything, my reading has become more desultory than ever. Only recently have I begun to read about music in I won't say a serious but in a fairly large-scale way. Once musical notation is put on the page, I am a goner, but I do enjoy reading about the lives of the great composers and the memoirs of the great performers. I always read a great deal of literary criticism, but now I read more music, art, and dance criticism. I like to read criticism, to watch a man or woman stand and deliver his or her understanding of how art works and how well a particular artist has brought it all off. The only criticism I do not read is that having anything to do with the Brontës. Why, you ask, exclude the Brontës? I don't really know, except that they are all so gloomy, and excluding one small body of writing makes me feel as if I have drawn at least one line and am in some sort of control of my reading life, which of course I am not.

As one grows older, reading becomes an even keener pleasure and an ever greater comedy. Part of the pleasure derives intrinsically from the activity itself; and part from its extrinsic rewards, not the least of which is knowing that there will always be plenty to read and so superannuation presents no real fear. (Great readers have this advantage over great lovers.) The comedy of reading is owing in part to one's memory, which in the natural course of things retains less and less of what one reads; and in part to that oldest joke of all, which Dostoyevsky insists comes to each of us afresh, I speak—hushed tones please—of death, which among other erasures rubs out all that one has read over a lifetime.

Still, as addictions go, reading is among the cleanest, least harmful, easiest to feed, happiest. As an addiction, however, one shouldn't underestimate its power. If reading has presented me with many of the most delightful moments in my life, there have also been times when I should rather read than be with a friend, or when reading about life has seemed more attractive than life itself, and I happen to be extremely fond of life. My heavy reading schedule keeps me from thinking too much about an afterlife, but it occurs to me that in the various descriptions I have read of heaven, no one ever mentions a library or bookstores there. Can it be that there will be no books or magazines in heaven? (Hell, I assume, will be full of newspapers, a fresh edition of each published every thirty seconds, so that no one will ever feel caught up.) If there is nothing to read in heaven, I am not sure I want to go. But should I ever be invited, I trust that whoever is sent to fetch me will at least have the common courtesy to allow me the few moments required to come to the end of my last paragraph.

(1989)

Livestock

My young friend," Aldous Huxley once instructed an aspiring novelist, "if you want to be a psychological novelist and write about human beings, the best thing you can do is keep a pair of cats." Whether this is good advice or not I do not know, but for me, a simple if more than occasionally pretentious essayist, one cat has done nicely. In recent years I have spent more time in the company of such a creature than I have with any human being, and, speaking for myself and not the creature in question, I find that it has its subtle compensations. It took me a long while to understand that a cat is the animal best suited to my talent and temperament. Since I have shown no talent whatsoever for training either children or dogs, having a cat, which is by nature intractable, has been a great relief. As for temperament, my cat and I share a penchant for being left alone for long stretches; neither of us is overly demonstrative in our emotions; and we are both quite good at gaining attention when we need it. Before leaving the matters of talent and temperament, I should add that

304

cats generally tend to be cleaner, better athletes, and on the whole more suited for the contemplative life than I.

I realize that owning up to a serious admiration for cats puts me in slightly odd company. Whenever I take my own cat to the veterinarian, at a place called the Chicago Cat Clinic, I feel myself in a somewhat unusual crowd. I will not be more specific than to say that, as a group, my fellow cat lovers show marked differences from the regular Sunday afternoon National Football League audience. Yet the admiration of cats does have a lengthy literary lineage. Ever since Montaigne struck off his famous sentence about his cat—"When I play with my cat who knows whether she diverts herself with me, or I with her!"—the link between literary men and women and cats has been forged. It has been notably strong in France. From Montaigne through Chateaubriand through Sainte-Beuve through Huysmans through Colette—ailurophiles all—cats have been on the scene to note some interesting literary composition. The literary history of France, it has been said, could be written through the nation's cat lovers.

They order these things differently in England. The English are most famously keen on dogs. Of all creatures great and small, to coin a phrase, the English seem most partial to their dogs. The pleasures of a small garden, the companionship of a dog, and most Englishmen, at least of recent past generations, felt life paradisical enough. To gain some flavor of the English love of dogs, I have just read for the first time the English writer J. R. Ackerley's *My Dog Tulip*, his account of life with his Alsatian bitch hound, a book that has long had the status of "one of the greatest masterpieces of animal literature," according to Christopher Isherwood. It does not have that status with me; much too much talk in it for my taste of micturition, defecation, impregnation, gestation, and parturition. Ackerley really wallows in all this, can't seem to write enough about it, but when he isn't doing so he does make vivid some of the strange enchantment that animals have for us, if not necessarily we for them. "How wonderful to have had an animal come to one to communicate where no communication is," he writes, "over the incommunicability of no common speech, to ask a personal favor." It is exactly so; and so, too, that "the only way to avoid the onus of responsibility for the lives of animals is never to traffic in them at all." This many of us cannot bring ourselves to do.

To avoid all such traffic is the perhaps sensible policy of the majority of men and women. With what cheerful disdain they are able to look upon those of us who have chosen to share our lives with animals. Gazing out a sixth-story window upon an ice-laden street on a below-zero morning at a shivering man waiting for a small Yorkshire terrier to do what is euphemistically called its "business" fills one with a reassuring sense of one's own prudence and the comic imbecility of advanced civilization. I have been both the man with that dog and the man in the window, and, while I can testify that life is more comfortable behind the window, I do not in retrospect regret my mornings with that Yorkshire terrier.

My only regret in this line has to do with another terrier I once owned, this one a wirehair, Sigmund by name, an affable fellow who one otherwise sunny afternoon was struck by a passing car. Great damage was done to the dog's leg. Many X-rays were required and no fewer than three operations and resettings of a pathetic cast that made a heartrending sound upon wooden floors. Expenses piled up; I have blocked the figures from my mind. A non-animal-owning friend with a cruel sense of humor suggested that there was a good man in Zurich to whom I ought to send the dog. After a lengthy and costly convalescence, Sigmund, I am pleased to report, regained full use of his injured leg—sufficient use, I am less pleased to report, to be able to run away, permanently and without so much as a by-your-leave. Farewell, ungrateful voyager.

I neglected to mention Sigmund's perfidious behavior to John Sparrow, Warden of All Souls at Oxford, who one night, awash with champagne, launched into a powerful and unrelenting attack on dogs in general. "So sycophantic," he exclaimed, "so hopelessly uncritical. Nothing more odious than a large dog, its tongue extended, drooling for its master's or anyone else's attention. Pathetic creatures, dogs, the playthings of those men and women who wish unqualified admiration and derive contentment from acting the part of lord over an ignorant, generally slobbering beast." On and on he went, warming to his subject with increasing intensity, so that toward the end of his tirade ownership of a dog seemed roughly comparable to membership in the Nazi Party through the war years. A dog owner myself at the time—the aforementioned Yorkshire terrier, named Max, was then in my possession—I felt I must at least bring this up, if not offer a full defense of dogs.

"Before you go further," I said, "I must report to you that I myself own a dog. He is a very small dog, true, but I am much enamored of him."

"Is he old?" the Warden inquired through a champagne-induced lisp.

"Nine years old."

"I see," said the Warden. "My advice is to keep him till he dies. But, pray, do not replace him."

As it happens, I never did. In the fullness of time—and not so full as all that—the charming and beloved Max departed the scene.

We later moved to an apartment where dogs were not permitted. Below-zero mornings I remained smugly indoors; returning late at night I felt a distinct relief at not having to brave the dark neighborhood streets. For a longish period I settled in without the company of animals. Without livestock, I won't say it was the good life, but it was a less-encumbered, a much simpler, life than I had become accustomed to.

Evidently I cannot stand too much simplicity. With children grown and gone, the element of tumult and even human traffic much diminished from daily life, I must have felt the want of a little additional complication. I began to notice myself considering other people's pets admiringly. A relative in San Francisco with whom I visited had a cat of such sweet temper, playfulness, and courtesy that I determined that I should begin to look for a cat of my own.

"A cat," said Edith Wharton, who all her adult life kept highbred small dogs, "is a snake in furs." Many people—technically known as ailurophobes—feel likewise. I never did, but I was for many years, given a choice, partial to dogs. Cats, though, have much to recommend them, especially for city living. A cat does not need to be walked; a cat is the only domestic animal I know who toilet trains itself and does a damned impressive job of it. A cat's requirement for attention is of an utterly different order from that of a dog. My cat seems to like my company but does nicely without my conversation. As I write, for example, she is asleep on my desk, atop correspondence I am late in answering and behind a small stack of books. Apart from her dubious value as a paperweight, I like her company, too, when she chooses to give it, though why it pleases me—no, make that comforts me—to have this sleeping creature on my desk is itself a mildly interesting question.

Before going any further, before I begin to give the false impression of vast sensitivity to all forms of animal life, I had better make it quite clear that you are a long way from reading an urbanized, Jewish, modern-day St. Francis. Many are the animals I wish had never made the ark. I have never met a rodent I liked; and rats drive me, as they did George Orwell, nearly ill with revulsion. Slobbering dogs are not my idea of a good time, either; I cannot see a Doberman pinscher without thinking of the gestapo; and Pekingese, of the kind that appear in several of Evelyn Waugh's novels, always suggest to me the possibility of furious nips at the back of one's ankles. Rabbits I can take or leave alone. Birds cannot be topped aesthetically, but I have never longed to own an aviary. Snakes I do not despise, though I much prefer them out of the grass and in zoos. Giraffes and penguins I adore for their lovely, elegant oddity. Monkeys and apes come too close to home.

Everyone can put together a similar list of zoological sympathies and antipathies—love iguanas, hate gophers—but some among us believe in something akin to a special, I hesitate to say mystical, perhaps the best word is romantic, relationship with animals, or at any rate with one animal. Sentimental, even sappy though I know this to be, I fear that, however tenuously, I myself hold this belief. In my case, I think it derives from a strong diet when young of animal movies and literature combined with an absence of any opportunity during these same years to live in a natural way with animals.

Walt Disney, with his fine anthropomorphizing hand, started me off nicely with Bambi, Dumbo, Jiminy Cricket, and other animal adorables now lost to memory. In the short subjects then known as serials, I recall being much taken with the high intelligence of Rin Tin Tin. The Lassie movies—*Lassie Come Home* and others—were even more affecting, for a collie, to a child's moviegoing eye, is incontestably more beautiful than a German shepherd. And the horses, the splendid, muscular, many-hued horses: my friend Flicka, Black Beauty, the dazzling palominos, the dangerous white stallions, the frisky pinto ponies, almost all of them ready to answer to the right human whistle, to count with their hooves, to gallop empty-saddled to the nearest town to bring back help.

Sabu, the Indian boy who could communicate perfectly with elephants, fed the belief not only in friendship between human and animal, but in their near-perfect understanding, given sufficient patience and kindness on the part of the human. This was greatly reinforced by the ever-ineloquent Tarzan, whose own unmelodious diction and brutish syntax, it occurs to me now, may have been formed by too much converse with apes, elephants, and other jungle denizens. Perhaps the only movie of my youth containing a heavy dose of truth about the relationship between man and beast was *The Yearling*, made from Marjorie Kinnan Rawlings's novel, about the sad consequences of a boy who, through love, wishes to domesticate a creature meant to live in nature.

It would be nice to be able to report that I have gotten over my infatuation with this sort of fare, but, alas, it is not so. Another boy-and-horse movie, this one entitled *The Black Stallion* (1979), did it to me again. The movie contains a roughly twenty-minute sequence of an eight- or nine-year-old boy riding upon the bare back of a Leonardoesque black horse plunging powerfully through the azure waters of the Mediterranean, lushly filmed from all possible angles, which I can only say, not very analytically, sends me each time I see it; and, owing to cassette tape, I have seen it four or five times. I gulp, I gush, I am a goner.

Perhaps only a city kid could fall so hard. In the solidly middle-class neighborhood in Chicago where I grew up, I have no recollection of any neighbors with dogs or cats, or scarcely any remembrance of animal life at all. World War II was on. It may well be that, with a scarcity of apartments, our building and those around it did not permit pets. Food was rationed, and meat for dogs and cats was not readily available. I was sent off to an expensive summer camp in Wisconsin when I was eight, but, owing to the war, we were told that the camp had had to cancel horseback riding. Meanwhile, all those movies, along with a fair amount of reading, stoked my untested regard for the companionship of living, non-human creatures. Pathetic to report, even grasshoppers interested me, and I tried to keep a few alive in a jar with a perforated top. I don't think I went so far as to name them; at least I hope I didn't.

When we finally acquired a pet, a dog, it seemed to come too late. We had moved to more spacious quarters, I was well into my adolescence, and the once powerful fantasy of an abiding friendship with an animal could not compete with rivaling fantasies about sports and girls. It was the early 1950s, and our dog was the popular dog of its day, a cocker spaniel. Cocker spaniels came in three colors, black, tan, and auburn, and were usually named, with extraordinarily unimaginative repetitiveness, respectively, Inky, Taffy, and Rusty. Ours was a Rusty. He wasn't a puppy, but five or six years old when we acquired him. Whatever the animal equivalent to personality is, Rusty's, near as I could make out, was singularly without interesting idiosyncrasy. A dull guy, Rusty. He was rather sniffy about food, and my mother, who had hitherto evinced no special sympathy for animals, cooked for the dog. The aroma of veal and hamburger sizzling in a heavy black skillet returns to me now; it and other viands were set before him. The result was a diet too rich for his system, and it threw off his toilet training habits. This vastly abbreviated Rusty's tenure with Swiss Family Epstein. In less than a year's time he was farmed out to the man who picked up and delivered our laundry, who lived in the country with a family of ten children. I hope Rusty lived out his days in dull contentment, but "Rusty come home" was never a cry that passed my lips.

Irving followed Rusty, at the goodly distance of some seven years. Irving was a black poodle, who was sold to me as a toy but turned out to be a standard. Nothing about poor Irving was quite licit, including my owning him in an apartment where dogs were strictly verboten. I had acquired Irving in the first place to please a woman with whom I was much taken, who was herself quite mad about domestic animals. She had earlier presented me with a hamster to whom, frankly, I was never quite able, as they say, to relate. Owing to Irving's precarious position in the apartment as, in effect, a stowaway, through no fault of his own he was never able to get the business of doing his business down pat. He had to be taken out at odd hours—when, specifically, the coast was clear—or often rushed out just before he was no longer able to control himself. Consequently, all his days he relieved himself nervously, never quite stationary in the act, always shuffling about slightly. Irving was eventually turned over to a childless aunt of mine who already owned a Chihuahua, whom she hand-fed and had named—so far as I could make out, without a trace of irony—Caesar. She treated Irving with surpassing kindness, for which I was immensely grateful, since I felt it let me off the hook a bit for what I had put him through.

The woman for whom I bought Irving and I went on to live in a state of holy matrimony and a condition of impressive chaos for nearly a decade. At one point we had three dogs (a mongrelized sheepdog named Luv, the feckless Sigmund, and dear Max) and two Siamese cats (Ralph and Clara were their names), not to speak of a thirty-gallon antique tank stocked with tropical fish. The Siamese cats had two different litters of kittens. (Ralph will always remain memorable to me for using a bathroom toilet to make water, a trick he must have picked up from the example of the boy children in the house.) One day I came home to discover an enormous collie that had been left at the Anti-Cruelty Society by a young man going off to Vietnam; it proved to be too much, and a few days later the collie was returned to the society whence it came. At various times during this marriage I felt less like a husband and father than a rancher.

"Divorced, no kids, no cats," with a few touches of anatomical description thrown in, is not an uncommon shorthand for one man formulating the situation of a woman to another, interested and eligible, man. My second (my current, my final, my dear and irreplaceable) wife was neither divorced nor had children, but she did have a cat, Ursula, when we married. I still had my main man, the Yorkshire terrier Max. Max and Ursula, Ursula and Max—either way it sounded like a delightful German film. Ursula was very black, very elegant, very independent, and not one to bestow affection thoughtlessly. Even now I recall the first time she climbed onto my lap, after I had been around her for some two years, and the enormous compliment I felt in the gesture.

Max, charming and not entirely resourceless, always desirous of friendship, put his best moves on Ursula. When she was sitting on a couch he would gently sidle up; when she was stretched out upon a rug he with tactful caution would approach. But it was no go; for his efforts, he got a hiss and a spit, or sometimes a declawed paw in the *punim.* We were pulling for Max all the way, hoping Ursula would relent, aching to witness the lion lie down with the lamb. Alas, he had no more chance than a fellow with a few gold neck chains and a lot of cheap astrology talk setting out to seduce Greta Garbo. Another animal fantasy blown out of the air.

But I wish to report a reformation of character, at least in this particular regard, with the entry into my life, some six years ago, of our cat Isabelle. I am not ready to go so far as those authors who, in their acknowledgments to their books, wish to thank their husbands or wives for making them warm and open and caring persons, but this cat has, I believe, taught me a thing or two about the proper relationship between human beings and animals. She has given me much quiet pleasure and no pain whatsoever. I am pleased to have earned her toleration and continue to be delighted by her not infrequent gift of affection. Her demeanor is a reminder that it is possible to get through life without having to be in the least obsequious. Her longish tail, which forms itself at its tip into a question mark when she walks with a certain confident gait, reminds me, when I note it, of the value of skepticism. To gaze upon her in certain of her moods, especially when she is sleeping, can render me almost instantly tranquil. I have decided that this little animal is for me the cat of cats, the long-awaited one, the animal who will mean most to me in my life and who is likely never to be replaced in my affection.

A cat, I realize, cannot be everyone's cup of fur. Alexander the Great, Napoleon, and Hitler are all said to have been ailurophobes. Scarcely shocking, this, for if one has a taste for command and a potent will to power, one does better without a cat for company. Cats resist compulsion and are by nature unpunishable; a grown man or woman yelling at a cat makes a ridiculous spectacle. It may be that you can't teach an old dog new tricks, but, unless one is fanatical, one cannot hope to teach a new cat old tricks. Besides, they have such interesting tricks of their own. You must either take a cat as she is or leave her alone. "A cat's game," a phrase from tic-tac-toe, means standoff, stalemate, forget about it. Even the notion of *owning* a cat seems faintly absurd; better to say that one is living with a cat and paying the bills.

When not long ago, after recounting how much pleasure Isabelle's company has given me, I advised a friend to consider acquiring a cat, he shook his head and replied, "I consider cats furniture." An amusing remark, and not without its quotient of truth. A cat can sit in the same place, awake yet supremely supine, longer than any breathing creature going. (As pure furniture, I should add, perhaps nothing surpasses the cat as the most decorative domestic item the world has thus far produced.) To admire this extreme talent for repose in cats, one must oneself have a certain aspiration for repose in one's own life. Schopenhauer spoke to this point of torpid contentment in certain animals—surely cats must have been uppermost in his mind, since he said that neither dogs nor apes had it—this enjoyment of life as simple existence, claiming that those animals command it who live outside anything beyond immediate motivation. "That is why," Schopenhauer writes in one of his aphorisms, "they find complete contentment in simple existence and why it suffices to fill their entire lives; so that they can pass many hours completely inactive without feeling discontented or impatient, although they are not thinking but merely looking."

I once remarked of William Maxwell, some of whose novels I admire, that if he had any serious flaw it was that he tended to anthropomorphize children. I am rather sorry I said that, for I now intend to anthropomorphize our cat. I often try to imagine what, if Isabelle had human speech, she would say. I assume that for the most part she would keep her own counsel, using language only with great precision and never needing to avail herself of words that end in "ism." Comparing hers to a human life, I sometimes envy her the leisure of her days and all the things she doesn't have to do: work her way through the turgid fatuity of a *New York Times* editorial, make a quarterly tax payment, meet a deadline, believe in progress, feign interest. She need give no thought to owning a fax machine or computer; she need not have anything to do with technical advances. "So that's the telephone," said Degas to Forain, when the latter was so proud of having had one installed in his house. "It rings, and you run." When my telephone rings, Isabelle doesn't even blink. Let us not speak of "call-waiting."

When I leave the apartment, I generally say goodbye to Isabelle, even if she is asleep. If this isn't anthropomorphizing, I'm not sure what is. Yet when I return, she generally walks to the door to greet me. (Felinomorphizing, perhaps?) Isabelle is a house cat; she only leaves the apartment in a carrying case—lined, to be sure, with a thick yellow towel—either to see a veterinarian, or to go off with us on a weekend visit, or to board with a relative when we are traveling. You probably ought to know, too, that her front claws have been removed; and she has been—a much less than apt word—"fixed." The declawing and the desexing were done more for my convenience than for hers. Letting her run free in our urban neighborhood carries less moral complication; to do so would be to invite her quick departure if not demise. Still, to put the question anthropofelinosophically, would I give up the right to claw and fornicate at will for a reasonable amount of security, food, and comfort? Don't look now, folks, but I believe I already have. In modern life, it is apparently civilization and its discontents for cats, too.

But enough of discontents, of which the world provides sufficient to go round. I don't think many are evident in Isabelle, who, at seven years old, is a cat full of fire, which is the way I prefer a cat. When the mood is upon her, she goes galloping down the long hall of our apartment, leaping onto the top of the back of a high wing chair. Or she will jump from my desk to a nearby file cabinet, thence to hop atop a bookcase. She has a lovely way of suddenly appearing—on my desk, on our bed, behind my reading chair—with an effortless little Balanchinian hop that I think of as her "star turn." When she does this, the impression I always get is that of a great ballerina suddenly emergent from the wings. All this while, with all this galloping, leaping, hopping, in a fairly tchotchke-laden apartment, Isabelle has never broken a single item.

This cat has given us no trouble over diet, having none of the finickiness about food for which domestic cats are infamous. She even defies the standard generalizations in this line. The essayist Agnes Repplier has remarked that she has "never known a cat that would touch ham": Isabelle relishes it, but then shows little interest in a bowl of milk. The cat, write Frances and Richard Lockridge, two popular writers on the subject, "is a great victim of the human inclination to generalize." Quite true; and her use to the essayist may be precisely that, in her conduct, she generally tends to defy all generalizations applied to her.

"We cannot," remarked the scientist St. George Mivart, "without becoming cats, perfectly understand the cat mind." Carl Van Vechten, author of *The Tiger in the House*, in my opinion the best of all books about cats, puts it rather better: "Faith is needed to comprehend the cat, to understand that one can never comprehend the cat." Whether cats "think" at all is, among ethologists, apparently a matter of serious debate. Yet if it is not thoughtfulness, what is it in Isabelle that has allowed her to become so keen—and she grows steadily keener—at sensing the moods of those into whose hands her fate has rather arbitrarily been tossed? She does not always come when wanted—and never on demand—yet she never arrives when unwanted, and, as it happens, is always wanted when she arrives. And why not? She has brought me, variously, tranquility, companionship, an enhanced sense of life's possibilities. All she in her turn asks is that I never impugn her independence.

Carl Van Vechten writes that the cat ought to serve as an inspiration to the writer, since the cat suggests grace, power, and beauty, and "the perfect symmetry of his body urges one to achieve an equally perfect form" in one's work:

> The sharp but concealed claws, the contracting pupil of the eye, which allows only the necessary amount of light to enter, the independence, should be the best models for any critic; the graceful movements of the animal who waves a glorious banner as he walks silently should stir the soul of any poet. The cat symbolizes, indeed, all that a good writer tries to put into his work.

Van Vechten goes on to say that the cat, with his reserves of dignity and urbanity, his magisterial calm overlaying his bountiful energy, "is as nearly as possible what many a writer would like to be himself." There's something to it.

There's something also to Van Vechten's adding that the cat can inspire literary creation on nearly any subject—"any subject, mind you, not necessarily on the cat himself." Part of the problem is that cats are a good deal more difficult to describe than are men and women. They are not so easily drawn or painted, either, at least in a way that captures the true individuality that anyone who has lived with a cat knows that his own cat possesses. Here it strikes me that the cat has been better drawn than painted, perhaps because in a drawing the element of character—or, more precisely, caricature—comes through more lucidly.

Close readers will have noted that thus far along I have shied away from describing anything about my own cat except the charming question mark that the end of her tail sometimes forms. Isabelle, you should know, is a tabby, with dark stripes predominating over a taupe background on her long, rather slender body. On her forehead she has the traditional M-shape marking of the tabby; and black lines, which shape themselves into slightly exotic wings, flare out in perfect (as opposed to William Blake's "fearful") symmetry along both her cheeks. Her whiskers are white and emerge from near a dotting or freckling along and just beneath her nose. Plenty of taupe plays about her face; her underbody is a mélange of different shades of taupe; her only white fur is under her chin. She has a small head, an extremely elegant one, in my opinion. I much prefer a cat with a small head, for too large a head not only seems indelicate in itself but is a bit too tigerish for my taste. I read into a large-headed cat the tableau of a tiger ripping the entrails of a gazelle near a brackish pond: red tooth of nature and all that, whereas my own clear preference runs to white tooth of dental floss and a warm bathrobe.

I have spent a fair amount of time gazing into Isabelle's face and must confess that I have not found there the least trace of what the

French poet Charles Cros suspects, in a white cat of his acquaintance, to be what we should nowadays call a hidden agenda: "*Je te demande, dans ces vers, / Quel secret dort dans tes yeux verts, / Quel sarcasme sous ta moustache.*" Nor, peering into Isabelle's blue-green eyes, have I ever discovered what it was that caused George Eliot to ask: "Who can tell what just criticisms the cat may be passing on us beings of wider speculation?" The great French draftsman Grandville claimed to have discovered seventy-five different expressions on the faces of cats. I have never counted those I have discovered on Isabelle, but among them have been neither uncritical adoration nor secret contempt, which seems to me fair enough.

Lots of music plays in this apartment, nearly all of it so-called "serious" music, much of it coming from radios dialed to classical music stations. This music seems further to becalm the already quite calm Isabelle, who appears especially taken with baroque music, with, I believe I detect, a particular partiality for woodwinds. So utterly content does she seem when lying on a bed or on my desk with music playing that when I have to leave the apartment briefly, I often leave the radio playing for her. Anecdotes about the enjoyment of music by cats are not uncommon. Théophile Gautier wrote charmingly about one of his cats' reactions to hearing singers whom Gautier accompanied on the piano in his apartment. The cat of the composer Henri Sauguet was bonkers for the music of Debussy. For a time I thought Isabelle quite gone on Bach's Cantata 147, "Jesu, Joy of Man's Desiring," in the Dame Myra Hess transcription. Desmond Morris, the zoologist, claims that "the musical sense of cats is just another feline myth." I am sure he is correct, but I prefer to cling, ever so lightly, to the myth. "Human kind," a certain lover of cats named T. S. Eliot once remarked, "cannot bear very much reality." Perhaps ailurophiles can bear just a jot less.

What may be at work here is the naive hope that a creature who has given me so much comfort and pleasure can herself take comfort and pleasure in some of the same things I do. For a long while I felt similarly about feline companionship for Isabelle and contemplated acquiring a second cat. She, Isabelle, spent the first months of her life in a bookshop—"Cat-free Bookstore" reads the sign in the window of an old *New Yorker* cartoon, suggesting that there aren't all that many of them—and the first time I saw her she was asleep entwined with a large, gentle marmalade-colored cat named Gingy. Two cats are said to be better than one, or so the current received wisdom has it, especially if one goes off to work and leaves a cat alone most of the day. Isabelle is not alone in this way, yet I have felt that in installing her in our apartment, perhaps I have cruelly deprived her of the company of her own kind.

Perhaps. Yet every time I have seen Isabelle with other cats, she has appeared either bored or put off by them. Feline sociability does not seem to be, as they said in the sixties, her "thing." Which leads me to wonder if perhaps it was I who really wanted yet another cat. Adding cats is not difficult to do. Ernest Newman, the music critic of the *Times* in London, longed for the day he could settle into a house and have a cat. He ended up with three. (Those cats must have heard some splendid music.) The decisive jump, I have always thought, is from two cats to three. If three cats, after all, why not five? And if five, why not eight? I would say that family therapy is strongly indicated somewhere around six cats, at least for apartment dwellers.

I hope that I have not given the impression that Isabelle is a genius among cats, for it is not so. If cats had IQs, hers, my guess is, would fall somewhere in the middle range; if cats took SATs, we should have to look for a small school somewhere in the Middle West for her where discipline is not emphasized. Isabelle eats flowers—though for some reason not African violets—and cannot be convinced to refrain. We consequently don't keep flowers in the apartment. Although my wife and I love flowers, we have decided that we love this cat more, and the deprivation of one of life's several little pleasures is worth it.

I am, then, prepared to allow that Isabelle isn't brilliant, but not that she isn't dear. She is, as I have mentioned, currently seven years old, yet already—perhaps it is a habit of my own middle age—I begin to think of the shortness of her life, even stretched to its fullest potential. Owing to the companionship of this cat, I have begun to understand friends who, having lost a dog or cat through age or illness, choose not to replace it, saying that they can't bear to go through it all again.

Solzhenitsyn remarks in one of his novels that people who cannot be kind to animals are unlikely to be kind to human beings. A charming sentiment, but far, I suspect, from generally true. ("I wanted you to see why I work with animals," says a female veterinarian in a novel by Jim Harrison. "I can't stand people.") Yet genuine kindness to animals is always impressive. One of the finest stories told about Mohammad has to do with his having to answer the call to prayer while a cat is asleep on the hem of his cloak; with scissors he cuts off the hem, lest he wake the cat, and proceeds on his way.

Searching for the cat who turned out to be Isabelle, I met a woman who had converted two of the three stories of her house in a working-class neighborhood over to the care of injured and deserted animals: three-legged cats, a blind German shepherd, an aged St. Bernard in a body bandage are among the animals I recall roaming the first floor. Something like eighty cats lived in the basement. The smell, expense, sheer trouble of it all overwhelmed me and I didn't hang around long. The existence of heaven, though, suddenly made a good deal of sense, for nothing less can be a just reward for such a woman.

Cats are said to be notably deficient in gratitude. Certainly they are nowhere near so efficient at sending thank-you notes as, say, members of the Junior League. But they have their own extraordinary ways of repaying such trivial debts as they accrue: through their example of repose, through the sensuous harmony of their elegant movements, through their gift of unpredictable but always welcome affection. I need call in no auditor to inform me that my debts to Isabelle vastly exceed hers to me, and that there is no way to pay them off except with a mute gratitude and an occasional privately uttered toast: "Here's to you, kid, than which few things give more pleasure."

(1990)

A Bonfire of My Vanities

A young woman with not a sexy but a very earnest voice telephones, announcing that she is a producer from the local
public radio station. She wants to tell me about something that
has been troubling her for quite a while. What has been troubling
her, it turns out, is political labels. The way people use such words
as *liberal* and *radical* and *conservative* and especially *neo-conservative*
seems to her so imprecise, slovenly, confusing. She would like to
do a radio show about it. What, she wants to know, do I think of
the idea? Not very much, I reply, for my sense is that such a subject
would make for deadly dull radio. To go into all the permutations
of meaning that the word *liberal* has acquired since it surfaced
in the nineteenth century seems to me, I tell her, up there with
juggling, fire eating, and bake-offs as activities that radio does
best to leave alone. She answers that she doesn't think so, adding
that her instinct about these matters is pretty good. Besides, she
says, I talk so well about the subject. Would I agree to go on an
afternoon public radio show, during which I would be interviewed

for roughly half an hour and then answer telephone calls from listeners for the other half hour?

I asked if there was any fee, though I was fairly certain that there would be none, and there wasn't. I said my time was very tight just now, for I was under the lash of a number of deadlines. I was told that this was no problem—along with "Have a nice day" and one of the several variations for "Kiss off," "No problem" is one of only three phrases an immigrant nowadays needs to make his way in this country—no problem, since the show would not have to be aired for another three or four weeks. My other objections were met with this same gentle but firm resolve on this young woman's part. Arrangements could be made, things worked out, nothing was impossible. Our conversation ended with my saying that I would think it over. She said she would call me early in the following week.

Once off the phone I began to feel that it might be useful if I— calmly, lucidly—set out a few important distinctions about these political labels and their derivations for an interested audience. A job was to be done here, a service delivered. Given the time it would take to travel down and back to the radio station and to organize my thoughts on the subject, it would no doubt mean the loss of a full day's work. I was not myself a regular listener of public radio, but it occurred to me that perhaps its audience is also my audience. I was, when I came to think about it, much impressed with this young producer's earnestness.

What I should have been impressed with, of course, was my own vanity. What made me think that I was in a position to instruct anyone, not to speak of a fairly large general audience, on a subject about which I had myself only a tenuous grasp? Apart from killing a little time for a radio station, what purpose would be served by trotting out my clichés—"Of course, the terms *Left* and *Right* derive from the division of seating arrangements in the French Assembly after 1848 (or was it 1789?), and the Left, partisan observers have been fond of pointing out, is the side of the heart, the Right that of the liver, heh, heh, heh"—except perhaps freshly to impress myself with my good-natured unwillingness to accept any intellectual limits on my learning this side of dividing fractions?

A day or so later, I came as near as a man with my size ego can come to his senses and decided that public radio could survive nicely without my wobbly pontifications and that only my really quite astonishing vanity had impelled me to consider prattling on in public in the first place. I was prepared to tell the earnest young producer when she called back, in the gentlest way, that it was a problem and so to kiss off and have a nice day. But I have to report that she never did call back. Clearly, she had found someone better for the job. If vanity had kidneys, mine could be said to have taken a furious rabbit punch thereat.

Vanity, vanity, vanity—vain, empty, and valueless, Webster calls it, and yet who is without it? Let him who is cast the first comb. Samuel Johnson spoke, iambic pentametrically, of "The Vanity of Human Wishes." Schopenhauer, raising the stakes, wrote "On the Vanity of Existence." Schopenhauer makes a fine distinction between vanity and pride in the book of essays called *Wisdom of Life*, where he writes that "*pride* is an established conviction of one's own paramount worth in some particular respect; while *vanity* is the desire of rousing such a conviction in others and it is generally accompanied by the secret hope of ultimately coming to the same conviction oneself."

Vanity, as with amusingly wicked accuracy Schopenhauer defines it, was the sole motive behind my readiness to go on public radio to discuss political labels. But what about two other invitations that I have recently been offered and have accepted? One is to appear on a panel sponsored by a university to discuss government support for the arts that is to meet in San Diego. The other is to be a moderator for a two-hour session in a conference on the arts sponsored by a foundation. In both cases I was offered a fee, though not a staggering one (given a choice, I prefer to be staggered). But the prospect of a visit to San Diego in the month of February to a man living in the fastness of the Middle West is itself a temptation to which it is easy to surrender. At the foundation's conference there was the prospect of seeing many friends who would also be there. Sunshine, renewed friendships, a bit of cash, none of these things preclude vanity playing a part in accepting these invitations, but because of them at least I can claim mixed motives. Or—another, slightly more complicated point to consider—is my bringing up these various invitations in the first place itself an act of vanity?

I must be watched very carefully in this essay. Suspend any good-will I may have earned with you. It is one thing for a writer to take up the subject of vanity generally; it is quite another for him to offer to consider his own. Be suspicious. Get the intellectual radar out and humming. Although everyone has vanity, I think it not unfair to state that writers figure to have rather more than other people; and if they are any good at all, they should be expert at disguising it. Don't be fooled. W. H. Auden put the case, if not the argument behind it, in the last stanza of his poem "At the Grave of Henry James," where, asking James to pray for still-living writers, he remarks that "there is no end to the vanity of our calling." No end? Well, none that I have ever seen.

"On the whole," the critic Desmond MacCarthy has written, "I rather suspect that the mainspring of the initial literary impulse is vanity." He goes on to say that he refuses to believe that most people set out to become writers because of an urgent sense of the significance of what they have to write. "They wish to assert themselves and impress others," he writes, "and if they believe otherwise, they deceive themselves." I hope this isn't universally true; I doubt that it's true of, say, Chekhov or Solzhenitsyn. I'm afraid, though, that it is altogether true of me. What I most remember about the emotions connected with my decision—it was more like a wish than a decision—to write was an eagerness bordering on lust to see my name in print. I envisioned my name appended to subtle stories in the *New Yorker*, to elegant poems in *Poetry*, to penetrating cultural criticisms in the old *Partisan Review*. What these stories, poems, and criticisms were about, I envisioned less lucidly. I was not aware of anything in particular that I wanted to write; I had no obsessions that needed to be worked out in print, no messages for mankind (let alone for García), not even anything resembling a pressing urge for expression. My name in print in the right places would have done it. What I wanted was to be among the fraternity of good writers—and I wanted this tremendously.

Not all human wishes are vain; nor is vanity behind all human wishes. My own heat to see my name in print had behind it a genuine if still largely inchoate love of literature. But my desire to be accepted as a good—more than a good, an elegant—writer was owing to a quality I have had for as long as I can remember: that of being self-regarding. I have always attempted to maintain a clear view of how I appear to other people—and, for the most part, I care considerably how I come off in their estimate. That I might seem coarse or insignificant would trouble me, perhaps inordinately. I say "perhaps" because I am uncertain if others are quite as vain as I. All human beings fall into one of two categories, I have heard it said: the vain and the extremely vain. Some people, disagreeing, say there is only one category into which we all fall: the extremely vain. About this I am less than sure, though I am ready to concede that I myself no doubt fall into it.

Clothes, haircuts, the way I look generally have never been a negligible matter to me. I do not need to be, and never have been, got up in the fashion of the moment. But it would pain me to wear clothes that I thought were ugly, shabby, or even drab. I am a man who feels a little worse for needing a haircut, and a lot worse for having got a bad one. When my shoes are not shined I feel, if not mildly depressed, at least a schlepper. But more is entailed in all this than merely wishing to avoid schlepperosity. Evidence of this resides in the fact that I have lately taken to buying Charvet bow ties, at nearly seventy dollars a throw. Seventy bones to show a bit of color at my throat is, I realize, ridiculous. Since it is bow and not four-in-hand ties we are talking about, I cannot even see these ties when I wear them. I wear them, apparently, not for myself but for everyone else. The price of seventy dollars frankly appalls me. I am not a rich man—only a vain one.

I assume that these French bow ties quietly announce me as a man of good taste and interesting style, that they help to separate me from the obviously coarse and insignificant. I say "quietly" because these extravagantly priced ties are rather understated. This is as I like it. If there were a machine that could measure vanity, as a polygraph is said to measure lying, I believe I could make such a machine hop and whirl and do as many mechanical gyrations as any man living. But my vanity, which is of a kind not at all uncommon among men, takes the form of pretending not to be vain. I want to appear subdued, not as some dude. I do not wish to stand out—except, decisively, a little.

In the 1960s, during the so-called Peacock Revolution in men's clothes, I went about disguised as a sparrow. Long hair, beards, denim, flowery shirts, great flapping bell-bottoms, boots, I eschewed them all, and without the least touch of regret. Instead of letting it all hang out, as the spirit of the day called for, I carefully tucked it all in. If there is a hell, and if I am assigned to it, as part of my punishment I suspect that I shall be required to dress for eternity in the standard getup of an assistant professor of English at the University of California (Berkeley) in 1969. My headband will bind, my beard will itch, the denim will chafe my skin, my boots will pinch, and I shall regularly trip over the generous expanse of my bell-bottomed jeans. All this will be hell enough, but what will really hurt will be my vanity. Why shouldn't there be vanity in hell, too? Vanity Fair, says Thackeray, who wrote the book, "is a very vain, wicked, foolish place, full of all sorts of humbugs and falsenesses and pretensions."

Male vanity, though it may be no more intense than female vanity, is rather more complicated, if only for its having no agreed-upon outlet. Women can choose either to dress for the attack or not. But men who are also on the attack do not always do well to dress for it. (I use the word *attack*, as does the novelist Anthony Powell, in connection with the attempt to conquer the attention of the opposite sex.)

Pandemic feminism to the contrary notwithstanding, great vanity in a woman, at least about outward appearance, appalls not and neither does it infuriate in the way that obvious great vanity in a man does. The resources open to women—in costume, in cosmetics, in conniving with one's physique generally—are well known and for the most part not disapproved. Less in this line is available to men, though they are striving to catch up: see here the men's fragrance section in any large department store.

Still, a too evidently vain man is a pathetic thing, subject to scorn and contempt, and generally receiving both. Something about a man fussing too greatly about his appearance is repellent. One shouldn't too easily be able to imagine a man standing before his mirror, manipulating the strands of his hair under the gale force of a blow-dryer. The working assumption is that a serious man ought to be more concerned about serious matters. Elegance, good looks, an agreeable appearance in a man ought to come easily or not at all. "A man of my limited resources cannot presume to have a hairstyle," Churchill once told his barber, hitting exactly the right masculine note. "Get on with it."

Fewer and fewer men nowadays are Churchillian in the sense of wishing to get on with it. They prefer instead to linger over it. Male vanities of recent decades have widened; much more leeway is allowed. Yet the chief item upon which masculine vanity is given exercise is the hair of head and face. A future historian of male vanity—what, one wonders, will he look like?—will want to discover the exact date on which the term *hairstyling* entered the language. I cannot make even a rough guess when it did, though I do recall, in the early 1960s, passing a barbershop on Lexington Avenue in New York and sighting men seated inside wearing hairnets. At the time it seemed remarkable to me that men would allow barbers to put hairnets on them and even more remarkable that they didn't mind being seen in this condition by people passing the shop on a heavily trafficked street. Men were not always so shameless.

The shift from getting one's hair cut to getting it styled was decisive, for it turned one's appearance over to a professional for what was in effect exterior decoration. Before, one combed one's hair as seemed most comely; and if comely wasn't a possibility, then as it appeared most seemly. One worked, as Churchill suggested, with the resources at one's disposal. "Don't take too much off the back," one might tell a barber. Or, "I like it full on the sides." Under the regime of hairstyling, your barber tends to tell you how he plans to cut your hair. And these fellows—many among them are women—have extraordinary ideas. It is owing to hairstyling that a vast number of men today walk the streets looking as if they are wearing someone else's hair. The results are frequently (unconsciously) comic, so that one sees a man with the body of Oliver Hardy wearing the hair of General George Custer, or a man with the natural refinement of a powerlifter wearing the pompadour of the Comte Robert de Montesquiou.

The comte, it will be recalled, was the principal model for Proust's Baron de Charlus, and it was to him that Degas declared, "Watch out, M. de Montesquiou, taste is a vice." Montesquiou, France's most perfect dandy, represented male vanity to the highest power. He had himself photographed more than two hundred times and painted by Whistler, Boldini, Helleu, and others. He wore astonishing getups and amazing ties, and he put more care into his mustache than most men do into their careers. Montesquiou's exorbitant aestheticism—Proust referred to him as Professor of Beauty—set him apart from all other men, even in that outrageously vanity-ridden day.

In our day, every man can be his own Montesquiou, at least from the neck up. Ours has been a time of great creativity in the fashioning of mustaches and beards. While women have cosmetics to alter their looks, men have facial hair. They have been availing themselves of this resource for some time now. I know men of my own age—all of them, it is true, academics—who have been wearing beards for more than a quarter of a century, so that I can scarcely remember what they looked like clean-shaven. I can recall, though, a time when a beard seemed a strange peculiarity, worn only by elderly Orthodox Jews, Monty Woolley, George Bernard Shaw, and the baseball team from the House of David. As for mustaches, they seemed a genuine masculine oddity—rare, rather European, and requiring a certain gravity of mien to bring off. They also presented rich comic possibilities, as Charlie Chaplin and Groucho Marx but not Adolf Hitler recognized.

In his autobiography, Carl Zuckmayer, the German poet and playwright who was born in 1896, recollects of his father's generation "how splendidly self-assured, vital, and conscious of success mustaches were in those days." Balanchine, in an interview published in the *New Yorker* not long before he died, said that he thought that the beards of his father's generation were quite authentic, but that all contemporary beards were fakes. I think what both Zuckmayer and Balanchine had in mind is that the mustaches and beards of an earlier time were integral to personality; they had to do with more than fashion, served a purpose greater than cosmetic; they in fact expressed inner conviction. Carl Zuckmayer said of his own father's mustache that "it reflected that naive faith in progress, that still unalloyed delight in the results of enterprise, which marked the period between the war of 1870 and the war of 1914." Today's mustaches and beards, where they are not grown to camouflage a long upper lip or a weak chin, seem more than anything else a form of fantasy. "Who the devil are you supposed to be," said a candid friend of mine to a London editor who had grown long thick sideburns to go along with his goatee, "Brahms or Trotsky?"

Great bushy muttonchops, subtle little imperials, lengthy rabbinicals, food-catching Nietzsches, chaste Amish-Solzhenitsyns, droopy Fu Manchus (or is it Fus Manchu?)—the possibilities in mustache and beard wear are considerable and tempting to the vain. As one of the vain, here I must confess that one summer, vacationing by a lake in the countryside of Wisconsin, I attempted a mustache. I had something rather English in mind: something on the order of a recently mustered-out World War I British cavalry officer now a fellow in classics at Trinity College, Cambridge. This mustache was envisioned as a piece of work at once aristocratic, debonair, intellectual. What in fact in ten or so days grew across my lip was something rather more Latin American in its effect; and I don't mean Cesar Romero Latin American, either. Instead I had the all-too-prominent beginnings of a mustache that looked as if it belonged to one of those anonymous *federales* in the movie *The Treasure of the Sierra Madre*. "No," as I once heard a young professor of English declare upon returning from an MLA meeting, "it wasn't what I had in mind." That mustache never left Wisconsin.

But even if it had appeared to work, if the mustache had been a perfect little objet d'art, it wouldn't really have worked. I am not a man who can grow a mustache one day, a beard a month later, and pop on an earring on Saturday night. I am what I am. From the age of roughly twenty my personal style, such as it is, has remained much the same. With only small variations, I wear the same kind of clothes now as then; I have my hair cut short and I brush it in the same undramatic style as I have since college. (A friend recently likened my hair, in its immutability, to Astroturf, which I took as a compliment.) A little dull I may be, but, as Napoleon must have thought when he was made emperor, I can live with that. Meanwhile my distinction resides in my being, as I like to think myself, the least likely man in America to show up in a ponytail.

But my vanity about my appearance is small-time stuff next to my vanity as an author. The vanity of authors is by now famous, or at least it ought to be. "But enough talk about me," the caption of a cartoon in *Publishers Weekly* ran, "what do you think about my new book?" Perhaps the reason behind authorial vanity has to do with writers working a good bit alone, often with doubt, not to say extreme dubiety, about the outcome. Perspective gets lost. The two quite contradictory notions that every writer must keep in balance in his mind at all times—that what he is writing at the moment is of thunderous importance and that it is most unlikely to have a long life—frequently get muddled. Add to this that in some circles—generally quite small ones—writers are greatly revered and hotly overpraised. All of which combines to make for a problem in self-esteem for many of us who write; the problem is that we have too much of it—self-esteem, that is.

At least I know I do, and not very deep down, either, but right up there near the surface. The other day, for example, I received in the mail a most friendly notice of a forthcoming book of mine; the notice begins by saying that I am "one of a handful of living Americans who have mastered the familiar essay." Nice, no? You would think that might please me. If you do, you show how little you know about the vanity of writers. I stopped upon reading that opening clause; I was "brought up by it," as used to be said. *A handful who have mastered the familiar essay*, I thought. *I didn't know there were others. Who*, I wondered, *might they be? I hope nobody thinks I am making this up.*

As with appearance, so with authorship: my vanity is the vanity of, above all, wishing not to seem vain. (If nothing so improves the appearance as a high opinion of oneself, it occurs to me that I ought to be better looking than I am.) When it comes to my writing, I prefer not to blow my own piccolo or, at any rate, not to be caught blowing it. "But it is more agreeable to preserve the modesty," says Agatha Christie's M. Hercule Poirot after explaining to still another ignorant Englishman that he is the world's greatest detective. Something about playing the great author—on television and radio chat shows, at bookshop signing parties—goes against my peculiar kind of vanity. So I do not promote my books, even though I could find uses for the additional money that promotion might bring in—visions of a closet filled with French bow ties dance in my head—and I am eager to have as many intelligent readers as possible.

My anti-vanity vanity, which begins to sound like reverse snobbery, runs to the details of book publication. I don't, for example, like to have my photograph appear on the dust jacket of my books. Better, in my view, to let readers imagine what the author they are reading looks like, better a vague apparition than the locked-in, visible definiteness of photography. In my own case, I find I don't particularly enjoy being photographed by professional photographers. Like barbers, tailors, and plastic surgeons, they live day in and day out with other people's vanity, and in their presence I find I grow anxious lest I expose mine. "That's good. Hold it. In this shot you look just like Camus," a photographer once told me. "And you look just like

Henri Cartier-Bresson," I replied, just to show him that two could play at this liar's game.

Then there is the matter of blurbs, which calls for asking other writers to indite a few promotional sentences on behalf of one's new book. I do not myself give blurbs and have never wanted them. When asked to write a blurb for someone's book by his publisher, I respond by saying that I only write blurbs for authors who have died and that my blurbs truly aren't worth dying for. I am embarrassed—which may be only another way of saying "too vain"—to ask other writers to supply blurbs for my books and have always chosen not to do so. But when I was about to have a collection of short stories published, and my editor, whose views I much respect, informed me that it would be immensely helpful to my little volume to have a few blurbs written in support of it, I agreed to go along. I am grateful enough that convincing blurbs were found, but the vainglorious truth is that there are only a few living writers of fiction from whom I should genuinely be pleased to have blurbs—Aleksandr Solzhenitsyn, V. S. Naipaul, Andrei Sinyavsky—and none of them, like me, so far as I know, dispenses blurbs.

But, then, truth to tell, I should prefer most of all to have blurbs from writers who are no longer blurbistically feasible, so to speak, because they are long dead. As for the blurbs I have in mind, they would read something like the following:

He is a writer I take very seriously indeed.

—*T. S. Eliot*

Il est un écrivain exquis.

—*Marcel Proust*

This guy cracks me up.

—*Franz Kafka*

Penetration and subtlety have never, in my experience, been so elegantly suffused with irresistible charm.

—*Max Beerbohm*

Now these are blurbs I can go with.

Koved is what the Jews call honor and glory, and I have not won enough of either to be vain about my own *koved*. I have been given an honorary doctorate from a university whose president would, I believe, be ready to allow that it is not yet first-class, and one of my books has won a regional prize. The only other award I have won is for tossing in twenty-one of twenty-five free throws at Green Briar Park in Chicago at the age of thirteen, for which I was supposed to receive a trophy but never did. All three of these awards have been immensely pleasing to me. Greater ones might have meant less. Such is my vanity that I don't think I care much to win honors that have been given to people before me who I don't think are fundamentally very honorable. By now, of course, nearly every prize in this nation has gone to someone or other whom your normally vain man is likely to find not only beneath him but also a touch beneath contempt. It is a problem, but not a deep one. "A man who pursues *koved*," I am told it says in the Talmud, "from him *koved* runs away." Let it run has become my view. I am for winning all possible prizes and awards, but at the same time I have reached an age where no prize or award will quell my doubts or satisfy my vanity.

"It is not possible," says La Rochefoucauld, "to enumerate all the kinds of vanity." Yet I feel I would be remiss if I didn't mention my vanity about what I take to be my general savvy about the world. There is no compelling evidence for my holding this belief, but hold it I do, quite in defiance of much experience to the contrary. Wary of being made a fool of—in modern life, my view is, paranoia is the better part of valor—I have not infrequently attempted to ward this condition off by attempting, ever so delicately, to fool others. Never shall I forget taking in a car to be repaired and telling the mechanic, lest he take me for a man entirely ignorant about cars (which of course I am), that I wasn't quite sure what was wrong, for I had only recently put in a throw-out bearing, faintly suggesting that I had done the job myself. In fact, I once had a throw-out bearing replaced in a car I owned, but what I didn't realize, and only later learned, was that a throw-out bearing is only required in a car with a clutch, and the car I was now bringing in for repair, having an automatic transmission, had no clutch. How the mechanic, over whose eyes I was attempting to pull the polyester, must have laughed and said confidently to himself, "Gotcha, buster!" "The surest way to be taken in is to think oneself craftier than other people," says (again) La Rochefoucauld. Thank you, my dear Duc, but if I want your advice, I shall ask for it.

One form of vanity I thought I was free of is family vanity. I hope my parents will forgive my saying so, but I come of a most non-distinguished family—if distinction be determined by achievement in public life, the arts, science, or commerce. In all these lines, we have, I can say without hesitation, done diddly. Not only did we fail to come over on the *Mayflower*, but we were lucky to have missed the *Lusitania*. I have often been at some confusion about describing my precise social class, until a short while ago when, reading an account of the life of Mrs. Humphry Ward, I noted Mrs. Ward described as being of "the cultivated middle class." On the spot I concluded that

I come from the "uncultivated middle class," or that class which lives in a certain comfort made possible by money but hasn't the least interest in culture. I have never had any shame about that, though no special pride in it, either. Life without ancestors, at least in twentieth-century America, is scarcely a hardship. But then I recalled a remark of Freud's, one doubtless intended to describe his own social condition, which was that better than having ancestors is to be an ancestor. Just so, *mais oui*, and eureka: I concluded that I, with a lot of luck, may just one day turn out to be an ancestor. Vanity, once more, finds a way.

When I was much younger, a famous novelist told me I was very worldly, and I have ever since been secretly vain about this. I have long thought myself a man of fastidious taste—"fastidiousness is the most pardonable of vices," said Chesterton, "but it is the most unpardonable of virtues"—and yet with a wide tolerance for taste less chaste than my own. A world where everyone dressed or felt about matters of taste as I did would be very dull. But so would a world where I couldn't make fun of those who don't, or they of me. Vanity is nothing if not invidious; nor is it known to obey the law of contradictions. My own vanity allows me to be tolerant yet hypercritical, reasonable yet perverse, worldly yet contemptuous of mere worldlings. Most convenient. I shouldn't know how to live without it.

"Vanity of vanities, saith the Preacher, vanity of vanities; all is vanity." That of course comes from Ecclesiastes, the book in the Old Testament that addresses itself to the question of vanity with rather depressing results, concluding over and over again: "Behold, all is vanity and vexation of spirit." The author of Ecclesiastes is not alone in his bleak views. As I have mentioned, Samuel Johnson wrote in rhyming couplets of "The Vanity of Human Wishes," and

Schopenhauer, who could take all the smiles out of Christmas, upped the ante in writing about "The Vanity of Existence," by which he meant all of it. Yet I wonder if it isn't closer to the truth to say not that human existence is vain but that vanity is part of human existence. I prefer Montaigne on this subject. In his essay "Of Vanity," he writes: "If others examine themselves attentively, as I do, they would find themselves, as I do, full of inanity and nonsense. Get rid of it I cannot without getting rid of myself. We are all steeped in it, one as much as another; but those who are aware of it are a little better off—though I don't know." I particularly like that final clause: "though I don't know." I don't, either, though I remain hopeful that awareness might make one perhaps a touch better off.

Montaigne's lengthy essay on vanity is highly digressive, even for him, who averred that his "ideas follow one another, but some-times it is from a distance, and look at each other, but with a sidelong glance." In fact, Montaigne's essay seems to be chiefly about death. Perhaps it is right that it should be so, for vanity, for all its inanity, at its best speaks to an avidity for the world; and it is in the light of death, as the author of Ecclesiastes well knew, that all seems vain. Yet anyone who is confident that vanity is purged by a recognition of death, even a very close recognition, may find himself surprised. I recall Sir William Haley once tell-ing me that, when he was editor of the *Times* of London, he one evening received a call from the butler of Lord X informing him that his lordship did not expect to make it through the night. What Lord X was doing in having his butler call was to give the *Times* a chance to get his obituary in good order, which strikes me as less astonishing than all too human.

Arthur Schopenhauer, Samuel Johnson, Edward Gibbon—I have

a distinct taste for these vanity-oh-all-is-vanity boys. They seem to have put so much energy into demonstrating that life is all a scam, a shuck, a silly if rather large-scale cosmic joke. Yet, if what they say was true, why did they themselves embark on such careful, monumental, furiously impressive works? I think it is because they didn't finally believe it. What they all knew and believed is that men and women are wondrous in their ability to take their eyes off the ball, to become wildly distracted, to believe astonishing nonsense, to let things get so badly out of hand that there can be little arguing with Henry James when, in an essay on Turgenev, he wrote: "Evil is insolent and strong, beauty enchanting but rare; goodness very apt to be weak; folly very apt to be defiant; wickedness to carry the day; imbeciles to be in very great places, people of sense in small, and mankind generally unhappy."

Schopenhauer, who was himself a meticulous dresser and who seemed to get so much pleasure out of showing why men are so miserable, may be quite right when he writes that vanity is "the appropriate term for that which has no solid or intrinsic value," but how much bleaker life would be without it. From Schopenhauer's perspective, we would all go under but for the agency of two simple impulses, hunger and the sexual instinct, "aided a little, perhaps, by the influence of boredom." Ought not vanity to be tossed in there, not only as a form of assuaging boredom (your vain man or woman is rarely bored, having him- or herself perpetually to contemplate) but in helping the world to go round, and for many of us to keep it spinning in the most amusing way?

Suggesting this redeeming social value for vanity is not intended as a provocation, a piece of intellectual perversity, like arguing that Mozart died too late or that we owe the invention of blood plasma to

Hitler. I quite mean it. Much of the little I have been able to accomplish thus far in life I find is owed in good part to vanity—with most of the remainder owed to guilt. Look to your own life to discover if it is much different. My bet is that it isn't. As for stakes, what about two of my French bow ties against your blow-dryer?

(1991)

Hair Piece

Plutarch, writing about Alcibiades, easily the most interesting if certainly not the most upright of fifth-century-BC Athenians, tells us everything about his adventures and quite a lot about his manner. The manner, there is reason to believe, was in good part the man. He was strikingly handsome; Plutarch, usually measured in his prose, goes so far as to speak of his "physical perfection." He writes: "As for Alcibiades' physical beauty, we need say no more than that it flowered at each season of his growth in turn, and lent him an extraordinary grace and charm, alike as a boy, a youth, and a man." So naturally elegant was he that even his physical defects came to seem attractive. "Even his lisp is said to have suited his voice well and to have made his talk persuasive and full of charm," notes Plutarch. Clearly, we are talking here about a nice-lookin' fella.

We are also talking about a fairly vain fella. Plutarch fills us in on the way Alcibiades wore his robes and on his disdain for the flute, which he refused to play because he felt that the instrument distorted the features of anyone who played it. He also makes plain that, owing to Alcibiades' radiant physical appearance, Socrates felt—wrongly, as we now know—that the young man must have natural virtue and sweetness of disposition. (No philosopher, you might say, like an old philosopher.) Plutarch tells us how many were the young Alcibiades's pursuers as well as the mature Alcibiades's admirers. But about the man's hair—its color, its texture, its length—not a word. Hirsutically, Plutarch has nothing to tell, except that when Alcibiades went to live among the Spartans, he wore "his hair untrimmed."

But what was Alcibiades' hair like when trimmed? Did he comb it forward or brush it back or over to the side? Was it curly or straight, wavy or lank, thick or fine? Black or blond or red or a shade of brown? Did he part it in the middle, or on one side, or not at all? Did his hairline recede as he grew older? (He died in his middle forties.) Did his hair turn gray? Did he carry a comb? Did he go in for oils, pomades, or other hairdressings, or did he leave his hair dry? Which did he prefer, Alcibiades, the wet or the dry look? If this man, noted for the excesses of his private life, was worried that playing a flute distorted his features, he couldn't have been unconcerned about the look of his hair. What a shame that we don't know how he dealt with the hair question! History, once again, leaves the significant facts blank.

Some writers are more hair-minded than others. Proust tells us little more of his M. Swann's hair than that it was red. Stendhal reports that Julien Sorel's hair is dark auburn in color, "growing down over his forehead [which] made it seem low, and gave him, in moments of anger, a rather forbidding, ill-natured air." Henry James could be—no doubt preferred to be—vague on the subject, never telling us the precise color of the Princess Casamassima's hair. Although James Joyce tells us everything else about Leopold Bloom—that he's five feet nine inches and 165 pounds, among other things—I'm not sure that he tells us anything about Bloom's hair.

I happen to be reading V. S. Pritchett's memoirs at the moment, and he is, so to say, a very hairy writer. In Pritchett's memoirs as well as in his stories men appear with forelocks and cowlicks and "waving mats of long thick white hair [with] a yellow streak in it" and "carefully barbered streaks over the long egg-like head." Pritchett remarks on his and his brother's youthful hair being "carefully greased by a hair oil we have invented: a mixture of olive oil and eau de Cologne, so that we smell like two young scented salads." Can it be that Pritchett, as a writer, is so attentive to other men's hair because his own, from the photographs I have seen, appears largely to have deserted him?

I would be inclined to think so, except that I am myself similarly attentive to this aspect of male plumage and always have been, without Pritchett's near baldness. My hair, like the nation at large, has been in a bit of a recession. Measured in hairline inches, I should say that, in my fifties, I have thus far along been allowed to keep roughly four-fifths of my hair, with a hairline that begins to resemble the southern portion of the continent of Africa, growing a bit thinnish around Mozambique. I shouldn't give, say, an index finger to have my lost hair restored to me, though I am generally pleased to have retained what hair I have.

I have been—how to say it?—hairdo observant all my days. When I was young I was even what I have seen described, in either *Esquire* or *Gentlemen's Quarterly*, as "hairdo intensive." In the earliest photograph of myself that I have seen, I have blondish hair combed into a large curl running the length of my head. Later my hair darkened and became not so much curly as wavy, but wavy understood in the context of stormy weather; unruly is probably the more precise word. Even today, in the somewhat impoverished condition of my scalp, if I fail to get regular haircuts, some impertinent and quite irrelevant wave appears atop my head, ready to crash against no known shore.

As a child I suffered no barber trauma. At least I can recall no tears at a barbershop. I do remember for a long spell in boyhood having to sit upon a board that raised me high enough for the barber to cut my hair, and I remember feeling that I had reached an important stage of maturity—perhaps at age seven or eight—when the board was no longer required. A boy's haircut was fifty cents when I was growing up, and then it shot up to seventy-five cents and then to a dollar. Once I began going to the barbershop on my own, my mother gave me an extra quarter and instructed me to tip the barber, unless he happened to be the owner of the shop, for it was thought undignified for the owner to accept tips. (My haircuts now cost twelve dollars, and I tip my barber three dollars.) The two rivaling barbershops of my boyhood were Levitan's and Ross's. I preferred Ross's, where the best barber was a tall, uncharacteristically (for a barber) reticent man named Dudley.

Dudley seems to me a fine name for a barber. So does the name Pete. I used to go to a barbershop called Pete's, where the owner, a very likable Austrian, cut my hair. I used sometimes to go in for my haircuts early in the day, at 9:30 or 10:00 a.m., in an attempt to avoid the rush; and more than once Pete, authoritatively flapping the sheet with which he covered his customers, asked, "Through for the day, Professor?" When he did this I wanted to but never did say, "Yes, Pete, except for my work on perfecting the hydrogen bomb, which is nearing completion and is there in my briefcase." A friend who also went to Pete's told me—when Pete had sold the shop to live nearer his son, an osteopath in Portland—that he had never had his hair cut by a barber whose name wasn't Pete. I told him to try the Yellow Pages. But he stayed with the new owner, an Italian named John.

My current barber, a West Virginian, is named Ralph, which strikes me as also a fine name for a barber. But then it may be that if you like your barber, as I do Ralph, whatever name he happens to carry will seem splendidly appropriate—just as, I have heard it said, the perfect title for any bestselling book is the title given to any book that happens to sell very well. The one barber in my past whose name I cannot remember was an elderly man in the basement of the old-fashioned barbershop at the Marion Hotel in Little Rock, Arkansas. He was frail and gentle, had rather fluffy white hair parted in the middle, and kept a portrait of Jesus next to his towels and barbering instruments and a pair of pajamas in the cabinet below his sink in case it snowed, which, in Little Rock, it almost never did. He had a memorably light and prettily rhythmic touch with the scissors.

I cannot say the same for Felix, a barber I went to in my young manhood. Felix used regularly to nick my neck and ears, and occasionally leave me with dried blood around and under my sideburns. He rarely gave me the same haircut twice. Like the man who said in defense of his continuing to go out with a notably unattractive woman that it wasn't the sex but the conversation afterward, so with Felix: it wasn't the haircuts but the laughter that went along with them that kept me coming back. An immigrant from Eastern Europe with a greenhorn's accent, Felix had my number; almost anything he said caused me to giggle. And much of what he said was what used to be called off-color—usually, let me add, way off, like chartreuse aquamarine or purplish magenta. I wouldn't say that Felix was lewd; he was the next two stages beyond lewd. No woman could pass his shop without Felix making an inappropriate comment. All his comments in this vein have left me, I am pleased to report, except for my memory of his once saying, as a woman who must have been in her nineties crept past his shop window, "Now dere, Epstein, is one built for speed."

Felix was also a super salesman, and I often used to leave his shop with conditioners, special shampoos, rubberized scalp massagers, tortoiseshell combs, and, on one notable occasion, condoms. Felix gave what I have elsewhere heard referred to, after the great power-tool company, as a Black & Decker haircut, and I finally left him when, one day, after catching the skin of my neck with his clippers, he caused me to take the name of the Lord in vain. I later discovered that, during this same haircut, he had badly, as I believe the term of art is, boxed off the hair at the back of my head, giving me a haircut that looked as if it had been acquired at the state prison at Joliet. I never returned.

I preferred smaller barbershops to larger, or what I sometimes think of as power, barbershops. Those were the shops where the atmosphere was generally a bit more Roman Empire (in decline) than I cared for. In such shops there were usually six or seven barber chairs, a manicurist (named—need I say?—Blanche), and at least one shoeshine man. I used to go to such a shop on lower Fifth Avenue in New York, and my mind retains the picture of many a businessman potentate having his hair cut while simultaneously taking a manicure and a shine, none of which distracted him from laying down the law on the forthcoming election or next Sunday's pro football game.

I enjoyed the spectacle provided by such shops—and I'm not sure many such still exist—but I couldn't quite partake in it. I have never had a manicure and think it safe to say that I shall go to my grave without having had one; somehow, I don't think there will be manicurists in the next world. I used to take shoeshines, but I no longer do, for getting one has become not only too expensive—two dollars and a one-dollar tip—but too fraught with social complications. In this realm as in many another we have come a long way from the time when the writer George Frazier could write a piece for *Esquire* entitled "The Second Greatest Shoeshine." (This shine was available in those days at the thirteen-chair shoeshine parlor in the Cleveland airport, where they used heat lamps on your shoes and a special blend of polish that didn't rub off on a clean handkerchief. The best shoeshine, as should always be the case with the best of anything, was, according to Frazier, in dispute, rivaling claimants being at the Waldorf, the Plaza, and a shop at the foot of Wall Street.) For some years now I have shined my own shoes and rather take pleasure in doing so.

But the great watershed moment in the history of men's hairdos, for me, came one day in Manhattan in the early 1960s when I passed a crowded barbershop on Lexington Avenue and through the window saw men in barber chairs getting their hair cut while wearing hairnets. I recall thinking that new heights of male vanity had been achieved. Arthur Koestler, I somewhere read, reported his anger when a rival for the affection of a beautiful woman told the woman that Koestler had slept in a hairnet. A filthy lie, Koestler claimed; the truth, he allowed, was that he only bathed in a hairnet. But now we had men sitting in plain public view in hairnets. A new age had arrived. *Fantastico!* The advent of male hairstyling was upon us.

Fancy male hairdos had existed in the past, beginning at least as early as the Persians, who cut off their hair and shaved the manes of their horses to lament the death in battle of a commander. In my own youth, there were ambitious pompadours, clean crew cuts, Chicagos (a flat crew-cut top with long greasy sides; in the city of Chicago, this hairdo was known as a Detroit), ducktails (to use the polite word), and a dramatic widow's peak with an added dippity-do effect at the front worn by the movie actor Tony Curtis, famous for the line, delivered in a movie to Debra Paget in the strongest possible New York accent, "Yonder lies da castle of my fadder the Caliph." If my own unruly hair could have supported a Tony Curtis, I, at the age of fifteen or sixteen, would have worn one proudly and looked, of course, perfectly ridiculous. Saved from this particular follicular folly, you might say, only by nature.

I wore my hair, as an adolescent, en brosse, with no part and no pomades. The great popular hair-taming potions of the day were products called Vitalis, Lucky Tiger, and Wildroot Cream-Oil; the last claimed it would give any man who used it the fairly serious social problem of keeping all the girls away. I note that in French *cheveux en brosse* means "crew-cut hair," but in fact my hair, though cut short and brushed back, wouldn't support a true crew cut, at least not one that gave a spiky stand-up effect, for which straighter hair than mine was required. Crew cuts were worn by athletes—the derogatory word *jock* had not yet come into being. Boys who were more interested in the girl chase wore more ambitious hairdos.

Hollywood led in this realm as in many another. In the movies, a leading man's hair was often big-city black and lacquered. The powerful movie hairdos were those of Clark Gable, Robert Taylor, Cary Grant, and Tyrone Power. Humphrey Bogart was an en brosse man, though closer observers than I inform me that he later wore a hairpiece, as did Bing Crosby. Gary Cooper's and James Cagney's hair seemed insignificant; so did Edward G. Robinson's and Jimmy Stewart's, though the latter took to wearing an unconvincing rug or toupee (pronounced among the cognoscenti as "toup"). Frank Sinatra was another big rug man and was said to have hired a woman, at a serious salary, to maintain his twenty-odd different hairpieces. John Wayne, too, wore a wig. In our own day, Burt Reynolds is of the wig party.

Clark Gable probably had the perfect movie star hair. In a number of his movies, owing to this hair, he was given the name Blackie. Lots of people took on nicknames from their hair, the most common, of course, being the name Red, which is a tough nickname to maintain once one's hair turns white. Some kids took the name Sandy from the color of their hair. A towheaded fellow, five or six years older than I, from my high school named Whitey Pearson went on to play basketball at the University of Kentucky. The language is deficient in not having a word, the visual equivalent of onomatopoeia, for things that sound as they look. I have in mind here a frightening character who roamed the halls of my high school who had the impressively menacing name of Whitey

Rasch. But the complications of race relations have put paid to the names Blackie and Whitey.

When I was in it, the military understood male vanity wonderfully well and, insofar as hair is a gymnasium for working out this vanity, made short work of it. One of the first events awaiting any military recruit is having his head shaved. The quickness of that first army haircut shocked. Three, perhaps four tracks across the scalp with a clipper—zip, zip, zip, zip—and one's individuality has suffered an immediate and powerful setback. That first military haircut was a great leveler, in a number of senses. All that careful coiffing was destroyed; all that empty vanity lay upon the floor. One felt so unsightly that one became almost automatically reconciled to the military life. With a haircut of this kind, where could one go anyway?

In the late 1950s and early 1960s, longish hair was not permitted in the army. I had a few sergeants, all of them black, who had mustaches. Nobody had a beard. I'm sure they weren't allowed. Today such restrictions would probably be subject to a civil liberties suit. I don't recall any bearded teachers at the University of Chicago when I was a student there, though there were a few with mustaches walking around. One of the most interesting mustaches, a small toothbrush job, belonged to the poet Elder Olson. The first man I knew with a beard was the literary critic Stanley Edgar Hyman. His was a brown beard, and it seemed right for him. Stanley was heavyish and had a good laugh and, when I saw him, wore three-piece brown suits, which rendered him a sepia and rather Jewish Santa Claus. In those days, the early 1960s, a beard was still a badge of bohemianism, an attention-getter, a conversation piece. People who invented personae for themselves wore beards—George Bernard

Shaw, Monty Woolley, Ezra Pound—and if one had a beard, it was somehow felt that one ought to have a sufficiently interesting personality to go along with it.

Student upheaval during the late sixties and early seventies put an end to that. As California may be credited with the great cultural advance of allowing a right turn on a red light, so the late sixties and early seventies may be credited with making long hair and facial hair not only acceptable but, in some settings, practically de rigueur. Beards and mustaches are fairly popular among men, but they seem especially so among academic men. Beards were a phenomenon once common among graduate students, and, as some of these students grew older and became professors, they kept their beards. Where I teach, roughly half the professors sport beards, mustaches, or hairdos befitting the Spanish conquistadores that most of them despise.

What is the significance of this? Perhaps it is in part a way of keeping allegiance with the spirit of protest of one's youth; or perhaps it is a way of belatedly getting in on the protest one never registered while meekly studying for one's doctorate. Perhaps it is meant to show that, given one's passion for learning, shaving can only be a time-consuming distraction and is better done away with. Recall in this regard Albert Einstein's uncombed hair. Montaigne, in his essay "On Educating Children," writes about "how many have I known in my time made as stupid as beasts by an indiscreet hunger for knowledge! Carneades was turned so mad by it that he could not find time to tend to his hair or his nails." Perhaps life is simply made easier for them by not having to shave. (Most academic beards are not carefully trimmed.) Perhaps, again, they are there out of pure vanity, because the people who sport them think themselves damned good-looking in them—or at any rate better looking than they would be without them. Perhaps some think beards and long hair make them look younger, though it is a discouraging fact that the hair on a man's face frequently turns gray before the hair on his head does.

My own sense is that the majority of men who grow beards tend only to add to their indistinctiveness. They become more Koren-ish—like those furry little figures in the cartoons of Edward Koren. (The combination of a woolly beard and a woolly head of hair reminds me of the child's game of men's faces that can be turned upside down and still show a face.) Some men experiment a good deal with different beards and mustaches. Facial hair is the poor man's version of cosmetic surgery, used to cover up a long lip, disguise a weak chin, camouflage bad skin. Beards taken on at midlife suggest discomfort with the way one has lived and looked in the first half of one's life. Too-frequent changes in the arrangement of a man's facial hair make him slightly suspect. One begins to feel about men who regularly experiment with different hairdos, beards, mustaches, and sideburns that they suffer a peculiar form of identity crisis—they don't know who they *aren't*.

The most recent trend in beardery seems to be the permanent one week's growth of facial hair. Show business once again set the precedent when an actor with the unpromising name of Don Johnson began wearing precisely such a scraggly beard on the television show *Miami Vice*. Yasser Arafat has long worn such a beard—and I call them, to myself, Arafats. How one sustains a permanent one week's growth of beard is not something I have been able to fathom. Long, unkempt hair and an Arafat can give a man what no advertising agency copywriter or designer has thus far thought to call "the homeless look," which, in a decadent society—who knows?—could become the rage.

George Balanchine, a very stylish and not notably hirsute man, once declared beards the very essence of stylelessness. His view was that the historical moment for beards had passed. They were authentic in his father's generation, but no longer. (Victorian men seem, somehow, appropriately hairy.) "All right," Balanchine said, "somebody wants to look like Christ, you know—the hair and all. But it's silly, it looks silly on people. It's all a fake."

And yet is it? I have known people, contemporaries, who have had beards for thirty years. (One of them once shaved the mustache portion of his beard and revealed that over the years he had developed a thin and disapproving upper lip; the mustache was returned instanter.) They will meet their maker in their beards. I should probably no longer recognize them on the street without their beards. Which reminds me of the joke, too elaborate to tell fully here, about the Hasid whom God does not allow in heaven because he fails to recognize him in an Armani suit and with his hair styled.

A beard, I feel, ought to be earned. Solzhenitsyn, in a Soviet labor camp, earned his beard and would seem quite unnatural without it. That he has an Amish look—a full beard with no mustache—seems even more appropriate. I have to strain to think of other earned beards. My own sense is that for a mustache to be earned, and not look fake, it probably ought to have been in place no later than 1947. Dean Acheson's Anglophiliac pencil mustache passed the test; so did Sidney Hook's small, dark, more Frenchified job. A mustache certainly ought not to have been grown after Robert Redford's mink-lipped appearance as the Sundance Kid in the movie *Butch Cassidy and the Sundance Kid*, which, because Redford looked so good in his, stirred many men to grow mustaches. Such a mustache, to work well, alas, requires the rest of Redford's face.

I once attempted a mustache, but a beard held no interest for me. I have never sported an Arafat, but years ago I used to prefer, if I had no social obligations, not to shave on weekends. No longer. Apart from occasional illness, I don't think I have failed to shave in nearly twenty years. I feel hygienically incomplete if I do not shave. A shave, like a haircut, has become something I look forward to, a positive pleasure. Now here, I do believe, is striking evidence of a quiet life.

I shave in the shower, afterward trimming my sideburns before the bathroom mirror. I use a safety razor. I regularly try new razors and new blades, though I secretly suspect that the companies who produce them do not provide improved products, but instead merely lower the quality of the ones previously on the market. At various times I have contemplated using a straight razor, but have decided against doing so, lest the probable consequence, that of cutting my own throat, make my insurance company uneasy.

I have been shaved by a barber with such a razor four or five times in my life, enjoying every moment of it each time, from the hot towels upon my cheeks and jaws to the brushing on of lather to the rustling sound of the steel razor scraping against my skin. I do not tend to yearn for the good old days, but being shaved every day by a barber, as many men once were, must have been a fine and refreshing thing. At the conclusion of a good shave I feel, as Henry James remarked when, late in his fifties, he shaved off his beard, "*forty* and clean and light."

Henry James was, from fairly early in life, bald. But he qualifies, I believe, as importantly bald. Churchill was importantly bald.

Edmund Wilson was, too. So were Montaigne and H. W. Fowler and Lenin, all of whom had well-trimmed goatees. Ralph Richardson was and John Gielgud remains not so much importantly as interestingly bald. In their own way, so were the novelist brothers Singer, I. B. and I. J., both of whom looked better bald than when, as young men, they had hair. (In his story "It May Never Happen," V. S. Pritchett describes "a stringy and dejected man, bald but not sufficiently so.") Robert Duvall, the actor, and Matt Williams, the third baseman of the San Francisco Giants, seem to me aggressively bald—bald men that you don't want to fool with. A. J. Liebling is not easily imagined with hair, nor is Socrates. Max Beerbohm, after he became bald, added a fine fluffy white mustache to his elegant getup. Varieties of baldness are considerable, nearly up there with those of religious experience. I do not say bald is beautiful, but it can be manly and impressive.

The first historical figure whom we know to have suffered psychologically from his baldness was no less a personage than Julius Caesar. He was, according to Suetonius, a bit of a dandy, "always keeping his head carefully trimmed and shaved" and even removing his body hair. Caesar's enemies apparently mocked his baldness, treating it as a disfigurement, and Suetonius goes on to report that "of all the honors voted him by the Senate and People, none pleased him so much as the privilege of wearing a laurel wreath on all occasions—[and] he constantly took advantage of it." Caesar was also the first major figure in history to avail himself of the hairdo known as the "comb-over," or "cover-up," or "McGovern" (after the former senator and presidential candidate). In the vain—in both senses of the word—attempt to hide his baldness,

Caesar used to comb the thin strands of hair that grew on the back of his neck forward. Napoleon, we know, was a comb-forward man; General Douglas MacArthur was a comb-over man, taking longish strands from the side of his head and pasting them across his scalp. From afternoons spent in athletic clubs, I have seen the intricate labors that go into such hairdos. The general anxieties of men who have chosen to wear them cannot, I think, be eased on windy days.

Few men take the loss of hair easily. For one thing, it is an early intimation of mortality, for as we come into the world nearly hairless, so do many of us depart it in something like the same condition. For another, baldness is viewed, in many quarters, as less than romantic. In the movies and theater, bald leading men are uncommon, though Yul Brynner, an exception, exhibited what most people would agree was virile baldness. Nowadays, too, many black athletes and white Olympic swimmers shave their heads. Yet, in television news, one never sees a bald anchorman. Without their hair and the careful coiffing expended upon it, Dan Rather, Tom Brokaw, and Peter Jennings, the major network anchormen, would have to sell neckties, which would be fine with me.

Wigs and rugs, toups and pieces are among the possibilities open to men greatly uncomfortable with their baldness. Hair plugs, a surgical implant procedure of some expense, is another. One can never predict what sort of men will avail themselves of such items. I know a podiatrist who is a hair-plugs man, a pharmacist who totes an ambitious widow's peak not of nature's making, the sweet father of a friend who dyed his hair shoe-polish black. "A permanent lifetime answer to baldness!" runs one advertisement seeking the shekels of the bald and balding. "Wake up to a full head of hair!" runs another. If the exclamation marks from such ads and the many thousands that have come before them could be used as hair, baldness would be at an end, for the growth of new hair has historically been one of the great fields of quackery. If anyone ever does discover a cure for baldness, his great-grandchildren and their grandchildren will be able to laugh from the penthouse balconies of apartments overlooking the world's most fashionable streets, so wealthy will he leave them. Customers will always be there.

Meanwhile, many men who lose their hair tend to go in for over-compensation. An unusually large number of men who wear pony-tails, for example, seem to be balding. Pulling their hair back in a ponytail is a mistake, I believe, for it seems chiefly to emphasize their hair loss. Besides, few things are more dispiriting than a gray ponytail. It suggests aging hippiedom, than which little is sadder: a flower child is one thing, a flower grandfather something else again. I have friends and acquaintances with mustaches and beards and comb-overs, but I don't, at the moment, know anyone who wears a ponytail. I do have a friend who tells me that, at his athletic club, he has encountered men who own and wear false ponytails. What a piece of work is man!

Not long ago, listening to the excellent Vermeer Quartet, I noted on my program that it is composed of two beards (second violin and cello), one male permanent (first violin), and one longish hair-over-the-ears arrangement (viola). The two bearded musicians are balding, the second violinist from the front, the cellist in the back. The violist, when bowing, revealed a monk's cap of baldness, and he may also be a hair-plug man, a judgment I make based on the preternatural evenness of the straight-across hairline situated midway back upon a high forehead. Longhair music has thus taken on a new meaning in our day. It is a cartoonist's delight.

I suppose the natural tendency is for each of us to consider others by the light of his own vanity. My own vanity, since becoming an adult, has directed me to appear as little obviously vain as possible. In my particular twist on masculine vanity, I seek a quiet, subdued, nicely understated elegance—and I am fairly confident that I don't quite bring it off. Pity. At the same time that vanity is the dealer in these hirsutical decisions, temperament, too, takes a hand. I would find it extremely difficult, soon after arising from sleep on a gray Chicago morning, with a vast quantity of obligations to fulfill, to look into the bathroom mirror and see staring back at me a gray Fu Manchu mustache, a thick set of snowburns (as I have heard white-haired sideburns called), and D'Artagnan-length hair waiting to be pulled back in a ponytail. No, with such accouterments festooned from my *punim*, I could not face the day. At the first glint of depression, I should doubtless shave it all off, and shave off the hair left on my head for good measure.

In these matters, one's own generation's ideal of masculinity also obviously plays an important role. One can either go with the flow or try to stop it. The first prospect renders a man ridiculous, the second hopeless. Yet another possibility is to take a seat on the sidelines, preferably in the shade, a glass of wine in one's hand, and not bark but laugh as the caravan passes. John Updike, writing in the *New Yorker*, after expressing the self-denigration that has become fairly standard with him, writes that "the impression has been growing upon me that I am surrounded by hostile haircuts," and he goes on to report that, in the wide range of male hairdos now current, "we're all butting for psychological space, and leading with our warheads." Something to it, perhaps. So many bizarre arrangements for male hair must have some meaning.

Peter the Great must have thought so in his time, for he, with his own hand, shaved off the beards of the boyars, which he thought a symbol of their backwardness. Montaigne, in his essay "On Ancient Customs," drew such a meaning from the dominant hairdos of his own day when he wrote: "Sidonius Appollinaris says that the ancient Gauls wore their hair long on the front of their heads and shaved close at the neck; that is precisely the hairstyle which has been brought back into fashion by the slack and womanish mode of our own century." We have here the hairdo view of history, which may be no goofier than many another put forward by postmodernist historians. (And who was it who said that the postmodernist always rings twice?)

True enough, our own century, or at any rate the last third of it, has seen some pretty wild do's. Blacks alone in this time have run through processed hair, the Afro, the drippy, the stack or muffin, cornrows, and dreadlocks, a hairstyle that is shared by black men and women and that is achieved by "dreading" one's hair. Some young blacks will tell you that a political statement is intended in many of these hairdos; others will say that it can all be chalked up to amusement. Certainly, the odious skinheads are making a statement, not to speak of a direct political identification, in shaving their heads as they do. Punk hairdos, among them high Mohawks, liberty spikes, and Day-Glo purple and orange dyes, are making a statement, too—one which I read to mean, "Look at me, Jack, test your own reaction, and get edgy."

But what does it mean that more working-class young men now seem to avail themselves of long hair than do young men of the middle class? Or that the two groups who seem to have the highest proportion of mustaches among them appear to be homosexuals and cops? Do you suppose that even to have a regular hairdo is to make a political statement, as Orwell—a high-pompadour and pencil-thin-mustache man—said that even to be apolitical is to be political, a formulation that, in my view, has more rhythm than truth?

Something rather unseemly there is about a man lavishing too much care upon his hair. In the end we are left with our prejudices, however implausible they might be. I prefer not to have waiters too much more fancily coiffed than I am. If I were a woman, I should prefer not to go out with a man who looks as if he has spent longer on his hair than I have. Worst of all is artificially induced naturalness. Carl Sandburg's rich mane of white hair is an instance of the artificial made to look natural. Sandburg must have felt that such hair was required of him in his persona as the "people's poet." Robert Frost, who almost specialized in put-downs of Sandburg (Sandburg was the only poet, said Frost, to gain in translation), once said of him that he was upstairs "trying to get the hair into his eyes."

"Behold my brother Esau is a hairy man and I am a smooth man," Jacob announces to his mother, stating a problem, but drawing no conclusions. Perhaps he ought to have done. People have for centuries been judged by their hair. Redheads were thought to be hot-tempered. There is practically a sociology of blond women, not much of it very complimentary, except that they are believed to have more fun. A high forehead was said to have been a sure sign of intelligence. Many of us who have had high foreheads conferred upon us by hair loss have an instinctive distrust of a man with too low a hairline. Think about these things long enough and the traditional spelling of "*hare*brained" begins to feel as if it ought to be changed to "*hair*brained." My own last words on the subject, which I hope to repeat many a time more, are "Short on top, fairly close along the sides, and not too high over the ears."

(1993)

Nicely Out of It

I have of late been feeling comfortably, luxuriously, really quite happily out of it. In wondering how this pleasing condition has come about, it occurs to me to ask an anterior question: Was I ever truly *in* it? Or, to keep my prepositions straight, Was I ever truly *with* it? I'll get to the meaning of that "it" presently, but the "with" speaks to a happy conformity, an almost total consonance, *with* one's own time. Carried to the highest power, being with-it calls for being a conformist just a little ahead of one's time, which is, come to think of it, a short definition of a trendsetter. I cannot say that I ever achieved such an exalted station, though I have the feeling that I might have had I stayed on the job. But I abandoned with-it-ry fairly early in life and hence, for better *and* worse, dropped out as a serious conformist.

I fear an air of put-down has crept into that paragraph, when all I intended was a mild whiff of self-congratulation. Let me attempt to make amends by saying quickly that I realize conformity, or living in spiritual consonance with one's own time, is no small pleasure. I myself last felt fully with-it nearly forty years ago, a period I often think of as the most pleasant in my life.

The "it" in "with-it" refers to life, life in its full and fine vibrancy, especially life lived at the very vortex of contemporary experience. To wear the clothes, to eat the food, to hum the tunes, to think the thoughts of one's own time, all perfectly unselfconsciously; to feel utterly at ease in the atmosphere in which one lives, without any complaint or fret; to be up to the moment, au courant, jollily, joyously with-it—all this is, no doubt about it, a delightful state in which to find oneself.

I was seventeen when last in this state. I thought that I knew pretty much all I needed to know about life, with only a little filling in required here and there. I picture myself as I was then, walking down the corridors of Senn High School, wearing a green-and-white letter sweater, Levi's, white sweat socks, loafers. At my side is a girl named Jackie, with a winning smile and a generous bosom draped in softest cashmere; in the background, the city of Chicago, which seems endless in the possibilities it offers a young man of adventurous spirit; ahead of me, an unclouded and entirely promising future. That happy fellow—me—now seems as distant, really quite as historical, as the head of a youth on an Antiochian coin of the second century BC.

What would have been the reaction of that serenely thoughtless young man had he, around that time, drawn a fortune out of his cookie that all too accurately prophesied: "You will soon and forever after live at a self-consciously oblique angle—skeptically, critically— to the life of your times"? "Whaddaya, kidding me?" he would likely have replied. Had I, knowing what I know now, been on the scene, I would have implored him, "Struggle against it, kid. Escape your fate. Don't, whatever you do, travel to Samarra. Forget the fortune, eat the cookie, pay your check, fight to remain pretty much as you are." But such advice probably wouldn't have mattered. Fate isn't so easily eluded.

When young I not only thought it important to be, but found no difficulty in staying, completely and cheerfully with-it. When I—not quite so young any longer—determined to become a writer, I fought manfully to stay up to the moment. By "up to the moment" I mean absolutely current in politics and popular culture. I felt under an obligation to know the key politicians as well as the popular songs; to go even to the bad movies; to listen to television talk shows; to glimpse most of the popular magazines, including the women's magazines, of the day. All this was done with deliberation and under the banner of keeping in touch with my country and its culture, which, as a writing man, I felt it incumbent upon me to do.

As best as I can date such an event, I believe I began to feel out of it roughly in 1966. Around that time the curtain fell, dividing the country between the young and the not-young, and I found myself, even though only twenty-nine, on the not-young side of that curtain. The student revolution had begun, and I—in taste, in temperament, in point of view—had ancien régime so clearly written all over me that I might as well have worn a powdered wig.

The unintelligible lyrics of rock music may have been the first inkling I had that I would fall further and further out of it. I continued occasionally to listen to country-and-western music with comic pleasure, learning that, as you yourself may not be aware, "God made honky-tonk angels" as well as that, what is perhaps more obvious, "everybody's somebody's fool." But listening to hard rock seemed more on the order of a punishment, and my desire to stay generally with-it, though still real, stopped short of masochism. (Masochist to sadist: Beat me. Sadist to masochist: No.)

I hope the following confession doesn't land me a job on the U.S. Supreme Court or even, God forfend, as president, but—you may as well know this up front, Senator—I have never smoked pot, another sign of my early out-of-it-ness. I have been in rooms where people seemed moronically happy puffing on the good stuff, as they called it; and I was once at a party where everyone sat in a circle and passed around a joint, but when it got to me I felt the whole ritual vaguely preposterous—your ironic man, poor chap, tends to eschew ecstasy—and passed it along without partaking.

Although I loved the movies of my youth, I found I couldn't take the movies of the 1960s and most of those that followed all that seriously. In fact, the more ambitious the intentions of these movies, the more they seemed like comic books to me. To prove my out-of-it-ness once again, in my pantheon Pauline Kael never came close to replacing Edmund Wilson.

I don't for a moment wish to give the impression that I live unrelievedly on the highbrow level of culture. I live there with a great deal of relief. In the realm of culture, I rather admire people whose standards are more stringent than my own. I was recently talking with a friend to whom I happened to mention the name Steve McQueen. He stopped the flow of conversation to ask who Steve McQueen was. I found it striking that a man in his late fifties could live all his days in the United States without having heard of Steve McQueen. I once asked this same friend, the music critic Samuel Lipman, not long after I had come to know him, if he ever went to the movies or watched much television. "I consider the movies and television," he announced, "dog droppings" (I euphemize). Not even to allow these major American forms of entertainment the dignity of horse or bull by-products seemed to me perhaps further than I wished to go, but his distancing himself from the seductions of popular culture seemed to me impressive nonetheless.

I still watch lots of sports on television and go to five or six baseball games a year. I am well known at my local video-rental store, where I often ask for assurance that the movie I am about to rent isn't all shooting and screwing. (I am usually told, rightly, that it isn't: the movie generally turns out to be only about 60 to 80 percent so.) I nowadays steer clear of all talk shows and am proud to report that a number of currently famous people are at least still obscure to me. Nevertheless, by osmosis of a mystical kind, I know rather more than I wish I did about people with no possible relevance to my life and whose minds I find more than a jot less than fascinating. I feel I would be living a better, a more elevated life if I didn't recognize the names Burt Reynolds, Marv Albert, Madonna, Connie Chung, Willie Nelson, David Gergen, Regis Philbin, and Dan Dierdorf. But, alas, I do.

In the progressive stages of out-of-it-ness, I not long ago crossed the line from merely being mildly out of it to taking a small but genuine pride in being out of it. I'm not sure I can convey how pleased I am at never having seen an Andrew Lloyd Webber musical, or the television show *L.A. Law*, or Arsenio Hall, or the Whitney Museum Biennial. How regrettable that I didn't take a pass on the Robert Mapplethorpe show, the last episode of *Cheers*, or Jay Leno! I suppose one can't be perfect—one can't, after all, hope to miss everything. More and more, however, I have begun to feel that it would be nice to try.

I feel I am progressing nicely when, standing in the checkout line at the supermarket, glimpsing the grocery store press (our version of England's gutter press), I don't recognize the names of people involved in scandals, or when I haven't a clue about the person on the cover of *People*. Yet there is no gainsaying that I do know the names Dolly Parton, Loni Anderson, and Tina Turner (not to speak of Keena Turner, the former San Francisco 49ers linebacker). So many, after all, are the old names I do not know enough about: Callimachus, Hypatia, Erasmus, Palestrina. I know, I fear, altogether too much about the Barbarians and not nearly enough about the Hellenes.

The names one must nowadays know to qualify as with-it lack not only quality but much in the way of staying power. In human typology, most are a little lower than I wish to go. If names there must be, let us have names of better quality. I even have a taste, come to that, for the gentle art of name-dropping. I wish I had a talent for it as sure as that of the late Ben Sonnenberg, the public-relations man, who specialized in what his son has called "the secondary name-drop." When asked if he knew George Gershwin, for example, Sonnenberg would reply: "*Know* him? I used to play gin rummy with his mother." He also once told an interviewer: "I know the difference between Irving Berlin and Isaiah Berlin, and I know them both." I shouldn't myself at all mind being able to say that I played Ping-Pong with their fathers—and beat both badly. I should mind this a lot less than having to confess, as I now do, that I know who Tommy Tune is.

One doesn't become out of it overnight. I happened recently to have been reminded that as long as fifteen years ago, when I was a mere slip of a youth of forty or so, I was called, by a book reviewer, "crankish" and "rearguard." This was distinctly not meant as a compliment, but, somehow, I didn't find myself taking offense. I even felt myself a touch precocious in being judged out of it so relatively young. If I lived to be eighty, there was no telling how far out of it I might eventually go; perhaps I could slip all the way back into the eighteenth century, which has always seemed to me a nice place to visit.

Apart from having a naturally conservative temperament, there are any number of reasons for falling out of it. One is that it might be part of some general personal breakdown. Staying with-it, after all, can be a terrible strain. When F. Scott Fitzgerald declared his crack-up—in *Esquire*, of all places—he was partially declaring his wish to be out of it, at least for a while. In a passage demonstrating that, even in the midst of a crack-up, he could continue to be charming, Fitzgerald wrote:

> Trying to cling to something, I liked doctors and girl children up to the age of about thirteen and well-brought-up boy children from about eight years old on. I could have peace and happiness with these few categories of people. I forgot to add that I liked old men—men over seventy, sometimes men over sixty if their faces looked seasoned. I liked Katharine Hepburn's face on the screen, no matter what was said about her pretentiousness, and Miriam Hopkins' face, and old friends if I only saw them once a year and could remember their ghosts.

Another reason for falling out of it is that you don't much like your times and wish, either gently or brusquely, to slip away from them. I have often enough felt sufficiently at odds with our times to have to consider this as an explanation for my slipping gradually out of it, though I don't, in my own case, think this the chief reason. Yet when I consider what it would take today to be considered with-it, the prospect, so pleasing to some, is to me, to put it gently, problematic. To begin with, there is the geographical problem. One cannot really be considered seriously with-it in, say, Minneapolis, or Salt Lake City, or Milwaukee, or Sacramento. One could perhaps qualify while living in San Francisco or Los Angeles; or, from a specialized standpoint (in outdoor living, in politics) in Seattle or Washington, D.C. Abroad, London, Paris, Rome, Florence continue to strike the gong as with-it cities.

But the with-it capital of America, probably of the world, is New York—more specifically, Manhattan—a fact that in itself may be enough to discourage many from the demands of a thoroughly with-it life. A great many people stand ready to put up with the punishing quality of quotidian life in New York—crime, filth, rudeness, high prices—in exchange for the reward of thinking themselves at the center of the action. I have known people who have left careers—in teaching, in publishing—rather than leave New York. What I believe alarmed them about the prospect was their sense that being out of New York meant, in the end, being out of it—and this, clearly, appalled. What price with-it-ry?

What, today, would a thoroughly with-it life look like? Much time, I imagine, would have to be spent at art galleries and shows looking at many doubtless extraordinary, mostly extra-aesthetic objects. Evenings would find one at a vast variety of new restaurants, tucking into all sorts of dubious delicacies. Either before or after dining one would be expected to buzz off to the Brooklyn Academy of Music for an evening of interminable avant-garde opera or to an unpleasant play on a terrifying subject Off-Off-Broadway. One would, as a man, be wearing the bulky, dark clothes of the kind I see advertised in *Gentlemen's Quarterly* or *Esquire*. One's hair would be pomaded and brushed back; a single earring as like as not would dangle from one ear. One would have to read a great deal of that journalism, companion sheets to the grocery press, that ought to go by the name of the with-it press: at a minimum, this includes *October, Details, Rolling Stone, W*, the *New Yorker, Vanity Fair*, the *New York Observer*.

As clearly as New York is the with-it capital of the United States, just so clearly is Chicago, my own city, nicely out of it. The pretensions of with-it-ry—in culture, in fashion, in social life—somehow don't seem to go down at all well in Chicago. Some people in Chicago do attempt to be with-it, but in the act of doing so they tend to seem faintly ridiculous. With-it clothes, for example, don't really succeed here. The characteristic male physique in Chicago is that of the Mayors Daley, *père et fils*, or the Brothers Belushi: chunky, short in the legs, thick in the chest, and not at all made for the clothes of the moment, or any moment that I know, except perhaps the Visigoth invasion of Rome. Chicago is a city where no one is going to look down on you if you are carrying around an extra twenty or thirty pounds. (The food of choice is pizza and Italian beef-and-sausage combination sandwiches, which tend not to conduce to that starved-to-perfection look that marks the with-it of our day.) Great cultural institutions exist—the Chicago Symphony, the Art Institute, the Lyric Opera— and a fair amount of serious art gets made, but, owing to the necessary exclusions of serious culture, it is understood that they are not as central to the city as are the Chicago Bears, Bulls, Cubs, White Sox, and Blackhawks.

But even in the fastness of Chicago, with its anti-chic spirit, it isn't always easy to turn your back on what the rest of the world construes to be with-it. A decade or so ago, for example, I discovered that I had ceased to read much contemporary fiction. Faster than you can say Italo Calvino, I had fallen two Malamuds, three Roths, a Bellow and a half, four Mailers, and five or six Updikes behind. I had let

John Irving pass me by. So, too, Ann Beattie, Joan Didion, Gabriel García Márquez. Every book you read is a book you don't read, by my reckoning, and there were too many important noncontemporary books I had not yet read. Life, as everyone knows, is short, and it doesn't take long to learn just how damnably long inferior art can be.

Still, I had a bad conscience about not reading these novelists. Apart from the aesthetic pleasures it brings, the novel, I believe, is a great instrument of discovery. When it is going well, the novel brings the news—to my mind the only enduringly serious news—about what is going on in the human heart. So, attempting to quiet my bad conscience, and turn a few bucks at the same time, I signed on with a magazine to become its critic of contemporary fiction, thinking to catch up with all the Malamuds, Roths, Updikes, Beatties, Didions, García Márquezes, and Mailers. And I did. On balance, I think I can report that it wasn't worth it. Either these writers had become worse or I had become smarter, perhaps a little of both, but I found they no longer spoke to, and certainly not for, me. As for the human heart, most of these writers turned out to be more concerned with organs four buttons below that.

I have begun to drop out again. I have taken a pass on what is promised to be the last of John Updike's Rabbit Angstrom novels: when Rabbit died, I failed to turn up at the funeral. I have not read Salman Rushdie's *The Satanic Verses*, and don't intend to. I recently reached page 110 of Philip Roth's novel *Operation Shylock* and I called it quits, having decided that to finish his books you have to be at least as interested in Philip Roth as is the author, which isn't easy. There is an American novelist named T. Something Boyle. The Something is a complicated name beginning with a *C* and has three or four syllables. I am perfectly content to think of him as T. Congressman

Boyle, not being sufficiently interested—or perhaps being too complacently out of it—to bother even getting his name right. This is the second time I have bailed out on contemporary novelists, and it seems to me increasingly unlikely that I shall bail back in. I may be beautiful, as the blues song has it, but I'm goin' to die someday, so, I now tell myself, how 'bout a little serious reading before I pass away?

If a loss of interest in the news is another sign of being out of it, I qualify here, too. Many years ago, living in New York, I used to read three newspapers a day. I now read one, the *New York Times*, and that I read reluctantly and, following the rule of prostitutes in Athens, never, never on a Sunday. I do not read a local paper, which renders me more than a little out of it in my own hometown. Not reading the *Chicago Tribune*, I usually do not know the names of the most recent serial killer in town, the most recently fired superintendent of schools, or the most recently traded hockey players. Somehow, though, despite this, I seem to get by.

I begin each day's *New York Times* by turning directly to the obituary page. This, I am told, is a standard old guy's move. So be it. Who died seems to me the most important news. I am interested not only in famous deaths but in quaint ones, such as that of Rita Ford, age ninety-two, who ran what sounds like a lovely store selling music boxes in Manhattan. The other morning I was surprised to find my own name on the obit page. Surely I hadn't become so out of it that I failed to notice my own death. I was relieved to discover that it was not I but a professor of philosophy at Amherst of the same name who had died. I hope my friends, reading this obituary, were similarly relieved. If my enemies were sorely disappointed, they should not worry: I promise to make it up to them eventually.

I next turn to the letters columns, looking for—and not very often finding—a man after my own heart. I glimpse the op-ed page, filled, as V. S. Naipaul once noted about a character he despised in his novel *Guerrillas*, with so many opinions that do not add up to a point of view. I read perhaps two editorials a week, usually not all the way through, but quickly turning to the last few sentences—the bottom line, you might say. I blaze through the foreign news, turning away with a wince from the standard stories of barbarity and natural disaster in the Third World. I read the national news for accounts of scandal, political squalor, decline and fall generally. I probably read the pages devoted to the arts—news and reviews of fiddlers and scribblers, daubers and dancers—more thoroughly than any others, though I come away from them no more satisfied for my greater effort. Like the eighty-year-old bachelor in a V. S. Pritchett story, I have begun to pick up each morning's paper searching for something that will annoy me—and, happy to report, I almost always find it.

Skimming the newspaper seems luxurious to me. Once, when I worked on a political magazine, I used to have to read the *New York Times* with great attention to stories that held no intrinsic interest for me. I had to note the exact spelling of the name of the latest ephemeral revolutionary party in Peru, the absence of N. V. Podgorny from the photograph of members of the Soviet Central Committee, the name and party affiliation of every member of the United States Senate. I was allowed to stop only at the prices of cocoa in Ghana.

Not long after I departed this job, letting natural interest be my guide, I began to eliminate entire categories of newspaper stories from my reading. Stories about agriculture went first. Space exploration followed. I soon ceased to read anything about central Africa. On the subjects of Latin America and the Indian subcontinent no one has ever accused me of being duomaniacal, and, based on my newspaper reading, no one ever will. I read stories about the environment only intermittently. I rarely read stories about the economy, contenting myself with knowledge at the headline level of detail; if professional economists can't understand the economy—as, clearly, they cannot—what chance have I?

I continue to read stories about blacks and Jews, murder and rape, the disgrace of politicians, the fall in educational standards, people making jackasses of themselves. I check the sports page, but, fortunately, the *New York Times* has so poor a sports page that it does not detain me long. My lapsed interest in the news might trouble me more if I didn't recall the novelist Isaac Bashevis Singer once telling me (I never played gin rummy with his mother, by the way) that he preferred the New York *Daily News* to the *New York Times*. "It's a vonderful paper, the *Daily News*, Mr. Epstein," I remember Singer saying in his strong greenhorn accent, "filled mid every kind of moider, scandal, and disgusting act. Just poifect for a novelist."

Reading the *New York Times* in so glancing a way, I find I no longer know many of the names of the paper's regular reporters and critics, where once I knew every last Drew, Brooks, Harrison, and Clifton among them. But then neither do I know the names of the editors of *Time* or *Newsweek*, where once I knew nearly the full mastheads of both magazines. I know a dentist who claims to have practically lost his practice when he canceled his office subscription to *People*, but in my dentist's office I am not even tempted by the rag. What's the point? If the redoubtable Cher were to move in with an elephant I suppose I would read about it, though before the day is out I am certain to have forgotten the elephant's name.

As a result of all this inattention to the news, I am not sure that today I can name more than twenty members of the United States

Senate, where once I knew them all. I know the name of my alderman, but I had lately to be reminded of the name of my congressman. I cannot tell you the names of the prime ministers of Italy, India, or Algeria, among other countries. With the exception of Kurt Waldheim, I cannot tell you the name of a secretary-general of the United Nations since U Thant. What I chiefly remember about Mr. Thant is that he allowed himself to be badly snookered by a New York landlord, and he wound up having to pay an outrageously high rent on his apartment. This incident made me think at the time that if you were ready to believe in the efficacy of the United Nations, you might be interested in some real estate I could show you.

I note, too, that I am less attentive to new slang and jargon than I once was. Even when I learn what new phrases mean, I don't use them, except for comic purpose. I don't mean merely the obviously stupid language of political correctness—with its silly *isms* (fattism, ageism, classism) and *ableds* (differently, otherly, uniquely)—which only an imbecile would take seriously anyway. I never say "focused" and, myself, try to stay "unfocused." (A recent *New York Times* obit for a professor of French at Columbia carried the subtitle "A Focus on Diderot.") I blanch at the new use of *fun* as an adjective, as in fun couple, fun time, fun run. Sometimes I find I not only dislike a term—*graphic* novel, for example, for a novel-length comic book—but the very thing it describes. This category includes "dramadoc" and "docutainments"; also, while the bad taste is still in my mouth, "infomercials" and "infopreneurs." Let us not speak—you won't catch me doing so—of "foodies," "compassion fatigue," "cruelty-free," or "cocooning." Hey, dude, I tell myself once I get going on this subject, chill out.

Reading the with-it press often doesn't chill me out but merely chills me. There I see and instantly forget the names of movie starlets of whom I have not previously heard. I read about young entrepreneurs—usually designers, or gym-shoe manufacturers, or "infopreneurs," many of them—who seem to me empty of everything but the harsh emotions connected with the kind of ambition that has nothing behind it but the sheer desire to get ahead. I thumb through an issue of *Esquire* or *Vanity Fair* and nothing, not even the ads, holds any interest for me. In the pages of these magazines, as a line from an old song has it, "I just don't see me anywhere."

For the first time I have begun to skim in my reading, often bottom-lining an article after giving it a three- or four-paragraph shot at arousing my interest. I bottom-line on the assumption that there is nothing useful I can learn from the article, or there is nothing sufficiently interesting to be worth stealing from its author's prose, or there is nothing in it that is going to stay in my mind anyhow. Skimming seems eminently sensible to me, but because it is something I never used to do—Justice Holmes claimed to finish every book he began and ceased to do so only in his seventy-fifth year—it also seems to me another sign of falling out of it.

Is this intensification of my out-of-it-ness no more than a sign of getting older? Getting older of course means—and here I do not euphemize—getting closer to death. In *The Sixties*, the last volume of his journals, Edmund Wilson, then in his late sixties and in poor health, comments again and again on how "the knowledge that death is not far away . . . has the effect of making earthly affairs seem unimportant. . . . And [it is] harder to take human life seriously, including one's own passions and achievements and efforts." Wilson attests to feeling "the *flimsiness of human life*," where, "surrounded by the void of the universe, we agitate ourselves, one sometimes feels, to very dubious purpose."

Death, even the hint of death, has a way of making nearly everything else trivial. I was walking away from reading a petulant review of a recent book of mine, beginning to work up a temporary but genuine sulk about it, when I met an acquaintance, who told me he had been discovered to have colon cancer. I'll take, I thought to myself, the bad review. Can it be that I am gaining a modicum of perspective, some distant hint of what is important and what is utterly beside the point in life? If so, this could be troublesome, for true perspective will put a person out of it faster than anything going. With perspective, one hears the dogs barking as the caravans hove out of sight and knows that future caravans will follow, each of them soon enough also to disappear. Why be one of the barking dogs?

As one grows older, there is, I suppose, something appropriate, even natural, about falling out of it. To be old and too much with-it, in the same way, can be quite unseemly. A man in his sixties ought not to write a book about Michael Jackson; a woman of seventy ought not to dress like Janet Jackson. (I wish I didn't know those two names.) The quickest way I know to be called Pops or Old-Timer is to show up at a rock concert wearing a ponytail when you're in your fifties.

I suppose a happy medium is possible in all this. I have friends in their seventies with a serious interest in the performing arts, who make it their business to see most movies, plays, and dance groups going—as sometime theatrical producers, they have a professional interest— and they do it with dignity and without any of the heavy breathing one generally hears when older people try to stay with-it. Edmund Wilson, too, attempted to stay with-it, within reasonable limits. He continued to go to the theater, to comedy reviews, to the movies, to the occasional nightclub (the tumult from which, he allowed, "stunned" him). But he reserved the right, sacred to the old, to find the young wanting, complaining at one point that he found it regrettable that so many of the young among the artists and intellectuals he knew in New York and Boston were in psychoanalysis.

In my own out-of-it-ness, though, I sense something more going on than my growing older and, hence, nearer to pegging out. I think a good bit about death, but do not do so, I believe, obsessively. While I have allowed that there is much about our time that is not to my taste, I am not in anything like the condition of Edmund Wilson's friend Dorothy Sharp, who, he says, "dislikes everything that is going on (but I and so many of my generation feel the same way). . . . It is plain that she is losing the will to live." A number of the acts featured just now in our cultural and political life may irritate me, but I still enjoy the show and have no intention of giving up my seat any sooner than I have to. No, something deeper is going on.

What it may be is a decisive change in sensibility, leading to a similarly decisive change in character, some of it generational, that makes it impossible for me to partake fully in contemporary culture. I have tried to formulate what is behind these changes, but without much success. Then, not long ago, I came upon the following interesting passage in an essay by Martin Amis, son of Kingsley. In an essay in the *New Yorker* in defense of the poet Philip Larkin, who had been posthumously under attack for improper opinions, Martin Amis writes:

> Larkin the man is separated from us, historically, by changes in the self. For his generation, you were what you were, and that was that. It made you unswervable and adamantine. My father has this quality. I don't. None of us [persons in Martin Amis's own generation] do. There are too many forces

at work on us. There are too many fronts to cover. In the age of self-improvement, the self is inexorably self-conscious. Still, a price has to be paid for not caring what others think of you, and Larkin paid it. He couldn't change the cards he was dealt ("What poor hands we hold, / When we face each other honestly!").

I wish Martin Amis had gone on to say more on this point, especially about those "forces at work on us" as well as about those "fronts" too numerous to cover. He does not specify what they might be, but I suspect he is falling back on all-too-vague military metaphors for the struggle to stay with-it in a culture that changes so rapidly. One of the reasons it changes so rapidly, of course, is that so many people—friends of Martin Amis if not of Philip Larkin—are ready to go along with every change, lest, terror of terrors, they be found out of it.

Yet who wishes to be with-it if the price is an almost endless changing of one's personality to accommodate those "forces" and those "fronts"? There are—perhaps there always have been—those who are ready to go with the flow, with its quick current, not particularly minding swimming amidst all the detritus in those muddy and churning waters. Such people pride themselves on being exceedingly knowing, above the ruck, with the show, perennial insiders over whose toes nobody but nobody pulls the wool. The aesthetic tends to be the chief criterion for such people. What is taken for style or taste is generally the basis for all their judgments; and style and taste, in the end, are made to stand in for virtue. To have opinions not congruent with theirs—however often theirs change—is, somehow, poor style and in bad taste.

It is unclear to what end all this knowingness and aesthetic judgment is directed. It is equally unclear to what end the self-improvement Martin Amis refers to is to be carried on. (Endless self-improvement always reminds me of Santayana, in his eighties, remarking, apropos of a physician suggesting that he lose twenty or so pounds, that he obviously wishes to have him perfectly healthy in time for his death.) The with-it of our day, as Martin Amis suggests, see no reason to play the cards they were dealt. Instead they see themselves in a game that might be called endless draw poker in which you keep turning in your cards till you find a hand that you can work with, always with the proviso that this, too, can be turned in at a later time should the aesthetic winds shift and leave you shuddering out in the cold.

I prefer being out in the cold with my own well-worn but comfortably out-of-it notions. These include: that there are a number of unchanging ideas—none of them particularly stylish—worth fighting for; that honor is immitigable; that so, too, is dignity, despite the almost inherent ridiculousness of human beings; that one's life is a work of art, however badly botched, which can be restored and touched up here and there but not fundamentally changed; that, in connection with this, integrity includes coherence of personality; that elegance, where possible, is very nice, but there are many things more important than style, loyalty, and decency among them; that a cello is a finer instrument than an electric guitar; and that a man ought to start out the day with a clean handkerchief. I hope I speak for others who are out of it when I say that we take these truths to be self-evident. And, as those of us who are out of it have learned, when it comes to most of the really important truths, no other kind of evidence is usually available.

(1993)

New Essays

The Bookish Life

The village idiot of the shtetl of Frampol was offered the job of waiting at the village gates to greet the arrival of the Messiah. "The pay isn't great," he was told, "but the work is steady." The same might be said about the conditions of the bookish life: low pay but steady work. By the bookish life, I mean a life in which the reading of books has a central, even a dominating, place. I recall some years ago a politician whose name is now as lost to me as it is to history who listed reading among his hobbies, along with fly-fishing and jogging. Reading happens to be my hobby, too, along with peristalsis and respiration.

Like the man—the fellow with the name Solomon, writing under the pen name Ecclesiastes—said, "Of the making of many books there is no end; and much study is a weariness of the flesh." So many books are there in the world that no one can get round to even all the best among them, and hence no one can claim to be truly well-read. Some people are merely better-read than others. Nobody has read, or can read, everything, and by everything I include only the good, the beautiful, the important books.

The first question is "How can one tell which books qualify as good, beautiful, important?" In an essay of 1978 called "On Reading Books: A Barbarian's Cogitations," Alexander Gerschenkron, a Harvard economist of wide learning, set out three criteria: a good book must be interesting, memorable, and re-readable. This is as sensible as it is unhelpful. How can one know if a book is interesting until one has read it; memorable until time has or has not lodged it in one's memory; re-readable until the decades pass and one feels the need to read it again and enjoys it all the more on doing so?

Not much help, either, is likely to be found in various lists of the world's best books. In 1771 a man named Robert Skipwith, later to be Thomas Jefferson's wife's brother-in-law, asked Jefferson to compile for him a list of indispensable books. Jefferson obliged with a list of 148 titles, mostly Greek and Roman classics, and some intensely practical treatises, among them a book on horse-hoeing husbandry. The *Guardian* not long ago published a list of the world's one hundred best nonfiction books in English, and while nearly every one seemed eminently worthy, one could just as easily add another hundred books that should have been on such a list, and this does not include all the world's splendid works of fiction, drama, and poetry, and not merely in English alone. In 1960, Clifton Fadiman, then a notable literary critic, produced a work called *The Lifetime Reading Plan*, a work of 378 pages, which I have chosen never to read, lest it take up the time I might devote to a better book.

Such lists reveal a yearning for a direct route to wisdom. Brace yourself for the bad news: none is available. If one wanted to establish expertise in a restricted field—economics, say, or art history, or botany—such a list might be useful. But for the road to acquiring the body of unspecialized knowledge that sometimes goes by the name of general culture, sometimes known as the pursuit of wisdom, no map, no blueprint, no plan, no shortcut exists, nor, as I hope to make plain, could it.

Bookish, which sounds a bit like Jewish, is the word I use to describe lives that are dominated by books. I grew up in a home proudly Jewish, but not in the least bookish. I don't believe we even had a dictionary in our apartment during the years I was growing up. The only books I can recall are a few volumes of a small-format, dun-colored, red-trimmed Funk & Wagnalls encyclopedia that my father acquired through a newspaper subscription. Both my parents were well-spoken, my paternal grandfather in Montreal published three books in Hebrew whose cost was underwritten by my father, and my mother was a near genius in her accurate judgment of other people, but reading books takes time, and neither of my parents found time for them.

As a young boy, I didn't find much time for books, either. Sports were all that interested me, and sports took up all four seasons of the year. I read only the sports pages in the *Chicago Daily News,* and I read lots of comic books, including classic comic books, which were useful for giving book reports in school. The first book that genuinely lit my fire—no surprise here, it was a sports book—was John R. Tunis's *All-American.* So enamored was I of the novel that I took out my first library card so that I could read the rest of Tunis's sports novels.

The next four years I spent as an entirely uninterested high school student. Shakespeare's *Julius Caesar,* George Eliot's *Adam Bede,* a few essays by Ralph Waldo Emerson, all offered as part of the required school curriculum, none of them so much as laid a glove on me. Willa Cather, a writer I have come to admire as the greatest twentieth-century American novelist, chose not to allow any of her novels put into what she called "school editions," lest young students, having to read her under the duress of school assignments, never return to her books when they were truly ready for them. She was no dope, Miss Cather.

Only after I had departed high school did books begin to interest me, and then only in my second year of college, when I transferred from the University of Illinois to the University of Chicago. Among the most beneficial departures from standard college fare at the University of Chicago was the brilliant idea of eliminating textbooks from undergraduate study. This meant that instead of reading, in a thick textbook, "In his *Politics* Aristotle held . . . ," or "In *Civilization and Its Discontents* Freud argued . . . ," or "In *On Liberty* John Stuart Mill asserted . . . ," students read the *Politics, Civilization and Its Discontents, On Liberty*, and a good deal else. Not only read them, but, if they were like me, became excited by them. Heady stuff, all this, for a nineteen-year-old semiliterate who, on first encountering their names, was uncertain how to pronounce Proust or Thucydides.

Along with giving me a firsthand acquaintance with some of the great philosophers, historians, novelists, and poets of the Western world, the elimination of that dreary, baggy-pants middleman called the textbook gave me the confidence that I could read the most serious of books. Somehow it also gave me a rough sense of what is serious in the way of reading and what is not. Anyone who has read a hundred pages of Herodotus senses that it is probably a mistake—that is, a waste of your finite and therefore severely limited time on earth—to read a six-hundred-page biography of Bobby Kennedy, unless, that is, you can find one written by Xenophon.

What is the true point of a bookish life? Note I write "point," not "goal." The bookish life can have no goal: it is all means and no end. The point, I should say, is not to become immensely knowledgeable or clever, and certainly not to become learned. Montaigne, who more than five centuries ago established the modern essay, grasped the point when he wrote, "I may be a man of fairly wide reading, but I retain nothing." Retention of everything one reads, along with being mentally impossible, would only crowd and ultimately cramp one's mind. "I would very much love to grasp things with a complete understanding," Montaigne wrote, "but I cannot bring myself to pay the high cost of doing so. . . . From books all I seek is to give myself pleasure by an honorable pastime; or if I do study, I seek only that branch of learning which deals with knowing myself and which teaches me how to live and die well." What Montaigne sought in his reading, as does anyone who has thought at all about it, is "to become more wise, not more learned or more eloquent." As I put it elsewhere some years ago, I read for the pleasures of style and in the hope of "laughter, exaltation, insight, enhanced consciousness," and, like Montaigne, on lucky days perhaps to pick up a touch of wisdom along the way.

The act of reading—office memos, newspaper articles on trade and monetary policy, and bureaucratic bumf apart—should if possible never be separable from pleasure. Twenty or so years ago there was a vogue for speed-reading. ("I took a speed-reading course and read *War and Peace* in twenty minutes," Woody Allen quipped. "It involves Russia.") But why, one wonders, would you wish to speed up an activity that gives pleasure? Speed-reading? I'd as soon take a course in speed-eating or speed-lovemaking. Yet the notion of speed generally hovers over the act of reading. "A real page-turner," people say of certain novels or biographies. I prefer to read books that are page-stoppers, that cause me to stop and contemplate a striking idea, an elegant phrase, an admirably constructed sentence.

A serious reader reads with a pencil in hand, to sideline, underline, make a note.

Nor, I suspect, is the bookish soul likely to read chiefly on a Kindle or a tablet. I won't go into the matter of the aesthetics of book design, the smell of books, the fine feel of a well-made book in one's hands, lest I be taken for a hedonist, a reactionary, and a snob. More important, apart from the convenience of Kindles and tablets—in allowing for enlarged print, in portability if one wants to take more than one or two books along when traveling—I have come to believe that there is a mysterious but quite real difference between words on pixel and words in print. For reasons that perhaps one day brain science will reveal to us, print has more weight, a more substantial feel, makes a greater demand on one's attention, than the pixel. One tends not to note a writer's style as clearly in pixels as one does in print. Presented with a thirty- or forty-paragraph piece of writing in pixels, one wants to skim after fifteen or twenty paragraphs in a way that one doesn't ordinarily wish to do in print. Pixels for information and convenience, then, print for knowledge and pleasure is my sense of the difference between the two.

I have heard many stories of intelligent people deriving much pleasure from listening to books, serious books, on their smartphones or other devices. I wish them joy of it, for I cannot find any. Many years ago a number of my own books were put on something then called "Books on Tape." Ordinarily I would have thought this a lovely ego sandwich, walking or driving about the city listening to my own words spoken by a (doubtless) out-of-work actor. On the contrary, I found I couldn't bear it. This stranger's reading rhythms were far from the rhythms I had put into my sentences; his pronunciations were sometimes off; listening to him I felt chiefly a sense of intrusion.

Besides, listening to someone read, not just one's own but any serious writing, doesn't allow one to linger, go back to reread, ponder an interesting passage. Reading and listening to someone else reading are two widely, I should even say wildly, different things.

In the risky generalization department, slow readers tend to be better readers—more careful, more critical, more thoughtful. I myself rarely read more than twenty-five or thirty pages of a serious book in a single sitting. Reading a novel by Thomas Mann, a short story by Chekhov, an historical work by Theodor Mommsen, essays by Max Beerbohm, why would I wish to rush through them? Savoring them seems more sensible. After all, you never know when you will pass this way again.

A great help in leading the bookish life is to recognize that as a reader, you might be omnivorous, but you can never be anywhere near omniscient. The realization removes a great deal of pressure. Some of this pressure derives from the claim of recent years that there is a much wider world than the Western one most of us grew up and were educated in. If one is not to be thought parochial in one's interests, the argument holds, one is responsible for knowing not Western culture alone but also the cultures of the Far and Near East. Yet when I think of all I haven't read in or about Western culture, I am perfectly prepared to take a pass on Islam, Hinduism, Shintoism, Buddhism, and the rich store of Chinese Confucian and contemplative literature. These and more will have to wait until I have read Pindar, Terence, Hume's *History of England*, Taine, Zola, and a few hundred other such items, not to speak of the books I should like to reread. They'll have to wait, it begins to look, until the next life, which, I like to think, will surely provide a well-stocked library. If it doesn't, I'm not sure I want any part of it. Hell of course will have a library, but one stocked exclusively with science fiction, six-hundred-odd-page novels by men whose first name is Jonathan, and books extolling the 1960s.

Rereading is a subject on its own. How many books you have read when young seem less impressive when you are older! The books of Ernest Hemingway and Henry David Thoreau are two instances that jump to mind for me. Hemingway's code of manliness and Thoreau's plea to simplify our lives both seem so much balderdash, fustian, rodomontade. Ralph Waldo Emerson left me cold as a kid and even colder now. While other books that one was less impressed with when young—Willa Cather's is my example here—now seem richly complex, deep, indispensable. Some of the best of all books are those one loved when young and finds even better in later life. Marguerite Yourcenar's novel *Memoirs of Hadrian* is such a book for me. The frisson afforded by rereading is the discovery not only of things one missed the first time round but of the changes in oneself.

When I was in grammar school, in the sixth grade, our class had a visit from a woman from the Chicago Public Library. She came to inform us, in a sanctimonious voice, that books will "take us to unknown shores, bring us treasures hitherto undreamed of. Yes, boys and girls," she said, "books are your friends." Marcel Proust, of all people, would have agreed, with a single proviso. He believed that books were in some ways better than friends. "In reading," he held, "friendship is suddenly brought back to its first purity." Unlike with friends, we spend time with books only because we truly wish to be in their company. We never have to ask what they thought of us. Clashes of egotism have nothing to do with the bookish relationship. Perhaps best of all, when we tire of books, unlike tiring of friends, we close them and replace them on the shelf. Friendship with books, Proust felt, though it may be one-way, is nonetheless an unselfish friendship.

Reading may not be the same as conversation, but reading the right books, the best books, puts us in the company of men and women more intelligent than ourselves. Only by keeping company with those smarter than ourselves, in books or in persons, do we have a chance of becoming a bit smarter. My friend Edward Shils held that there were four modes, or means, of education: that in the classroom, that through superior newspapers and journals, that from the conversation of intelligent friends, and that obtained from bookstores and especially used bookstores. The so-called digital age, spearheaded by Amazon, is slowly putting this last-named mode out of business. With its ample stock, quick delivery, and slightly lower prices, Amazon is well on its way to killing the independent bookstore. But the owners of these stores are not the only losers. Readers, too, turn out to be ill-served by this bit of mixed progress that Amazon and other online booksellers have brought.

I have seen used bookstores described as places where you find books you didn't know you wanted. I recently went into a neighborhood used bookstore just to browse, and came out with two books I hadn't, until I had them in my hands, known I'd wanted: Lesley Chamberlain's *Nietzsche in Turin* and Barry Strauss's *The Battle of Salamis*. I regularly make such unexpected discoveries. A few years ago, in another used bookstore, in its classics section, I came upon a book entitled *Rome and Pompeii* by a writer I had never heard of named Gaston Boissier (1823–1908). I opened it, was pleased by the few passages I scanned, and bought it. I have subsequently read two other of Boissier's books, *Roman Africa* and *The Country of Horace and Virgil*, both of which gave much satisfaction. Without coming upon Boissier in a shop, holding his book in my hands, examining it, I should have missed out on a splendid writer.

As you will have gathered, correctly, I am far from a systematic reader. I read only books on subjects that interest me, and my interests tend to rove all over the intellectual and aesthetic lot. These interests tend to come in phases, sometimes resulting in reading binges. Not uncommonly a broad general subject will absorb my interest—the history of Rome, the Austro-Habsburg Empire, the belle epoque—and I find much of my reading devoted to it. Within the last few years, for example, caught up in a passion for all things Roman, I read Sallust, lots of Cicero, a great deal of Livy, some Appian, Polybius, Plutarch, Tacitus, Seneca, Pliny the Younger, Suetonius, Edward Gibbon, Theodor Mommsen, Ronald Syme, and more. I read all this not to gain mastery over the subject but for pleasure and what I hope is the occasional insight into human nature across a vast stretch of time that reading about Rome brings. I know no better ways to spend my days.

"I hate to read new books," William Hazlitt began an essay called "On Reading Old Books." He closes the essay with a brief listing of many of the books he would still like to read: Clarendon's *History of the Grand Rebellion*, Guicciardini's *History of Florence*, the plays of Beaumont and Fletcher, the speeches in Thucydides, *Don Quixote* in the original Spanish, and more. Reading that list, I immediately feel an intellectual kinship with Hazlitt.

I cannot say that I hate to read new books; since I write a few of them, this would put me in an awkward position. But as one grows older and recognizes that one's time isn't infinite, one is more likely to choose to read the three volumes of Mommsen's *History of Rome* over the five volumes of Robert Caro's *The Years of Lyndon Johnson*, the poetry of Wallace Stevens over that of John Ashbery, the novels of Marcel Proust over those of Jonathan Franzen.

We all live in the contemporary world, but that doesn't mean that we have to restrict our reading to that world, which is doubtless already too much with us. "The art of not reading is a very important one," Schopenhauer wrote.

> It consists in not taking an interest in whatever may be engaging the attention of the general public at any particular time. When some political or ecclesiastical pamphlet, or novel, or poem is making a great commotion, you should remember that he who writes for fools always finds a large public. A precondition for reading good books is not reading bad ones, for life is short.

I know of no better advice for taking a pass on just about everything on the *New York Times* bestseller list.

If you happen to be in search of an example of the word "desultory," allow me to offer my own current reading. On or near my bedside table I have bookmarks in the following books: Paul Johnson's little book on Mozart, John Aubrey's *Brief Lives*, A. J. P. Taylor's *The Habsburg Monarchy, 1809–1918*, William Rothenstein's *Men & Memories, 1872–1938*, and Robert Burton's 1,381-page *The Anatomy of Melancholy*. I've twice before made a run at Burton's book, but it now begins to look as if I may have to finish finishing it in the next life. In my bathroom astride the back of the commode sits Ernst Pawel's *The Labyrinth of Exile: A Life of Theodor Herzl*, André Maurois's *Byron*, and the *Journal de l'abbé Mugnier*. (As for reading in the bathroom, one of the highest compliments I have had came from a reader of a magazine I edited when he told me that he took it to the bathroom.) Elsewhere round my apartment, I have bookmarks in studies of Catullus and Alcibiades, a recent biography of Brutus, G. K. Chesterton's *Saint Francis of Assisi, The Reflections and Maxims of Luc de Clapiers, Marquis of Vauvenargues,* two slender volumes on Proust by Princess Marthe Bibesco, and Cornelius Nepos's *Lives of Eminent Commanders.* If you can make sense of this jumble of subjects, yours is a keener mind than mine.

Which brings me to the clutter that books can bring into a home. *Books Do Furnish a Room* is a truism as well as the title of the tenth novel in Anthony Powell's twelve-volume *A Dance to the Music of Time* novel cycle, but it needs to be added that books can also take over a room—and not one room alone. Harry Wolfson, the Harvard scholar and philosopher, is said to have used both his refrigerator and oven to store books. I tell you this so your feelings shouldn't be hurt if, had you happened to have known him, Professor Wolfson failed to invite you to dinner.

I have myself twice sold off large numbers of my books. I had hoped to keep my own collection of books within respectable bounds—down, say, to the two or three hundred of the books I most love—but have found that impossible. I also instituted a failed policy of telling myself that for every book I brought home, I would get rid of one already in my possession. Meanwhile, over the years, I seem to have acquired two thousand or so books. Publishers and people send me books. Like an incorrigible juvenile delinquent who can't stay out of pool halls, I wander into used bookshops and do not often emerge empty-handed. Books in my apartment continue to multiply. Some of them, I suspect, do it overnight, in the dark, while I am asleep.

As a book accumulator, I am a piker next to Edward Shils, who in a capacious three-bedroom apartment in Chicago had a library of roughly sixteen thousand volumes, in three languages, all of them serious, with another six thousand books stored in a house he kept at Cambridge in England. In one of the two bathrooms in his Chicago apartment, Edward had bookshelves built over and above the bath and commode. No flat surface in his apartment, including his dining room table, was uncovered by books or magazines or papers.

I am Edward Shils's literary executor, and in his will he noted that he wished his personal library to go to Hebrew University in Jerusalem. When I wrote to a former student of his, himself now a teacher at Hebrew University, to inform him of this bequest, he called back to say that, though he was touched by Edward's sentiment, the library at Hebrew University couldn't find the space for so many books, nor the money—he estimated it at $100,000—needed to ship and catalogue them, but would accept a few hundred or so books that they would set out on shelves under his name. I eventually sold the bulk of the books to a private dealer, for the sum of $166,000, which went into Edward's estate, but I also felt a touch of sadness that this great personal library, reflecting a powerful thinker's intellectual autobiography, would now be broken up.

Nietzsche said that life without music is a mistake. I would agree, adding that it is no less a mistake without books. Proust called books "the noblest of distractions," and they are assuredly that, but also more, much more. "People say that life is the thing," wrote Logan Pearsall Smith, "but I prefer reading." In fact, with a bit of luck, the two reinforce each other. In *The Guermantes Way* volume of his great novel, Proust has his narrator note a time when he knew "more books than people and literature better than life." The best arrangement, like that between the head and the heart, is one of balance between life and reading. One brings one's experience of life to one's reading, and one's reading to one's experience of life. You can get along without reading serious books—many extraordinary, large-hearted, highly intelligent people have—but why, given the chance, would you want to? Books make life so much richer, grander, more splendid. The bookish life is not for everyone, nor are its rewards immediately evident, but at a minimum, taking it up you are assured, like the man said, of never being out of work.

(2018)

Learning Latin

S ome people acquire foreign languages more easily than others. I, alas, am one of those others. I cannot truly say that I have possession of any foreign language. I have perhaps two hundred or so words of Yiddish—just enough to fool the Gentiles into thinking I know the language, but not enough to speak to real Jews. When I was a boy, I was sent to Hebrew school. But Israel only recently having become a state, Hebrew was still thought of chiefly as a liturgical and scholarly language, and not yet as a spoken one. So my fellow students and I learned pronunciation and prayers, this in preparation for reading our Torah portions at our bar mitzvahs, but regrettably we did no translation. I have sufficient French to read Pascal and La Rochefoucauld, but not Montaigne nor Proust. Owing to the elision so rampant in French speech, I do not hear spoken French very well. On the few occasions when I have been called upon to speak French, I sounded, I have a sad hunch, *comme une vache espagnole.*

When I was coming out of grammar school, those thought to be among the more promising students were directed to take Latin.

Some earnest young boys, at age fourteen already intent on a medical career, were instructed to take German, useful, it was said, for reading scientific papers later in life. The dullards among us did Spanish. I took it for two years in high school. *El burro es un animal importante* is pretty much all that remains of my Spanish, not a sentence I have found much use for in later life.

Is there any connection between facility with foreign languages and other skills and aptitudes, such as is sometimes thought to be true of a linked aptitude for mathematics with that for music? I have heard it said that acting ability, the skill of turning oneself into someone else, is aligned with that of acquiring foreign languages. In one of the most delightfully risky generalizations I have come across, Anthony Powell in *A Dance to the Music of Time* describes a character—X. Trapnel—as able quickly to acquire speaking knowledge of foreign languages, and, the narrator of the novel goes on to say, like all people he has known who have this gift, "he was fundamentally untrustworthy." If this is so, then I must be among the most trustworthy people in the land.

The multiest-lingual person I have known was a man of no otherwise great intellectual distinction named Thomas Donovan, who seemed to have *all* languages. When I asked him how he did it, Thomas replied that it was no big deal. "I just acquire a novel in the new language I am trying to learn and a dictionary of that language," he told me, "and, with the dictionary's help, work my way through the novel." This suggests an intrinsic, universal understanding of all grammar, and a powerful capacity to accommodate several different vocabularies.

In my mid-twenties, I made a stab at learning Russian, toting around a small Russian grammar, which I read on coffee breaks at my job. This set in motion the rumor, started by a fellow worker I shall call Schmuckowitz, that I was a communist. A couple of decades later, I audited a course in ancient Greek but, owing to the press of other work, had to drop out. I recall being very impressed by the instructor, a man named Stuart Small, who told us not to be concerned overmuch about our pronunciation of ancient Greek, for we needn't worry about communicating with the great Greek writers but about their communicating with us. Sound advice, I thought at the time, and still do.

If I had a family crest, *Ne ex experientia umquam discas*, or "Never learn from experience," would be the motto inscribed upon it, for two years ago, at the age of eighty-one, I set out to learn Latin. Why Latin? And why so late in life? The short answer is that I found not knowing Latin a deficiency, especially in a person of my rather extravagant intellectual and cultural pretensions. I also felt I had a fair chance of mastering the language. Latin presents the same alphabet as English. The language also offers no strenuous problems in pronunciation. One will never be called upon to speak it (except of course, in the bad old joke, to Latin Americans). Then there is the fact that for centuries, from Roman times through the Middle Ages, Latin was the language of the educated. As for taking up Latin so late in life, my response, which comes from St. Edmund of Abingdon, is: *"Disce quasi semper victurus; vive quasi cras moriturus,"* or "Learn as if you will live forever; live as though you would die tomorrow."

Another incitement to learning Latin is that I had for some while been on a binge of reading Roman history. I had read Sallust, Cicero, Livy, Tacitus, Suetonius, Pliny the Younger, and Seneca among the Roman writers, and Edward Gibbon, Theodor Mommsen, Ronald Syme, Arnaldo Momigliano, and Peter Green among the writers about Rome. I have long felt a minor but nonetheless nagging disappointment in reading Catullus, Virgil, and Horace in English and wondered if they were not among those writers who had to be read in their original language to be appreciated. (The greatness of the small handful of truly great writers—Homer, Cervantes, Tolstoy—survives even poor translation.)

Latin, or specifically the study of Latin, has its proponents, its proselytizers, its propagandists. One among them who is all three is N. M. Gwynne, a retired businessman who had gone to Eton and thence up to Oxford. Before taking up *Gwynne's Latin*, modestly subtitled *The Ultimate Introduction to Latin*, I had earlier read *Gwynne's Grammar*, an unapologetic defense of standard English in which its author defines grammar as being "simply the correct use of words" and expresses the refreshingly retrograde belief that "pictures in textbooks actually interfere with the learning process."

Gwynne holds that the study of Latin provides "a training and development of the mind and character to a degree of excellence that no other mental or physical activity can come anywhere near to bringing about." The study of Latin, he believes, concentrates the mind, exercises the memory, improves the facility of analyses and thereby the solving of problems—and through all this enhances "the powers of attention to detail, of diligence and perseverance, of observation, of imagination, of judgment, of taste."

This may seem to be going a bit far. But then, when I think of it, at the time I began university teaching in the early 1970s, my best students—they could write grammatically, they knew how to argue—were often those who had received a Catholic education, which in that day still meant four years of Latin. In England of an earlier day, by the time a student had arrived at Oxford or Cambridge he had taken seven or eight years of Latin and Greek. This surely must have gone a long way toward helping create brilliant generations of English historians, philosophers, and literary critics. Today, alas, neither in most Catholic high schools nor in English public schools is such training in Latin any longer part of the regular curriculum.

After setting out all that is to be gained by learning Latin, Gwynne then goes on to note that—pause here for a clearing of the throat— "no modern language comes close to approaching Latin in difficulty." This is doubtless so. Latin does without definite and indefinite articles and often dispenses with pronouns. Inflection, or cases—nominative, genitive, dative, accusative, ablative, vocative—is crucial to the language, and there are no fewer than five different declensions of nouns and four different conjugations of verbs. Toss in that all nouns are assigned a gender—masculine, feminine, neuter—and that there are six tenses among verbs. About pluperfect past participles, gerundives, locatives, deponent and semi-deponent verbs, and the ablative absolute, let us not speak.

Latin is, moreover, without the straightforward syntax—subject, verb, direct or indirect object—that is at the heart of the English sentence. In Latin, verbs tend to appear last in a sentence, adjectives (some of them) before nouns, adverbs (usually) to follow verbs. But clauses arise without commas separating them, and phrases (clauses without verbs) can pop up anywhere. Every Latin sentence of any complexity is therefore within itself a small puzzle awaiting solution. In *Long Live Latin*, his excellent study of Roman writers and their use of Latin, Nicola Gardini writes: "Latin resists linearity, straightforwardness, immediacy. On the contrary, it pursues allusiveness and multiplicity."

Gardini's account of the rewards of Latin goes less to developing character, à la Gwynne, and more to pure aesthetic pleasure. Learning Latin, he holds,

> is a highly exciting process of selection and decision making. Logic is involved, but logical skills alone are not enough. Learners of Latin must use intuition and imagination, be ready to take chances and be daring. . . . Latin is here to remind us that meaning is not to be taken for granted; that words are complex entities, almost like living creatures, and therefore have memories and intentions of their own.

Even in the hobbled condition of my own Latin, I agree entirely.

I began my study of Latin by auditing a first-year class at Northwestern University, where I had myself taught for thirty years, a class taught by a woman with the mellifluous name of Francesca Tataranni and the charming Italian accent to go with it. The class met at 10:00 a.m. and had twelve students. After asking Professor Tataranni for permission to audit, I also asked her if she would be so kind as to not call on me in class, for I feared not knowing the answer to one of her questions and thus appearing a lunkhead, which at my august age would mean a hopeless lunkhead. She, kind woman, agreed.

I bought the text, *Wheelock's Latin*, seventh edition, and began attending the four-day-a-week, one-hour class. Professor Tataranni proved a sound and sensible teacher. I did each night's homework, not always flawlessly, and showed up for every class. But I soon found that attending class, even though only a few blocks from my apartment, and doing homework was taking up roughly four hours of my day, and those the hours in which I generally did my own work. So

I quietly but reluctantly dropped out of the course and decided to continue studying Latin on my own.

This meant acquiring other Latin textbooks. Along with *Gwynne's Latin*, these included Eleanor Dickey's *Learn Latin from the Romans*, Reginald Foster and Daniel McCarthy's *Ossa Latinitatis Solas*, Robert J. Henle's *First Year Latin*, Basil L. Gildersleeve's *Latin Grammar*, and a few supplemental volumes including, yes, *Latin for Dummies*. I ranged round in these, passing from one to the other. I listened to *Wheelock's* pronunciation guide online. I translated all the sentences—Latin to English, English into Latin—in *Gwynne's Latin*. I made endless notes about vocabulary, third conjugation verbs, fourth declension nouns. I did my best to remember to discriminate among *docere* (to teach), *discere* (to learn), *ducere* (to lead). I memorized adverbs (*iam, etiam, forsitan, denique*), did the same for prepositions (*ad, ab, sub, de, in, post, ante, ex*), tried to keep straight yesterday (*heri*), today (*hodie*), and tomorrow (*cras*). Then there were all those *Q* words: *numquam, umquam, quoniam, quis, quod, quam, quid, quoque*, and so on into the night.

Many English words derive from Latin, of course—as many, I read somewhere, as 65 percent—which is a help in grasping their meaning. But many Latin words are, in the French phrase, *faux amis*: Why should *neuter* mean "neither" and not "neutral" or even "spay," or *tandem* mean "at length" and not "paired together"? Why should *placenta* mean not what one thought it obviously should mean but instead mean "cake," and why should *opera* turn out not to mean the English word "opera" at all but "labor," "trouble," "difficulty"? *Cum, tum, dum; tam, nam, tamen; hic, haec, hoc; ille, iste, idem; vox, vix, vae!*—in and out the mind the words come and go, and they ain't speaking of Michelangelo.

The usually subtle Nicola Gardini pauses in his book to state the

Joseph Epstein

obvious: "Learning Latin demands attention and memory." The memory of a man in his eighties is not famously efficient. In a charming book called *Living with a Dead Language: My Romance with Latin*, by Ann Patty, I learned that people who are on the autism spectrum tend to be good at Latin because of their powerful memories. The memory of the very young is also said to be capacious, perhaps because there is less already there to crowd things out, which is no doubt why Latin and ancient Greek were staples of English public school education, and why the young often acquire languages fairly easily. Montaigne, a prominent figure in my own small pantheon of cultural gods, grew up speaking Latin at his father's insistence before acquiring his native French. I found my own memory unsteady. I could make out the passive and subjunctive verb forms on the page, but if you asked me to give you the third-person plural subjunctive of the verb *habere*, I'd doubtless stammer.

Much of education is divided between that centered on memory and that centered on the conceptual. When at eighteen I went off to the University of Illinois, at a time when the school accepted anyone who lived in the state and was said to flunk out roughly a third of each year's entering freshman class, much of my first year's education was based on memory. Biology, in those pre-DNA days, was chiefly devoted to learning the phyla, with the dissection of a sad frog tossed in at no extra charge. My introductory French course was also chiefly based on memorization. Thanks to a reasonably good memory, I did well enough to avoid the disgrace of flunking out. But then, such was my fear of failing, I believe I could have taken a course in the telephone book and gotten at least a B.

In more advanced education, the role of memory becomes less important. When I transferred after my freshman year to the

University of Chicago, the emphasis switched from learning chiefly based on memory to that of making intellectual connections. Making dazzling connections is what marks the intellectual giants, from Tocqueville through Max Weber through Sigmund Freud, all central figures in the University of Chicago undergraduate curriculum.

Literary intellectuals of generations earlier than mine had vast quantities of poetry in their heads. (I always thought that before his death Harold Bloom ought to have recorded himself reciting Wordsworth's *Prelude* from memory. What a splendid device that would have been for ending dull parties!) Apart, though, from remembering historical facts—the line of kings and queens of England, the dates of the American, French, and Russian Revolutions, the names of great works, recalling what Aristotle thought, Shakespeare wrote, Churchill said—memory is not the name of the game in intellectual life.

In the early stages of learning a language, memory is crucial. I followed the instructions of my textbook and teachers and memorized as best I was able the various declensions, conjugations, tenses, and moods of Latin. I often wrote them out. Too often I found that what I thought I had locked into memory escaped, departed—what was it *nikmi* means? what is the future infinitive of *currir*?—gone where notes of music go. Would it have fled so successfully from the fourteen- or twenty-year-old me? I suspect not.

Meanwhile, I stagger on. I should like to be able to say that I am up to Book VI in my translation of the *Aeneid*, and believe I am doing things in my English version of the poem that have never been attempted before. Unfortunately, not true. Closer to the truth to say that my Latin may not be good enough to take Professor Tataranni's first-quarter final. What has grown is my love for this language in which I am fairly certain I shall never achieve anything resembling the equivalence of fluency in reading. "It is astonishing," wrote Basil Gildersleeve, "how much enjoyment one can get out of a language that one understands imperfectly." The love of Latin in my case is in good part love for the precision of the language. One cannot guess at the meanings of Latin words, but must know their meanings by their inflections, tenses, genders. The virtue of Latin being a dead language is that the meanings of its words do not change in the way that words in contemporary languages do. No Roman, after all, ever said that at the end of the day he was weaponizing multiple existential threats to ensure a level playing field.

My dream in taking up Latin was to achieve an easy mastery of the language. I imagined myself picking up a Latin version of, say, Tacitus, whose Latin is notably difficult, and casually reading two or three paragraphs in the washroom. I can perhaps now do that, but the effort would be far from casual and is likely to have me in the House of Commons, as Dylan Thomas called the washroom, for more than three hours. I cannot yet say that I can really read Latin, but merely that I can, given time and with the help of my iPhone Latin app, figure it out.

Will I, in the unknown amount of time left to me on the planet, ever master Latin? Perhaps strangely, I find I do not much care. I simply enjoy working—or is it playing?—with the language, testing my memory, puzzling out complex sentences, marveling at its orderly richness. The idea of a good time for many people my age is to do crossword puzzles, play bridge or Scrabble, hit golf balls. I prefer to wrestle with this long dead but still magnificent language. Like the man said, *De gustibus non est disputandum.*

(2020)

Living in a Cathouse

In the risky-generalization department, Alexandr Solzhenitsyn wrote: "If we stop caring for animals, we will stop caring for people." Whatever the truth quotient here, many people do indeed care for their animals passionately and often at great expense. While on a book-promotion tour in California, I was driven by a woman who told me that she had just spent $6,000 for chemotherapy for her twelve-year-old wirehair terrier. Years ago, it was a sign of perfect looniness when an elderly spinster left her (sometimes sizable) estate to her beloved cat. Today, this seems a touch more sensible than leaving money to one's university or college.

To offer a risky generalization of my own: one of the major differences between people who have pets—and perhaps among humankind in general—is that between those who favor dogs and those who favor cats. Many, myself among them, like both, but never equally. Those who favor dogs are surely in the majority. Dog owners expect, and generally receive, pleasing affection from them. Unalterable devotion is the last thing one is likely to receive from a cat. Affection one might receive, but entirely on the cat's terms, which is to say when it is in a mood to dispense it. Cats are independent in a way no domesticated dog is likely to be. Unless they are sure of a reward, they tend not to come when called, and are intractable generally. Cats do not travel in packs and as often as not eschew the company of other cats, whom they often fear will horn in on their territory. Cats, in short, are for the most part in business for themselves.

Worshipped in ancient Egypt as the animal of the gods, if not gods themselves, cats throughout history have also been despised, loathed, thought evil incarnate, tortured. The cause of cats is not helped by the fact that something on the order of 10 percent of the population is said to be allergic to them. No word exists to describe those who fear and sometimes hate dogs, while "ailurophobe" describes the more common phenomenon of someone with a strong antipathy to cats. "Ailurophobia," writes Carl Van Vechten in *The Tiger in the House*, perhaps the best book ever written about cats, "is a stronger feeling than hate; it is a most abject kind of fear." Van Vechten goes on to describe the extreme reactions of ailurophobes, from nervous worry to violent terror to actual convulsions at the mere sight of a cat. Only snakes and rats are hated more than cats.

History's most famous ailurophobe was probably Napoleon. The sixteenth-century French poet Pierre de Ronsard expressed his hatred of cats in the following quatrain:

> There is no man now living anywhere
> Who hates cats with a deeper hate than I;
> I hate their eyes, their heads, the way they stare,
> And when I see one come, I turn and fly.

And yet, for the past two decades, I have lived with a cat. With three different cats, to be precise; two calicos, one tabby, all females. I prefer female to male cats; feline, after all, suggests femininity. The tabby, Isabelle by name, had to be put down, her body riddled with cancer at age thirteen. The first of the two calicos, Hermione, I found one morning dead at the age of five under a chair in our living room, presumably from an aneurysm. The third, Dolly, we adopted five years ago from the Evanston Animal Shelter when she was seven. No two cats are quite alike, and that has certainly been true of the cats rooming chez Epstein. Isabelle tended to be elegantly passive and accommodating, allowing strangers and children to pet her. Hermione was rambunctious, awakening my wife at 6:30 a.m. for her own breakfast, going bonkers when a can of tuna was opened, forever attempting to escape into our outer hallway. Dolly has been impressively patient and charmingly content. Her manner and the pleasure she brings I should like briefly to describe.

Most people prefer to adopt kittens, but when I first saw her, I found Dolly's rich coat and intelligent face irresistible and, on a subsequent visit, so did my wife. She is brilliantly tricolored—black, white, marmalade orange, all prettily melding into one another—with a small head and pleasingly plump body. I frequently describe her as one of those fat cats from city hall. Little is known of her previous history. She was apparently left in a cat carrying case one evening on the steps of the Evanston Animal Shelter. Perhaps her owner had died, or moved, or married an ailurophobe. A college student who was a volunteer at the shelter and who took Dolly home for a brief period left only the information that she, Dolly, liked to be brushed. Adoption, of animals as of humans, is always a crapshoot, but in Dolly, a cat perfectly mated to us, the roll came up a solid seven.

When I brought Dolly home to our apartment, I showed her the placement of her litter box in our main bathroom, and no further tour was required. On her own she discovered the three bowls—one for water, another for dry food, a third for a small daily portion of moist food, collectively known as the buffet—that lie on the kitchen floor to the left of the refrigerator. She took over her predecessor Hermione's bed. She cased the joint, soon picked out a few favorite spots, and has ever since walked about it as if she held the mortgage.

Dolores was her name when we brought her home. Dolores, however, sounded too dolorous, and my wife quickly changed her name to Dolly. This allowed me to master and not infrequently sing to her the Jerry Herman lyric of "Hello, Dolly!": "So nice to have you back where you belong." The naming of cats is a serious business. My own belief is that cats are too dignified for overly affectionate names. Hippolyte Taine kept three cats, named Puss, Ebène, and Mitonne. None, in my view, is sufficiently stately. I know a young man who acquired a sphynx, or hairless cat, and named him, cruelly, Chemo. I like an earnest, adult name for a cat: Linda or Clara, say, or Ralph or Sidney. T. S. Eliot, in "The Naming of Cats," puts this serious matter in comic terms:

> The Naming of Cats is a difficult matter,
> It isn't just one of your holiday games;
> You may think at first I'm as mad as a hatter
> When I tell you, a cat must have THREE DIFFERENT NAMES.
> First of all, there's the name that the family use daily,
> Such as Peter, Augustus, Alonzo, or James,
> Such as Victor or Jonathan, George or Bill Bailey—

All of them sensible everyday names.
There are fancier names if you think they sound
    sweeter,
Some for the gentlemen, some for the dames:
Such as Plato, Admetus, Electra, Demeter—
But all of them sensible everyday names.
But I tell you, a cat needs a name that's particular,
A name that's peculiar, and more dignified,
Else how can he keep up his tail perpendicular,
Or spread out his whiskers, or cherish his pride?

Dolly is one cat that curiosity will never kill. Friends or strangers come into our apartment, and she does not stir to greet them. She has never shown the least interest in life in our outer hallway. She spends a fair amount of time atop the back of the couch, which we have come to call the mezzanine, in the room where we keep our television set, viewing the street six stories below or napping off when the mood strikes her, which it frequently does. She is alarmed only by the noise of vacuum cleaners or thunderstorms, both of which drive her into one of our closets or under our bed until the havoc caused by either passes. While she can flick a paw or turn over her body quickly, I have never seen Dolly run; a brisk waddle is the best she does. Although possessed of a full set of claws, in the five years she has lived with us, she has caused no damage of any kind, not the least scratch on any of our furniture, not a single tchotchke knocked over or chipped. Through the day she gives off an aura of calm, serenity even.

Soon after I arise and head toward the kitchen to prepare my tea and toast, Dolly puts in her first appearance. I fill the dishes of her buffet. She nibbles a bit of this, a touch of that, and follows me to the chair in my living room, where I do an hour or so of morning reading. She appears at my feet, asking with her eyes to be picked up and set upon my lap, which I am more than pleased to do. There she sits, gazing outward at the street, purring gently as I stroke her back and administer further strokes under her chin, which she seems especially to like.

With Dolly on my lap in the early morning, my head clears and random thoughts begin to flow. Among them thoughts about her life, her happiness being alone with two older human beings, desires she might have or once have had that cannot any longer be satisfied. After twenty minutes or so, she departs my lap and waits upon a nearby rug for me to brush her. She will sometimes wait as long as forty-five minutes for a five-minute brushing. Whence did this patience derive? I suspect from her months in a small cage at the Evanston Animal Shelter. After the grooming, we proceed into the kitchen, where she gets her morning reward of six chicken-flavored Greenie treats.

Much of the day Dolly sleeps. Does she dream? And if she does, of what do these dreams consist? A freer life? Memory of kittens to which years before she may have given birth? At dinner she now sits on my lap, which makes eating a touch awkward, but I find the honor of her wanting to be there worth the awkwardness. In the evening she lies between my wife and me on the couch, where we sit to watch television. Here she tends to nuzzle up to my wife. (Sisterhood, after all, is powerful.) Something immensely becalming there is about having her there with us as the television set blares away at English detective stories or Chicago Cubs or White Sox games. Her day ends with six more Greenie treats. On winter nights she sometimes sleeps at the end of our bed. Otherwise she sleeps in her own bed or on a wing chair facing a bank of windows.

Why does having Dolly with us give such pleasure? In *Feline Philosophy: Cats and the Meaning of Life,* John Gray, a retired professor of European thought at the London School of Economics, helps answer the question. Toward the close of his brief and well-written book, he writes that "while cats have nothing to learn from us, we can learn from them how to lighten the load that comes with being human." Cats are Gray's ostensible subject, but his true subject is human nature: "If cats could look back on their lives, might they wish that they had never lived? It is hard to think so. Not making stories of their lives, they cannot think of them as tragic or wish they had never been born. They accept life as a gift," he writes, with the implication that human beings do not.

Throughout his pages, Gray distinguishes the differences, social and philosophical, between cats and humans. Cats do not form social groups, or recognize leaders, including human leaders. Nor do they know jealousy or boredom. They show few signs of sharing the feelings of others. Altruism, a word coined by Auguste Comte in the nineteenth century, is unknown to cats, which means neither are those programs for the improvement of life that have caused so much trouble for human beings. "Cats are happy being themselves," Gray writes, "while human beings try to be happy by escaping themselves." Cats, he notes, have no need to go to the opera. Cats, unlike us, have no self-image. "Their senses are sharper and their waking attention unclouded by dreams. The absence of a self-image may make their experience more intense."

In their dealings with human beings, cats, according to Gray, "may come to love human beings, but that does not mean that they need them or feel any sense of obligation to them." They appear to love, again unlike human beings, not out of motives of despair, loneliness, or boredom, but chiefly in reaction to kindness. All they want from human beings, Gray writes, "is a place where they can return to their normal state of contentment. If a human being gives them such a place, they may come to love them."

They seem to be without family feeling. Once their kittens are ready for the world, they take off on their own, without, so far as we know, any regrets on either side. Cats "show no signs of experiencing guilt or remorse, any more than they do of struggling to be better than they are," writes Gray. "They do not exert themselves to improve the world, or agonize over what is the right thing to do." They are not immoral but amoral, quite content to be themselves, which is of course what most human beings should like, but find it so difficult to be.

Cats do not worry, at least not such that we can notice. (If Dolly has any worries, perhaps it is only that I shall forget her treats.) Above all, they do not seem to share that greatest and most ubiquitous of human fears, that of death. So far as we know, only human beings live with an awareness of their decease. "The human being who thinks nothing of death does not exist," John Gray notes, adding that "humankind is the death-defined animal." He also reminds us that if human beings are prepared to die for their ideas, they are also ready to kill for them. "Killing and dying for nonsensical ideas," he writes, "is how many human beings have made sense of their lives." When cats die, on the other hand, it is generally "because they no longer want to live." While human beings attempt to take consolation from philosophy —the late Roman politician Boethius wrote a book during a jail term called "The Consolation of Philosophy"—cats live on nicely without such support. As psychoanalysis was said by Karl Kraus to be the disease of which it purports to be the cure, for Gray, "philosophy is a symptom of the disorder it pretends to remedy." Human beings have philosophy; cats have the simple enjoyment of everyday life.

Could my regard, bordering on reverence, for Dolly have anything to do with my being a writer? Writers have claimed not merely affection for but affinity with cats. They have been an almost standard subject for poets to write about; cats appear, for example, in many of Baudelaire's poems. "As an inspiration to the author I do not think the cat can be over-estimated," Carl Van Vechten writes. "He suggests so much grace, power, beauty, motion, mysticism." The cat, he adds, may even serve as a model for the critic: "The sharp but concealed claws, the contracting pupil of the eye, which allows only the necessary amount of light to enter, independence, should be the best of models for any critic." Over the years, French writers have shown a particular partiality to cats, many of them—Chateaubriand, Colette, Pierre Loti—adding substantially to the felinature, or literature about cats. Among the English, a famously dog-loving nation, Jeremy Bentham and Samuel Butler, neither of whom were high on human beings, turn out to have been ailurophiles. American cat-loving literati have included Edgar Allan Poe, Mark Twain, Henry James, Sarah Orne Jewett, and the essayist Agnes Repplier.

As I come to the end of this essay, Dolly, having been brushed and treated, is currently asleep on the mezzanine. She will leave a time or two before the morning is out for a trip to the buffet for a nibble and a sip of water, after which she often cleans herself. She is likely to put in an appearance while we are lunching at our kitchen counter. The most unobtrusive of creatures, she requires little attention, asks nothing of us. She makes no noise, apart from the pleasing tap-tap of her clawed paws against our wooden floors on her way to her litter box. Later she will join us to watch the evening news. What the stock market has done, how great the rising murder toll in Chicago, the latest scurrilous lies of politicians, the unending anger of victim groups, about all this Dolly couldn't care less, while we human beings care a great deal, though we can do little or nothing about any of it. Makes one wonder whether she, Dolly, a mere creature, and not we, despite calling ourselves *Homo sapiens*, hasn't got it right.

(2021)

Good Grief

Fortunate is the person who has reached the age of fifty without having had to grieve. To be among the grieving, the bereaved, is an experience most of us go through, excepting only those who die preternaturally young and are themselves the cause of bereavement. The death of a parent, a husband or wife, a brother or sister, a dear friend, in some ways saddest of all, a child, is among the major causes of grief. May grief be avoided? Ought it to be? Is there any sense in which, as Charlie Brown's favorite phrase had it, there is good grief?

Socrates held that one of the key missions of philosophy was to ward off our fear of death. Upon his own death, by self-imposed hemlock, he claimed to be looking forward at long last to discovering whether there was an afterlife. Montaigne wrote an essay called "To Philosophize Is to Learn How to Die," in which, as elsewhere in his essays, he argues that, far from putting death out of mind, we should keep it foremost in our minds, the knowledge of our inevitably forthcoming death goading us on the better to live our lives.

But no one has told us how to deal with the deaths of those we love or found important to our own lives. Or at least no one has done so convincingly. The best-known recent attempt has been that of Elisabeth Kübler-Ross, a Swiss psychiatrist, in her 1969 book *On Death and Dying* and in her later book, written with David Kessler, *On Grief and Grieving* (2005). Kübler-Ross set out a five-stage model for grief: denial, anger, bargaining, depression, acceptance. Yet in my own experience of grieving, I went through none of these stages, which leads me to believe there is more to it than is dreamt of in any psychology yet devised.

Or, one might add, in any philosophy. In *Grief*, Michael Cholbi, who holds the chair in philosophy at the University of Edinburgh, informs us that philosophy has never taken up the subject of grieving in an earnest way. He attempts to make the positive case for grief: "The good in grief, I propose, is *self-knowledge*." Cholbi defines grief as "an emotionally driven process of attention whose object is the relationship transformed by the death of another in whom one has invested one's practical identity." As for the term "practical identity," it was coined by the American philosopher Christine Korsgaard, who writes that it is "a description under which you value yourself, a description under which you find your life to be worth living and your actions to be worth undertaking." The value of grief, then, according to Cholbi, is that "it brings the vulnerability, and ultimate contingencies of our practical identities into stark relief" and, ideally, "culminates in our knowing better what we are doing with our lives."

In our secular age, the dead are thought generally to go into the ground, up in flames, or into the heads of others. But what about grieving those who believe in an afterlife, which usually entails their going to a better place? Ought we to grieve their deaths, or rather to celebrate them? Cholbi writes that "the fact that believers in the afterlife genuinely grieve is difficult to reconcile with the notion that they grieve for what the deceased have lost by dying." I had a neighbor named Dee Crosby, an earnest, daily Mass–attending Catholic, unmarried, a former schoolteacher, ten or so years older than I. I recall her once telling me that she had no fear of death. She hoped to avoid a painful or a sloppy passing, but she was confident about where she was headed after death. When she told me this, I felt a stab of what I can only call faith envy.

Cholbi makes the useful distinction between grieving and mourning, the former being personal, the latter public. Victorian women had set rituals for mourning: withdrawal from social life for a year, then two years appearing in public only in black. Mourning can be spontaneous, as it was after the death of Abraham Lincoln, or elaborately staged, as it was for John F. Kennedy after his assassination; it can also be elaborate but still perfunctory, as it is after the death of most politicians.

In our day, there are what seem almost concerted efforts to turn grief public. Courts now allow victim statements, which are statements of losses by families of murder victims. One sees something similar on local television stations, where the mothers, fathers, brothers, siblings, aunts, even friends of murder victims are televised setting out their loss, usually by gang members and other murderers, as often as not weeping while doing so. We now have a set of clichés to accompany grief; invariably "the process of healing," "the need to be made whole," "coming to closure," "the end of the journey" will be hauled out. When a grammar or high school student dies unexpectedly, school administrators call in grief counselors. There are even grief workshops.

With Jessica Mitford's *The American Way of Death* six decades ago, we learned how grief was exploited by funeral homes throughout the country. Evelyn Waugh's novel *The Loved One* features a cruelly comic account of grief sentimentalized. Grief counseling has become a substantial part of the psychotherapy industry.

Like death itself, grief is too manifold; it comes in too many forms to be satisfactorily captured by philosophy or psychology. How does one grieve a slow death by, say, cancer, ALS, Alzheimer's, Parkinson's; a quick death by heart attack, stroke, choking on food, car accident; death at the hands of a criminal, which in our day is often a random death; death at a person's own hands by suicide; death in old age, middle age, childhood; death in war; yes, death by medicine tragically misapplied. Grief can take the form of anger, even rage, deep sorrow, confusion, relief; it can be long-lived, short-term, almost but never quite successfully avoided. The nature of grief is quite as highly variegated as its causes.

Grief, like the devil, is in the details. I have a good friend whose son committed suicide at age forty-one. A young man devoted to good works, he ended his life working for an international agency in central Africa. At his suicide, the only note he left was about what he called "this event" having nothing to do with his work. To this day, then, his father and other relatives do not know the reason for his taking his own life, which adds puzzlement to my friend's grief, a puzzlement perhaps never to be solved.

Then there is the complex question of the purpose of grief, with all the various emotions it brings in its trail. Cholbi quotes a philosopher named Robert Solomon on our moral obligation to grieve. "The right amount of grief," Solomon holds, "speaks of a person and his or her caring for others." But what is the right amount? Religious Jews say kaddish daily for a year for their dead; if Orthodox, they say it three times a day. My father, who did not say kaddish for his Orthodox father, used to refer to me, half-jokingly, as his kaddishim. Alas, I did not say kaddish for him or my mother, though I loved both and felt, and continue to feel, myself fortunate in what I think my winning ticket in the parents' lottery.

My mother died at eighty-one, after a roughly two-year bout with liver cancer. She never quite came to terms with her own death. "Whoever thought this would happen to me?" she said on more than one occasion in my hearing. Someone suggested to me that I recommend a support group for the terminally ill for her. I can all too readily imagine my mother's response to such a suggestion: "Let me get this straight. You want me to go sit in a room with strangers and listen to their troubles and then tell them my own, and this will make me feel better? This is what you want? This is the kind of idiot I have for a son?"

My father lived to ninety-two, and died, at home, of congestive heart failure. His last few years he required a caregiver, the first a black man with the oddly Jewish name of Isaac Gordon, the second a woman, an Albanian physician unlicensed to practice medicine in the United States. Henry James wrote that "you are rich if you can meet the demands of your imagination." By this criterion, my father was rich. He could give ample sums to (mostly) Jewish charities, he could help out poor relatives, he could travel to exotic foreign lands after his retirement, he could supply his wife with jewels and furs and other prizes that their generation was enamored of. What offended my father most about his illness in his last years was his loss of independence. He disliked relying on others; he preferred to be someone others relied upon.

Orphaned at the generous age of sixty-two, I cannot say that I deeply grieved either of my parents. I did, though, and continue to, miss them. And I felt—one of the stages left out by Kübler-Ross—remorse. I wish I had asked my mother several questions, among them whether she believed in God. I never thanked my father for his generous support and for supplying me with an impressive model of manliness. I never got round to thanking him for this and for much else.

Two dear friends, Hilton Kramer and John Gross, I do not so much grieve as sorely miss. I miss their humor, their brilliance, and their unfailing kindness and generosity to me. Hilton had put me up for the job of editor of the *American Scholar*, a job I held for some twenty-three years, and he encouraged my writing in his own magazine, the *New Criterion*. I first came to know John during his days as editor of the London *Times Literary Supplement*, to which he often invited me to contribute. After a year or so of formal correspondence, John began a letter to me, "How I wish I could, as Henry James said on a similar occasion, leap the bounds of formality and address you by your first name." He would occasionally call me from London, usually with some delicious piece of gossip: "Joe, bet you can't tell me with whom Fidel Castro is sleeping." (Kathleen Tynan, wife of Kenneth Tynan, it turned out.) With both Hilton and John, I recall lots of laughter and a nearly perfect rapport

More recently Midge Decter, a dear friend, died at age ninety-four. One cannot be shocked, or even surprised, by the death of someone who has attained her nineties, yet one can nonetheless feel the subtraction created by her absence. I loved to invoke Midge's intelligent laughter, and it would never occur to me to attempt in any way to dupe her full-court-press savvy. One of the sad things about growing older is that one runs out of people to admire, as I admired Midge, for her good sense, her wit, her intellectual courage.

In a book called *Geometry of Grief*, Michael Frame writes: "Times folds up. So many ghosts crowd into my head. Parents, grandparents, aunts and uncles, dear friends, students. . . . And far too many cats." Live long enough oneself and one realizes that half or more of one's friends and relatives have departed the planet, "summoned," as the poet Robert Southey had it, "on the grand tour of the universe," before one. One lives with it, saddened yet grateful oneself still to be in the game. Yet some holes never successfully fill up.

In my case, that hole is the death of the younger of my two sons, who died at twenty-eight, rendering me officially a member of that least enviable of all clubs, parents who have buried children.

When strangers or distant acquaintances ask me whether I have children, I say that I had two sons, though one died young. When, with the inevitably sad look on their faces, they ask how he died, I lie and say in a car accident. In fact, my son Burton died from an opioid overdose, alone, in his apartment in Hyde Park in Chicago. I lie about the cause of his death because I do not wish to seem more pitiable than I am; and I lie because to admit that one's son played around with drugs suggests that one was not the strong parent every child needs.

Burt was a wild kid. He didn't care much about school, got into fights, yet could be immensely charming. Early in life, in an accident with a so-called safety scissors, he lost an eye, and henceforth wore a glass eye, which didn't in any obvious way slow him down; it may even have made him wilder. Bored by school, he decided not to go to college, but after a year or so working in Las Vegas, he changed his mind and called to ask if I could get him into a college. I was able to help him get into Drake University in Iowa (his ACT scores were impressively high), which he left after a year to attend and finish his bachelor's degree at the University of Massachusetts. He majored in history and was an admirer of Tolstoy's novels. Once out of school, he became a salesman, working in real estate. Then, cashing in some Israeli bonds that had come due that his grandfather had bought for him, he bought two limousines and went into the limo business. For reasons I am not fully aware of, this didn't work out. He had a pretty girlfriend named Paula Black, who suffered depression and killed herself when he was away, leaping from the balcony of his ninth-story apartment on Sheridan Road.

When I learned about my son's death, I was, somehow, not immediately plunged into grief. In a reversal of the way grief is supposed to work, it has been with the passing years that my grief has slowly increased. When I go to my semiannual cemetery visits and note his gravestone (Burton Epstein—1962–1990), all I can think of is waste, of all the years he missed out on. I keep a photograph of him as a smiling boy of perhaps eight or nine on a bookcase shelf near my desk. I incorporate his name into my various computer passwords. He would be sixty if he were alive today, but I have no strong notion of what kind of man he would have grown to become. I never talk about him with anyone except his daughter. He died before she was a year old, and for her, a beautiful, intelligent, artistic young woman who never knew her father, I supply anecdotes and stray facts about him.

The only memorable condolence note about my son's death came from my friend Norman Podhoretz, who wrote that the one bit of solace I might take from the death of a child is that nothing so sad was ever again likely to happen in my life. The writing of condolences to the grieving is perhaps the most difficult of all compositions. Platitudes must be avoided, clichés eliminated, all false feeling excluded. Yet what can one write that is likely to provide anything like real solace? Politicians and television news anchors, when announcing a death, mutter the perfunctory "Our thoughts and prayers go out to the family," which merely reveals their own thoughtlessness and want of true reverence.

The same holds true for funerary eulogies, which, frequently delivered by clergymen who did not know the deceased, often descend into little more than platitudes strung together by stale metaphors. Such empty eulogies are nicely blasted by the story of Mr. Birnbaum, who asks his rabbi to say kaddish for his recently dead dog, Buster. The rabbi tells him that Jews do not say kaddish over animals. Birnbaum pleads with the rabbi, informing him that he has no surviving family and that in recent years Buster was all the family he has had. He then offers the rabbi a check for $20,000 for his inner-city youth fund if the rabbi will accommodate him. The rabbi, begrudgingly, agrees. The next afternoon in the synagogue's private chapel, the rabbi spends twenty minutes saying kaddish and eulogizing Buster. At the end, Mr. Birnbaum, in tears, mounts the bimah, hands the rabbi his check, and thanks him profusely, adding, "You know, Rabbi, until this afternoon I had no idea how much Buster had done for Israel."

In *On Grief and Grieving*, Kübler-Ross and Kessler, themselves grief therapists, call upon therapy, either through private counseling or in bereavement groups, as the ultimate balm for grief. They also encourage crying, on the part of men and women both. They allow that grief is "a reflection of a loss that never goes away." They suggest a proper, or adequate, kind of grief, but never quite succeed in setting out what it might be. They even make grieving seem a self-improving exercise: "Grief presents us with a rare opportunity to relate to ourselves more fully, rationally, and lovingly." And they write: "For in fact we have an imperfect duty—or short of that, a strong moral reason to grieve, rooted in our larger duty to pursue self-knowledge. In grieving, we show both love and respect for ourselves." That last sentence is echoed, word for word, by Michael Cholbi in *Grief.*

Cholbi, while allowing that grief is "perhaps the greatest stressor in life," finds it neither a form of madness nor worthy of being medicalized, grief being neither a disease nor a disorder. He finds it instead part of "the human predicament," a part that eludes even philosophical understanding. "We can grieve smarter," he writes. "But ultimately, we cannot outsmart grief. Nor should we want to." We do not ultimately recover from grief; if lucky, we merely at best are able to adjust to it.

On my desk sits a bill for $150 from the Waldheim Cemetery for plantings on the grave of my maternal grandmother, a woman who died when I was a very young child and left no memories in my mind. Her own husband had died young, and, a true materfamilias, she raised five children. My mother, I know, greatly admired her mother. As for my mother, I pay each year for plantings on her grave, though not on the graves of my father and son at Westlawn Cemetery, whom when alive I don't feel would care about such things. But what to do about the grandmother I never knew, who is buried in Waldheim Cemetery? One hundred and fifty dollars is not a staggering yet also not a trivial sum. Shall I pay it?

In *The Ancient City,* Fustel de Coulanges reminds us that the ancient Greeks, the Latins, and the Hindus believed that the soul was also buried with the body and was divine. They left food at the graves of the dead, pouring wine upon their tombs. Euripides's character Iphigenia exclaims, "I pour upon the earth of the tomb milk, honey, and wine; for it is with these that we rejoice the dead." Religious sentiment appears to have begun with worship of the dead. "It was perhaps while looking upon the dead that man first conceived the idea of the supernatural, and began to have a hope beyond what he saw," wrote Fustel de Coulanges. "Death was the first mystery, and it placed man on the tract of other mysteries. . . . It raised his thoughts from the visible to the invisible, from the transitory to the eternal, from the human to the divine."

I shall write the check to Waldheim Cemetery today.

(2022)

Taste: What Is It? Who Needs It? How Do You Acquire It?

No accounting for taste," the best-known words on the subject run, and indeed it turns out that not all that many people have actually attempted to account for taste. Apart from that pertaining to gastronomy, taste has not been a subject much explored. Yet what a significant subject it seems, for there is taste in books, art, ideas, humor, companions, clothes, and just about everything else the world has to offer.

De gustibus non est disputandum—"there is no disputing taste"—is the longest-standing aphorism about taste, though of course people dispute it all the time. "You say there can be no argument about matters of taste," Nietzsche wrote in *The Gay Science*. "All life is an argument about matters of taste." Without disputes over taste, criticism would be out of business. The avant-garde is about changing taste, sometimes radically. Arguments about taste may be the most passionate arguments of all. I, for one, should rather be told that my political opinions are wrong than that my apartment is drab or my favorite poets third-rate. I have the support here of La Rochefoucauld, who wrote, "Our self-love can bear less to have our own tastes than our opinions condemned."

Taste can mystify understanding, and often does. For example, I cannot grasp the aesthetics of tattoos, or understand why anyone finds them attractive, yet their popularity has greatly increased in recent years. Nor do I understand the pleasure derived from rap music or why men, many famous athletes among them, find that wearing earrings is elegant. Neither can I work up much interest in Bob Dylan, whom I am prepared to let blow in his own rather pretentious wind. None of his songs seems to me authentic; all seem pseudo-profundities acquired secondhand from Woody Guthrie and others. Taste—go figure!

Along with Nietzsche, David Hume was among the major philosophers who wrote about taste. Hume chiefly attempted to establish an objective basis for taste. Opposing taste to passion, he held that the former enlarged "the sphere both of our happiness and our misery, and makes us sensible to pain as well as pleasures, which escape the rest of mankind." He set out the standards for fair-minded taste. According to Hume, the problem of taste is that "among a thousand different opinions which different men may entertain of the same subject, there is one, and but one, that is just and true; and the difficulty is to fix and ascertain it." Hume is less incisive on how to acquire true taste than he is on those things that get in the way of establishing it, with prejudice high among them.

"Prejudice is destructive of sound judgment," Hume wrote, "and perverts all operations of the intellectual faculties: It is no less contrary to good taste; nor has it less influence to corrupt our sentiment of beauty." Good taste, for Hume, is bound up with a sound understanding. Both go into making what he calls "delicacy of taste." This delicacy of taste "is requisite to make him [the critic, or anyone else with genuine good taste] sensible of every beauty and every blemish, in any composition or discourse."

Many things stand in the way of attaining true delicacy of taste: one's nationality, one's social class, one's age, one's temperament, the time in which one lives. Of the last, Nietzsche wrote: "One has to get rid of the bad taste of wanting to be in agreement with the many. 'Good' is no longer good when your neighbor takes it into his mouth." The taste of the majority, Nietzsche is saying, rarely if ever qualifies as good taste.

Jean-Jacques Rousseau thought that taste finally eluded definition. "The further we go in search of a definition of taste," he wrote in *Émile*, his study of the education of youth, "the more we are bewildered; taste is only the power of judging what will please or displease the greatest number. Go beyond that and no definition is possible."

Tastes of course vary, widely and wildly. "One person is more pleased with the sublime," Hume writes, "another with the tender; a third with raillery. One has a strong sensibility to blemishes, and is extremely studious of correctness: Another has a more lively feeling of beauties, and pardons twenty absurdities and defects for one elevated or pathetic stroke." Hume concludes: "Such preferences are innocent and unavoidable, and can never reasonably be the object of dispute, because there is no standard, by which they can be decided."

Then there is fashion, which often plays a significant role in the formation of taste. The fashions that prevail at a given moment mark their time as surely as its ideas or anything else about it. Fashion can pervert taste. When fashion leads, Rousseau felt, "the object of taste changes: Then the multitude no longer has judgment of its own. It now judges only according to the views of those whom it believes more enlightened than itself. It approves not what is good but what they have approved. In all times, see to it that each man has his own sentiments, and that which is most agreeable in itself will always have the plurality of votes. Here people often defer in their tastes to those they think better informed than themselves, approving not what they think superior but what others do." Hence the power of persuasive critics to form taste.

"The rich, in order to display their wealth, and the artists, in order to take advantage of that wealth, vie in the quest for new means of expense," Rousseau wrote. "This is the basis on which great luxury establishes its empire and leads people to love what is difficult and costly. Then what is claimed to be beautiful, far from imitating nature, is beautiful only by dint of thwarting it. This is how luxury and bad taste become inseparable. Wherever taste is expensive, it is false."

Not entirely true. Many expensive things can be in good taste: splendid houses facing water, pleasing paintings, artistically designed jewelry, elegant automobiles, certain items of clothing. One, of course, may have a taste for many things one cannot afford. Rousseau, a thinker who never seemed to mind going too far, adds: "A taste for ostentation is rarely associated in the same souls with a taste for honesty. No, it is not possible that minds degraded by a multitude of futile concerns would ever raise themselves to anything great. Even when they had the strength for that, the courage would be missing."

As for how tastes change, Nietzsche felt that change in taste is more powerful than a change in opinion, and that what changes taste is the views of powerful and influential men who "announce, without any shame, *hoc est ridiculum, hoc est absurdum,* in short, the judgment of their taste and nausea; and then they enforce it tyrannically." When people talk about tastemakers, they are really talking about taste-changers, with the obvious proviso that not all changes in taste are changes for the better. What is a tasteful opinion? In *The Gay Science*, Nietzsche cites one: "Above all, one should not wish to divest existence of its *rich ambiguity*: that is a dictate of good taste, gentlemen, the taste for reverence for everything that lies beyond your horizon." A distasteful opinion, one with a wretched history, would be anti-Semitism.

The evidence of changing taste is ubiquitous, perhaps never more so than at present. In television interviews, athletes now commonly use such phrases as "kick ass" and "pissed off"; on some cable television shows, the f-word appears more frequently than many common prepositions. A current television commercial invokes you to "put your keister in a Honda." In the middle-class suburb in which I live, men in their fifties and beyond go about in cargo shorts, tank tops, and flip-flops—clothes my father, not a notably formal man, wouldn't have worn to take out the garbage.

Taste runs the gamut from bad to good, vulgar to exquisite, sound to precious. We all like to think of our own taste as at least sound, with perhaps a few thinking theirs exquisite. But how can we be certain? Apart from examining our taste item for item, I'm not sure we can. "Taste," Rousseau believed, "is natural to all mankind, but they do not possess it in the same degree. . . . The degree of taste which it is possible for us depends on our innate sensibility; its development and form depend on the societies in which we live." The development of taste, Rousseau held, depended on living in large enough societies that allow us to make comparisons among things, and these must be societies that allow for amusement and idleness, "for those of business are not regulated by pleasure, but by self-interest."

In their very personae, people can themselves seem in good or bad taste. Fred Astaire always seemed an emblem of good taste, aristocratic yet very American. A run of English actors—Ronald Colman, Douglas Fairbanks Jr., David Niven—seemed to embody good taste, at least on-screen.

As for bad taste, one doesn't have to go any further than our current and previous American presidents. Nearly everything about Donald Trump suggests bad taste, from his hairdo to his views about women to his crude put-downs of anyone who disagrees with him. The bad taste inherent in Joe Biden is perhaps less obvious but no less pervasive. Bad taste in Biden ranges from his endless recounting of his parents' advice to him when he was a boy—"Joey, my father used to say to me . . ."—to his bringing up the death of his son Beau on every possible occasion to show his own sensitivity to the world's sadness. (No Irishman, it is said, is ever taken in by the charm of another Irishman, but in Joe Biden's case, one doesn't have to be Irish to be impervious to his attempts at charm.) Beyond bad taste, both men, Trump and Biden, have been accused of being sexual predators. No one would ever accuse either man of even lapsing into good taste. Perhaps when people in polls declare they don't like the direction in which the country is headed, what they really mean is that our recent presidents, our national leaders, in their differing ways, have been in appallingly bad taste.

Which brings up the question of what taste has, if anything, to do with character. One would like to think that a person of good character would also be a person of not necessarily flawless but at least generally sound taste. A man or woman of exquisite taste and bad character is easily imagined. One of life's little disappointments is the discovery that some people can attain to high culture and in all other realms be without taste. Less easily imagined is a man or woman of good character but vulgar tastes. One of life's pleasant surprises is that some people, quite without culture, can be generous and in every way good-hearted.

Rousseau thought a distinction needed to be made between taste and morals. In *Émile*, he notes that "taste is no more than self-knowledge in regard to little things" and adds that "since it is on the sum of little things that pleasure of life depends, attention to them is by no means a trivial matter. From it we learn to drink deep of the good things which lie within our reach and go drain from them all the meaning which they can have for us." He then proceeds to skid off the track by declaring that one should "consult the taste of women in physical matters, which pertain to the judgment of the senses, and that of men in moral matters, which are more dependent on the understanding."

Do I, I ask myself, have what David Hume called "the delicacy of taste"? Here are a few of my own preferences. In the realm of culture, I prefer Mozart over Beethoven, Raphael over Michelangelo, Hazlitt over Emerson, Tennyson over Walt Whitman, Paul Klee over Pablo Picasso, Marcel Proust over James Joyce. As you might have guessed after reading my animadversions about rap music and the songs of Bob Dylan, my taste in popular music runs to the singing of Nat King Cole and Rosemary Clooney, Ella Fitzgerald and Bing Crosby, Frank Sinatra and Sarah Vaughan. La Rochefoucauld again: "Tastes in young people are changed by natural impetuosity, and in the aged are preserved by habit."

After graduating from the University of Chicago, where an interest in material objects was regarded as opposed to an interest in truth, beauty, and goodness, I found myself purposely buying dullish cars— Chevy Malibus, Oldsmobile Cutlasses—lest I be thought taken in by the low-grade status conferred by the possession of a flashy or elegant auto. When the price of an Olds Cutlass exceeded $20,000, I shed my concern about such matters and bought a 3 Series BMW. I next jumped up to 5 Series BMWs, and thence to S-Type Jaguars. Apart from gazing out the rearview mirrors of these cars, I never looked back.

My clothes are a throwback almost to my high school days. While I own no jeans, I mostly go about in chino, or khaki, wash pants, penny loafers, and polo shirts and (in colder weather) sweaters worn over them. I have had the good luck not to have had to work in an office since 1970, and suspect that such suits as I own have by now gone out of style. I have bought a number of items—a suede jacket, a winter coat, a double-breasted blazer—in vintage clothing stores. I have never had a beard or mustache, and tend to believe, with George Balanchine, who allowed none of his male dancers to have beards or mustaches, that there is something slightly false about them in the modern age.

As for tasteful speech, in recent years I have attempted to eliminate the use of what Clifton Fadiman called the "coital intensifier," or the f-word. The same goes for other readily available four-letter words. I try my best only to say "yes" and never "yeah." I hope I am a good listener. Like many an older gent, I fear I too often repeat my repertoire of anecdotes. I may well tell too many jokes? I worry, perhaps not sufficiently, about being a bore.

How does one attain to David Hume's "delicacy of taste"? Rousseau thought a first step was to go off to live in Paris. "Perhaps there is no civilized town where the general taste is worse than in Paris," he wrote, "yet this is the capital where good taste is trained, and few books of note have lately been written in Europe of which the author has not been to Paris to form his taste." Can Paris, or life in any other city, imbue good taste? I have lived much the better part of my life in Chicago, never a citadel of good taste. In Chicago, one can drive ten miles down most of the city's main streets and not encounter a person tastefully attired. New York has long been thought more sophisticated than Chicago, but also more aggressive—"Can you tell me how I can get to the Empire State Building," a visiting Hoosier asks a native New Yorker, "or would you prefer I go screw myself?"—and aggression is not usually in good taste.

Good taste, David Hume's "delicacy of taste," if it is to be acquired, must be acquired on one's own. The only way to do so is make a conscious attempt to eliminate all that is distasteful in one's public presentation. Prejudice has to go. So, too, narrow views. One's opinions must not be too firmly pressed; nor must one live to win arguments, political or other. Charm, if one can command it, may be taken on, and with it quiet elegance, though neither in a too obvious way. Any hint of vulgarity must be effaced.

Or perhaps no program of this or any other kind is needed. Good taste is instead to be had, more simply, by invoking one's better instincts, putting other people's feelings on a par with one's own, being generous in one's impulses, kindly with everyone, above all never hurting or humiliating others. Social sensitivity, generosity, kindliness, gentleness in all one's dealings—here, surely, are the ingredients, the ultimate prescription, for the best of all good taste.

(2023)

About the Author

Joseph Epstein is the author of thirty-one books, among them works on divorce, ambition, snobbery, friendship, envy, and gossip. He has published seventeen collections of essays and four books of short stories. He has been the editor of the *American Scholar*, the intellectual quarterly of Phi Beta Kappa, and for thirty years he taught in the English department at Northwestern University. He has written for the *New Yorker*, *Commentary*, *New Criterion*, *Times Literary Supplement*, *Claremont Review of Books*, *New York Review of Books*, *Poetry*, and other magazines both in the United States and abroad. In 2003, he was awarded the National Humanities Medal.